TO
START
A WAR

ALSO BY ROBERT DRAPER

Pope Francis and the New Vatican (with David Yoder)

Do Not Ask What Good We Do:
Inside the U.S. House of Representatives

Dead Certain:
The Presidency of George W. Bush

Hadrian's Walls

Rolling Stone Magazine:
The Uncensored History

TO
START
A WAR

How the Bush Administration
Took America into Iraq

ROBERT DRAPER

PENGUIN PRESS

NEW YORK

2020

PENGUIN PRESS
An imprint of Penguin Random House LLC
penguinrandomhouse.com

LIBRARY OF CONGRESS CATALOGING-IN-PUBLICATION DATA
Names: Draper, Robert, author.
Title: To start a war : how the Bush Administration
took America into Iraq / Robert Draper.
Other titles: How the Bush Administration took America into Iraq
Description: New York : Penguin Press, [2020] | Includes index.
Identifiers: LCCN 2020001715 (print) | LCCN 2020001716 (ebook) |
ISBN 9780525561040 (hardcover) | ISBN 9780525561057 (ebook)
Subjects: LCSH: Iraq War, 2003–2011—Causes. |
Iraq War, 2003–2011—Decision making. |
Bush, George W. (George Walker), 1946—Military leadership. |
United States—Politics and government—2001–2009.
Classification: LCC DS79.757 .D73 2020 (print) |
LCC DS79.757 (ebook) | DDC 956.7044/310973—dc23
LC record available at https://lccn.loc.gov/2020001715
LC ebook record available at https://lccn.loc.gov/2020001716

Printed in the United States of America
1   3   5   7   9   10   8   6   4   2

Book design by Daniel Lagin

To Kirsten

A man is not deceived by others; he deceives himself.

JOHANN WOLFGANG VON GOETHE

CONTENTS

AUTHOR'S NOTE

===

This is a story bracketed by the two defining tragedies of the twenty-first century. The first was an unprovoked attack on America's homeland that left nearly three thousand dead. The second, eighteen months later, was an act of war by America against a sovereign nation that had neither harmed the United States nor threatened to do so. The death toll from the latter would ultimately eclipse that from the former by more than a hundredfold.

The two grim events are unalterable facts of history. What took place between them, connecting the one to the other, is arguably the looming riddle of our time, for all that it asks about America's self-awareness and moral presence in the world today. I've attempted to solve that riddle here.

Necessarily at the center of this tale is President George W. Bush. Profoundly unpopular when he left office in January 2009—in no small measure due to the events described here—Bush has since benefited from time's leavening of passions, as well as a nationwide yearning for the kind of decency that his family long epitomized. This book seeks to contribute to history's understanding of America's forty-third president. I hope to do so through the careful telling of Bush's single most consequential act: a long and costly war waged by a commander in chief who sincerely believed he had little choice in the matter.

The decision to invade Iraq was Bush's alone to make. But he had an abundance of help. Some in the upper tiers of the administration vigorously urged that decision. Others did what they could to make his decision less difficult. None of them advised him to decide otherwise. Those lower down the Bush administration's food chain who would have counseled against the decision variously did not speak up or were not given the chance to speak or did speak but went unheeded.

The story I aim to tell is very much a human narrative of patriotic men and women who, in the wake of a nightmare, pursued that most elusive of dreams: finding peace through war.

TO
START
A WAR

CHAPTER ONE

=====

IDÉE FIXE

A t first Paul Wolfowitz mistook the tremors in the Pentagon for an earthquake. Such an event would have been rare in the nation's capital, but far more fathomable than what had in fact occurred at the opposite end of the building. It took a few bewildered seconds for him to connect the sudden pandemonium just outside his doorway with the events in New York he had seen on his office television less than a half hour earlier.

Uniformed officers entered the deputy secretary of defense's office and instructed him to evacuate immediately. Wolfowitz and his staffers hurried down the E Ring corridor. The entire Pentagon work force, thousands of them, assembled outside on the parade grounds.[1] Black smoke swirled over the western side of the building where American Airlines Flight 77 had completed its path of destruction a few minutes before, at 9:37 on the morning of September 11, 2001.

Even when he was intended to be the center of attention, Wolfowitz cut an indistinct presence. He was fifty-seven and a father of three, recently divorced, a slight, fast-graying academic for whom certain big thoughts were all-consuming and everything else—manner of dress, posture, hair care, time of the next appointment, sleep—were relegated to afterthought. His default expression was one of mildly skeptical consideration, as if perusing the menu at an overpriced restaurant.

For the past three decades, he had been a sort of backstage eminence in the Washington hierarchy, an important man to more important men. That was about to change. But at this moment, Paul Dundes Wolfowitz was just another vulnerable federal employee standing under an empty blue sky with the ruins of his office building before him.

A half hour before, he had just concluded a breakfast in the Pentagon with Defense Secretary Donald Rumsfeld and nine Republican members of the House Armed Services Committee. At some point during the breakfast, Rumsfeld had predicted that, while Americans were currently luxuriating in peacetime, "an event somewhere in the world will be sufficiently shocking that it will remind the American people and their representatives in Washington how important it is for us to have a strong national defense."[2] Rumsfeld was given to such proclamations, at once sage and lacking in utility. The remark did not take on any added significance a few minutes after he uttered it, when a military aide handed Rumsfeld a Post-it note informing the secretary that some type of aircraft had apparently struck the North Tower of the World Trade Center.[3]

Eventually, after several helpless minutes on the parade grounds, Wolfowitz insisted to his aides that he be allowed to return inside. They escorted him to the National Military Command Center, in the basement. Rumsfeld was already there, along with Richard Myers, the vice chairman of the Joint Chiefs. They were discussing United Flight 93, which had just crashed "somewhere northeast of Camp David," according to the Air Force's Northeast Air Defense Sector. At issue was whether to elevate the nation's threat level to DEFCON 3.[4] Jet fuel fumes had overtaken the entire building. The command center was filling up with senior Army personnel whose offices had just been destroyed. Reports were coming in—among them that an explosion had taken place outside the White House. Recognizing that Rumsfeld was sixth in line to the presidency, military officers anxiously informed the secretary that he needed to leave the Pentagon. Rumsfeld refused.[5]

Wolfowitz saw their plaintive expressions. He murmured to his boss, "You and Myers should really get out of here."

Rumsfeld ignored him. After a few minutes, the deputy secretary tried again. Then a third time.

The secretary then snapped, "No, *you've* got to get out of here."[6]

Wolfowitz and his senior military aide were ushered to the helipad. Hovering for a moment over the ghastly spectacle of the acrid plumes rising from the nation's defense headquarters, the helicopter then moved quickly, seventy-five miles in forty minutes' time, cityscape giving way to the deep green ridges of Appalachia. They touched down at the Raven Rock Mountain Complex, also known as Site R, six miles from Camp David on the Maryland–Pennsylvania state line.[7]

It was not yet noon when the deputy secretary was led into the underground nuclear bunker. He was shown a room with cots. There was no computer for Wolfowitz to use, only landline phones. He tried to call his children, but the cell phones in the Washington, D.C., Beltway had ceased to function.[8]

At that moment, the deputy secretary of defense knew little more than the rest of America did. Soon the nation would be at war. Within a year and a half's time, that war would expand dramatically—beyond Afghanistan, the country that had harbored the 9/11 attackers, to a country nearly 1,500 miles away, Iraq.

In the months and years that followed, it would be almost universally stated—or, rather, overstated—that Paul Wolfowitz was the "architect" of this fateful expansion. Two facts belie this characterization. First, the decision to invade Iraq was one made, finally and exclusively, by the president of the United States, George W. Bush—whom Wolfowitz had known for only the past two years, and not very well at that. Second, Bush made his decision without benefit of an architect's blueprint; and, to the extent that there was such a document, it was not one that Wolfowitz would have drawn up.

Still, it was Paul Wolfowitz who, more than perhaps any other American, had spent the past decade crusading for the overthrow of the Iraqi dictator Saddam Hussein—lending an otherwise beleaguered cause both intellectual brawn and moral ballast and, finally, a political path to realization. That same path would begin on September 11 with Wolfowitz's small error in judgment about an earthquake—and then, a few hours later, with him alone and in the dark, miserably sequestered somewhere inside a mountain, an early prisoner of war starving for information.

Late that evening, he would let the intelligence analysts back at the Pentagon know exactly what information he was seeking.

OUTSIDE THE MOUNTAIN, A COUNTRY TREMBLED.

The attacks had come when all was orderly and ordinary: a Tuesday morning, millions on the streets and in the offices of Manhattan under a lidless blue sky. The first plane, the one that plowed into floors 93 through 99 of the World Trade Center's North Tower, was an astonishing spectacle. New Yorkers stopped in their tracks to gape at it. Gray smoke poured out of the tower, progressively darkening. Fire truck sirens screeched from every direction. For sixteen minutes, the city remained baffled and shaken, but for the most part unafraid.

At 9:02 a.m., with millions of Manhattanites and nearly every television station around the world fixated on the flames leaping out of the North Tower, a second plane materialized from nowhere. Faster and lower than the first plane, it burst into the South Tower. In that instant, tragedy was unmasked as something far worse. Debris spewed out of the buildings. A man jumped from a window and hurtled one thousand feet.

The men and women charged with reciting the news of the day to TV viewers across America were at pains to convey meaning to the live images. Their sentences were spare and futile: "Oh, my goodness." "That's absolutely inexplicable." "It looks like a movie." "This looks deliberate, folks." "What we have been fearing here for the longest time has come to pass."

All traffic stopped. The subway trains stopped. Cell service stopped. The taxis disappeared. More bodies dropped out of the two flaming buildings. From the wreckage, hundreds upon hundreds of office workers staggered uptown or over the Brooklyn Bridge on foot, covered head to toe in ashes.

Crying, screaming, the wailing of sirens. A monstrous white cloud rose up as the South Tower crumbled to the ground. Then the North Tower collapsed. New York's skyline was decapitated.

Meanwhile, reported sightings of the next calamity were spreading from coast to frenzied coast. Rogue jets screaming toward the White House and the Capitol. A car bomb detonating at the State Department. No visual images, no proof—perhaps they hadn't happened? But something had; and, it now seemed inevitable, something else would. Who would dare say otherwise? That wide-angle spectacle of a great city under siege was like a winged monster that had swooped down from the skies and swallowed up America's adolescent sense of imperviousness.

Now anything was possible.

THE FIRST TIME PAUL WOLFOWITZ HAD EVER BEEN A WITNESS TO HISTORY, he was pulled to Washington rather than away from it. He was nineteen and a sophomore at Cornell University on the evening of August 27, 1963, and he had convinced fellow classmates to board a bus carrying mostly African Americans and drive all night from Ithaca to the capital.[9] They arrived the next morning at the Lincoln Memorial. Standing in the back among nearly 250,000 strangers, Wolfowitz could plainly hear Martin Luther King Jr. deliver his "I Have a Dream" speech. Having recently read King's "Letter from the Birmingham Jail," the brilliance of his message that day did not astonish Wolfowitz so much as the orator's elemental power. One man, it suddenly seemed to him, could make the earth tilt.

Wolfowitz's father had not particularly approved of this road trip. Though Jacob Wolfowitz was a Polish émigré whose family had been decimated during the Holocaust, he was also a disillusioned left-winger and leery of King's fellow travelers. As always, the young Wolfowitz listened respectfully to his mathematician father, then went his own way. He chose political science as his vocation. On campus he organized against fraternities that discriminated against blacks.[10] At Cornell and later at the University of Chicago, Wolfowitz fell under the spell of Cold War–era academic giants—Allan Bloom,

Albert Wohlstetter—and at some point during Reagan's presidency he decided that he was a Republican. In his fundamental conviction that governments should intervene to preserve social justice, however, he was and would
remain, in his Cornell classmate Fred Baumann's words, "a bleeding-heart
liberal."[11]

After five years' worth of assignments in the Far East policymaking
bowels of Reagan's State and Defense departments, Wolfowitz received his
first plum assignment. In March 1986, he became the U.S. ambassador to
Indonesia, less than a month before Reagan was to visit the country for the
first and only time in his presidency.[12] Wolfowitz would later term it the best
job of his life.[13] It was not simply that the ambassador threw himself into
Indonesian culture: learning the language with the help of his driver and
with flash cards he took with him to interminable meetings; attending recep-
tions for local authors; winning third place in an Indonesian cooking contest
while his then wife, Clare, an anthropologist, took up Javanese dance. Indonesia was also his first experience as a Jew living in a predominantly Muslim
country.[14]

"Ambassadors are supposed to be careful about falling in love with the
country," he later said. "But I admit that I did nevertheless. And it was partly
because they're very hospitable and were very friendly to me, but mostly it
was because I saw a remarkable religious tolerance, which, it was already clear
to me at the time, was becoming a major issue for our era." At the same
time, Wolfowitz could plainly see, in the wake of the toppling of the shah of
Iran in 1979, the early stirrings of Islamic extremism. Even as the ambassador stood up for the rights of Indonesian journalists under the repressive
Suharto regime, he worked quietly to send some of the country's young
scholars to American universities so that they might gain exposure to moderate interpretations of Sharia law.[15]

The job was also Ambassador Paul Wolfowitz's personal introduction to
power. Unlike other diplomatic postings, where one's duties consist chiefly
of chaperoning big-shot visitors, he had become *the* American face in Indonesia. Years after his assignment had come to an end, in 1991, a colleague
would recall walking with him down the streets of Jakarta and seeing

everyday Muslims flock to the Jewish public servant, exclaiming, "Mr. Ambassador! Mr. Ambassador!"

Recalled the colleague, "They revered him."[16]

THOUGH WOLFOWITZ WOULD DESCRIBE HIS THREE-YEAR TENURE IN JAkarta as "life-changing,"[17] it was his next job that began to define his career. In early 1989, he was confirmed as the George H. W. Bush administration's undersecretary of defense for policy, the third most powerful position in America's largest government agency. His new boss, Defense Secretary Dick Cheney, admired Wolfowitz's creative thinking. But another quality would make just as lasting an impression. As Cheney would recall more than a decade after he hired Wolfowitz, "He was tenacious. Sometimes he'd come in and I'd throw him out. It never fazed him. He'd come back the next afternoon and hit you again. That was invaluable. He had enough conviction and enough self-confidence that even if he'd come in and he'd triggered a negative reaction from me, it didn't bother Paul."[18]

As it was for President Bush and Secretary Cheney, Wolfowitz's chief foreign policy preoccupation was the collapse of the Berlin Wall in 1989 and management of a new post–Cold War order. The invasion of Kuwait by the Iraqi Army on August 1, 1990, had gone largely unforeseen by the intelligence community. On February 24, 1991, following months of diplomatic entreaties, and with the help of an international coalition of thirty-five countries that included armored divisions supplied by Syria and Egypt, Operation Desert Storm entered its ground assault phase and proceeded to expel Iraqi forces from Kuwait. One hundred hours later, Saddam Hussein agreed to a cease-fire.

At the time, the decision not to follow the retreating Iraqi troops into Baghdad, thereby allowing Saddam to remain in power, was not controversial. Secretary Cheney supported Bush's decision to withdraw.[19] So did Undersecretary Wolfowitz.[20] The widely held assumption was that the Iraqi dictator would surely not survive this international humiliation—particularly given that U.S. commanders had finished off the one-hundred-hour war by bombing every structure that had buttressed Saddam's power base, including Baath Party headquarters in Baghdad.[21]

Wolfowitz was nonetheless horrified by what transpired within days of the cease-fire agreement. On February 15, 1991, days before the ground assault in Kuwait, President Bush had publicly urged "the Iraqi military and the Iraqi people to take matters into their own hands and force Saddam Hussein, the dictator, to step aside."[22] The long-oppressed Shiite majority took Bush's words to heart. They commenced an uprising near the southern city of Basra on the day of the cease-fire. The next day, March 1, Bush at a news conference repeated his earlier sentiment: "I've always said that it would be—that the Iraqi people should put him aside."[23]

The undersecretary for policy argued to Secretary of State James Baker that the United States should do more than stage a pep rally for the insurrection—it should enforce a demilitarized zone in the south. The American commander of Desert Storm, Norman Schwarzkopf, maintained that such a plan lacked military value. Baker sided with his victorious general. A few days later, Saddam's military made use of the helicopters they had been permitted to keep in the cease-fire agreement, proceeding from the sky to massacre the dissidents by the thousands.

Wolfowitz received a phone call from a friendly reporter who described to him a humanitarian crisis in the making. Some twenty thousand Shia refugees had massed on the Iraq–Saudi Arabia border near Safwan. Without military protection, they were sure to starve or be slaughtered.

Wolfowitz called his boss. Cheney agreed to lean on the Saudis to set up a refugee camp. Already, however, Wolfowitz was gloomily contemplating the famous observation made during the French Revolution, following Napoleon's ill-advised execution of the Duke of Enghien: "It is worse than a crime. It is a mistake."[24]

TWO YEARS LATER, THE BRANDEIS UNIVERSITY ISLAMIC SCHOLAR AND IRAQI native Kanan Makiya came to Washington to give a speech about the atrocities committed by Saddam Hussein's regime. Makiya's 1989 book, *Republic of*

Fear, had chronicled those profuse acts of torture, terror, and mass killings with such unsparing exactitude that he had been compelled to publish it under the pseudonym Samir al-Khalil, for fear of bringing harm to members of his family who still lived in Iraq.

The book had become a bestseller during the Gulf War; al-Khalil was hailed as Iraq's Aleksandr Solzhenitsyn. Now the author, self-revealed as Kanan Makiya, was in Washington promoting a new book about the regime, *Cruelty and Silence.* Several hundred attendees listened raptly to the famed and no-longer-anonymous writer, whose denunciation of Saddam was at once methodical and electrifying.

At the end of his talk, Makiya looked up to see a man heading toward him. The man offered his hand and said that he was Paul Wolfowitz. When it was evident that the name was unfamiliar to Makiya, the man went on to say that he had been the undersecretary of defense for policy during the Bush administration.

Then Wolfowitz said, "I want to apologize on behalf of the United States government for its failure to support the uprising." The Bush administration, he added, had let the Iraqi people down.

Wolfowitz then said goodbye, leaving Kanan Makiya dumbstruck. As he would recall, "I'd never then, nor ever after, heard someone say something like that. It was quite moving."[25]

AFTER EIGHT YEARS IN THE WILDERNESS OF BILL CLINTON'S PRESIDENCY, Paul Wolfowitz was among the hordes of conservatives eager to regain influence in a Republican administration. In the interim, the former third-ranking DOD man had achieved platinum status as a foreign policy mandarin. As dean of Johns Hopkins University's Paul H. Nitze School of Advanced International Studies (SAIS), Wolfowitz presided over an academic juggernaut of post–Cold War conservative thought.[26] He lent his foreign policy views to Bob Dole's unsuccessful 1996 presidential campaign. Two years later, Wolfowitz was among nine congressional appointees to the bipartisan Commission to Assess the Ballistic Missile Threat to the United States, also known as the Rumsfeld Commission after its chairman Donald Rumsfeld, the former defense secretary in the Ford administration. That same year, he joined a different bipartisan group of foreign policy luminaries in calling for Poland, Hungary, and the Czech Republic to be admitted to NATO.

Wolfowitz had remained haunted by Iraq in the decade since the Gulf War's tragic aftermath. Saddam continued to be a scourge to his own people and a bellicose malefactor in the Middle East. But Wolfowitz had come to view the dictator through an even darker lens after meeting a former Harvard professor named Laurie Mylroie.

Mylroie was convinced that Saddam had orchestrated the failed World Trade Center bombing plot of 1993. Her obsessive research on this matter took on a more farcical shape to some when she also maintained that Saddam was responsible for the 1995 Oklahoma City bombing.

Wolfowitz chose to overlook the latter claim and embrace the former. He and his then wife, Clare, became friends with Mylroie, who would thank them effusively in the acknowledgments of her 2000 book *Study of Revenge: The First World Trade Center Attack and Saddam Hussein's War Against America.* (Two others Mylroie singled out for praise were colleagues of Wolfowitz's from the first Bush administration: his deputy, Scooter Libby, and John Hannah, from the State Department's policy planning group.)[27]

There were in fact two leads connecting Saddam to the failed 1993 World Trade Center attack. The FBI had looked into both of them. One of the seven plotters was an American-born Iraqi named Abdul Rahman Yasin. (The other conspirators hailed from Egypt, Palestine, Kuwait, and Jordan.) He had cooperated with federal authorities and been permitted to relocate to Baghdad. Another, Mohammad Salameh, had placed forty-six calls on his phone to Baghdad in the eight months leading up to the attack—many of them to his uncle, a former Palestinian terrorist. "We can only speculate about what Salameh told his uncle," Mylroie wrote. Not surprisingly, her speculation pointed to Saddam's culpability.[28]

But Salameh and his housemates had placed hundreds of calls all over the world—perhaps to raise funds for the plot, or just as likely to pass the time with friends overseas. Iraq, in any event, quickly receded as a promising angle. When the plot's mastermind, a Kuwaiti named Ramzi Yousef, was arrested in 1995, Mylroie called the Bureau's New York office in near hysterics: "You've got the wrong guy!" She insisted that the actual leader was an Iraqi agent whose identity Yousef had assumed—a theory that was soon disproved by fingerprints that matched the man in custody to evidence found in the vicinity of the bombing.[29]

Wolfowitz nonetheless believed that Mylroie was onto something. While serving on the ballistic missile commission in 1998, he and Donald Rumsfeld requested a briefing on how the bomb in the 1993 attack had been delivered. Wolfowitz asked the CIA briefer who had been behind the plot.

Al Qaeda was the reply.

"Could Iraq have been behind it?" Wolfowitz pressed the CIA briefer.

"We've examined all of Laurie Mylroie's evidence," he was told. "And she's free to make her case."

Wolfowitz had not brought up Mylroie's name and was stunned by the analyst's dismissiveness.[30] He emerged from the session convinced that the CIA was not taking Saddam seriously.

No one could say the same of Wolfowitz. The SAIS dean would conduct strategy sessions in which, recalled one participant, "I'd get into huge fights with Paul, who was convinced Saddam was the cause of all, and I mean *all*, of the problems in the region."[31] Wolfowitz coauthored, with Zalmay Khalilzad, a story in the December 1997 issue of the *Weekly Standard* succinctly entitled "Overthrow Him."[32]

The following year, while testifying before a House committee, he called upon the Clinton administration to "liberate ourselves, our friends and allies in the region, and the Iraqi people themselves, from the menace of Saddam Hussein."[33] The solution, Wolfowitz repeatedly stated, was not an all-out U.S. military invasion. Rather, it was to do what he believed should have been done in 1991: "support the many Iraqis who desperately want to overthrow this tyrant, but who have so far found the United States stinting and unreliable in the support we have provided them."[34]

His stature demanded that he at least be heard out. "Paul Wolfowitz was going around Washington saying that he had this idea of how to take out

Saddam," recalled General Joseph W. Ralston, who at the time served as vice chairman of the Joint Chiefs of Staff. "He's a respected man, so I called Paul and asked him to have lunch with me in the Pentagon. He brought in a Kurd and a Shiite and a military officer. He had a concept that you could get Kurds, Shias, and disaffected military officers to come together and take out Saddam, and with our support form a new government.

"It seemed off-the-wall to me. He was passionate about it, but I was not at all convinced that this was the right way to go."[35]

EARLY IN 1999, WOLFOWITZ RECEIVED A PHONE CALL FROM CONDOLEEZZA Rice, who had served on the National Security Council during the Bush administration. The former president's son, Texas governor George W. Bush, had decided to run and had named Rice his chief foreign policy adviser. In putting together her advisory team, the first call Rice made was to Wolfowitz.[36]

Bush, an extrovert driven by his viscera, the Bible, and a love for baseball, had almost nothing in common with the man he called Wolfie. The governor's worldview was, broadly speaking, Reaganite. He had a welcoming attitude toward Texas's neighbors to the south, and a frequently espoused conviction that freedom was God's gift to the world and not just to America.

Otherwise, Bush's foreign policy slate was almost perfectly blank. Many of Wolfowitz's colleagues found this quality off-putting. Some of them, like *Weekly Standard* editor in chief William Kristol, threw their support behind an underdog candidate, Senator John McCain, a Vietnam War hero and unambiguous hawk.

Wolfowitz stuck with the front-runner. He marveled at Bush's unrehearsed rapport with the public, a quality that both the father and Dole had sorely lacked. One day on the campaign trail, the governor asked Wolfowitz what job might interest him in a new Bush administration.

"I'm not looking for a job" was his careful reply—adding that the one job he did *not* want was that of CIA director. Espousing a belief he held at the time, Wolfowitz said, "It would ruin my academic career to have a CIA affiliation."[37]

Wolfowitz did not know the candidate well enough at the time to realize that he had committed a faux pas: in attempting to get on Bush's good side, one did not telegraph to Bush that one was already contemplating a life after Bush. He had also failed to tell the candidate plainly what was widely suspected—namely, that Wolfie himself harbored aspirations of becoming secretary of defense.

That scenario seemingly became more plausible in July 2000, when the Republican nominee picked Wolfowitz's former boss at the Pentagon, Dick Cheney, to be his running mate. Cheney, in turn, selected one of Wolfowitz's former college students and DOD subordinates, I. Lewis "Scooter" Libby, to be his chief of staff and to help oversee the transition.

Yet the fix was not in for Wolfowitz. Even his greatest admirers could not envision the notoriously disorganized intellectual overseeing a bureaucracy of more than two million employees. In the end, the job went to Donald Rumsfeld, whose résumé trumped Wolfowitz's: mentor to Cheney in the Nixon White House, formerly Gerald Ford's secretary of defense and chief of staff, chair of the 1998 ballistic missile commission on which Wolfowitz served, a CEO of two large companies. Cheney urged Wolfowitz to accept the cabinet-level post of ambassador to the United Nations.[38] Instead, he became Rumsfeld's deputy.

Wolfowitz was confirmed on March 2, 2001, arriving six weeks into the Bush presidency. Unglamorous tasks consumed the deputy secretary's first months. After learning that the Army was about to purchase several hundred thousand black berets that were made in China—just on the heels of a U.S. surveillance plane crew being detained in that country—White House spokesman Ari Fleischer pulled Wolfowitz from a meeting and said incredulously, "Paul, are you guys serious?"

Wolfowitz killed the purchase order.[39] He also ended bombing exercises on Puerto Rico's Vieques Island after a series of protests and arrests. Both President Bush and Secretary Rumsfeld were clamoring for Wolfowitz to identify outdated weapons systems to redline and replace with newer technology. The Pentagon's collective energy was focused on developing a Quadrennial Defense Review as well as a missile shield system.

Of course, Wolfowitz brought his fervor for Iraqi regime change into the Bush administration. Now that the new deputy secretary had a daily CIA briefer whose job was to answer whatever questions were on his mind, among Wolfowitz's first such questions to her was, "What do you make of the phone calls that Mohammed Salameh made to his uncle in Baghdad before the '93 World Trade Center bombing?"

The briefer submitted that question to the agency's analysts. The reply came back to the deputy secretary in writing. The CIA did not know anything about such phone calls. Wolfowitz would need to ask the FBI (apparently because such information fell under the Department of Justice's control). The reply went on to say—using almost the identical words spoken by the CIA briefer to the Rumsfeld Commission three years earlier—that the agency had examined all of Laurie Mylroie's evidence and concluded that she had failed to make her case.

Wolfowitz later complained to the CIA director, George Tenet, at the end of a meeting both attended with Rumsfeld. He showed Tenet the photocopy of Salameh's phone bill reprinted in Mylroie's book as evidence that the agency had left at least this one stone unturned. It got back to Wolfowitz that Tenet had later asked Rich Haver, one of Rumsfeld's close associates who had also been in the same meeting, "Can you help me get Wolfowitz back in his box?"[40]

The deputy secretary's tenacity on the subject was not readily subdued, however. In April, his first full month on the job, Wolfowitz asked his senior military assistant, John Batiste, to gather whatever intelligence there was to support Laurie Mylroie's claims. Batiste sent out a tasking to the Defense Intelligence Agency.[41] Wolfowitz brought that information into his first NSC Deputies Committee meeting that month—only to find, to his frustration, that the NSC counterterrorism specialists at the meeting insisted on focusing on Osama bin Laden rather than the true overlord of terrorism, Saddam Hussein.[42]

Wolfowitz searched within the Pentagon for sympathizers. One day he asked a Clinton administration holdover, Austin Yamada, the deputy assistant secretary for special operations and combatting terrorism, to read Mylroie's book. After Yamada had completed his homework, Wolfowitz summoned him to his office to hear what the deputy assistant secretary thought.

What Yamada thought was: *Why is this book not in the science fiction section?* What he said, politely, was: "I'm not sure I buy the connection."

Wolfowitz countered with several tantalizing specifics in Mylroie's narrative. His subordinate did not change his assessment, however. "Well, thank you very much, Mr. Yamada," the deputy secretary finally said. Wolfowitz never consulted with Yamada after that.[43]

His experiences with Yamada, the CIA, and the NSC specialists typified Paul Wolfowitz's Sisyphean quest to dethrone the Iraqi dictator. Though much would later be made of early National Security Council discussions about Iraq, the framework was unswervingly Clintonian: *Saddam is in a box. Keep him there.*

Like most new presidents, Bush's early priorities revolved around domestic issues—specifically, education reform and tax cuts. Regime change, one of the administration's "small subset" of Iraq hawks would flatly state, "was not where the president was. It's not where Cheney really was."[44] The vice president and Scooter Libby shared Wolfowitz's contempt for Saddam, but both could see that Bush had little appetite for adventurism. Secretary of State Colin Powell and National Security Adviser Rice strongly favored containment of the Iraqi dictator. Rumsfeld, for his part, was critical of the current arrangement but had no concrete remedy to offer.

The Wolfowitz solution—train, fund, and in other ways support an Iraqi opposition to overthrow Saddam—had very few takers in the administration. There was John Hannah, Cheney's Middle East adviser (and friend of Laurie Mylroie), who for years had maintained close relations with Iraqi opposition leaders. There was Zalmay Khalilzad, Wolfowitz's "Overthrow Him" coauthor and former policy aide in Cheney's Defense Department, whom Libby installed in Condi Rice's National Security Council. There was Doug Feith, who now had Wolfowitz's previous job as undersecretary of defense for policy—and who, like Wolfowitz, Libby, and Khalilzad, had lent his signature to blue-ribbon petitions in 1998 calling for Saddam's ouster[45]— but who had only been confirmed in July and was still learning his way around the Pentagon. And there were other Iraq hard-liners scattered at the periphery of power: Bill Luti and David Wurmser in Feith's policy shop, Richard Perle chairing the Defense Policy Board, Harold Rhode in the DOD's Office of Net Assessment.

But none of these individuals, including the deputy secretary of defense, succeeded in leaving so much as a fingerprint on the new administration's Iraq policy. By the summer of 2001, one of Washington's leading proponents of regime change in Iraq, Danielle Pletka of the American Enterprise Institute, would recall thinking, "Oh, fuck. This is going nowhere."[46] The torpor was exactly what some Iraqi opposition figures had feared would eventuate from a candidate who had declared himself averse to "using our troops as nation builders."[47] For this very reason, many of them had hoped that Bush would lose to Al Gore.[48]

The early months of the Bush administration thus constituted, as one of the administration's Iraq hawks would recall, "a period of real frustration."[49]

LATE INTO THE EVENING OF SEPTEMBER 11, 2001, A LINEBACKER-PROPORTIONED Defense Intelligence Agency senior officer by the name of Gary Greco was sitting among the jet fumes and smoke in his Pentagon office, drawing up a crisis schedule for his team. For the past decade, Greco had been among a dozen or so members of the U.S. intelligence community whose principal job was tracking the activities of Al Qaeda. In recent years and with accelerating frequency, Greco and his colleagues had sent up urgent communiqués about the imminence of a major attack, most likely on American soil. Their warnings had largely gone unheeded.

Earlier in the afternoon, Greco had seen a passenger manifest provided by the FAA, listing the suspected hijackers behind the attacks in Washington and New York that morning. The names were instantly recognizable to him as Saudi. Surprise was one of the few things he did not feel.

At about two in the morning, Greco looked up from his crisis schedule to see a deputy holding out a piece of paper. It was the printout of an email from a Joint Chiefs of Staff intelligence officer who was stationed at Site R, time-stamped at 1:26 a.m., relaying an oral request that had been issued by Paul Wolfowitz:

> From DepSec Def, Hot!!! Tasking: Providing information,
> paper format, history and assessment of Iraqi involvement in
> terrorism since Gulf War.

Greco read the note with odd dispassion. As it happened, he knew quite a bit about Iraq. In December 1998, Greco had been involved in the planning and execution of Operation Desert Fox, in which Saddam Hussein's weapons facilities were bombed by U.S. forces. In the three years since Desert Fox, Greco had frequently checked in with the UN's weapons inspectors. His conclusion was that Saddam was a regional bully, an occasional ally to the PLO and other extremist groups in the Middle East, and no friend of the United States—but no threat, either. And while following the activities of Osama bin Laden, Greco had willingly chased down any discernible trail. No such trail led to Iraq. What Wolfowitz was doing, it seemed to Greco, was changing the subject while pretending not to do so.

Still, Greco was a student of war history. He knew that countries under attack did not always respond in rational and proportionate ways. Sometimes they lashed out where they knew they could land a swift and satisfying retaliatory blow.

Greco's deputy stood over his shoulder and read the email along with his boss. "What the hell does it mean?" the deputy asked.

Greco tersely replied: "It means we're going to war with Iraq."[50]

ON THE MORNING OF SEPTEMBER 15, 2001, PRESIDENT BUSH CONVENED HIS National Security Council in the Laurel Lodge conference room at Camp David, the presidential retreat situated six miles from where Wolfowitz had briefly been sequestered at Site R. Bush wanted to discuss a military response to the 9/11 attacks. The briefing that CIA director George Tenet had prepared for the meeting was entitled "Destroying International Terrorism." It focused on Afghanistan, where Al Qaeda had been given safe haven by the Taliban.[51]

After the conclusion of Tenet's briefing, Rumsfeld spoke up. "If it's a global war on terror, you need to show it's global," the secretary of defense reasoned. He then raised the possibility of military action against Iraq.[52]

Secretary of State Powell cautioned against Rumsfeld's proposal. He had already described in elaborate detail the other countries that were prepared to ally themselves with the United States against the 9/11 perpetrators. That coalition, he warned, would fall apart if America invaded some other, apparently unrelated country.

"Then maybe it's not a coalition worth having," replied Rumsfeld.[53]

Now Rumsfeld's deputy spoke. In fact, said Wolfowitz, Saddam Hussein might very well have been involved in the 9/11 attacks. It seemed unlikely that Al Qaeda could have pulled off such a deviously orchestrated scheme all by themselves. Saddam, in the network of global terrorism, was "the head of the snake." Wolfowitz reminded the participants that while countries all across the world, including Iran and Libya, expressed sympathy to America for the nearly three thousand who had perished in the attacks, Saddam stood alone for his churlish response: "The United States reaps the thorns its rulers have planted in the world." And while bombing Afghanistan would largely be a futile exercise in pounding sand, Iraq offered a wealth of promising targets, an opportunity to send a potent message to adversaries around the world.[54]

Tenet traded astonished glances with the two other CIA officials who had joined him at Camp David: What the hell was Wolfowitz talking about?[55]

One of them raised his hand. "Yes, Cofer," said the president.

Cofer Black was the director of the CIA's Counterterrorism Center (CTC). Tenet had brought him along to furnish specifics about Al Qaeda sanctuaries in Afghanistan. Since Tenet was a polished briefer, Black's main contribution up until now had been to roll a tennis ball over to Bush's

Scottish terrier Barney, a furtive act that seemed to have pleased both the dog and its owner.

But the assertions being made by Wolfowitz had alarmed him, all the more so because none of the principals—not Powell, not Rice, not his boss Tenet—had spoken up to denounce them. They flew in the face of everything Black had come to know in his nearly decade-long pursuit of Islamic extremists. Like Gary Greco at the DIA, Black believed that, after what had occurred four days prior, there was only one subject at hand, and Paul Wolfowitz had just changed it.

"Mister President," the CTC chief said, slowly and emphatically, "we were attacked on September 11 by Osama bin Laden and Al Qaeda in Afghanistan. Saddam Hussein and Iraq have nothing whatsoever to do with this."

Wolfowitz responded crisply, "We have intelligence that Saddam's intelligence service sent senior representatives to Khartoum and met with bin Laden, and a union was formed then."

Black was startled when he heard that. "That intelligence was collected by Khartoum station in 1995," he said, referring to the CIA's office in Sudan. "And I was the chief of that station."

Black then explained what the 1995 intelligence had determined. "Iraq officers came to Khartoum. They met with bin Laden. They attempted to subordinate him. Bin Laden and Al Qaeda rejected it. They were happy to take Iraq's weapons, but not to subordinate themselves to a secular Saddam Hussein. And so that was that."[56]

"Okay," said the president with finality. "We'll leave Iraq for later."[57]

The large group did not discuss Iraq from that moment onward. JCS chairman Hugh Shelton would later write that, during a break in the meeting, Bush had pulled him aside and said of Wolfowitz's comments, "What am I missing here, Hugh?"

Shelton responded that there was nothing to miss—Iraq had nothing to do with the 9/11 attacks—and that he was right to stay focused on Afghanistan.[58] Vice Chairman Myers would recall that Bush had decisively put an end to any further talk about Iraq,[59] and Rice would write that Bush had instructed Chief of Staff Andy Card to tell Wolfowitz to refrain from further interjections.[60]

"Atmospherically, it was, 'Let's move on,'" Rice would recall.[61] Powell left the meeting "pretty dismissive" of Wolfowitz's argument, convinced that the president had not taken it seriously, according to one of the secretary's top aides.[62] And though a top government official would remember Cofer Black still muttering to her almost three months later about Wolfowitz's outburst,[63] Black himself never heard Tenet or anyone else at the CIA mention the matter—leaving him to assume at the time that the issue of Iraq was dead.[64]

IT WAS FAR FROM DEAD.

Late that same afternoon, after the day's meetings at Laurel Lodge had concluded, President Bush sat by the fireplace drinking coffee. His attorney general, John Ashcroft, was playing spirituals on the piano, while Rice and a few others sang along.[65] Cheney, Libby, and Wolfowitz joined Bush by the fireplace.

If the deputy secretary had in fact been upbraided by Card a few hours earlier, he did not seem particularly chastened by the experience. Wolfowitz told the president that he had not been particularly impressed by the Afghanistan bombing plan that Shelton and Myers had recommended. He doubted that blowing up a few tents in the desert would accomplish much.

Well, Bush replied pointedly, it wasn't as if anyone had presented an Iraq bombing campaign that was any more impressive.

Wolfowitz was ready for that one. "Well, how about this," he said, then proceeded to describe the concept he had been promulgating for years—one in which a southern enclave could be created in Iraq for the purposes of training and equipping an indigenous fighting force.

But he added a detail that might capture the imagination of the former Texas oilman. "Half of Iraq is always under Kurdish control," Wolfowitz said. "The other half is within sixty kilometers of the Kuwaiti border. It wouldn't be difficult to liberate that portion of Iraq and control all of Iraq's oil." Such a maneuver, Wolfowitz argued, would both isolate Saddam and cut off his chief revenue stream. He would become little more than "the mayor of Baghdad."

"Why didn't you say that in the meeting?" Bush asked, clearly intrigued by the idea.

"It's not my place to contradict the chairman of the Joint Chiefs," Wolfowitz replied—at least, he added, not without Rumsfeld's permission or direction.[66]

The very next day, Sunday, September 16, Wolfowitz received precisely that from the secretary of defense. At Rumsfeld's urging, Wolfowitz and the undersecretary for policy, Doug Feith, met that evening with General Gregory Newbold and General John Abizaid, respectively the JCS's director of operations and its director of strategy, plans, and policy.

Both of them had a history with Wolfowitz. Following the Gulf War in 1991, General Abizaid and his 325th Airborne Battalion Combat Team had hunkered down in northern Iraq to protect the Kurds from Saddam's attacks. The successful humanitarian mission in the north would inspire Wolfowitz to champion the concept of a similar operation in southern Iraq.[67]

Wolfowitz had been less admiring of Newbold's work during the first Bush administration. The latter, a midlevel staffer in the JCS at the time, had coauthored a paper advocating a policy of "peaceful engagement" through which the United States could spread its influence in non-military ways after the collapse of the Soviet Union. The concept had won some admirers in the Pentagon, but Wolfowitz was not one of them. Whether this was because the JCS authors had stepped out of their lane into the forbidden realm of strategic thinking or because the idea itself appeared too dovish, Newbold did not know. The Marine general remained an admirer of Wolfowitz's intellect, though their prior disagreement was tame compared with the differences that would soon develop between the two men.[68]

"We had a useful talk about more creative approaches to Iraq and possibly other state supporters of terrorism besides Afghanistan," Wolfowitz wrote the next day in a memo to Rumsfeld. He added, "We explained that you want options to introduce more creative ideas to the President, not to

conform to whatever ideas someone thinks the President may already have."
Newbold and Abizaid had made clear that they took direction from the Joint
Chiefs, "who as a rule, will formulate that direction from what they infer is
the President's thinking."[69]

In other words: in order for there to be any forward movement on a bold
military initiative such as aggressive action in Iraq, the commander in chief
would first have to describe to his top generals what he had in mind.

And that was exactly what happened the day after Wolfowitz's meeting
with the generals. On Monday the 17th, Bush convened his National Security Council. Afghanistan dominated the discussion, as it had at Camp
David. This time, however, the president issued an additional directive: even
as the CIA and the Pentagon endeavored to lay siege to Al Qaeda, Bush
ordered that the Defense Department consider a plan that might include
occupying Iraqi oil fields.[70]

At last, after ten years of evangelizing, Paul Wolfowitz's lonely crusade
had made its way into the White House agenda. His task now was to make
it stay there.

CHAPTER TWO

===

A MAN IN AMERICA

Three days after that NSC meeting, on September 20, 2001, President Bush tried out the idea of going after Saddam's oil fields on the visiting British prime minister, Tony Blair.[1]

Blair maintained his poker face as he listened to Bush. Word had already reached him—from his foreign minister, Jack Straw, who had heard from Straw's friend Colin Powell—of what Paul Wolfowitz had been pushing for at Camp David.[2] The prime minister implored the president to exercise restraint. *You need to have public opinion with you,* Blair cautioned.

The two leaders, along with the senior staffers, had convened for an early dinner of veal scallops and salad in the White House residence. Blair and his subordinates had just flown in that afternoon and would be leaving late that same night, after attending the president's nationally televised address to the joint session of Congress. Their brief appearance in Washington was meant as a show of transcontinental solidarity with the Americans in the wake of the 9/11 attacks. But Blair was also there to (as he would tell his aides) "try to steer them in a sensible path," lest the world turn against Bush, a man he was only just getting to know after years of friendship with the previous president, Bill Clinton.[3]

Over dinner, Bush was calm and even reflective. He described to his British guests what had gone through his mind on that sunny Tuesday morning as he sat in an elementary school in Sarasota, Florida—how he had assumed the first plane to hit the World Trade Center was an accident; how his chief of staff, Card, had later whispered in his ear, "America is under attack, sir"; how Bush instantly knew that what lay ahead would be the greatest challenge of his life.

With Powell and Rice (but not Cheney or Rumsfeld) seated within earshot, the president acknowledged to the guests that some in his administration were agitating for him to turn America's sights on Iraq. For that matter, Bush said, Israel's prime minister, Ariel Sharon, wanted to use 9/11 as a pretext for going after the Palestinian leader, Yasser Arafat. Meanwhile, Russian president Vladimir Putin was warning about the Islamic extremists in Chechnya.

Bush's own tough talk was for the benefit of Middle America. Most of his countrymen, he explained to the Brits, had never heard of Osama bin Laden. They knew only that America had been attacked, that thousands of Americans had been killed. The public wanted Bush to inflict some payback. They wanted it done the day before yesterday, he said.[4]

And so that evening, as he stood before Congress, with Blair seated next to First Lady Laura Bush in the balcony, the president channeled the vengefulness of his fellow Americans. To the Taliban, the president issued a grave ultimatum: "Deliver to United States authorities all of the leaders of Al Qaeda who hide in your land. . . . They will hand over the terrorists, or they will share in their fate."[5]

But then, in the very next breath, the Texan offered words that no sitting American president—much less one under whose watch thousands of fellow citizens had just been killed by Islamic extremists—had ever uttered. "I also want to speak tonight directly to Muslims throughout the world," Bush said, in a voice that was prayerfully somber. "We respect your faith. It's practiced freely by many millions of Americans, and by millions more in countries that America counts as friends. Its teachings are good and peaceful, and those who commit evil in the name of Allah blaspheme the name of Allah. The terrorists are traitors to their own faith, trying, in effect, to hijack Islam itself.

The enemy of America is not our many Muslim friends; it is not our many Arab friends. Our enemy is a radical network of terrorists, and every government that supports them."

Bush's paean to Islam was striking. The greater American public had not asked for it, and some among the conservative intelligentsia found it cloying. ("And why must we constantly repeat that we are not at war with Islam?" demanded *Washington Post* columnist Charles Krauthammer.)[6] But Bush intended to be bigger than his country's smaller impulses. Reports of hate crimes targeting Muslim Americans immediately after 9/11 had alarmed him. Laura Bush suggested that he visit a mosque.[7]

On the afternoon of Monday, September 17, the presidential motorcade drove three miles to the Islamic Center of Washington. Bush took off his shoes, walked into the prayer hall, and, in his black socks, stated flatly that America's millions of Muslims "need to be treated with respect. In our anger and our emotion, fellow Americans must treat each other with respect." Attempting to harass women in head scarves, he said, "should not and will not stand in America." Lashing out in such a manner "represents the worst of humankind, and they should be ashamed of that kind of behavior."[8]

Bush's four-minute monologue at the Islamic Center was destined to fade from history's spotlight, upstaged by his many famous utterances both before and after it. But his remarks there were among the most meaningful he would give that month. After Bush's admonition, attacks on Muslims in America plummeted by roughly 50 percent.[9] What Americans heard, then and three days later in his speech before Congress, was a president who believed himself duty-bound to preserve the nation's moral goodness.

They also saw a skilled politician who understood the electoral value of faith-based constituencies. Having seen his father place a dismal third in the 1988 Iowa caucuses, behind Senator Bob Dole and televangelist Pat Robertson, the son quietly but assiduously courted conservative Christian leaders during his own presidential run.[10] He did the same with Jewish voters, telling British foreign minister Jack Straw that "my dad got burned by the Israeli lobby in 1992, and I don't want to fall into the same trap."[11]

When Bush decided to run for president, his political adviser Karl Rove

quickly identified Muslim voters as a key constituency that had been given
the cold shoulder by the Gore campaign. The candidate received Muslim
leaders at the governor's mansion in Austin. In speeches, he repeatedly used
the novel if somewhat cumbersome term "Judeo-Christian-Islamic America." At the Republican convention in Philadelphia, the Bush team saw to it
that the opening day began with a Muslim prayer. During one of his debates
with Gore, Bush brought up and denounced racial profiling of Arab Americans. Two weeks before the election, he received the endorsement of the
American Muslim Political Coordination Council. After the Florida recount was settled in December 2000, Bush carried the state by a margin of
537 votes. Given that, according to exit polls, the vast majority of Florida's
sixty thousand Muslim voters had cast their ballots for Bush, White House
political director Ken Mehlman was not speaking hyperbolically in saying,
"Muslim Americans got us here."[12]

Bush had in fact been scheduled to meet with several Muslim leaders in
the White House on the afternoon of September 11. The events of that morning foreclosed the gathering. Still, just a few hours before Tony Blair arrived
at the White House on September 20, the president received several religious
figures in the Oval Office. Among them were Reverend Franklin Graham,
Cardinal Bernard Law, and Hamza Yusuf Hanson, an Islamic scholar and
founder of the Zaytuna Institute, in Berkeley, California. Hanson was meeting Bush for the first time, but the president was impressed by his poise (and
proficiency in Spanish). That evening, he would be Laura Bush's personal
guest at the speech in the Capitol.

Bush told the religious leaders that the ensuing military campaign to
defeat America's enemies would be called Operation Infinite Justice. Hanson
advised against this. "It would be very offensive to believers," the Berkeley
imam warned Bush.

"Really?" said the president.

"Only God's justice is infinite," said Hanson.

Bush wheeled to an aide. "Call and get that changed," he instructed.

Smirking, he added to his guests, "We don't have any theologians at the
Pentagon."

Bush told Hamza and the other religious leaders that America would need their guidance in the days ahead. He shared with them a sentiment that he would soon be repeating incessantly, in speeches and to foreign leaders: "Through my tears, I see opportunity." But he also offered to these holy men a confession that few others would hear.

"I'm having difficulty controlling my bloodlust," the president said.[13]

THE MEN AND WOMEN IN THE FEDERAL GOVERNMENT WHO WITNESSED THE conduct of George W. Bush during the first days of the 9/11 crisis would later profess amazement at the forty-third president's leadership abilities. Some of them had not voted for the man, viewing him as too conservative, inexperienced, and not especially bright—a winner by birthright (and crafty lawyering in Florida) rather than by merit.

Even when they discovered that the Texan was not only personable but quite intelligent, they saw nothing in him to foreshadow the piercing clarity of purpose that he exhibited after the most calamitous event in American history since the Civil War. An intelligence official who listened in to Bush's conversations on Air Force One throughout much of the day on September 11 would recall, "I didn't vote for him, but hearing him talking to Cheney and Rumsfeld totally put me in the bag for Bush. He knew what to do, what to ask. I mean, he was the fucking president of the United States."[14]

Said Cofer Black, of the CIA, "In the meetings, I was thinking, *You're watching greatness here.* He was calm, not flustered, measured—his thought process was good and solid. He was the most impressive of anybody."[15]

Bush was presiding over a badly rattled White House. While Air Force One underwent an eight-hour odyssey through suddenly vacant skies, his aides had been evacuated from the building, rushing past Secret Service members crouching in the corridors with long guns. At least one of the president's senior staffers, Brad Blakeman, had lost a family member in the World Trade Center.[16] Other aides were Muslim and fearful of retaliation.

The privileged burden of the everyday White House experience was now tinged with what press secretary Ari Fleischer would term "a heart-heaviness."

Aides were apprised from September 12 forward that the prospect of a second attack on America was not a question of *if*, but *when*. As a physical reminder of this, on September 13 the Secret Service expanded the security perimeters of 1600 Pennsylvania Avenue out into Lafayette Park. That same day, an aide in the Situation Room alerted Andy Card to a report that a truck bomb was barreling down the Baltimore–Washington Parkway, bound for a hospital where the president was visiting first responders who had been injured at the Pentagon.[17]

Throughout, the president displayed calm as well as focus—going so far as to tell his White House communications team one morning, "Let me tell you how to do your job today."[18] Rarely in those initial weeks did he let his emotional reflexes get the better of him. One exception took place during a break at the Camp David meetings on September 15, when a senior State Department official approached the president and emphasized that his first interaction with the Taliban needed to be diplomatic rather than an act of aggression. After watching the official go, Bush said to the two CIA officials who had been standing beside him, "Fuck diplomacy. We are going to war."[19]

BUSH HAD NEVER BEEN TO WAR. HE HAD AVOIDED DEPLOYMENT TO VIET-nam by enlisting in the National Guard. His foreign affairs experience had consisted of little more than playing tennis on the Beijing embassy court when his father served as U.S. ambassador to China and, later, as governor dedicating a water treatment plant at the Mexican border town of Nuevo León. Bush in 1994 had beaten the incumbent Texas governor, Ann Richards, by focusing militantly on four issues: education, juvenile justice, welfare, and tort reform. Six years later, he endeavored to win the presidency in the same minimalist manner. Not surprisingly, his path to the White House entailed a self-designed obstacle course of foreign policy gaffes: confusing Slovakia and Slovenia, failing to know the names of foreign leaders, terming Greeks "Grecians" and Kosovars "Kosovians."

Bush's choices for his foreign policy team reflected some self-awareness about his own shortcomings. He delegated enormous power to Cheney, to whom he had said more than once during his search for a VP, "You know, you're the solution to my problem"—that problem being inexperience.[20] For his first cabinet nominee, Bush selected as the first-ever African American secretary of state Colin Powell, whose 83 percent Gallup approval rating dwarfed Bush's. Powell and Cheney had a history, as did Cheney and his mentor Donald Rumsfeld, Bush's secretary of defense, though of a different sort.

Bush was aware but not fully appreciative of that history. It was irrelevant, to his mind. They all reported to him now. Foreign policy would proceed with hierarchical locomotion, as his domestic policy did—except perhaps on a more modest scale, with any disputes among his foreign policy team ably mediated by Bush's national security adviser, Condoleezza Rice, who happened to possess only a fraction of their experience, another fact that the new president failed to appreciate.

Before and just after Bush took office, much was made of the fact that, in stark contrast to a famously undisciplined Clinton presidency, this was to be the first-ever administration presided over by a Harvard Business School alumnus. Meetings were to be short and focused, with punctuality zealously enforced. No one could enter the Oval Office without a coat and tie. Upholding the dignity of the office functioned as proof of a well-oiled executive apparatus. It was also widely noted that Bush was a deeply competitive man who relished smoking his aides in mountain bike rides at his Texas ranch under withering August heat and who—unusual for a Republican—unabashedly saw himself as an "activist" executive.[21]

Such characteristics, combined with Bush's unique experience of having been a president's son, created the illusion of extraordinary competency and engagement. The paradox of this star-studded but tragically dysfunctional administration begins with the deceptively complicated personality of a man whose energies tended toward compulsiveness: several drinks too many in an earlier era, chop-chop hyperefficiency and maximal calorie burning later in life. The way Bush ran meetings constituted a tell. Often, they started and concluded earlier than scheduled, as if leading the free world amounted to a series of daily sprints. When moved to do so, Bush could pick apart an aide's flimsy presentation. Just as often, however, he would conclude with a brisk "Anything further? Okay, thank you"—and then early to the next meeting.

Could someone so clipped and propulsive also be regarded as somehow complacent? A recurring leitmotif in the life of George W. Bush was that of a son of privilege whose favoring of the easy road could lead him astray. A famously undistinguished pupil in Ivy League institutions, Bush as an adult was a somewhat more dutiful student but still glided over details whenever possible. He hated "small ball," a phrase he used interchangeably with "tactics." His natural realm was "strategy," or "vision." He also looked skeptically on "nuance," which to him often meant "bullshit." Bush excelled at detecting bullshit, of which there was no shortage in Washington, just as he possessed a gift for grasping and articulating the larger stakes.

But not everything small lacked significance. His tendencies served as an occasional excuse to avoid nettlesome specifics. Five months into his presidency, after spending ninety minutes with the Russian leader Vladimir Putin—in which Bush implored his counterpart not to "get stuck in history" but instead to join him in "making history together"[22]—Bush declared to the press that he had looked into the former KGB agent's eyes and "was able to get a sense of his soul."[23]

Similarly, during the summer of 2001, Bush interrupted a monologue by his CIA briefer Michael Morell with a curt "Okay, Michael. You've covered your ass."[24] The topic had been Osama bin Laden's threats against America. Recounting this moment in his 2015 book—which had been carefully reviewed before publication by Deputy National Security Adviser Steve Hadley—Morell assured readers that the president was only joking. At the time, however, Morell was dismayed by Bush's flippancy, and said so that afternoon to a fellow CIA briefer.[25]

Bush had been hearing such warnings about bin Laden for a year now. On September 3, 2000, the Republican nominee, Rice, and policy adviser Wolfowitz received a briefing from CIA deputy director John McLaughlin at Bush's ranch in Crawford, Texas.[26] During the four-hour briefing, McLaughlin informed the candidate, "Governor Bush, if you are elected, the

United States will experience a serious terrorist attack during your time. That's where we are in this battle."

Bush did not respond to the CIA deputy director's dark prediction.[27] Nor did he issue any remarks about Al Qaeda thereafter during the campaign. (His spokesman during the campaign, Ari Fleischer, would recall hearing the term "Al Qaeda" for the very first time in June 2001—uttered not by Bush but instead by Putin, in reference to extremist activity in Chechnya.)[28] When asked, during the final presidential debate on October 17, about violence in the Middle East following the recent bombing of the USS *Cole* off the coast of Yemen, candidate Bush did not reply with any thoughts about terrorism. He did, however, observe, "Saddam Hussein is still a threat in the Middle East."[29]

To a significant degree, Bush's relative disinterest in Islamic extremism reflected the priorities of his foreign policy team. Those views held by Cheney, Rice, Rumsfeld, and Powell had been forged during the Cold War. Their concerns centered on America's vulnerability to ICBMs, not on asymmetric warfare waged by terrorists.[30] Among Bush's national security team, only Powell and his deputy, Richard Armitage, took the briefing on Al Qaeda offered during the transition by NSC counterterrorism adviser Richard Clarke.[31] And throughout the first eight months of the Bush presidency, only a smattering of questions about terrorism were asked by Rice, Rumsfeld, and Cheney during their daily CIA briefings.[32] So threadbare was their concern that the agency's analysts joked mordantly among themselves that whenever the Texas president did eventually offer up a query relating to "the Gulf states," he would probably be referring to Alabama or Mississippi.[33]

The joke, in the end, was unfunny. Repeatedly, Director George Tenet would mutter to his analysts after briefings, with palpable chagrin, "They don't get it."[34]

The resident counterterrorism experts at the NSC, CIA, and DIA struggled to understand the new administration's disengagement. Perhaps, they thought, Bush and his lieutenants regarded terrorist-inflicted mayhem as a kind of abstraction, since such a tragedy had yet to occur on their watch. Perhaps, to their Western minds, terrorists were exotic anomalies like Carlos the Jackal. Perhaps the occasional terrorist attack on an American embassy was seen by them as the cost of doing business overseas. And perhaps the much despised Clinton administration's obsession with bin Laden served as proof, to Bush and his fellow Republicans, that it was a foolish preoccupation.[35]

"You give bin Laden too much credit," Wolfowitz had argued to Clarke during the former's first Deputies Committee meeting, in April 2001, adding that a "little terrorist in Afghanistan" lacked the means to pull off a major attack, at least without a state sponsor.[36] Cheney and Rumsfeld openly speculated that bin Laden's activities were merely a ruse, an attempt to force the government to waste resources on a bogus threat. It was, in fact, their pronounced skepticism about Al Qaeda's seriousness that compelled Morell's briefing—the one to which Bush had responded with his regrettable you've-covered-your-ass retort.[37]

In a final effort to convey to Bush the direness of their intelligence warnings, the CIA took the unusual step of partnering with the FBI to produce a brief, on August 6, 2001, entitled "Bin Laden Determined to Strike in US." The two-page paper, briefed by Morell to Bush while the latter vacationed in Crawford, warned of "suspicious activity in this country consistent with preparations for hijackings or other types of attacks, including recent surveillance of federal buildings in New York."[38] As Morell, Rice, and others would later point out, the brief cited no specific date, city, or target. (Seldom, however, does intelligence arrive in such granular form, a senior analyst would argue: "Exact place and time—in the history of the planet, you don't get that.")[39]

Nor, however, did the president and his advisers press for more information—or, at minimum, for continued interaction between the FBI and the CIA. The Al Qaeda specialist who had been the author of the brief would recall thinking, as follow-up questions failed to eventuate, "So what is this—you're not even *curious?*"[40]

Five weeks and one day later, on the afternoon of September 11, George W. Bush received his CIA briefer Morell in the airborne office of Air Force One. The number of casualties in New York and the Pentagon had yet to be determined, but it was already clear that the total would be in the thousands.

To the very analyst who had given him repeated briefings on Al Qaeda's malevolent intentions, Bush asked, "Who did this, Michael?"[41]

NOTHING CHANGES EVERYTHING. AMERICA'S AIRPORTS RETURNED TO BUSI-ness on September 13. Six days after the September 11 attacks, the New York Stock Exchange reopened and Major League Baseball resumed. The next day, Tuesday the 18th, *Style 24/7* magazine featured Jennifer Aniston on the cover to showcase "100 Celebrity Looks," while on the CBS morning game show *The Price Is Right,* the inhumanly tanned host Bob Barker exhorted contestants to "spin that wheel" in hopes of winning a fifty-five-inch high-definition TV valued at $6,498. On September 23, the national flags outside of federal buildings that had been flying at half-staff for the previous eleven days were hoisted to their customary height.

Three months after the attacks, it was Christmastime. The UK's minister of defense, Geoffrey Hoon, called an American friend who lived in Kentucky to wish him season's greetings. The friend volunteered to Hoon that he and his wife had only just started going out in public again.

Hoon was stupefied. His friend, a law professor, was hardly an ignora-mus. But he lived eight hundred miles away from Ground Zero. It then oc-curred to Blair's defense minister that, as he would later reflect, "we Europeans had not really grasped the level of shock that 9/11 had caused to ordinary Americans." That shock, Hoon predicted to his colleagues in the Blair ad-ministration, would dramatically alter decision-making in Washington.[42]

The capital city had not been assaulted by a malevolent force since British troops torched the White House and the Capitol in 1814. To Washington's governing elites, "crisis"—a recession, a presidential sex scandal, an election decided by the Supreme Court—was something to cluck about from an im-pervious remove. As a British study would conclude, European policymakers tended to fear terrorism even more than average citizens did.[43] That phenom-enon would prove just as true in Washington, a center of power whose marble fortress now seemed as collapsible as the Twin Towers.

But the blow struck by bin Laden's hijackers was not simply an attack on America's national security. In a deeper sense, the 9/11 aftershocks exacerbated the same decades-long cultural drift that candidate George W. Bush had vowed to bring to a halt. Though his father and Clinton had presided over a decade of post–Cold War triumphalism and prosperity, the United States had lost its ideological foil and in its place experienced, perhaps, a certain forlornness on the mountaintop. As the British sociologist Frank Furedi would observe, "In many respects, American moral superiority was contingent on the moral inferiority of the Soviet empire. Once that was gone, one got the sense that American political culture was running on empty."[44]

The country was thrown into a deep state of shock and disorientation after 9/11. An enemy bearing neither flag nor uniform had crashed America's planes into America's buildings. Their first weapon of choice had been an American invention from the 1920s, the box cutter.[45] The possibilities of danger now seemed almost limitless. In anticipating the unfathomable, the first casualty was expertise. What might come next was anybody's guess.

Fear of "the next wave" consumed the White House. There was a credible threat that the White House food supply had been poisoned, and another suggesting that the building had been infected with botulinum toxin. Another lead pointed to a bombing device in midtown Manhattan. An imminent smallpox attack was also reported. "People were losing their minds on this," recalled Roger Cressey, the NSC's director of transnational threats.[46] A different NSC official would say, "What I noticed most strongly at the time was how really scared everybody senior in the Bush administration was."[47]

Bush, in seemingly inverse proportion to his pre-9/11 detachment, was now immersed in reports of suspected terrorist activity. In addition to the Presidential Daily Briefing furnished by the CIA, the FBI now supplied the president with a daily threat matrix. The intelligence in it was raw, closer to rumor than to fact. "If some nutcase was going to blow up Sears Tower from a phone booth in Minnesota, it was on the president's desk," Rice recalled.[48]

The specter of the commander in chief poring over such harrowing minutiae struck some of his senior aides as ill-advised.[49] Still, though it was never like George W. Bush to publicly admit failure, the buck stopped with the impassive recipient of repeated pre-9/11 warnings. Now he heeded them with a penitent's grim fervor.

How to manage so fearful a climate? The president, famously averse to what he called "navel gazing," instead strove to reclaim a sense of normalcy. He ate comfort food. He prayed. He exercised. He watched baseball. And he preached for the nation as a whole to do the same. "The American people have got to go about their business," he said at a press conference exactly one month after the attacks. "We cannot let the terrorists achieve the objective of frightening our nation to the point where we don't conduct business, where people don't shop."[50]

That last sentiment invited ridicule from the left. But Bush understood something that his critics did not. In America, in Washington, and in the White House, reorienting oneself to the strange new contours of a post-9/11 climate resembled a kind of surrender. The president strove to flatten meaning. America had done nothing to deserve this evil. The nation's goodness, its rightness, was unassailable. Correspondingly, the perpetrators and their sympathizers did not merit any deeper understanding. "We have seen their kind before," Bush would say in his joint session speech, and then liken the terrorist creed to "fascism, Nazism, and totalitarianism"—the familiar templates of evil.[51] (Some American religious leaders would conflate Islamic extremists with another great destroyer of innocence: pedophiles.)[52]

But entangled with the encompassing fear, and a desire to overcome it, was an intense yearning for revenge. As Colin Powell would later reflect, "The American people wanted somebody killed."[53] For George W. Bush and his national security team, the means to regain America's primacy lay in seeking out a more comprehensible foe—a reversion to familiar and more favorable territory, involving wartime parameters that the world's lone superpower had long mastered.

The Bush administration did not have to look far for such an obliging target. The nemesis in question had resided in the president's muscle memory for years now and was still around, sneering at America's misfortune, all but begging for one more fight.

HOW DEEP AND LASTING WAS THE BUSH FAMILY'S ANIMUS TOWARD SADDAM Hussein?

On April 18, 2006, Jeb Bush, the governor of Florida and younger brother of the president, traveled to Iraq with three other governors to visit the troops over Easter. As the C-130 conveyed them from Kuwait to Baghdad, Bush and one of the other governors, Joe Manchin of West Virginia, fell into conversation.

"How's my brother doing in your state?" the Florida governor asked.

"Well," Manchin replied, "when it comes to the war on terror, West Virginia is behind the president all the way."

Manchin paused, reflecting on their destination, now a land of chaos with daily eruptions of roadside bombs and guerrilla attacks causing public support for the American military presence there to plummet to all-time lows. "But as for the war in Iraq . . ." His voice trailed off, and he shook his head.

Jeb Bush then said something that astonished his West Virginia counterpart. "You know, he tried to kill my father," he said. "I was on that trip, too." So were Bush's mother, his brother Neil, and his sister-in-law Laura, the first lady. "All of us could've been killed."

Manchin knew what the younger Bush was referring to. On April 15, 1993, during a three-day trip by former president Bush to Kuwait, the country he had liberated from Saddam, several suspected terrorists were arrested by the Kuwaiti authorities. The suspects confessed that they had been recruited by the Iraqi Intelligence Service to detonate explosives packed inside a Toyota Land Cruiser that would be parked on Bush's motorcade route. Should the bomb fail to go off, one of the suspects, a thirty-six-year-old Iraqi named Wali al-Ghazali, had been instructed to detonate his suicide belt. The plot was a marvel of ineptitude and unraveled before its inception. The Bushes left Kuwait none the worse for the wear on April 16.

Nine days passed before news of the assassination attempt made its way into a London-based Arab newspaper. A week later, the FBI verified that the 170-pound bomb in the Land Cruiser matched Iraqi explosives that had been recovered after Desert Storm in 1991. Two months after the arrests, thirteen defendants were found guilty in the aborted plot. Five of them, including al-Ghazali, were sentenced to death in Kuwait.[54] Immediately after the trial, on orders from President Clinton, U.S. Navy ships fired twenty-three Tomahawk missiles, leveling Iraqi Intelligence Service headquarters in downtown Baghdad.[55]

The Iraq government insisted that it had been framed by the vengeful Kuwaitis. Regardless, Saddam faced no further reprisals. The assassination attempt, grievously bungled as it was, failed to animate the Iraqi leader's ardent foes in the way that his attacks against his own people had. But to the Bushes, the Kuwait episode was not readily forgotten.

"I'd take 'em out—I'm surprised he's still there," presidential candidate Bush said of the Iraqi dictator during a debate in New Hampshire in December 1999. (Bush later insisted that he meant he would take out Saddam's weapons of mass destruction. But the remark nonetheless took his own press spokesman by surprise.)[56]

Two months later, in the heat of the South Carolina primary, Bush's hostility toward Saddam remained undisguised. "I'm just as frustrated as many Americans are that Saddam Hussein still lives," he said to PBS newscaster Jim Lehrer. If Saddam was found to possess WMD, Bush vowed darkly, "I'll deal with him in a way that he won't like."[57]

Still, Bush's disdain of Saddam fell well short of all-consuming. Not once during the 2000 campaign did he advocate regime change in Iraq as his goal. Quite the contrary: in 2000, Condi Rice wrote an essay for *Foreign Affairs* that was widely viewed as the intellectual framework for a Bush administration national security agenda. The passage pertaining to Saddam was notably restrained: "The first line of defense should be deterrence—if he does acquire WMD, his weapons will be unusable, because any attempt to use them will bring national obliteration."[58]

And on January 11, 2001, when the president-elect received his first briefing on current U.S. military activity by the Joint Chiefs of Staff, in the JCS conference room known as "the tank," he listened with skepticism to the descriptions of the no-fly zone operations taking place over northern and southern Iraq.

"How much are those operations costing us?" he asked. When informed of the expense—roughly $700 million to enforce the southern no-fly zone alone—Bush's pursed expression made clear his disfavor of the operation.[59]

Three days later, on January 14, the soon-to-be-inaugurated president welcomed two *New York Times* reporters, Frank Bruni and David Sanger, to his ranch at Crawford. During their lengthy interview, Sanger asked Bush about Iraq.

"He basically shrugged," Sanger would recall. With his dog Barney on his lap, the president-elect replied that something needed to be done to strengthen the sanctions on Saddam's regime that had begun during the first Bush presidency. He seemed otherwise indifferent on the subject—so much so that the reporters did not include anything about that exchange in their story.[60]

Just a month later, on February 16, the new president chose for his first foreign visit a familiar destination: Mexico. At President Vicente Fox's ranch house in San Cristóbal, the Texan wore his cowboy boots, tried out his Spanish (while declining to try on a sombrero), kissed the Mexican president's elderly mother, and winked a great deal. It was a new leader wading gingerly into the baby pool of diplomacy—a breezy day trip with little opportunity for misfortune.

But the first question that Bush took from the press that afternoon did not involve U.S.-Mexico relations. Instead, a Mexican reporter asked about a breaking-news development on the other side of the globe. "What does the United States want to send to the world as a message with the new bombing of Iraq?" the reporter wanted to know. "And above all, why, Mr. Bush, at this point, when you are establishing a dialogue with the president of Mexico? Why? Is this the beginning of a new war?"[61]

Only a few moments earlier, during the presidential meet-and-greet, NBC White House correspondent Campbell Brown had whispered into Ari Fleischer's ear, "Why are we bombing Iraq?" The spokesman had no clue. He motioned frantically for Rice to leave Bush's side. By the time she had made her way to him, Fleischer had heard from other reporters.

"Why are we bombing Baghdad?" he asked the national security adviser. Rice had no ready answer.[62]

In fact, Rice and one of her senior staffers, Frank Miller, had been briefed on the matter a few days earlier by General Gregory Newbold. The JCS director of operations informed them that Iraqi forces—most likely reflecting Saddam Hussein's desire to test the resolve of a new administration—had been firing antiaircraft artillery and surface-to-air missiles at American and British aircraft enforcing Iraq's no-fly zones with increasing frequency since Bush's inauguration. As a result, the JCS had designed a bombing response that would be "quite robust."

"What will Saddam's reaction be?" Rice asked.

"He is going to scream," Newbold replied.

Rice and Miller approved the package. Subsequently, they briefed the president. What none of them had anticipated was that some of the Tomahawk missiles would overshoot their targets and set off air raid sirens in Baghdad while killing two Iraqi civilians and wounding twenty others. What had begun as an antiseptic military strike triggered howls of humanitarian outrage and upended Bush's first foreign visit.[63]

Cheney, for his part, was delighted by the jut-jawed message to Saddam conveyed by the bombing.[64] Powell, at the State Department, was far less pleased. The aggressive response had been roundly condemned, from France to China to Egypt. Thousands of Palestinians marched in the streets, burning American flags.[65]

The State Department was focused on modifying the U.S. government's ongoing Iraq sanctions policy, which had evolved into a PR nightmare in the Arab world, one in which America was seen to be denying food to Iraqi children in the name of a vendetta against Saddam. Powell's "smart sanctions" would allow more consumer goods to flow into Iraq while clamping down on imports that could be used for weapons systems.

At the same time, Powell's policy planning director, Richard Haass, had been quietly talking to the CIA about the feasibility of staging a coup against Saddam. Haass ultimately informed Powell in a memo that search-ing for an obliging Iraqi general to dethrone the dictator was not a viable option.[66]

Still, Paul Wolfowitz was sufficiently alarmed by the scenario—one that might simply replace one evil Baathist with another—that the deputy secre-tary ordered a rebuttal to Haass's memo. The April 23, 2001, countermemo, entitled "A Strategy to Liberate Iraq," argued Wolfowitz's familiar position of financing and training an indigenous opposition force that would over-throw the dictator with the help of limited U.S. military strikes.[67]

But Wolfowitz's boss, Donald Rumsfeld, remained as unconvinced of a liberation scheme as he was of Powell's sanctions policy and continued no-fly-zone enforcement. The defense secretary himself espoused no comprehensive Iraq policy, only a Rumsfeldian galaxy of possibilities—including, as he wrote in one memo to Rice, "to take a crack at initiating contact with Saddam Hussein."[68] Though Wolfowitz and other Iraq hawks advocated tougher re-sponses to no-fly zone violations—a departure from "pinprick bombings" in favor of a provocation that might trigger some fatal reciprocation by Saddam—Rumsfeld cautioned against this. The defense secretary's reason-ing was simple: it would be irresponsible to push the Iraqi dictator to the brink of military conflict if the president himself had no appetite for war—which, by all indications, he did not.[69]

Sitting in the Oval Office one morning in the spring of 2001, Bush confided to his CIA briefer Michael Morell that a day would come when Saddam's provocations would necessitate military action from the United States. "It is not a question of *if* but only a question of *when*, Michael," said the president.[70]

But he voiced the prediction as an abstraction. Bush's current pursuits focused on education reform and tax cuts. After August recess, the White House would throw itself into immigration reform. As he woke up in Sara-sota, Florida, on the morning of September 11, the forty-third president's Iraq policy was the same as the forty-second president's. Saddam Hussein was a problem to be managed—and, whenever possible, ignored.

———

"SEE IF SADDAM DID THIS," BUSH SAID TO RICHARD CLARKE IN THE SITUA-tion Room on the evening of September 12, 2001.[71]

Clarke was startled but not completely surprised. The previous evening, in a conference room adjacent to the Situation Room, the NSC counter-terrorism chief and two of his aides had overheard the president and Rums-feld quietly discussing Saddam's possible involvement.[72] A transcript of the dictator's uniquely brutish intimation that America had deserved to be at-tacked had been widely circulated around the White House. Clarke was thoroughly convinced that Al Qaeda was the sole perpetrator. Still, the com-mander in chief's order was nonnegotiable.

"Paul, you run this process," he said to his deputy, Paul Kurtz, who had just walked into the conference room as Bush was leaving.

Kurtz, who had spent a great deal of time in Iraq as a weapons inspector following the Gulf War, quickly convened a secure video teleconference, or SVTC, with Iraq specialists from the CIA, FBI, NSA, and State Depart-ment. After three days, Kurtz compiled the analysis from each agency, which Clarke immediately forwarded to Deputy National Security Adviser Steve Hadley. The three-page memo Kurtz produced reflected the unanimous conclusion that Iraq did not have any involvement in the 9/11 attacks.

A day or two later, Hadley sent the memo back to Richard Clarke with a note attached. "Please update," it said. Clarke interpreted this as his team not having produced the answer that the White House wanted. Clarke did not hear anything further about Kurtz's memo.[73]

On the morning of Wednesday, September 26, Bush summoned Rums-feld to the Oval Office for a private conversation. I want you to look into our military plans regarding Iraq, he instructed the secretary of defense.[74]

"I just think the president was covering his bases," Rice would say later of Bush's scattered utterances about Iraq in the days and weeks following 9/11. Emphasizing that she saw the president numerous times every day, Bush's national security adviser would insist that Iraq "was not on his mind.

It just wasn't . . . Any human being has only so much bandwidth. And his bandwidth was 'Are we going to get attacked again?'"[75]

In the main, this was true. The president's schedule for the first ten days of September 2001 and that of the last nineteen days of the same month would look like agendas from entirely different epochs. Bush's presidency had changed irrevocably.

But it had not changed completely. He was, out of necessity, more than a war president. His "bandwidth" still included room for bill signings, staff appointments, proclamations of Family Day and National Historically Black Colleges and Universities Week, and baseball.[76]

All the same, Bush did not ask members of his administration to investigate Libya's or North Korea's possible involvement in the attacks on America. He did not request creative options for military action against Iran. Alone among nations, it seemed, Iraq took up residency in a dark corner of George W. Bush's consciousness even as he threw his energies into defending a wounded nation.

AS IT HAPPENED, THE GREATER AND LESSER PREOCCUPATIONS SOON CON-verged. On the morning of October 4, 2001, the presidential motorcade stopped off at Foggy Bottom. Bush was visiting the State Department to thank its employees for working long hours in building a global coalition to fight terror, and to announce that the United States would be sending $320 million in humanitarian assistance to the people of Afghanistan. During his remarks, the president became emotional and began to tear up. After returning to the White House, he motioned for Fleischer to follow him into the Oval Office.

Bush's shoulders were slumped as he stared out the window onto the Rose Garden. "We've got a report in Florida this morning of an anthrax case," he told his press spokesman. The man afflicted with it was in grave condition. Bush speculated that this could be the second wave of attacks.[77]

The Florida man died the next day. Within a week's time, envelopes stuffed with anthrax would materialize in the offices of media outlets in Boca

Raton and New York. Speculation soon turned to Saddam Hussein, who was known to have stockpiled biological weapons while waging war with Iran throughout the eighties. When British reporter David Rose of *The Guardian* called former CIA director Jim Woolsey on October 13, Woolsey—who had bonded with Paul Wolfowitz over their contempt for Saddam—said that only Iraq was known to have the capability to produce airborne anthrax spores. "Iraq Behind U.S. Anthrax Outbreaks" was the headline blaring from *The Guardian* the next day.[78]

Three days later, while traveling on Air Force One to Travis Air Force Base, in Northern California, Bush called Prime Minister Blair. He told Blair that the anthrax was weapons-grade. In all likelihood, said the president, its source was Saddam, who he believed had given the anthrax to bin Laden to spread throughout America.[79]

How Bush had arrived at this conclusion was never made clear. (Though he was not the only politician to do so. The next day, while appearing on *Late Night with David Letterman,* Senator John McCain claimed that "there is some indication that some of this anthrax may—and I emphasize *may*—have come from Iraq.")[80] By the end of the month, the Bush White House had accepted the prevailing view of the intelligence community that the anthrax had been produced domestically.[81]

Still, the anthrax attacks sent Washington into cascades of near hysteria. The offices of Senator Patrick Leahy and Senate Majority Leader Tom Daschle had been exposed to anthrax. So had an Air Force mail room that received packages intended for the White House. Five people died from anthrax inhalation, and numerous others were hospitalized. Though President Bush felt certain that, as he put it in an interview, "people are going to tire of the war on terrorism,"[82] what he had yet to recognize was that the nation's capital had fallen prey to a siege mentality. The Pentagon had been attacked; but for the heroics of United Flight 93's passengers, the Capitol might have been hit as well. Washington Reagan Airport had been shut down for more than three weeks. Now newsrooms and Senate offices had been targeted by a bioweapons terrorist.

For the first time since 1861, insulated Washington found itself on the

front lines. Unaccustomed to such vulnerability, the city took leave of its native skepticism and fell in line behind America's protector, George W. Bush,
with his approval rating of 90 and his equally stratospheric self-confidence,
which, for the moment, felt entirely comforting.

IN AN ADDRESS TO THE NATION ON OCTOBER 7, 2001, BUSH BEGAN BY SAYING,
"Good afternoon," then got right to the point: "On my orders, the United
States military has begun strikes against Al Qaeda terrorist training camps
and military installations of the Taliban regime in Afghanistan."[83] Operation
Enduring Freedom had begun. America was officially at war.

Over the next two months, a U.S.-led coalition that included troops
from the UK, Germany, Italy, France, Turkey, Canada, Australia, and the
Netherlands deluged Afghanistan with air and ground strikes. On December 7, the Taliban stronghold of Kandahar fell. The Taliban's founder, Mullah Mohammed Omar, and Al Qaeda's two top leaders, bin Laden and
Ayman al-Zawahiri, had somehow managed to escape the country. But Afghanistan was no longer ruled by supporters of terror. Its new leader, Hamid
Karzai, was sworn into office on December 22, 2001.

Once the Taliban's demise seemed imminent, David Friend, an editor at
Vanity Fair, approached Bush's media adviser, Mark McKinnon. Friend
wanted to know if the president and his war council—Cheney, Rumsfeld,
Powell, and Rice—would agree to be photographed by Annie Leibovitz for
the cover of an upcoming issue.

The idea was audacious in the extreme. Bush's combativeness toward the
press, going back to his days as troubleshooter for his father the president,
had not mellowed with time. A glammed-up treatment in *Vanity Fair* seemed
even more dubious a pursuit for a president with war on his mind. McKinnon
advised the editor to take it up with Bush's counselor, Karen Hughes, as well
as Cheney's communications director, Mary Matalin. Friend met with them
more than once. He emphasized the need to capture the gravitas of the moment, the iconography of American history makers.

Bush himself made the call: he and his national security team would be photographed. On a Monday morning in early December, they promptly filed into the Cabinet Room, all dressed in black. "You're gonna need a lot more makeup on this guy!" Bush guffawed while a makeup artist dabbed at Rumsfeld's face. The defense secretary's eye was bloodshot from a broken blood vessel. Bush's immense belt buckle sported the presidential seal. Powell asked Leibovitz what she wanted their expressions to convey.

"Resolve," she replied.

Just before shooting was to begin, the president called for someone to fetch his chief of staff and his CIA director. The tableau would now be hopelessly overcrowded, but Bush was emphatic: Card and Tenet belonged in the frame.[84]

The resulting cover shot—five men and one woman staring intently into the lens, with Rumsfeld squinting off to the side at some unspecified "known unknown"—was, indeed, a portrait of collective resolve. But for others in the Bush White House, the image on the cover of the February 2002 *Vanity Fair* conveyed the makings of hubris. Before 9/11, Bush's domestically oriented agenda had relegated his national security team to the back pages. Now they were on the cover. Wartime had conferred on Cheney, Rumsfeld, Powell, and Rice the mantle of celebrity. They had become, in the caustic words of one White House senior staffer, "barons of power, projecting the image of war. She can't make them pose in ways they don't want to."[85]

Another senior administration official who saw how the president's war council had responded to the limelight said, "The Annie Leibovitz photo shoot took it to another level—to being on steroids. And the irony is, the person who saw it the least was Bush."[86]

SADDAM'S SPITEFUL COMMENT ON SEPTEMBER 12, 2001, THAT AMERICA "REAPS the thorns its rulers have planted in the world" was immediately echoed in the state-controlled Iraqi press. The 9/11 attacks, proclaimed the newspaper *Al-Iktisadi*, constituted "God's punishment." Said another Iraqi daily, *Alif-Ba*, "The real perpetrators are within the collapsed buildings."[87]

Just as quickly, the regime went silent. Attacks by Iraqi aircraft on aircraft enforcing the no-fly zone immediately plummeted after 9/11.[88] On September 27, one of Colin Powell's top deputies, Assistant Secretary of State for Near Eastern Affairs Bill Burns, received a letter from an old friend, former Reagan national security adviser Frank Carlucci. Saddam's deputy prime minister, Tariq Aziz, had sent Carlucci a note, which the latter now forwarded to Burns, followed by a second missive a week later. The message in both was clear: despite the initial anti-American bluster, Saddam's regime was not looking for trouble.

In the first note, Aziz maintained that the Iraqi regime was "ready to meet any American official, publicly or secretly, to discuss issues of mutual concerns. At any rate Iraq has suffered from terrorism," including, he claimed, several assassination attempts against Saddam. The second note emphasized that Iraq "is very eager to get involved in a positive manner." Apparently in reference to the incendiary earlier comments about 9/11 in the Baathist press, Aziz said that such public statements "should be disregarded . . . Iraq is very eager for a dialogue opening."[89]

The sincerity of the Iraqi deputy prime minister's overture was debatable. It was also too late. On November 21, 2001, the president celebrated Thanksgiving with the Army troops stationed at Fort Campbell, Kentucky. With Operation Enduring Freedom nearing its victorious end, Bush now endeavored to stay on offense as a means of staving off any further attacks on the homeland. "Afghanistan is just the beginning of the war on terror," he proclaimed that day. "There are other terrorists who threaten America and our friends, and there are other nations willing to sponsor them. We will not be secure as a nation until all of these threats are defeated."[90]

What the commander in chief did not tell the troops was that earlier in the day, following an NSC meeting, he had pulled Rumsfeld aside and asked him, "Where do we stand on the Iraq planning?"[91]

With twenty-seven of Afghanistan's thirty provinces liberated from Taliban rule, Bush now felt comfortable turning his attention to the next in what he termed "a variety of theaters." He did so with the certitude of a man who believed in the justness of his newly found cause. For perhaps the first time in his political life, and owing to the historic fulcrum on which America now pivoted, George W. Bush had begun to see himself in comparison to other consequential figures. While hosting several Asian journalists in the Oval Office the day before flying to Shanghai, Bush, unprompted, began to talk about leadership.

Pointing to a painting of Abraham Lincoln on the wall, he said of the Great Emancipator, "He took a position in what he thought was right and stuck by it. He was severely criticized. They made fun of him, the press did. They treated him—they accused him of not being able to put sentences together sometimes. Sounds familiar. But he turned out to be a great president, because he did what he thought was right."

Bush then gestured to a painting of Winston Churchill and another of George Washington—both leaders in wartime. "You notice I don't have people in this office who tried to figure out what was right," he said pointedly. Leaders took stands, often unpopular ones. "But at least by taking a stand you believe in," he went on, "you'll be able to live with yourself, which ultimately, to me, that's what's most important for a leader, to be able to be comfortable about who you see in the mirror when you wake up in the morning."[92]

Had Bush been that man in a more innocent time, just a couple of months earlier, on the early morning of September 11, when, after a predawn jog[93] and breakfast, he found himself thumbing through a paper on smart sanctions in Iraq and mulling over the prospects of containing Saddam Hussein?[94] Regardless, he was that man now: a leader who knew who he was and who knew what was right. And what he knew was that the time had now come to confront Saddam Hussein.

SHORTLY BEFORE CHRISTMAS OF 2001, BUSH SUMMONED CONDI RICE AND HIS chief speechwriter, Michael Gerson, to the Oval Office. His first State of the Union address was more than a month away. But the president already knew what its focus should be. It was, in fact, something he had been thinking about for the past several weeks: the deadly hijackings would have been far more devastating had Al Qaeda been in possession of chemical, biological, or nuclear weapons. "Given the means," Bush warned on November 6 to foreign leaders at the Warsaw Conference, "our enemies would be a threat to every nation and, eventually, to civilization itself."[95] Hostile state actors providing terrorists with weapons of mass destruction—this was the nightmare scenario Bush wished to talk about in the next month's address to the nation.[96]

That such a scenario had never occurred before—that there was no intelligence to indicate any likelihood that it *would occur*—was irrelevant to Bush. Never again would he fall a step behind the enemy. The president indicated to Gerson which state sponsor of terror he had in mind: Iraq. To avoid anyone reaching the conclusion that Bush had already decided to go to war with Saddam, the president agreed with Rice's suggestion that other hostile nations be named as well. Iran and North Korea became the nominees.[97]

One of Gerson's deputy speechwriters, David Frum, proposed a catchy term to describe this nexus between terrorists and state sponsors: "axis of hatred." "I hate 'hatred,'" groaned Matthew Scully, one of the other speechwriters—adding that in this context, the word seemed like the kind of timid label Bill Clinton would use. Scully offered a substitute that he knew Bush would go for: "evil."[98]

BUSH SPENT CHRISTMAS WITH HIS FAMILY AT HIS RANCH IN CRAWFORD, Texas. On the morning of December 28, he received two guests at the "Western White House": General Tommy Franks, head of the U.S. Central Command (CENTCOM), and his deputy, General Gene Renuart. Leading them into a secure videoconference room, Bush punched a button and several faces appeared on his plasma screen: Rice, Powell, Card, and Tenet in the White House Situation Room; Cheney from his home in Wyoming; and Rumsfeld from his ranch house in Taos, New Mexico.

For the next hour, Bush and his war cabinet listened as Franks briefed them on a possible plan for invading Iraq, should Bush choose to do so. What Franks laid out was not Wolfowitz's modest scheme of establishing an enclave in southern Iraq, seizing Saddam's oil fields, hammering Baghdad with air strikes, and then largely standing back while an indigenous opposition army swarmed the capital city and toppled the regime. Instead, it was a "commander's concept" for "regime change and WMD removal" involving more than 100,000 combat troops. It constituted a U.S. commitment to war.

Bush, Cheney, Rice, and Powell all asked several questions during the course of the briefing. But two matters of looming consequence went almost entirely undiscussed. After Franks had gone through his briefing slides, the president addressed the CIA director. "George, your people have done a great job in Afghanistan," he said. "What do you have in Iraq?"

"Iraq's a different situation, sir," Tenet replied. With the UN weapons inspectors having vacated Iraq three years prior, the agency lacked human assets inside the regime and was largely reliant on allies with embassies in Baghdad. "Our human intelligence capability is thin," he acknowledged.[99]

Bush had heard an even starker assessment almost a year before this, just before his inauguration, during a CIA briefing at Blair House, across the street from the White House. "We do not have the resources there," Jim Pavitt, the deputy director of operations, had flatly told Bush. "We can't get access to the people."[100]

In fact, the agency had a grand total of two human sources operating inside Iraq. One of them could convey information to the Americans only when he traveled outside of the country, which was every six months. The other passed coded writing through Yemen, but the process was laborious and the information tended to be outdated by the time it arrived. A third source, a former Iraqi intelligence officer, had seemed promising—that is, until he defected to Virginia with his family after one of Saddam's sons had taken a lascivious interest in his daughter.

Tenet's "Iraq's a different situation" description did not come close to capturing just how difficult it was to gather intelligence inside that country. As one senior agency officer would put it, "The only thing we had to offer these guys was money. Meanwhile, they know the price—'We'll blow out your kneecaps, rape your daughters, burn your house down, and throw salt on your farmland.' The likelihood of recruiting anyone is slim."[101]

The U.S. government's complete inability to monitor a country being targeted for possible invasion did not seem to concern Bush at the time. Nor, for that matter, did the briefing slide Franks characterized as "Phase IV— Post-Hostility Operations." The timetable for this post-combat phase was marked "Unknown."[102]

Bush concluded the videoconference by saying that he hoped war would not prove necessary—that perhaps Saddam would succumb to international pressure and turn over his deadly arsenal without a shot being fired. But the president did not sound especially optimistic about this eventuality. Instead, he invoked his nightmare scenario: "We cannot allow weapons of mass destruction to fall into the hands of terrorists. I will not allow that to happen."[103]

The president and his CENTCOM commander then walked outside and held a twenty-five-minute press conference. The subject of Iraq did not come up.[104]

ON JANUARY 29, 2002, BUSH STOOD BEFORE CONGRESS AND SOBERLY IN-formed his fellow Americans that the war on terror had only just begun. "Our discoveries in Afghanistan confirmed our worst fears," the president stated to a hushed audience. Some of the details he relayed—such as the claim that "tens of thousands" of terrorists had been trained in Afghanistan—had been wildly hyperbolized by the speechwriters, over the futile objections of the CIA.[105] But Bush was determined to jar the American public out of compla-cency.

He then turned to the matter of regimes hostile to American interests. Bush described North Korea as "a regime arming with missiles and weapons of mass destruction, while starving its citizens." Iran, he then warned, "ag-gressively pursues these weapons and exports terror, while an unelected few repress the Iranian people's hope for freedom." Each summation had con-sisted of a single terse sentence.

By conspicuous contrast, Bush then lavished five sentences' worth of condemnation on the third regime. "Iraq continues to flaunt its hostility toward America and support terror," he began, before elaborating on

Saddam's pursuit of WMD, his murderous treatment of innocent Iraqis, and his refusal to permit weapon inspections in his country. "This is a regime that has something to hide from the civilized world," said Bush.

Thereupon he proceeded with one of the most memorable lines of his presidency: "States like these, and their terrorist allies, constitute an axis of evil, arming to threaten the peace of the world."[106]

The noun in Frum's original construction that had survived all edits—"axis"—was freighted with World War II connotations. Yet no one from the State Department, the NSC, the Pentagon, the CIA, or the White House who read the final version seemed to consider how deeply it might register, particularly to foreign ears.

The worldwide frenzy touched off by the axis-of-evil formulation—which had been misinterpreted by many as suggesting that Iraq, North Korea, and Iran had formed among themselves an unholy alliance—in turn set off a mild panic within the Bush White House. Rice had expected that the portion of the State of the Union address to garner headlines would be Bush's stated intention to "take the side of brave men and women who advocate these [democratic] values around the world, including the Islamic world."[107] White House officials discreetly attempted to walk back the axis-of-evil phraseology.

Bush was furious when he learned about this. "No backing off," he ordered Fleischer, his press secretary.[108] The president had fully expected—and, in fact, wanted—the passage to seize the world's attention.[109] And as Bush himself would later write, "There was a larger point in the speech that no one could miss: I was serious about dealing with Iraq."[110]

Everyone now knew where he stood—including, presumably, Saddam Hussein.

CHAPTER THREE

═══

THE SUPERVILLAIN

O ne cool evening in Baghdad in the fall of 1979, just weeks before sixty-six Americans were taken hostage in Tehran, the eleven U.S. diplomats stationed in Iraq's capital city attended the finals of an international military wrestling competition. The match, held at night in an outdoor tennis stadium, pitted an American Marine from Peoria, Illinois, against an Iranian wrestler. Thousands of Iraqis were in attendance, more than the stadium could safely hold: an overhang collapsed, causing several dozen who had been perched on it to be hospitalized.[1] While the diplomats cheered fervently for the Marine, they were stunned to find their voices drowned out by Iraqis who were chanting just as they were: "USA! USA! USA! USA!"

The crowd exploded when the referee signaled that the American wrestler, Jeff Simons, had defeated the Iranian. Most of them stayed for the medal ceremony. After the Marine accepted his gold medal, the Iraqi band performed a flawless version of "The Star-Spangled Banner." Deeply moved, one of the diplomats, Ryan Crocker, stammered out his appreciation to Iraq's deputy foreign minister.

Solemnly, the latter replied, "They've been practicing it for months."[2]

———

THE OUTPOURING OF AFFECTION FOR AN AMERICAN WRESTLER BY AN IRAQI audience reflected the seismic shift that had convulsed the Middle East in 1979. Until that year, the United States and Iraq had enjoyed testy relations at best. Out of contempt for Israel, the Iraqi government foreswore any diplomatic relations with the United States following the Arab-Israeli War of 1967.[3] A year later, the nationalist Baath Party—"Baath" being Arabic for "renaissance" and thus evoking a new Arab kingdom—seized power under the leadership of Ahmad Hassan al-Bakr and his thirty-one-year-old kinsman Saddam Hussein.

Relations didn't improve when, in 1972, the Baathists took control of Iraq's oil sector—in the process nationalizing operations by Exxon and other Western firms[4]—and signed a "friendship" treaty with the Soviet Union, in which the latter pledged to join the "struggle against imperialism and Zionism."[5]

American policymakers were not terribly fazed by the Baathist bluster. After all, they had in their corner Mohammad Reza Pahlavi, the secular shah of Iran, around whom U.S. policy in the Middle East had been built. Still, the State Department encouraged entrepreneurs to spread capitalistic diplomacy wherever they could. Boeing operated a branch office in Baghdad. Throughout the seventies, Iraqis bought American chicken—which, though fatty to their tastes, was deemed superior to Chinese poultry, which was commonly raised on fish meal. The Baathist government purchased U.S.-made audiovisual equipment for its new national theater. Wine researchers were hired by Iraqis to see if a drinkable wine could be fermented from local dates. (It could not.)[6] An enterprising catfish farmer from Arkansas pursued considerable, if ultimately vain, efforts to wean Iraqi consumers off their beloved Tigris carp.[7]

For any Western visitor, the pulverizing grip exerted by al-Bakr's young strongman Saddam Hussein was invisible yet impossible to miss. Jittery locals avoided being seen near Americans. Purges of perceived Baath Party foes were frequent, comprehensive, and capricious. In other oppressive regimes, such as Syria or East Germany, a bureaucrat or military officer might dare to mutter a sidelong crack about their leader. Not in Iraq, where whole families were known to disappear over a cousin's ill-chosen comment.[8]

Because Saddam was a Sunni Muslim, precautions especially had to be taken by Iraqi Shiites—and even more so by the Kurds, having launched an uprising in 1973, with CIA assistance, in a fruitless effort to establish autonomy in the north.[9] So enraged was Saddam by the Kurds' quest for independence that in 1975 he and al-Bakr agreed to give Iraq's hated neighbor, the shah, control over a major border river, Shatt al-Arab, in exchange for Iran's relinquishing any support for the Kurdish population in the north. At the shah's behest, the CIA withdrew its assistance to the Kurds as well, prompting a humanitarian disaster. A U.S. official at the time, thought by many to be President Gerald Ford's national security adviser, Henry Kissinger, explained unsentimentally to a congressional committee that "covert action should not be confused with missionary work."[10]

Despite such accommodations, by the end of the 1970s the Cold War lines in the sand seemed immutable. Iraq had the USSR's Kalashnikov rifles and its oil dollars. Iran, three times Iraq's size, had the West and therefore called the shots in the Middle East. It seemed a small if spiteful thing at the time that Iraq had provided safe haven for much of that decade to the shah's other foe, Ayatollah Ruhollah Khomeini. Only too late did Saddam realize that he had unwittingly abetted an Islamic revolution that seized power in Iran at the beginning of 1979.[11]

That July, Saddam himself formally took power in Iraq, rising on a red tide of summary executions. Practically overnight, jittery state propagandists proceeded to mythologize the new Iraqi ruler as the one true descendant of ancient Mesopotamian kings. A State Department official would recall seeing Saddam strutting into the presidential guesthouse to greet a visitor, letting the gold-bordered cape fall from the shoulders of his Pierre Cardin suit—knowing that there was an underling there to catch it. ("The man was a king, he was an emperor, he was a prince, he was a god.")[12] Frescoes ubiquitously featured Saddam in a range of deified postures: in full military regalia, in an Armani suit, in Bedouin commoner's garb, in baggy Kurdish trousers, or hovering reverently above a Shia mosque.[13]

Among those sentenced to death by Saddam's leadership were numerous Shia Islamists suspected by the new president of posing a threat to secular Arabism. The ayatollah of Iran took notice. Having once been protected by Saddam, Khomeini now declared himself the dictator's nemesis.[14] But after November 4, 1979, when students in Tehran stormed the American embassy and proceeded to take hostages, Iran had earned itself a new foe as well.

In a year's time, all geopolitical norms had been turned upside down. Iraqis were now chanting *"USA! USA!"* Warily, America began to engage with the enemy of its enemy.

IN THESE, THE BEST OF TIMES, SADDAM REMAINED A BEWILDERING FIGURE to his American counterparts.

He was the son of a Tikriti peasant who died of cancer before the boy's birth. According to lore, young Saddam was transfixed by a cousin who knew how to read and write, inspiring him to abandon his stubbornly illiterate immediate family for the apprenticeship of a well-educated and highly nationalistic uncle. His known travels outside of Iraq took place in 1959, when the twenty-two-year-old Baathist fled to Syria and Egypt after attempting to assassinate Iraq's military ruler,[15] and sixteen years later, when Iraq's leader-in-waiting flew to Paris to purchase two nuclear reactors from President Jacques Chirac.[16]

Otherwise, he saw and knew only Iraq. Saddam married his uncle's daughter and surrounded himself with sycophants from Tikrit. Though he had dabbled in law and would later try his hand at writing fiction, his genius proved to be lording over a country that had been haphazardly put together by British colonizers in 1922, following the collapse of the Ottoman Empire at the end of World War I. Saddam scrupulously fractured Sunni tribal structures while brutalizing restive Kurdish villages and Shia clerics whose followings he deemed too large for his comfort.[17] It was also the case that Kurds, Shiites, and Christians all served in his administration. The dictator was a murderer but not a genocidalist. Those who swore fealty to him, whatever their denomination, were free to go about their lives. Those who challenged or otherwise found fault with the regime were targeted for extinction.

Though Saddam and his Baath cronies hoarded wealth, he was not a kleptocrat like Mobutu in Zaire or Amin in Uganda. The state's oil revenues paid for highways, airports, and hydroelectric dams. Iraqis feared him but were also placated by excellent state-furnished health care and education; as a former U.S. government official who spent considerable time in the country would observe, "Saddam didn't wake up every morning saying, 'I'm going to be the best homicidal maniac on the planet.'"[18]

His focus on the new Mesopotamia came at the exclusion of nearly everything else. As a psychological study of the dictator by the UK's Joint Intelligence Committee (JIC) would dryly conclude, "Much of Saddam's anxiety and intense distrust of others emanate from this narrow view of the world."[19]

His self-image was that of a latter-day Nebuchadnezzar, conqueror of Jerusalem.[20] Of course, Arab purity yielded to his native insecurities. To Western visitors, Saddam could not resist showing off his well-tailored suits, his diamond cufflinks, and his Dunhill pipes.[21] He was an avid admirer of *The Godfather*[22] (and in 1981 bankrolled his own $30 million clunker of a film, *Clash of Loyalties*, starring the British actor Oliver Reed[23]). At bottom, however, as the JIC assessed, "Saddam is driven by three enduring factors: personal survival, survival of his regime, and an Iraqi led Arab unity."[24]

In September 1980, Saddam blundered into war with Iran. Officially, the Reagan administration stayed neutral. But after a wave of Iranian counterattacks in the spring of 1982, forty thousand Iraqi troops had been captured and it seemed likely that Iran would be victorious by summertime. U.S. policymakers pondered the implications and concluded that America could no longer remain on the sidelines.[25] The CIA sent a senior operative to Baghdad to provide satellite imagery of the Iranian army's advance. Saddam suspected that the intelligence was a ruse, that the United States and Iran were conspiring to deal his regime a death blow. The CIA operative was turned away. Ultimately, Iraqi's military commanders prevailed upon the party leaders. The Iranian troops were repelled and the CIA was permitted to have a semiregular presence in Baghdad.[26]

By this time, Saddam's forces had already been using riot-control spray against Iran. It deployed mustard gas on the battlefield in 1983—the same year that a State Department emissary named Donald Rumsfeld returned from a meeting with Saddam in Baghdad declaring confidently that "there were more areas of agreement than disagreement."[27] In early March 1984, Iraq became the first country ever to use nerve gas in combat.[28] Rebuked by the State Department, Saddam yet again angrily accused the United States of taking sides with Iran.[29]

Seeking to mollify the dictator, Deputy Prime Minister Tariq Aziz was granted an audience with President Reagan and Secretary of State George Shultz in the White House, where they announced that the United States had decided to restore diplomatic ties with Iraq after a seventeen-year estrangement.[30] Still, the Iraqi regime's barely disguised use of prohibited chemical weapons against its neighbor portended a bilateral relationship of fraught ethics and gritted-teeth realpolitik.

In March 1988, the Iraqi army assaulted the northern town of Halabja with mustard gas, sarin, and other nerve agents—ostensibly to repel Iranian soldiers but with the specific intention of killing approximately five thousand Iraqi Kurds who had joined forces with the Iranians.[31] The UN declined to assign blame for the Halabja massacre. State Department officials protested Iraq's "particularly grave violation" of the Geneva Convention ban.[32] Campaigning for president that same year, Vice President George Bush vowed that he would make weapons treaty violators like Iraq "pay a price."[33]

In fact, Iraq had been paying a price for its weapons technology for some time—to the Swiss, the Germans, the British, and the Americans.[34] Some of these transactions had been unwitting, as in 1985, when the Centers for Disease Control, in Atlanta, provided Iraqi scientists with three express-mail shipments containing West Nile virus agents, thinking they were for research purposes. Intelligence sources later indicated that Iraq had procured the agents to make biological weapons at its Salman Pak laboratory.[35] It was nonetheless the case that several Western firms sold Iraq "dual use" technology that could invariably be applied to ballistic missile systems and weapons laboratory equipment.[36]

Saddam therefore had the receipts to challenge the West's professed piety. The Americans could not restrain him. On July 21, 1988, Ayatollah Khomeini glumly agreed to a cease-fire with his mortal enemy, saying, "Taking this decision was more deadly than taking poison."[37]

The Iraqi dictator proclaimed victory. He celebrated it five days later by lobbing chemical weapons on the five main valleys of the Kurdish territory.[38]

"I'VE COME HERE WITH PRESIDENT BUSH'S INSTRUCTIONS THAT WE DESIRE to have good relations with you," said John Kelly to Saddam Hussein on February 12, 1990.

"You say this," replied the Iraqi dictator, "even as you are trying to undermine me."

"We're not trying to undermine you," protested the assistant secretary of state for Near Eastern and South Asian affairs.

"Well, I have reason to believe that you are," said Saddam.

Sitting with Kelly was his deputy, Skip Gnehm, and April Glaspie, the U.S. ambassador to Iraq. The meeting was in Baghdad. Exactly where was impossible for the three Americans to determine, given that they had been hustled by heavily armed Iraqi officers from vehicle to building to another vehicle to another building and then finally to a third car and third building. But its purpose was clear. For the past decade, the U.S. government's relationship with the Baath Party leader had been an uneasy but important one, born out of a common foe: Iran.

Now that alliance wobbled on a knife-edge. Saddam Hussein had emerged from the eight-year war as an incalculable new force, one swimming in a roiling pool of triumphalism, recrimination, and paranoia. For a decade now, the United States had tolerated his parochial brutishness. At an NSC meeting in 1989, President George H. W. Bush had wondered aloud of Saddam, "Can a leopard really change his spots?"[39] Though the question answered itself, the American policy had remained one of wary engagement. Now, however, Saddam's erratic behavior was seen by many in Washington as a threat to American interests in the Middle East.

Saddam sat behind a desk. He wore a crisp military uniform and a mustache scrupulously manicured in the manner of Stalin. His dark-eyed stare was unyielding. The hands of his interpreter visibly trembled.

Suddenly the dictator fell into an animated dialogue with himself: "Hey! . . . What do I see when I look south? Lots of ships . . . Lots of ships, yes! They're warships. Naval ships . . . Whose ships are they? . . . I believe they're American warships! . . . Why would there be so many warships in the Gulf when there is no war? Could it be that they are aiming at me?"

The Americans sat in stupefied silence. Gnehm finally spoke up. U.S. Navy ships had been patrolling the Persian Gulf since 1948, he said, albeit in drastically reduced numbers today. Gnehm added, "I'm going to predict that they'll still be there long after we're gone."

"There's no need for them to be there," the dictator said flatly. With the Soviet Union's demise, America could now exert its will with impunity, he observed. The question was whether the lone superpower wished to behave—as he had put it in a recent speech—"in a just and morally correct manner."[40]

His impudence suggested a palpable vulnerability. Kelly sought to return the conversation to the current precarious state of U.S.-Iraq relations. In the past year, the U.S. government had removed Saddam's country from the State Department's list of state sponsors of terror. It was continuing to extend agricultural credits to Iraq. Still, the subject of cooperation between the two countries was a delicate one and would become even more so in the coming days, when the State Department would publish its appraisal of Iraq's human rights record. Kelly felt duty-bound to warn Saddam about the report, which would refer to the regime's treatment of the Kurds as "abysmal."

Defiantly, the ruler replied, "The Kurds love me." He would be only too happy to take his visitors to a Kurdish village, where "the people come out and kiss my hand."

The Americans struggled to disguise their incredulity. They departed Baghdad the next day pessimistic about the prospects for what the Bush administration hoped would be "normalized" relations with Iraq.[41]

Two months later, it was Senator Bob Dole's turn to seek out Saddam's rational side. The Republican Senate minority leader brought with him a bipartisan delegation of four other senators to Mosul early on the morning of April 12, 1990. Dole had been thoroughly briefed by Ambassador Glaspie. "Shrewd, smart, well-read (in Arabic), Saddam is also deeply provincial and ignorant of cultures other than his own," she wrote to Dole the day before his visit, "which is why he often blunders badly in international affairs." The dictator coveted strong ties to the West, "and especially the U.S." He hated Communists and professed happiness at seeing the USSR self-immolate (now that Iraqi forces had all the Soviet military hardware they required).[42] But, Glaspie wrote, he clung to the suspicion that America "would drop Iraq if it has a chance to improve relations with Iran." He also nurtured fears that American Zionists would support Israel's attacking the regime, as it had in 1981, when Israeli aircraft destroyed Iraq's nuclear reactor at Osirak but faced no repercussions from the United Nations for doing so.

With the long war against Iran now behind him, Saddam saw himself "as potentially the premier Arab leader," the ambassador wrote. But for all his bluster, the theocracy in Tehran had not been defeated. Iran remained a threat, one that only technological superiority via Western assistance could overcome. Saddam needed America, though he would be loath to say so. Dole therefore arrived in Mosul believing that, as he would later say, "there might be a chance to bring this guy around."[43]

Saddam wore for this occasion an expensive blue double-breasted suit. He was not in good humor. "We are aware a large-scale campaign is being launched against us from the United States and Europe," he asserted.

"Not from President Bush," Dole insisted. "Yesterday he told us he does not support this."

Saddam was unmoved. The Western press had seized upon a remark he had made in a state radio address on April 1: "I swear to God that if Israel dares to hit even one piece of steel on any industrial site, we will make the fire eat half of Israel." The Western media and the Zionists, he said, had twisted his words to mean that he intended to launch an unprovoked strike against Israel using his chemical weapons—which, by the way, he had no intention of surrendering, not unless Israel relinquished its own weapons of mass destruction. The dictator had brought with him the tape of his original statement. "I said, 'If Israel strikes, we will strike back,'" he said. "I repeat now, in your presence, that if Israel strikes, we will strike back. I believe this is a fair stand."

Alan Simpson, the tall and folksy senator from Wyoming, saw an opening. "I believe your problem is with the Western media, not with the U.S. government," he said. The press, Simpson continued, "is spoiled and conceited. All the journalists consider themselves brilliant political scientists. They do not want to see anything succeeding or achieving its objectives. My advice is that you allow those bastards to come here and see things for themselves."

Dole had a more incisive point to make. There had been a report by Fred Francis of NBC News of a biological weapons plant south of Baghdad, in the city of Salman Pak. Perhaps, he said, the Iraq government should permit the press to inspect Salman Pak and thereby report the truth.

But Senator Simpson had given Saddam the rationale he needed to dismiss this suggestion. Journalists, said the dictator, "are like a spoiled child. If this child is given a sweet in response to his desires and cries, he will continue to cry and demand more." The two-and-a-half-hour meeting concluded without any diplomatic advances.[44]

Still, the Bush administration continued to believe that Saddam could be reined in. In May 1990, a month after Dole's delegation visited Mosul, Secretary of State Jim Baker's subordinates conducted a war game in the operations center of the State Department's headquarters. The scenario involved an invasion of Kuwait. But the invading country was not Iraq; rather, it was Iran.[45]

Instead, Saddam's belligerence escalated. He refused to accommodate further inquiries into his alleged biological weapons program. U.S. intelligence reports indicated that radical Palestinians such as Abu Nidal had opened offices in Baghdad. The State Department was obliged to reconsider its list of terrorist sponsors.[46]

More alarmingly, 100,000 Iraqi soldiers had been deployed south to the Kuwait border. Economically hobbled by the Iran-Iraq War, embittered by the Arab world's insistence that Iraq repay loans that he believed had been grants, and enraged by the Gulf states' insistence on driving down the global price of oil with excessive production, Saddam, it now appeared, was poised to claim Kuwait's Rumaila reservoir as territory that (in his view) British colonialists should have bequeathed to Iraq in the first place.

On July 25, 1990, the day after the two Iraqi divisions were deployed to the border, Glaspie again met with Saddam in hopes of lowering the temperature. In keeping with Bush administration policy, the U.S. ambassador uttered the fateful words "We have no opinion on the Arab-Arab conflicts, like your border disagreement with Kuwait."

The dictator responded with a rambling reassertion of his country's rights and the economic injustices heaped upon his people by the Kuwaitis. He vowed that "Iraq will not accept death."

But, he also said, Iraqis were willing to sacrifice their lives for this cause. Was America? "I do not belittle you," Saddam said to the American diplomat. "But I hold this view by taking the geography and nature of American society into account. Yours is a society which cannot accept 10,000 dead in one battle."[47]

One week later, Iraqi forces invaded Kuwait. The faint hope of Saddam Hussein as an American ally became permanently irretrievable. As the United States assembled a coalition of twenty-eight countries willing to provide combat troops, the dictator brashly predicted "the mother of all battles." Instead, after enduring five weeks of an 88,500-ton aerial bombardment, followed immediately by a crushing ground assault by 670,000 troops that lasted all of one hundred hours, the fourth-largest army in the world had been devastated.

At that moment, President George H. W. Bush was faced with a decision. He could order an encirclement and subsequent destruction of Saddam's elite army, the Republican Guard. For that matter, he could test—many would say violate—the UN mandate and continue into Baghdad, hell-bent on ending Saddam's regime.

As it stood, the coalition's mission had been achieved. Kuwait was liberated. And Bush was on the cusp of a psychological achievement as well: he could, by declaring victory and withdrawing from Iraq with a mere 147 combat-related deaths to grieve, exorcise the ghost of the Vietnam War from the American conscience.

But for now, Iraqi troops were fleeing in droves along Highway 80, which connects Kuwait to Iraq. Mowing them down would amount to a "turkey shoot," a macabre spectacle sure to be captured live by CNN and broadcast around the world. As Joint Chiefs of Staff Chairman Colin Powell reminded the president—appealing to Bush's experience as both a World War II pilot and a patrician subscriber to noblesse oblige—"There is chivalry in war."[48]

It should come as no surprise that the beneficiary of Bush's decision to halt hostilities, Saddam Hussein, did not consider the withdrawal of coalition troops to be an act of mercy. He viewed it as a sign of weakness. After all (as his lieutenants would explain years later to their American captors), Saddam was convinced that what had really dissuaded Bush from marching into Baghdad was his legendary arsenal of chemical and biological weaponry.[49] "Yours is a society which cannot accept 10,000 dead in one battle" were his taunting words to the U.S. ambassador in the summer of 1990.

Now Bush had proved him right. Baghdad had been spared. Saddam remained in power. Victory, he boasted, was his.

ONE OF THE MOST FLABBERGASTING PARADOXES IN THE HISTORY OF AMERI-can foreign policy came to pass in the years following the conclusion of Operation Desert Storm. From 1991 until 1998, under the terms of Iraq's surrender, an inspection team known as the United Nations Special Commission, or UNSCOM, scoured the defeated country for evidence of Saddam's weapons program.[50] UNSCOM's team—twenty-one of them at its inception, and eventually over three times that amount—included several American inspectors; embedded in their ranks were a few CIA analysts pretending to be inspectors. U-2 reconnaissance aircraft watched from above, videotaping imagery that would later be reviewed by the inspection teams. It was a period of maximum visibility, an unprecedented seven-year window into the military ambitions of Saddam Hussein.

Somehow, the United States managed to peer into that window and misunderstand nearly everything there was to see.

In April 1991, Saddam convened his Revolutionary Command Council. He emphasized to them a singular postwar goal: to get out from under the economic sanctions set forth by UN Resolution 687. This would mean complying with the UNSCOM inspectors—but only up to a point. Because Saddam's army had been decimated by the Gulf War, and because Iran had massed more than a million troops at the border, the dictator wanted to maintain both an operational ballistic missile capability and enough chemical weapons to blunt a military assault. Thus, he instructed his RCC: *Declare as little as possible. Get them in and get them out, and then the shackles will come off.*

The Iraqis offered up a weapons declaration that, in its dubiousness, UNSCOM deputy executive director Robert Gallucci would term "laugh-out-loud funny."[51] The Iraqis declared only about half of its Scud missile inventories. Unnerved by the realization that the UN inspectors possessed better intelligence than anticipated and that an armada of naval ships had been moved into the Gulf, the Iraqis revised their declaration a year later. Even so, the inventory was still incomplete: the Iraqis had divulged their destroyed missile sites but not the purchasing documents—apparently because they hoped to be reimbursed for a few undelivered parts after sanctions were lifted.

The Iraqis claimed to have only a peaceful nuclear program. In short order, inspectors with the International Atomic Energy Agency (IAEA) discovered two facilities that were not on the list provided. Then, inside a supposed petrochemical building in downtown Baghdad, the inspectors discovered four trunks of documents describing just what the two facilities were. One was a uranium enrichment plant, the other a nuclear weapons development facility. After two months' worth of denials, the Iraqis acknowledged the true purpose of the structures.

The Iraqis claimed, in a 1992 declaration, to have only a very limited chemical weapons stockpile. Unfortunately for them, UNSCOM would soon be in touch with the companies that had sold Iraq the chemicals in question. Confronted with the gaping discrepancies, Saddam's bureaucrats cobbled together a new declaration in 1995—and then, after being caught in more lies, a third inventory. Though Iraq's principal chemical weapons complex at Al Muthanna had been bombed during the Gulf War, many of the bulk containers full of mustard, sarin, and tabun had been buried to escape damage. UNSCOM excavated more than seven hundred tons of chemical agents and chemicals.[52] The inspectors did not, however, discover any chemical weapons. The Iraqis claimed to have already destroyed their entire CW arsenal. Given their early prevarications, UNSCOM had just cause for skepticism.[53]

Finally, the Iraqis claimed to have "obliterated" their biological weapons program immediately after the war. It took a tip from Israeli intelligence officials in January 1995 for the inspectors to learn about the thirty-nine tons of bacterial growth media that Iraq had imported from a British company during the 1980s. Traces of that bacteria had been found earlier, at a rather peculiar research laboratory at Al Hakam, where an unprepossessing female scientist named Dr. Rihab Taha worked. The inspectors decided to look at U-2 imagery of Al Hakam. They were stunned to discover on the roof of the modest facility, as UNSCOM's director, Rolf Ekéus, would recall, "an extremely advanced system of aerial ventilation, among the most expensive in the world."[54]

In August of that same year, Hussein Kamel—Saddam's son-in-law and the head of Iraq's Military Industrial Commission—defected to Jordan. Panic-stricken, the Iraqis accosted Ekéus as he prepared to board a flight from Baghdad to Amman to debrief Kamel. The Iraqis confessed that they had some explaining to do. Over the next several days, they pronounced their initial BW declaration "null and void." The new disclosure was staggering. As one of the lead inspectors, Rod Barton, would write, "Iraq told us that some 8500 liters of concentrated anthrax, almost 20,000 liters of concentrated botulinum toxin and 2200 liters of aflatoxin were produced and stored."[55] The Iraqis also drove Ekéus to the defector Kamel's chicken farm, where they helpfully unearthed over one hundred metal footlockers containing documentation of a WMD program that, the Iraqis maintained with a straight face, Kamel must have ordered all on his own. The following year, UNSCOM demolished Al Hakam. Its superintendent, Rihab Taha, thereafter came to be known in the Western press as "Doctor Germ."

The deceptions continued, however. And because they did, it followed logically that Saddam's regime had something to hide. But what was that something? Could it be that the numerous chemical agents not accounted for might actually be a result of . . . poor postwar accounting? Could it be that two outstanding tons of anthrax were never inventoried because . . . they had hurriedly been dumped near one of Saddam's palaces, a hanging offense had the dictator learned of the act? Could it be that the undeclared VX nerve gas residue found on fragments of destroyed warheads in early 1998 proved . . . merely that the Iraqis had been reluctant to admit to a program that they had already furtively destroyed?

Of course, the only straightforward explanation for such deviousness was that Iraq was hiding both an active weapons program and substantial weapons stockpiles. It did not occur to the UN inspectors and American policymakers that in authoritarian Iraq, the truth was necessarily nonlinear, lurking in the shadows. The irony, as UNSCOM deputy chief inspector Charles Duelfer would come to realize only years later, was that "Saddam's compliance had been going up, while at the same time our confidence and willingness to give him the benefit of the doubt was going down."[56]

Something else had not occurred to the inspectors. Already the so-called 661 Committee—set up by the United Nations in 1990 to enforce sanctions against Iraq under UN Resolution 661—was withholding basic goods from the Iraqi population until Saddam's government could prove that such goods would not somehow be used to make weapons. According to one of the committee's members, "We were watching everything that came in like a hawk. We questioned the ink used for pens. We questioned plastic bags used for urine collection at hospitals. At one point, we moved to stop Iraq from obtaining powdered milk because we said it contains casein, which is a growth medium. It wasn't like when Reagan said to the Soviets, 'Trust but verify.' Because we offered the Iraqis no trust at all."[57]

The inspectors did more than simply reinforce the view that everything the regime did warranted suspicion. Their invasive and at times arrogant behavior—ripping open a door with an ax when a site supervisor was
slow to bring a key; prowling around a mosque that was not under suspicion
of hiding weapons—bred hostility and, in turn, recalcitrance of the very sort
that would lead UNSCOM to conclude that Iraq must be hiding something.[58] On January 22, 1998, following accusations by UNSCOM that
Iraq was maintaining a secret VX nerve gas program, Saddam ordered a
freeze on further inspections.[59] It was clear to the Iraqis that they were paying
for their early deceptions and that the Americans would never take them at
their word. As Deputy Prime Minister Tariq Aziz would say years later to
Duelfer, "Iraq could have sanctions with inspectors or sanctions without
inspections."[60]

At the same time, the Iraqis maintained that their punishment represented a cruel double standard. True, they had not always been honest with
inspectors. Yes, they had failed to obey UN resolutions, but couldn't the same
be said of countries favored by the West, such as Israel? As Iraq's chief scientist, Dr. Amer al-Saadi, pointed out to the inspectors, "When Israel hit
our atomic reactor [in 1981], it was a transparent program, a civil contract that
was well known. Our intention was to go about this in a legal way under
international safeguards . . . and what happened? In front of the whole world,
the reactor was bombed. But instead of the world condemning it, they were
cheering it. What are treaties worth?"[61]

At the urging of the Clinton White House, nearly a hundred permanent
staffers of UNSCOM quietly evacuated Baghdad overland to Amman in
December 1998.[62] Operation Desert Fox followed, involving four days of
bombing—the targets ostensibly being Iraqi weapons sites, but of course if
any such sites had been known, the UN inspectors would already have visited
them.

Not surprisingly, Saddam did not permit the inspectors to reenter Baghdad after the bombings. UNSCOM was disbanded in 1999 without fanfare. A
new, more internationally diverse inspection body, the United Nations Monitoring, Verification and Inspection Committee, or UNMOVIC, immediately

took its place but likewise could not gain entry. Once again, a heavy curtain fell over Iraq.

BEHIND THE CURTAIN WAS A BROKEN COUNTRY.

Iraq's infrastructure had been laid waste by Desert Storm's aerial bombardment. Saddam's army was now a mere fraction of its prewar fighting strength. Underpaid soldiers in the regular army were known to beg at the mosques for food.[63] Completely unbeknownst to the outside world, the dictator's fearsome WMD arsenal was a paper tiger.

In keeping with the dictator's most urgent priority—his personal survival—Saddam's domestic intelligence agency, Mukhabarat, remained strong. But because "they sent their third-rate people overseas," in the words of one high-ranking CIA official, Iraq's overseas spy network was comically ineffectual.[64] Inside, the country had descended into a dysfunctional "snake pit of competing mafias," according to another CIA official—one that positioned Saddam's two sons, Uday and Qusay, against each other and occasionally against their father.[65]

Saddam was a survivor, of course. He had survived war with Iran, war with the United States, and a bloodless slog under the UN's inspections microscope. He was also surviving international sanctions, thanks to an "oil-for-food" loophole granted by the UN in 1995 for humanitarian purposes and then cleverly retrofitted by the dictator to line the pockets of his regime. Knowing he had amends to make in the Arab street after his aggression in the Gulf, Saddam performed several deft gestures of appeasement. After having conferred holy status on his "mother of all battles" by incorporating *"Allahu akbar"* ("God is great") into the national flag on the eve of Desert Storm, Saddam postwar began to (selectively) encourage the building of mosques in Iraq. For a time, he indulged the growing popularity of Najaf-based Shia ayatollah Mohammed Sadiq al-Sadr—at least until February 1999, when al-Sadr was gunned down by unknown assassins.[66]

And beginning in 2000, Saddam found a more practical means of ingratiating himself with the Arab world: he became a noisy benefactor of

Palestinian radicals, awarding checks as great as $25,000 to the families of suicide bombers in Gaza and the West Bank.[67] (As was always the case with Saddam, there was ample reason to doubt the extent of his largesse to the Palestinians. And in any event, the three biggest donors to radical Palestinian causes were American allies: Saudi Arabia, Jordan, and Egypt.)[68]

But perhaps the strongest guarantor of Saddam Hussein's survival was the status afforded him by the world's lone superpower. Speaking at the Pentagon in February 1998, President Bill Clinton elaborated on what he termed "predators of the twenty-first century," saying, "There is no more clear example of this threat than Saddam Hussein's Iraq. His regime threatens the safety of his people, the stability of his region, and the security of all the rest of us."[69] The next day, Clinton's three top foreign policy officials—Secretary of State Madeleine Albright, Secretary of Defense William Cohen, and National Security Adviser Sandy Berger—traveled to Ohio State University to host a town hall on the unique threat posed by the Iraqi dictator. (To personalize the matter, Cohen warned the audience—in a manner that would eerily foreshadow a more famous presentation by Secretary of State Colin Powell five years later—that a five-pound bag of the anthrax believed to be in Saddam's WMD stockpile "would kill half the population of Columbus, Ohio.")[70]

Later that year, Congress passed the Iraq Liberation Act (ILA) by a 360–38 majority in the House and by unanimous consent in the Senate. Signed into law by Clinton on October 31, 1998, the bipartisan bill made it official U.S. policy "to support efforts to remove the regime headed by Saddam Hussein from power in Iraq and to promote the emergence of a democratic government to replace that regime."[71]

The ILA's only vocal opponent was the Texas congressman Ron Paul— who, in the predictable manner of libertarians, blamed Saddam's animus on persistent U.S. interventionism: "Why is it that terrorists want to go after Americans? Because we are always dropping bombs on people and telling people what to do; because we are the policemen. We pretend to be the arbitrator of every argument in the world, even those that have existed for 1,000 years. It is a failed, flawed policy." (In his remarks on the House floor, Paul also made passing reference to an Arab jihadist whom the United States had supported against Russia in the nineties: "I hope we make a better choice than we did with bin Laden. I mean, he was our close ally.")[72]

Of all the autocrats in the world, only Saddam Hussein's regime had been legislated against by the United States government. He had become America's supervillain. The Arab world found this incomprehensible. When Madeleine Albright's assistant secretary of state for Near Eastern affairs, Edward Walker, traveled to the Middle East in August 2000, one Arab leader after the next told him, *The real danger in the region isn't Iraq—it's Iran.* After Walker protested to the ruler of the United Arab Emirates, Zayed bin Sultan Al Nahyan, that Saddam remained a continuing threat to the Gulf, the eighty-two-year-old sheikh shook his head.

"You Americans have weakened him so much already," he said.[73]

Saddam was delighted to be perceived otherwise, of course. At long last, he and the U.S. government had managed to find agreement in a shared illusion. His regime did not let on that his UN representative, Nizar Hamdoon, had discreetly reached out to the CIA throughout the nineties, seeking some kind of common ground with the United States.[74] The dictator had risen to embrace the mantle of strongman of the Arab world by the time of George W. Bush's inauguration. On the final day of 2000, the Baath government performed Iraq's most expansive military parade in at least a decade, a four-hour procession featuring a thousand tanks rolling through downtown Baghdad (and conspicuously featuring numerous state-of-the-art propeller missiles), with Saddam waving to the masses in his three-piece suit.[75] Less than two weeks later, outgoing secretary of defense Cohen warned, without presenting any evidence, that Saddam had already rebuilt Iraq's weapons infrastructure.[76]

Four days before the 9/11 attacks, the State Department's in-house Bureau of Intelligence and Research (INR) produced a secret document entitled "Iraq—Saddam Riding Higher Than Ever." Listing the progress made by the dictator in recent years—improving relations in the Arab world, circumnavigating sanctions while keeping weapons inspectors at bay—the paper noted ruefully, "Saddam no doubt takes great satisfaction in the gains he has made."[77]

And seven months after that memo, a cable to Secretary Powell described the twenty-two-hour parade celebrating the Iraqi dictator's sixty-fifth birthday, which also featured the cutting of a gigantic pink cake in his hometown, Tikrit.[78]

In these final moments of power, Saddam Hussein's Potemkin show of indomitability would prove to be his masterwork, and also his undoing.

CHAPTER FOUR

===

"ABOVE ALL, PRECISION!"

Secretary of Defense Donald Rumsfeld squinted at the slides of the plans for invading Iraq—six months of deployment time, 500,000 troops on the ground—and through his wire-rimmed glasses awarded his briefers a look that would curdle plutonium. "This is just ridiculous," he snapped. "Who would come up with a plan like that?"

It was late September 2001, shortly after President Bush had first asked Rumsfeld to examine the Pentagon's existing war plan. The two briefers, Joint Chiefs of Staff vice chairman General Richard Myers and JCS director of operations General Gregory Newbold, looked sidelong at each other. The war plan, developed in 1998, was indeed outdated. No one, including the plan's originator, General Anthony Zinni, would dispute that Iraq's army was now a shadow of its former self and that U.S. military technology had improved greatly in the past few years.

Carefully, Myers asked, "Well, Mr. Secretary, how big do you think it ought to be?"

"I don't know," Rumsfeld replied. Then he said, "How about 150,000?"

Newbold gave momentary thought to saying, *Uh, Mr. Secretary, please, we've got your guidance. Faster, lighter—we get it. But let's not put some artificial number on it right now.* Instead he elected to keep this thought to himself, believing that this was just another disposable impulse on Rumsfeld's part. *After all,* figured the general, *who cares about Iraq?*[1]

As it would develop, for Rumsfeld, the arbitrary projection of 150,000 troops on the ground was not his idea of the floor. It was the ceiling. Later, he would endeavor to push the deployment force to well below six figures. After one such demand by the secretary, the recipient of the order, CENT-COM commander General Tommy Franks, hung up the phone and sputtered out a few expletives.

Then Franks said with disgust, to a CIA official who happened to be in his office, "He just whipped that number right out of his ass."[2]

DURING THE MONTHS SPENT REINVENTING A MILITARY PLAN TO INVADE Iraq, there were some who regarded Donald Rumsfeld's chesty critiquing of his generals with a certain admiration. "Rumsfeld kept pushing Tommy: 'Go lighter.' My sense is that he did an excellent job," said one White House of-ficial who knew nothing about war planning but who sat in on a few of the CENTCOM meetings and appreciated the secretary's native skepticism of institutional thinking.[3]

Others involved in the planning had their doubts but could see the mer-its of challenging the status quo, even the intellectual exercise of "forcing us to think about risk factors and operating at the edge of our comfort level," as CENTCOM's director of operations, General Gene Renuart, would tact-fully put it.[4]

Others still viewed Rumsfeld's tinkering as nothing more than a vanity project; as one Bush administration official who got along with the secretary would say, "I'm convinced Rumsfeld's primary motivation was the transfor-mation of the U.S. military, and he didn't give a shit what war it was. He wanted some kind of conflict to enable that metamorphosis."[5]

But there was also an air of disingenuousness that accompanied Rums-feld's inquest—a pretense of truth-seeking to justify deeply rooted precon-ceptions. As one high-ranking Defense Department official would recall,

"He had a way of calling the generals in and asking the first in line, 'Hey, how many troops is it going to take to get into Baghdad?' And he'd find one who gave him the right answer. From my vantage point, he manipulated the guys in uniform so that he could say, 'Well, I'm just saying what the generals told me to do.'"[6]

Myers, who offered no reservations about Rumsfeld's push to downsize the invasion force, became the secretary's handpicked choice to succeed Hugh Shelton as chairman of the JCS on October 1, 2001. Newbold—who, the Defense Department official recalled, "took the high road, gave honest answers"—would not attain such favored status.[7]

Instead—in what would become a recurring motif throughout the months following the 9/11 attacks—those like Newbold who did not assume a deferential posture to Rumsfeld, who not only disagreed but dared show even so much as an ankle flash of independence, were mocked or marginalized by the secretary for their trespasses. On October 16, 2001, a little over two weeks after Newbold and Myers presented the 1998 Iraq invasion plan to Rumsfeld, Newbold briefed reporters on the bombing campaign in Afghanistan. The general described efforts "to destroy the Al Qaeda terrorist infrastructure." Then, speaking about recent air strikes in the northern Afghanistan city of Mazar-i-Sharif, Newbold said that "the combat power of the Taliban has been eviscerated."[8]

His remark was factually accurate. Still, he had erred twofold. First, the general had failed to recognize that his comment might be misconstrued by some to suggest that the war was all but over. This offended one of the many adages that constituted what the secretary touted as Rumsfeld's Rules—in this case, "under-promise and over-deliver!"

But Newbold had also, with his hundred-dollar verb "eviscerated," violated an unwritten Rumsfeld Rule: *Don't upstage the boss.* So it was that nine days after Newbold's remark, Rumsfeld himself conducted a press briefing, during which he acknowledged that the Taliban had been "dogged" in clinging to power. A reporter asked him how to reconcile that viewpoint with Newbold's previous observation that the Taliban had been "eviscerated."

"Oh, look," chuckled the secretary. "We are trying to have daily briefings. There's been an enormous appetite for daily briefings. And when I get
up in the morning, I say, 'By golly, we're going to feed that appetite!'"

The press was laughing along with him—laughing far more than he was.
Rumsfeld continued by praising the "darned good job" done by those conducting the daily briefings. Then he said, with squinty understatement,
"Sometimes they might use a word that I might not, or sometimes they might
use a word that they won't again."

Again, the reporters present laughed loudly.[9] But back at the Pentagon,
recalled General Mark Hertling, the chief of war plans on the Joint Chiefs
of Staff, "that sent a signal. You just called out maybe the smartest guy in the
entire military for using a big word? It was a classic bullying technique."[10]

AMONG THE MOST UNEXPECTED CONSEQUENCES OF THE ATTACKS ON SEP-
tember 11 was the instant celebrity conferred on Donald Rumsfeld in their
wake.

He had spent the previous forty years largely unknown outside Washington, a walking resume of a man who was a ubiquitous witness to American history but had not yet truly shaped it. Still, as a congressman, White
House chief of staff, NATO ambassador, and CEO of several large companies, Rumsfeld epitomized experience for a new president who himself lacked
that quality. A quarter century before, he had served as the country's young-
est secretary of defense, under Ford. Now, at age seventy, Donald Rumsfeld
was the nation's oldest to occupy the post.

His manner of speech was a mothballed quilt of *by-gollys* and *gosh-darns*
and *my-heavenses*. His wardrobe was equally timeworn. Once, in the presence of Powell and Rice, the secretary felt the need to ask Bush's communications director, Dan Bartlett, "Danny, remind me—how old are you?" When
Bartlett replied that he was thirty-four, Rumsfeld looked at the others and
exclaimed, "Good God! I've got suits that are older than you are!" Bartlett
fingered Rumsfeld's lapel and retorted, "Yes, Mr. Secretary, and this must be
one of them."[11]

But, like the president he now served, this brilliant and difficult man had discovered his moment. In the aftershocks of 9/11, a reeling America found itself steadied by blunt-talking alpha males whose unflappable, crinkly-eyed certitude seemed the only antidote to nationwide panic.

Rumsfeld never panicked. Staring somewhere between the clouds and the television cameras—a Reaganesque hint of modesty, though to his detractors it came off as a self-satisfied above-it-all-ness—the secretary articulated his musings slowly, almost lovingly, as if the audience were unshakably his and he could stop time with a wish. His resolute antiquatedness was comfort food in a world gone post-postmodern. The secretary's press conferences were now labeled by *The Wall Street Journal* "the best new show on television," the secretary himself "a rock star" (CNN) and "a babe magnet for the 70-year-old set" (Fox News).[12] The *Saturday Night Live* impressionist Darrell Hammond perfectly captured Rumsfeld's folksy condescension behind the podium in a cold-open skit two months after 9/11.[13] Recognizing his preeminence, the secretary not-so-humbly instructed his office to "write the Bible" on wartime communications and "get the rest of the government doing it right."[14]

Forgotten, somewhere along the way, was the ignominy of Donald Rumsfeld's pre-9/11 tenure. He had not been Bush's first choice, nor even his second. Senator Dan Coats of Indiana, a traditional defense hawk who had forcefully denounced President Clinton's attempts to allow gays to serve in the military, had been the front-runner. But Coats's relationships in the Pentagon were few, and advocates of the other contender, Paul Wolfowitz, had begun a whisper campaign about the senator's "fitness."[15] Vice President–elect Cheney, who oversaw the presidential transition process, happened to be sitting in during Coats's audition with Bush on December 18, 2000. Cheney favored Wolfowitz, his former undersecretary of defense for policy, and was now in a position to put his thumb on the scale.

Yet Cheney also knew that the rap on Wolfowitz—his disorganized manner—was a valid one. While conservatives saw in both Wolfowitz and Coats a suitable ideological counterweight to the moderate incoming secretary of state, Powell, Cheney knew from experience that it was Powell's

Beltway cunning, his close ties on the Hill and in the media, that would have to be parried. Wolfowitz had one other strike against him: Bush's roster of Cheney, Powell, and Rice was already looking like a reassembly of his father's administration. Moreover, even overlooking Wolfowitz's perceived shortcomings, Cheney had never forgotten who it was that had given an obscure Wyoming political novice a plum job in the Ford administration.

On December 22, the day Bush announced that he was delaying his decision for secretary of defense, Donald Rumsfeld flew to Austin and was smuggled into the governor's mansion. "He had to be aware that I did not have a close relationship with his father," Rumsfeld would later write in his memoir. This was a colossal understatement: during Ford's presidency, the politically ambitious Rumsfeld was widely thought to have recommended that the elder Bush be appointed CIA director, which, because of the agency's low standing during the seventies, was thought to have canceled out Bush as a presidential competitor. But the president-elect did not raise the issue during the job interview. He let Rumsfeld do most of the talking.[16]

The day after Christmas, Rumsfeld was at his ranch in Taos when he received a call from his protégé Cheney. Bush wanted Rumsfeld. The news surprised him. "I'd told Joyce," he wrote in a memo two days later, referring to his wife, "that since Governor Bush was spending the Christmas holidays with his family I was pretty sure it wouldn't work."[17] But the father had apparently given his blessings, and so, on December 28, 2000, Donald Rumsfeld became the last high-profile appointee of George W. Bush's administration.

Still, he had arrived late to an administration that was already taking shape. For his deputy, Rumsfeld was informed by Cheney that he had two options: Wolfowitz or Richard Armitage, another Bush campaign adviser who also happened to be Powell's close friend. Rumsfeld, of course, selected Wolfowitz, whom he knew only somewhat.[18] For his second-most-powerful subordinate, undersecretary for policy, Rumsfeld had in mind his friend Richard Perle, one of Washington's most prominent defense hawks. Perle demurred but recommended his understudy, Douglas J. Feith, a floppy-haired and bespectacled lawyer and former Pentagon official in the Reagan administration. After an awkward twenty-minute interview, Rumsfeld dismissed Feith. The incoming secretary also interviewed a former Cheney staffer, Zalmay Khalilzad. He, too, failed to impress. Perle persuaded Rumsfeld to give Feith a second chance. Rumsfeld then offered Feith the job, though the decision came a full two months after Bush had been inaugurated.[19]

The new secretary believed he had a mandate from the president to transform the military but would claim (as he wrote in a memo to himself), "The second a question is raised about any current policy or any current process, the response is immediate and violent; 'You must not change anything.'"[20] Immediately he formed a host of advisory groups—and just as immediately they were dismantled, as Rumsfeld had done so in violation of the Federal Advisory Councils Act.[21] He found inefficiency everywhere he looked, as reflected in the daily avalanche of "snowflakes" issued from his office, rattled off by him into his Dictaphone. "Do we need all these inspectors general?" "What do we do about Pentagon bureaucracy?" Upon learning that fifteen DOD personnel were stationed in Western Sahara, he wrote, "Is there any way we can reduce that number?"[22]

Al Qaeda had not been his focus. When briefed on the matter by his predecessor, Bill Cohen, the incoming secretary in his notes misspelled bin Laden's name.[23] His impulse, hours after the 9/11 attacks, had been to find targets to hit and to "move swiftly," according to notes taken by an aide that afternoon, with one candidate being Saddam Hussein's Iraq: "Hit S.H. @ same time—Not only UBL," referring to the common abbreviation for bin Laden.[24]

This was his deputy's preference, of course, to the consternation of Bush's national security adviser. A week after 9/11, Condi Rice called Wolfowitz and asked, "When are you getting going on Afghanistan?"

"I thought we were still considering a broader range of options," said Wolfowitz.

No, Rice said emphatically. *The president has decided to target Afghanistan.*[25]

The problem for Rumsfeld was that there was no Afghanistan war plan sitting on a shelf. There had been no Paul Wolfowitzes in the conservative

foreign policy community fixating for years on how to attack Al Qaeda's base
of operations the way they had obsessed over Iraq. When the secretary summoned General Charles Holland, his commander of Special Operations
Command (SOCOM), on September 23, 2001, to be briefed on potential
bombing targets, Rumsfeld was informed that Al Qaeda had elements and
allies in Sudan, Somalia, Indonesia, and the Philippines and scattered throughout Latin America.

We should hit all of them, the secretary said. He envisioned doing so
immediately.

"Sir," Holland replied, "we don't have the actual intelligence where we
can strike those people anywhere. Not even in Afghanistan."

The disclosure that the Pentagon lacked intelligence of its own sent
Rumsfeld into apoplexy. "What—I have to ask George Tenet permission to
go fight a war for America?" he sputtered. The supine posture of his combat-
ant commanders was unacceptable. They were, he said that day and frequently thereafter, "like little birds, and until the mama bird, the CIA, puts
the worm down their throat they can't do anything!"[26]

Everyone scrambled to accommodate the impatient secretary. Undersecretary Feith produced a memo suggesting other countries to hit in addition
to Afghanistan. Not surprisingly, Iraq was on the list.[27] Navy admiral Dennis
Blair, the commander of the U.S. Pacific Command (PACOM), went so far
as to suggest sending a special operations team into the Indonesian island of
Sulawesi to spy on a potential terrorist training camp.[28]

Rumsfeld could tell what he did not want. He had no interest in conventional "lead-bomb" options.[29] And when the CIA's chief of station in Pakistan, Robert Grenier, suggested that a bombing campaign in Afghanistan
be halted for a few days to give the Taliban time to huddle and discuss handing over bin Laden, Rumsfeld scoffed that the plan sounded to him like the
bombing pauses during the Vietnam War. "We're not going to do that,"
he said.[30]

Rather than wait for Rumsfeld to settle on a plan of attack in Afghanistan, Bush handed the lead to Tenet and the CIA. U.S. Army Special
Operations Forces would follow. The ensuing campaign was not entirely

seamless. Early on, as the Afghan opposition fighters known as the Northern Alliance made their way toward Kabul, General Franks's inability to halt them infuriated Rumsfeld to the point that Franks's job appeared to be in danger.[31] Later, Rumsfeld's reluctance to permit artillery to flow to the 101st Airborne during the ground battle known as Operation Anaconda may have contributed to U.S. military casualties.[32] Most notably, the leader of Al Qaeda, Osama bin Laden, had managed to escape Afghanistan through the mountain creases of Tora Bora.

Still, Rumsfeld found good reason to be satisfied with Operation Enduring Freedom. Against fretful predictions that Afghanistan would prove to be a quagmire for the United States, as it had been for the Soviet Union during the 1980s, the Taliban abandoned Kabul and Kandahar a mere two months after the operation had begun.

Almost as significant was how victory had been achieved. Operation Enduring Freedom was not a feat of Gulf War–style "overwhelming force;" rather, it was led by a combination of Army Special Forces on horseback and indigenous Northern Alliance forces, augmented by high-tech firepower such as daisy cutter bombs. By the end of 2001, an Afghan, Hamid Karzai, was running the country's affairs. The lightness of America's footprint in Afghanistan was thoroughly Rumsfeldian. "It was," the secretary marveled in a long essay he wrote in 2002 for *Foreign Affairs,* "the first U.S. cavalry attack of the twenty-first century."[33]

But to the war planners at CENTCOM now mulling over a new scheme for invading Iraq, the Afghanistan experience loomed as an implicit template. "The plans we would develop—they'd say, 'Oh, that's too slow, too long, too many forces,'" a member of the CENTCOM team recalled. "Some people in the Pentagon fell a little too much in love with the model of Special Forces guys riding into Afghanistan on horses and beating the Taliban."[34]

THE MONUMENTAL INFLUENCE THAT DONALD RUMSFELD WOULD EXERT over wartime policy in the months ahead owed to several interwoven factors. But with one glaring exception—the insistence on a smaller, fleeter combat force—ideas were not among them. This is not to suggest that he lacked ideas: Rumsfeld fairly exploded with them. It is that he was reluctant to stake his reputation on any one of them, preferring instead to be seen as a visionary in the broadest of terms while merrily shredding the ideas put forth by others.

Rumsfeld was a peerless articulator of paradoxes. On the afternoon of 9/11, he had sagely predicted to JCS vice chairman Myers, "One week from now, the willingness to act will be half what it is now." Yet, four days later at Camp David, when President Bush asked the top five members of his war cabinet—Cheney, Powell, Rumsfeld, Rice, and Card—for their opinions on whether to attack Iraq in addition to Afghanistan, the vote was unanimous against doing so. Unanimous, that is to say, except for Rumsfeld. He had abstained altogether from voting.[35]

Rumsfeld's silence was its own statement. He intended to maintain a posture of extreme neutrality, the better to maximize his value to the president. The secretary scrupulously cared for and fed their relationship. He did not personally leak to the press, nor did he break the president's confidence to members of his senior staff. He took pains not to get out in front of policy or otherwise upstage the commander in chief—except perhaps when it came to press conferences, for which the secretary was given a pass. Bush admired Rumsfeld's cussedness with the media, his flip disregard of public opinion.[36] (This indifference was entirely feigned: Rumsfeld paid considerable attention to how he was portrayed in the Washington press.)[37]

As a routine, the two men met weekly. From Rumsfeld's perspective, these get-togethers were not ideal, as National Security Adviser Rice and Chief of Staff Card were also in attendance. Rumsfeld's quest for one-on-one time with Bush, often pursued through back and side channels and with quasi-legalistic rationales at the ready—for example, the secretary's aide would inform the NSC that Rumsfeld wished to discuss "military policy," as distinguished from "national security"—was a continual source of amusement to Rice's staff. ("It was this constant cat-and-mouse game," one of her senior staffers recalled.)[38]

For Rumsfeld, maximal influence was achieved not only by managing up. One also had to subjugate the lateral competition—meaning his fellow principals, Cheney, Powell, Rice, Tenet, and Card. Cheney was of course both protégé and patron, not to mention a former defense secretary who sympathized with the difficulties of the job. Powell, on the other hand, was fated to be Rumsfeld's worthy adversary. But, Rumsfeld could see over time, the secretary of state possessed a potentially fatal weakness—namely, an unwillingness to develop warm relations with their boss, as Rumsfeld had done.[39]

Rumsfeld could be brusque and bullying toward Tenet. He assumed that posture full-time when it came to Rice and Card. Both individuals, in Rumsfeld's view, were institutionally offensive, in that they interposed themselves into the chain of command between the secretary of defense and the commander in chief. "You have no idea how to do your job," the secretary once told Andy Card—adding helpfully, "You should resign."[40]

Rumsfeld's contempt for Rice was both withering and undisguised. On one occasion, he flipped off the lights in her office as he stalked out the door. To the NSC senior staffer who witnessed this, Rice's lack of outrage was indicative of "her remarkable capacity for serenity."[41] But to another subordinate, such condescension begged the question "Why does she take this shit from him?"[42]

The secretary chronically complained to Rice and her deputy, Steve Hadley, that the NSC process was "broken."[43] He was in fact its breaker in chief. During meetings, the secretary answered questions with questions of his own. When briefing the president, Rumsfeld would send over the materials at the last possible minute—"literally while the president was just taking his seat," recalled an NSC aide. "And then he would direct me right after to collect all the copies and destroy them."[44] He insisted that no one had given him briefing papers in advance, then maintained that he had no time to read them anyway. He complained about those who had been allowed to attend a meeting (such as other people's deputies) and those who hadn't (such as his deputies). If a rule were declared by Rice or Hadley, it would be Rumsfeld's way to refuse to agree to it. And to those things he did agree to, it would also be Rumsfeld's way to contend later that in fact he had agreed to no such thing.[45]

Rumsfeld's counterparts tended to believe that his carping served some larger strategic objective—that the secretary, a former wrestler, was grappling to keep his opponents off-balance. On that score he often succeeded, though not necessarily in a way that benefited Rumsfeld's commander in chief. More than once before the beginning of an NSC meeting, Rice would alert Bush that he would likely be hearing a disagreement between Rumsfeld and Powell on a particular issue. But then the two men would show no such signs of disharmony in front of the president. It was Rice's suspicion that Rumsfeld's Socratic style of argumentation had simply worn Powell down. The result was that at least four people in the Situation Room—the president, his national security adviser, the secretary of defense, and the secretary of state—were aware of a difference of opinion that was never aired and that none of them thought to bring up.[46]

But there was a third component to Rumsfeld's management style—one that would prove perhaps even more consequential in the Iraq debate. In addition to managing up and elbowing laterally, the secretary's bullying propensity for kicking down and disempowering subordinates meant that dissent on critical issues was close to nonexistent in the Pentagon. Things would be done Rumsfeld's way, often by Rumsfeld himself—at times in a way that would have been comical if the stakes themselves weren't as high as they were.

The secretary was a very impatient man. Demands on his time were incessant, as he was quick to remind others: "Well, *I've* just been to three countries—what have *you* been doing?" Succinctness was not enough. "Above all, *precision!*" Rumsfeld would declare, gesturing upward like a conductor—a mantra that Feith would soon adopt as his own. Indeed, the undersecretary saw Rumsfeld's ongoing quest for precision as a means of bonding with his prickly boss. Others in the building could supply Rumsfeld with funny stories or military expertise. Lacking either, Feith instead put his lawyerly acumen to use. The two men would go line by line over a speech draft, side by side at the secretary's standing desk; when Feith happened upon a word that was not quite right, just short of precise, he would swoop down with his pen, scribbling in his tidy handwriting the one verb or preposition that would instantly bring precision to the offending phrase, and the secretary would murmur, as if in the presence of art, "Wow. Great." Such moments offered the closest thing to a genuine compliment that Doug Feith received from Donald Rumsfeld.[47]

If an idea did not immediately catch the secretary's fancy, that made the idea an imposition, an affront. He stormed out of briefings after they had barely begun. He dressed down generals in the presence of his civilian deputies, ripped into his deputies in front of generals. Once, he angrily tossed briefing papers into the chest of a stunned senior officer and snapped, "This meeting's over." Was it a repetitive briefing slide? One acronym too many? (In that instance, Rumsfeld later acknowledged to Feith that he might have been too harsh and would apologize to the officer.) That men who had served honorably in combat might take umbrage at this belittling did not move Rumsfeld in the slightest. His battlefield was Washington, where reptilian old warriors were as useless as (he would say) "a one-armed paperhanger."[48]

The secretary did not believe in apprenticeship. One swam or one sank. He wanted his meetings to be kept small, the better to minimize leaks— though this, of course, made it more difficult for those excluded to understand his mind and his needs. (Rumsfeld compensated for this physical distancing with his daily blizzard of snowflakes, which General Abizaid, the JCS's director of strategic plans and policy, would wearily disperse among the Pentagon staff.)

In his personal dealings, he could fairly be termed arrogant. "It's really good that you and I met, so that I can improve you," Rumsfeld would say, only half-joking. But if he was not quite intellectually humble, the secretary nonetheless was bedeviled by what he did not know and could not see—the feared "unknown unknowns"—and to that end he was welcoming, even craving, of input . . . provided it was short, precise, and brilliant, in which case one could expect that Rumsfeld would appropriate the idea as if it were his own.[49]

It was perhaps a fair criticism that the uniformed officers who did not test their opinions with the secretary were simultaneously hidebound and thin-skinned. Stories were plentiful of those who stood up to Rumsfeld and were rewarded, or at least not fired, for doing so. One Navy lieutenant who briefed the secretary, a counterterrorism specialist named Christopher Carney, was introduced as "also a college professor."

A bemused smirk formed on Rumsfeld's face. "College professor, eh?" he said. "Are you tenured?"

"Yes, sir," came Carney's reply.

"I hate tenure," said Rumsfeld. "I think it's for the weak."

Standing nose to nose with the lieutenant/professor, he added, "If you were any good, you'd give up tenure."

Instead of retreating, Carney grinned broadly. "I think tenure's great," he said. "It enables us to think different thoughts—like the ones I'm about to tell you right now."

A light went on in the secretary's eyes. The two got along well after that.[50] Still, Donald Rumsfeld's desire for dominance at times hindered his desire for information—except, of course, around the president, at which time he became a model of self-restraint, leaving Bush at a loss to understand how anyone could find fault with his genial SecDef.

Over time, a close observer of Donald Rumsfeld—which Feith and Wolfowitz were, by necessity—understood that, while any number of things might set him off, a few in particular were guaranteed to do so. The first of these was to assume that alliances were hallowed objects, never to be tampered with. Ten days after the 9/11 attacks, the secretary issued a new Rumsfeld's Rule, via snowflake: "The mission determines the coalition. Don't let the coalition determine the mission."[51] This new dictum had been on Rumsfeld's mind after the preceding weekend at Camp David. That was when Powell had argued that going after Iraq would destroy any effort to build a vast post-9/11 coalition. "Then maybe it's not a coalition worth having" had been Rumsfeld's rejoinder. The notion that the outside world should be dictating America's goals mortally offended his sensibilities. And, as Feith would observe, "it didn't matter whether the topic was North Korea, Iraq, or Timbuktu."[52] For in the end, Rumsfeld believed, one's intentions were themselves sovereign states.

Another grave mistake was to assume that some small decision might be unworthy of Rumsfeld's time. This was almost never the case. If something of even the slightest significance was to be decided, the secretary wanted to know about it—and early, "when the clay is wet" and he could still shape the contours of the matter.[53]

Having the secretary's fingers sculpting the daily DOD minutiae was a fact of life to which many career staffers struggled to adjust. At times, they pushed back against doing so. A major source of friction was the "dep book," the bulging file of deployment orders coordinated by the Joint Chiefs and the Office of the Secretary of Defense. Rumsfeld insisted on approving all troop movements. Some, of course, were major and well deserving of the secretary's input. Most, however, were logistical necessities—training missions, repositioning of military police from one base to the next—that would seem not to rise to the secretary's level.

Such judgments, however, were for Rumsfeld to make. Each and every mission throughout the world would grind to a halt as the secretary squinted at the dep book. Recalled one Pentagon official, "He would either sit on things or flat-out reject them, or ask question after question: 'Why are we doing this?' Push came to shove, and we were really having trouble getting forces deployed, even on training missions. It became a real issue. Here we had folks prepared, trained, literally on the tarmac at times, waiting for the go-ahead and not getting it. And we were getting hard questions from the JCS as to why OSD couldn't get the dep order signed. We became aware that it was just a game the secretary was playing: *If I don't sign this, who's going to scream the loudest?*"[54]

During one senior meeting, the deputy assistant secretary for special operations and counterterrorism, Austin Yamada, wondered aloud whether it was really necessary for the secretary to sign off on a deployment order to send two special operations personnel to Norway. "It's a stagnant process," Yamada said, "that we believe is not worthy of the SecDef's personal approval." That authority should be delegated, Yamada said.

Rumsfeld stood and glared at the deputy assistant. Then he looked around at the others in the room. "Well," the secretary announced, "I think that's a bad idea. Does anybody here disagree with me?"

The room was silent, since of course the question really was: *Who in the Pentagon would like to stand up and say that the secretary of defense should be less in charge of the Department of Defense?*[55]

A third mistake was to assume that the "mama bird," the CIA, knew what it was talking about. This was one error that neither Wolfowitz nor Feith was likely to commit. Wolfowitz, who had his own disappointing experiences with the agency during the first Bush administration, had served on the 1998 ballistic missile commission that Rumsfeld chaired. Both had taken turns chiding a senior intelligence official whose testimony they found wanting. "These guys are keeping banking hours," Rumsfeld had muttered, adding that he held the briefer in "minimum of high regard."[56]

Feith was even more militant than his boss when it came to appraising the work of the CIA. In the undersecretary for policy's view, the agency was good for capturing telephone conversations and satellite imagery, the spycraft stuff. But its analysis—particularly political analysis, and especially as it related to closed societies like Iraq—Feith found to be no better than the average pundit's. Certainly no better than his. When George Tenet definitively informed the president on September 13, 2001, that the perpetrators of the attacks were Al Qaeda, Feith (as he would later write in his memoir) "wondered how solid the CIA's information was."[57]

The undersecretary had his own opinion. He had flown into Washington from Germany on September 12, aboard a KC-135 tanker, along with two of his top aides, Peter Rodman and Bill Luti, as well as General Abizaid. They spent hours discussing the previous day's attacks and how best to respond to them. At one point Feith said, "I think the Iraqis are involved in this." Astonished, Abizaid replied, "No way. No way. The Iraqis aren't involved in this. The Iraqis don't support Al Qaeda. They don't support Islamic groups, and they wouldn't do anything as reckless as this."

The result, Abizaid would recall years later, was "a pretty heated debate" between him and Feith.[58] The undersecretary's fervor did not end on the September 12 plane ride. A day or two later at the Pentagon, General Newbold was briefing Feith on bombing options in Afghanistan. The undersecretary was puzzled. "Afghanistan?" he said. "Why are you going after Afghanistan? We ought to be going after Iraq."[59]

During the same period, Feith held a meeting with several of his senior aides. Quietly, with the door closed, he told them, "We've got to find proof that Saddam was involved in this."[60] In the coming weeks, Feith would establish the Policy Counter Terrorism Evaluation Group, a small in-house shop to analyze terrorism-related intelligence—or more to the point, according to one of PCTEG's members, to be "looking for the connections between Iraq and Al Qaeda."[61] Of course, this was the CIA's job. But, as Feith had shrewdly come to recognize, for all of Rumsfeld's professed disdain of bureaucratic thinking, the secretary was happy to build bureaucracies of his own—particularly if they circumvented someone else's bureaucracy.

By coincidence rather than design, Rumsfeld had selected two deputies for whom toppling Saddam Hussein was a core mission. Feith, whose father had been a committed Zionist and whose grandparents had been murdered in concentration camps, was an ardent supporter of Israel and believed Saddam to be that country's greatest foe. Wolfowitz, with his long crusade against Saddam, "spoke for that very large group of people who felt that regime change was an important piece of unfinished business," said Marc Grossman, at the time Powell's undersecretary for political affairs.[62]

Rumsfeld lacked such sustained animus toward Saddam. As a government emissary in 1983, he shook the hated dictator's hand. Rumsfeld had been out of government during the Gulf War. He had not written op-eds on the horrors of the Iraqi regime throughout the nineties, as his deputies had. And in the first year of his second tenure as secretary of defense, Rumsfeld's musings about the Iraqi ruler had been notably scattershot. Engage with Saddam? Bomb him? Persuade him to leave Baghdad? When the subject of whether to declare war on Iraq had come up at Camp David, Rumsfeld had voted neither yea nor nay, perhaps for tactical purposes but also for the simplest of reasons: he had not decided.

Wolfowitz and Feith could see this about the secretary. Rumsfeld might well be inclined to support regime change, but only on terms that were his.

If his deputies could demonstrate that the intelligence community was yet again miscalculating a threat—that Rumsfeld's people knew better than Tenet's—they had license to do so. If they could form a mission that did not require one of Colin Powell's unruly international coalitions, Rumsfeld would likely be receptive. And if they could execute that mission with agility, swiftness, and innovation befitting a post-9/11 landscape?

That was a war to which Donald Rumsfeld could subscribe.

ON JANUARY 19, 2002, GENERAL TOMMY FRANKS RECEIVED A VISITOR AT CENTCOM headquarters in Tampa. The guest, an Army colonel named Doug Macgregor, had a benefactor in former House Speaker Newt Gingrich, who was close to Rumsfeld and shared the secretary's appetite for shredding conventional wisdom. Macgregor had written a paper arguing that Iraq could be overtaken with fewer than 35,000 troops. Much impressed, Rumsfeld had forwarded the briefing to Franks—who, knowing an imperative when he saw one, gamely invited the colonel down to Tampa.[63]

Franks's small team had been working around the clock for the past two months, trying to come up with an Iraq war plan that was both logistically feasible and tailored to Rumsfeld's less-is-more specifications. Macgregor was now telling them that they should—as his memo from that afternoon said—"strike suddenly and without warning directly at Baghdad to induce a complete collapse of the Iraqi regime." The day of the attack would be eight and one-half months from then, on October 1, 2002.

The CENTCOM team responded with numerous operational concerns. Coming directly into Baghdad with so small a force, in a month that happened to be when Saddam's three best divisions typically achieved peak readiness, was immensely risky. The large logistics tail—food, fuel, and other supplies—needed to protect the troops was not accounted for in Macgregor's scheme. What galled the fatigued planners most, however, was the sheer effrontery of an Army colonel who had never commanded a brigade telling a four-star like Tommy Franks how to fight a war. One of them stormed out midway through the meeting. Another who was involved in war planning would declare that Macgregor was "the most pompous asshole I've ever met—Feith times five."[64]

Still, Macgregor's six-page memo of the meeting was delivered by Gingrich to Wolfowitz. The deputy, in turn, forwarded it to Rumsfeld—noting in a cover memo, "It is fairly encouraging about the state of Tom Franks' thinking, but a little less so about the thinking of his staff."[65]

The immediate result of Macgregor's report was that Rumsfeld dispatched two of Feith's subordinates, Abram Shulsky and Bill Bruner, to Tampa, ostensibly to serve as planning aides. Once it became evident that the two had very little of substance to contribute other than to eavesdrop on conversations and report back to the secretary, they were sent back to the Pentagon.[66]

But the more insidious effect was the toll that such prodding had taken on CENTCOM's operations. Rumsfeld and his deputies were getting their way, but at a cost. Franks himself revealed this on February 19, 2002, when another guest showed up to MacDill Air Force Base a month after Colonel Macgregor's visit.

The guest was Bob Graham, a U.S. senator from Florida and the chairman of the Senate Select Committee on Intelligence. Graham had expected the visit to be routine. But after receiving the standard military briefing, Franks led the senator into his office and closed the door.

"Senator," he said, "we are not engaged in a war in Afghanistan." CENTCOM's chief resources there—Predator drones to monitor terrorists at large, and high-end special operations forces to kill the terrorists—were all being diverted to Iraq.

Graham was stunned. President Bush had given his "axis of evil" speech just three weeks earlier. Dialogue on what to do about Iraq had not even begun. And already critical military resources were being deployed there?

It was worse than that, the general said. Echoing Tenet's words during the briefing to the president two months prior, Franks told Graham that the U.S. intelligence in Iraq was "very unsatisfactory." The general then said to the Florida senator, "It's a big mistake. We can finish this job in Afghanistan, if we're allowed to do so." At that point, if hunting down Al Qaeda and their affiliates was truly the mission, Franks said, his choice would be to conduct military operations in Somalia and, after that, Yemen.

"Not Iraq," the general finished.

Graham left the base brooding, and would realize only later that he had failed to ask the CENTCOM commander an important question: Had Franks conveyed these concerns to Secretary Rumsfeld?[67]

But, of course, the question answered itself.

CHAPTER FIVE

THE MAN WHO FEARED TOO MUCH

On March 12, 2002, Vice President Dick Cheney flew to the Middle East to confirm to the Arab world what they already suspected—namely, that Bush was now weighing whether to bring the war on terror to Iraq.[1]

An unspoken trepidation loomed over Cheney and his fellow passengers aboard Air Force Two, including his wife, Lynne. Of the eleven countries they would be visiting following a stopover in London, four bordered the sovereign nation that Cheney now maintained was America's greatest threat. Journeying to the mouth of the volcano may have been a logical culmination to six months of threats, building evacuations, anthrax scares, nerve-shattering daily briefings, and overnights in undisclosed locations—a coda to Cheney's plain-faced remark to Tim Russert on NBC's *Meet the Press* five days after the 9/11 attacks: "We also have to work, though, sort of the dark side, if you will."[1]

Still, Cheney and his accompanying staffers—his chief of staff, Scooter Libby; assistant national security adviser Eric Edelman; Middle East adviser John Hannah; and speechwriter John McConnell—were civilian policymakers. None of them had served in the military or were habitués of danger zones. "You don't have to go, you know," Libby had said to McConnell. The speechwriter replayed that offer in his head on the fourth day of the trip, when Air Force Two received a credible report of an Al Qaeda threat, requiring a diversionary second plane and a corkscrew landing in Yemen.[2]

Cheney had been here before, literally. In August 1990, the then secretary of defense had traveled to Saudi Arabia and Egypt to enlist support for expelling Saddam from Kuwait by military force. King Fahd bin Abdulaziz Al Saud and President Hosni Mubarak had assented without hesitation.[3] Now he would again be seeing these men, along with leaders from Jordan, Oman, the United Arab Emirates, Yemen, Bahrain, Qatar, Kuwait, Turkey, and Israel.

Cheney carried with him a list from General Tommy Franks. The CENTCOM commander wished to secure overflight, landing, basing, and other logistical concessions in several countries, should the decision be made to invade Iraq.[4] Cheney's mission was to take temperatures, listen closely, and offer assurances that nothing would be decided rashly—but also to make clear that the president sought no one's permission to defend America from harm.

Two recent events had occasioned Cheney's trip. The first was the conclusion of Operation Enduring Freedom. Even as Bush returned to something resembling a peacetime agenda—advocating welfare reform, promoting an economic stimulus, appointing a director of faith-based initiatives, and speaking at a cattle industry convention[5]—he continued to declare, "And we're just beginning. Afghanistan is the *first* theater in the war against terror."[6]

The second event was a series of discoveries after the Taliban fell. CIA teams had interrogated numerous Al Qaeda detainees and recovered documents and computer drives in safe houses throughout Afghanistan. "What we discovered stunned us all," CIA director Tenet would later write.[7] Bin Laden was well on his way to developing an advanced chemical and biological weapons program. Even more intently, Al Qaeda's leader was seeking a nuclear capability. For Dick Cheney, the follow-up question was obvious: What rogue actor was likeliest to furnish such weapons to a fellow hater of America?[8]

Among the passengers on Air Force Two was an interloper of sorts: Bill Burns, Powell's assistant secretary of state for Near Eastern affairs. Burns, too, had been here before—two months beforehand, in fact. In both Bahrain and the UAE, their message to him was clear: *Saddam is containable. You don't need to overthrow him. And you'd better be careful about what comes after you do so.*

"Maybe Cheney will hear what I've been hearing," Burns said hopefully to Powell's deputy, Rich Armitage. "Maybe it'll change his mind."

Armitage, a bald and oversize cinder block of a man, growled, "Nope, that's not how it's going to turn out."[9]

Both men were right. Cheney did hear much of what the assistant secretary had been hearing—though spoken to him with a great deal more restraint than the Arab leaders had used weeks earlier when they expressed their reservations to Burns—and he left the region just as resolved against Saddam as when he entered it.

In Amman, Jordan's King Abdullah made clear his distaste for war against his oil-supplying neighbor.[10] In Cairo, Mubarak indicated that he would not stand in the way of a military invasion and would assist within reason. But the Egyptian leader also issued caution. As an Egyptian Air Academy pilot, he had done some of his training in Baghdad. Mubarak had left that experience concluding that Iraqis were among the most violent people in the Arab world. He did not quite say to Cheney what he had spelled out explicitly beforehand to American and British diplomats: "If you go into Iraq, you will create one hundred Osama bin Ladens."[11]

Cheney's visit in Jeddah with the ailing King Fahd's son, Crown Prince Abdullah, was particularly touchy. During Operation Desert Fox, in December 1998, the Saudis had refused to let the U.S. military conduct air strikes against Iraq from their bases.[12] Tamping down the Wahhabi fundamentalists in Saudi Arabia was incompatible with embracing an American attack on an Arab country. Abdullah was not looking to stir up a fight, either with Saddam or with the "street."[13] And though the country's voluble ambassador to the United States, Prince Bandar bin Sultan Al Saud, often ingratiated himself with the Bush administration with words they wished to hear, the words most emphatically expressed by the Saudis were echoed throughout Cheney's ten-day tour of the Middle East: *You must first work to resolve the crisis between the Palestinians and the Israelis.*[14]

The West Bank and Gaza roiled with violence during the Second Intifada. Cheney had been warned by a CIA analyst weeks earlier that the bloodshed would shape the thinking of Arab leaders. His reply had been dismissive: "Well, the last administration spent forever trying to get a deal. They couldn't get it. They had their chance. I'm not interested in that issue."[15]

On the flight from Kuwait City to Tel Aviv, Burns tried to convince Cheney to agree to an ad hoc meeting with Palestinian leader Yasser Arafat. Libby, Edelman, and Hannah vehemently protested. But the admonition of Abdullah and others had registered with him. The vice president announced that he would meet with Arafat if the Palestinians would agree to a ceasefire. They did not, and Cheney thereby managed to avoid the meeting. Still, the intifada "ended up hijacking the trip," according to one of its participants.[16] At an NSC meeting the day he returned, March 21, the vice president somberly reported that deposing Saddam Hussein was not uppermost among the Arab world's concerns.[17]

Bush had breakfast with Cheney that same morning. Though the president was not disinterested in what Abdullah, Mubarak, and the others had to say, he had not sent Cheney on a listening tour. He reminded the press that morning after their breakfast that "this is an administration that, when we say we're going to do something, we mean it; that we are resolved to fight the war on terror; that this isn't a short-term strategy for us; that we understand history has called us into action, and we're not going to miss this opportunity to make the world more peaceful and more free."

Bush then added, "And the vice president delivered that message."[18]

IN EARLY 2001, THE UK'S PERMANENT SECRETARY AT THE MINISTRY OF DEfence, Kevin Tebbit, was in New York for a United Nations event when he ran into his old friend Brent Scowcroft, the former national security adviser to both Reagan and the elder Bush. Tebbit was curious to hear what Scowcroft had to say about the new Bush administration. "You've got Rumsfeld on one hand and Powell on the other," Tebbit said. "Seems like a strange thing. How do you suppose it'll work?"

"I wouldn't worry," Scowcroft assured his British friend. "The vice president will be a moderating voice between those two."

Exactly one year later, at the same UN event, Tebbit sought out Scowcroft. "Well, Brent, what happened?" he exclaimed.

The man who had served with Defense Secretary Cheney sighed. "When you have a quadruple bypass operation, it can change your character," Scowcroft replied. "It happened with Al Haig when he was secretary of state. I can only assume that's what happened here."[19]

Scowcroft had misjudged Dick Cheney the first time around. The defense secretary had to tread carefully in an administration where Scowcroft and Secretary of State Jim Baker enjoyed unusually close relations with the elder Bush. But in truth, the only thing "moderate" about Cheney had been his tolerant views on gay rights, no doubt influenced by his lesbian daughter, Mary. As Wyoming's congressman from 1979 to 1989, he'd had a voting record so far to the right that he felt compelled to warn George W. Bush about it when the latter asked him to be his running mate in 2000. ("No, I mean *really* conservative," he told him.)[20] Most notably, Cheney decried the War Powers Act and other post-Watergate constraints on executive authority. (Writing the minority report after the House held hearings on the 1987 Iran-Contra scandal, Cheney struck a sympathetic tone regarding the Reagan administration's penchant for secrecy, ascribing it to a "legitimate fear of leaks.")[21] And while serving with Scowcroft in the first Bush administration, the defense secretary oversaw a 1992 Defense Planning Guidance coauthored by Paul Wolfowitz and Scooter Libby, in which Cheney's preference for an unapologetic aggressiveness in foreign affairs was made manifest.[22]

What had changed was not the person but the circumstances. Until September 11, 2001, his life had been marked by extraordinary luck. Two drunken driving offenses, two expulsions from Yale, avoidance of the Vietnam draft, and four heart attacks barely jostled his ascent. Instead he benefited from the scandals of others: first, Nixon's resignation, at which point Rumsfeld became President Ford's chief of staff and brought in his protégé

Cheney to serve as his deputy; and fifteen years later when George H. W. Bush's first pick for defense secretary, John Tower, was torpedoed by the latter's history of overdrinking and womanizing, thereby necessitating an easily confirmable alternative, which Republican House Minority Whip Cheney happened to be.

Cheney's one term as secretary of defense had coincided with the fall of the Soviet Union and Saddam's foolhardy invasion of Kuwait. After Bush was defeated by Clinton, he considered running for president, thought better of it, and instead took the offer to be CEO of Halliburton, despite having no experience in the oil industry.

By 2000, Cheney was rich and content. In the end, however, the chance to be vice president for a man who lacked a background in national security and wanted a strong governing partner was too tempting to forgo. Bush afforded his VP remarkable latitude in personnel decisions and policy portfolio. (When requested by White House Deputy Chief of Staff Josh Bolten to spearhead an offshoot of Al Gore's "reinventing government" movement, Cheney simply refused, and that was that.)[23]

Unlike Rumsfeld at the DOD, Cheney wasted no time exerting his influence. He and Libby ran the transition, installing favored personnel in key slots, such as Zal Khalilzad and Elliott Abrams at the NSC and the sharp-elbowed conservative lawyer John Bolton at State. ("Dick said to me, 'You really need to find a place for Bolton, because he did such a good job for us in the Florida recount,'" Powell recalled. "He was saying, 'You don't have any far-righters over there; you need someone who represents the right wing of the party.'")[24]

Most of all, he stacked the Office of the Vice President with intelligent and driven staffers who would not be shy about exerting their will on his behalf. (His chief counsel, David Addington, took this mandate to an extreme early on, by proposing that Cheney chair the Principals Committee meetings instead of Rice. Upset by this perceived power grab, the national security adviser took up the matter with Bush, who sided with her.)[25] It would be said of Dick Cheney that he endeavored to repurpose OVP as his own hulking shadow government. In fact, the VP's operation was no bigger

than Al Gore's. His speechwriter (McConnell) and communications director (Mary Matalin) were essentially half-time employees who spent the rest
of their time working for the president.

Being a proud man with a politician's ego, Cheney did little to discour-
age the media depiction of him as the White House's resident necromancer.
But the source of his power was there for all to see: Cheney had immense
national security experience, while Bush had very little of his own. Recognizing this, the NSC interwove itself with OVP. "The NSC staff was told
in no uncertain terms from day one that the OVP were coequals," recalled
one senior NSC staffer.[26] Arguably, Cheney's office had the advantage over
Rice's. For while the NSC had only limited visibility into OVP's machinations, the NSC was expected to be transparent toward Cheney and his chief
of staff. "The vice president and Scooter were on every memo that went up to
the president," Steve Hadley said. "They got a copy."[27]

Meanwhile, the most antagonistic figure in the Bush administration,
Donald Rumsfeld, "was very deferential to Cheney, and Cheney to him," said
Edelman.[28]

As Addington liked to say, Cheney never forgot that his job title began
with the word "vice" before "president."[29] Theologically wedded as he was to
the concept of paramount executive authority, and having forsaken for good
his own presidential ambitions, Cheney made clear to Bush that he well
understood who the boss was. He offered himself up as the lone adviser who
represented no agency's interest and could therefore give the president "the
pure, unalloyed national security perspective, stripped of the politics and the
bureaucratics," as Hadley would put it.[30] Then, as Cheney vowed, "once he's
made a decision, I'll salute smartly and support the policy."[31]

Of course, Cheney was hardly a fact-dispensing automaton. His predi-
lection for a muscular American foreign policy had not changed since Wolfowitz and Libby drafted his Defense Planning Guidance in 1992. Another
thing had not changed: Saddam Hussein remained in power. That fact
gnawed at him. Just a few days after Bush's inauguration, the DIA received
a request from the Office of the Vice President: Cheney's office wanted a
memo on Iraqi support of terrorism and Saddam's involvement in both the

Bush assassination plot of 1993 and the first World Trade Center attack that same year.[32]

"Cheney was very focused on the Saddam problem from the moment he came in," Edelman would say.[33] But that focus was subservient to Bush's agenda, which did not include toppling Arab dictators.

Then came 9/11, and Dick Cheney's fortunate life experienced a trauma far more profound than his heart attacks.

A FEW DAYS AFTER THE DEADLY HIJACKINGS, THE VICE PRESIDENT CAME TO CIA headquarters at Langley to receive a briefing. The agency was in a frenzy to anticipate more terroristic activity by Al Qaeda. But Cheney believed the agency might be missing something obvious. Was Saddam involved?

His briefer, a counterterrorism analyst, informed Cheney of her group's unanimous opinion: There was no evidence to suggest Iraqi involvement in the attacks. (As one analyst in her group would say, "It's like asking, 'Did Belgium do this?'")[34] The vice president's displeasure with her answer was evident; "the briefing was a disaster," recalled another analyst who had helped prepare the briefing materials.[35]

In the weeks that followed, Cheney's daily intelligence briefings, normally a half hour in length, would sometimes go on for hours.[36] Cheney had always been a voracious consumer of intelligence data—Libby's deputy, Edelman, kept seven vaults that were full of CIA reports—and briefers found his questions particularly incisive. But now these dialogues began to take on an edge. On more than one occasion while sitting in on the president's briefings, Cheney would ask about Iraqi support for terror groups. When the briefer replied that such a scenario was unlikely—that Iran was more likely to confederate with Al Qaeda—"it was obvious that's not the answer the vice president wanted," said an attendee of these briefings.[37]

The belief was dawning on Cheney and his nimble-minded chief of staff, Libby, that the agency had become captive to its own bureaucratic dogma. As Cheney reminded Tenet and his deputy, John McLaughlin, the CIA had failed to recognize the advanced state of Saddam's nuclear program until IAEA inspectors stumbled upon it after the Gulf War.[38] But to Libby, the problem went beyond ignorance. It was not just that, in his view, an analyst's "assessment" was not much better than a semi-educated guess. It was that biases had overtaken the agency's ability to assess with any accuracy the threats now facing America. And chief among those biases was the stubborn conviction by CIA analysts that a secular dictator would never, under any circumstances, consort with Islamic extremists.

But Cheney and his staffers were themselves guided by collective assumptions, beliefs, and fears. Unlike the president, the vice president was not animated by the desire to see freedom take root throughout the world. He did not share Wolfowitz's belief that humanitarian outrages warranted regime change. And though he accepted the logic of Rumsfeld's desire to transform the military, it was not the vice president's pet cause, not even when he had been defense secretary.

What motivated Cheney was America's vulnerability to another sensational attack, and the necessity of the United States overcoming that vulnerability without impediments. Even before 9/11, Cheney and Libby had studied with great interest a simulated biological-attack exercise conducted at Andrews Air Force Base in June 2001 known as "Dark Winter." (The actors in this simulated production included Senator Sam Nunn as president, James Woolsey reprising his role as CIA director, and New York Times reporter Judith Miller playing herself.)[39] After the attacks, the vice president established his own homeland security advisory team headed by WMD experts Carol Kuntz and Seth Carus, both of whom had worked for Cheney at the Pentagon. He and Libby immersed themselves in briefings relating to biological warfare and the potential for contaminating the U.S. food supply. Some of these briefings took place in Cheney's West Wing office, others at undisclosed locations to which the Secret Service had dispatched the vice president as credible threats continued to roll in.[40]

One Saturday morning at the Naval Observatory, where the vice president resided, his CIA briefer, David Terry, was reciting the Presidential

Daily Briefing when Cheney happened to notice that the family Labrador, also named Dave, had just come inside from playing outdoors and had his muddy paws on the sofa.

"Dave, get down!" Cheney yelled, whereupon Terry dove to the floor.[41]

Levity of this sort was scarce in the quaking ecosystem of the Office of the Vice President. After 9/11, OVP emerged as the Bush administration's think tank of the unthinkable, where apocalyptic scenarios became objects of obsession, no matter how unlikely—and, in the case of Saddam's possible relationship with Al Qaeda, *because* supposed experts at the CIA had deemed it unlikely.

The only recourse, in Dick Cheney's view, was to unleash America's own apocalyptic might. Though he believed himself to be a principled man, principle was not at stake here. What hung in the balance was "the safety and survival of civilization itself."[42]

One of Cheney's subordinates vividly described the OVP's atmospherics:

> Putting yourself in that time after 9/11, where even for those of us who sort of knew about Al Qaeda, you were really almost operating in the dark. And then these goddamn books that come in every day. They're binders filled with threats. These are the daily threat matrixes that nobody could really make heads or tails out of. Nobody really has the organization mapped out in a good understanding of where they are, who they are. Everybody's anticipating another hit, another major operation, so it's all in that kind of fevered swamp of fear and genuine threat, and uncertainty about what could be coming. Everyone has some degree of, I don't know whether it's guilt or something else, but "My God, we let this happen to the country. We sort of had some warnings. Obviously, nobody put together the dots. Can't allow that to happen again."[43]

Divining what the "again" might be was now mission central for OVP. And though it would frequently be said in later years that the staggering mistakes committed in assessing the threat posed by Saddam Hussein seemed to constitute a "failure of the imagination," in reality the opposite had occurred. Imagination rather than facts had driven policy. Largely forgotten, for example, was a rather glaring omission in the cache of Al Qaeda material discovered in Afghanistan that had prompted Cheney's trip to the Middle East. Though the voluminous evidence left no doubt that bin Laden intended to acquire weapons of mass destruction, not a single document or detainee made mention of Iraq as a potential supplier of such weapons.[44]

Save one. In December 2001, Al Qaeda senior operative Ibn al-Shaykh al-Libi was captured by the Americans and interrogated. After failing to reveal anything of material value, he was handed over to Egyptian interrogators. Within days, al-Libi confessed that he had heard from an unnamed associate that two Al Qaeda recruits had been sent to Baghdad in December 2000 to be trained in building and deploying chemical and biological weapons.

Al-Libi's confession, uncorroborated by any other detainee, struck many in the CIA and DIA as highly suspect. Later it was determined to be a fabrication, extracted from him under torture by the Egyptians. The CIA renounced the bombshell—but not until March 2004, well after the detainee's coerced flight of imagination had achieved the status of fact, thereby buttressing the case for war.[45]

CHAPTER SIX

"HISTORY HAS CALLED US"

On Sunday, March 17, 2002, Christopher Meyer, the British ambassador to the United States, hosted Paul Wolfowitz for lunch at his residence on Embassy Row.

Meyer had first met Wolfowitz five years before, when the former had just arrived in Washington and the latter was dean of the Johns Hopkins School of Advanced International Studies. It had struck Meyer as a bit on the fringe for a respected scholar to argue, as Wolfowitz had one day in 1998, "We should invade southern Iraq, seize the old fields, base ourselves in Basra and from there launch raids in Baghdad, and little by little we will bring the regime down." Even more startling to the ambassador was learning through back channels that Deputy Secretary of Defense Wolfowitz had urged that very same plan of attack to President Bush at Camp David three years later, on September 15, 2001.[1]

Meyer nonetheless liked Wolfowitz a great deal. His bearing was that of a reasonable man, and Meyer knew that his views on Iraq, however provocative, were born of a deeply held belief that Islam and democracy were compatible.[2]

And in any event, the subject of Iraq was no longer an avoidable one for the Brits. Three weeks from now, on April 5, 2002, Prime Minister Tony Blair would be visiting Bush at his ranch in Crawford to discuss the Saddam problem. Blair wanted a preview of what the Americans were thinking. Three days earlier, Meyer had joined his colleague David Manning, the UK foreign policy adviser, for lunch with Condoleezza Rice. "Condi's enthusiasm for regime change is undimmed," Manning would later report to Blair in a memo. But, he added, "from what she said, Bush has yet to find the answers to the big questions"—chief among them "how to persuade international opinion that military action against Iraq is necessary and justified. . . . He is still smarting from the comments by other European leaders on his Iraq policy."[3]

But Blair also needed to hear from those in the Bush administration who were urging the president to charge ahead, heedless of the outside world's response. Hence Meyer's lunch with Wolfowitz. The deputy secretary listened appreciatively to the UK ambassador's message: Prime Minister Blair favored regime change. But the plan needed to be "clever." To Meyer, this meant establishing a legal case against Saddam to present to the UN.

Wolfowitz was noncommittal on that last point. His position, he said, was somewhat different from the view held by others in the Bush administration. Their focus was on Saddam's weapons—and, he said, in building the public case for regime change, that topic was obviously important. But, as Meyer would later write in a memo to Manning, "Wolfowitz thought it indispensable to spell out in detail Saddam's barbarism. . . . Wolfowitz thought that this would go a long way to destroying any notion of moral equivalence between Iraq and Israel" in the skeptical eyes of the Arab world.[4]

Meyer himself suspected otherwise. The British ambassador had become an astute observer of the American political scene during his five years in Washington. He had watched Bush grow in stature since September 11. The president's approval ratings now hovered in the upper seventies. "Bush has successfully defined himself as the commander in chief of the war on terrorism," the ambassador wrote in a cable to Blair's senior staff two weeks after his lunch with Wolfowitz. Cowed by wartime atmospherics, the Democrats had awarded Bush a blank check. The president, Meyer observed, "faces few domestic constraints."

But, he continued, the vice president's tour of the Middle East had been a splash of ice water: "And as Cheney found out recently, it is only Washington ideologues who think that Iraq is a feasible option while Palestine burns." With exquisite insight, Ambassador Chris Meyer described the predicament of the man Tony Blair would be visiting in four days:

"At Crawford, the prime minister will find the president fully engaged as commander in chief of the war on terrorism. But while the early months after America was attacked played to Bush's talents for instinctive leadership and moral certainty, sustaining the momentum poses new and more complex tests."[5]

Whether Bush could manage "more complex tests," Blair and his team did not know.

THEY KNEW THAT HE HAD PLEASANTLY SURPRISED THEM BEFORE—REALLY, from the outset. Wistful about the departure of the Clintons, Blair's Labour Party team eyed the Texas Republican warily. But as was so frequently the case, the Brits had "misunderestimated" Bush's political skills—how he spoke confidently and without notes, how he remembered names, how present he was in his dialogues.[6] After 9/11, Blair had feared the worst from the hot-blooded president. "My God, fasten your seat belts," the prime minister had moaned to his staff after a phone conversation with Bush three days after the attacks. And on September 20, after hearing Bush relay Wolfowitz's proposition about seizing Saddam's oil fields, Blair's chief of staff, Jonathan Powell, mordantly recalled to Blair's communications chief, Alastair Campbell, how Margaret Thatcher had advised the elder Bush before Operation Desert Storm, "This is no time to wobble, George."

Said Powell, "This IS a time to wobble."[7]

Bush, they could see, was weathering the crisis of the attacks better than other members of his administration. Alastair Campbell could plainly see how shell-shocked the president's longtime adviser, Karen Hughes, was when he visited her in the White House six full weeks after the attacks. This was all very different, she acknowledged to Campbell, from running a Texas political campaign.⁸ For that matter, Bush's receptiveness to Blair's opinions on Iraq stood in marked contrast to Cheney, who had visited the prime minister on March 11, just before flying to the Middle East. Sitting stiffly in the White Room of No. 10 Downing Street, the vice president informed Blair, "A coalition would be nice, but not essential." ("Their jaws dropped," recalled Colin Powell's assistant secretary Bill Burns, who was in the room.)⁹

Still, Blair knew that the pressure on Bush to extend the war on terrorism to Iraq was not coming from just Cheney and Wolfowitz. The American public, so wounded and at the same time so invested in the ability of its military to unleash vengeance, was unlikely to be satisfied with a torturous manhunt for bin Laden. As Cheney himself said to the *Washington Post* reporter Bob Woodward, in obvious frustration, "They have nothing to defend. You know, for 50 years we deterred the Soviets by threatening the utter destruction of the Soviet Union. What does bin Laden value? There's no piece of real estate."¹⁰ The desire to do more than simply "pound sand" had become a nationwide yearning.¹¹

The prime minister saw his role as one of reminding the president that the world was watching, and that all sympathy for America would collapse if the White House started recklessly seeking out bombing targets outside of Afghanistan. On October 11, after spending the day with President Mubarak of Egypt and Sultan Qaboos bin Said of Oman, Blair wrote a note that began "Dear George," sent via a secure White House link: "There is a real willingness in the Middle East to get Saddam out but a total opposition to mixing this up with the current operation. . . . The uncertainty caused by Phase 2 seeming to extend to Iraq, Syria etc. is really hurting [Arab leaders] because it seems to confirm the UBL propaganda that this is West vs. Arab. I have no doubt we need to deal with Saddam. But if we hit Iraq now, we would lose the Arab world, Russia, probably half the EU and my fear is the impact of all that on Pakistan. However, I am sure we can devise a strategy for Saddam deliverable at a later date."¹²

Delaying that "later date" became Blair's objective. When he flew to Washington to meet with Bush on the afternoon of November 7, he handed the president a four-page list of foreign policy tasks that the two leaders went over together. Toppling Saddam Hussein was not on the list. Instead Blair's note suggested a milder alternative: "New UN Resolution on Iraq."[13]

The stalling tactic did not work, however. Two weeks after Bush's get-together with Blair, the president requested that Rumsfeld and Franks begin updating an Iraq war plan. Word of this reached the prime minister quickly. On December 4, Blair again wrote to Bush. His seven-page memo, entitled "The War Against Terrorism: The Second Phase," was an acknowledgment that Bush's attention had turned to Saddam. Still, the strategy he counseled was attuned to global wariness: "[B]uild this over time until we get to the point where military action could be taken if necessary; but meanwhile bring people towards us, undermine Saddam, without so alarming people about the immediacy of action that we frighten the horses, lose Russia and/or half the EU and nervous Arab states and find ourselves facing a choice between massive intervention and nothing."

Blair concluded with "Sorry to be a bore on this. The Middle East is set for catastrophe. . . . The issue is whether a process of sorts can be put back on track. If it isn't, this will complicate everything in the Middle East for a wider struggle."[14]

Blair himself was anything but an apologist for Saddam. Nearly two years before Bush became president, the prime minister delivered a fiery speech in Chicago in which he implied that the actions of the "dangerous and ruthless" Iraqi dictator warranted intervention.[15] Even so, the political climate in the UK did not favor foreign adventurism. Three weeks before Blair set out for Texas, a poll by *The Guardian* indicated that only 35 percent of British voters supported U.S. military action in Iraq; 51 percent opposed it.[16] Some members of Blair's own cabinet were outright opposed to the UK joining a military invasion. His defense minister, Geoffrey Hoon, pointed out, in a memo to Blair, "In objective terms, Iran may be the greater problem for the UK. . . . Ironically, we have Saddam Hussein bound into an established control mechanism."[17]

Bush's "axis of evil" speech had only sown confusion, argued Blair's foreign minister, Jack Straw. It would be hard, Straw wrote to Blair, "to show why military action against Iraq is so much more justified than against Iran and North Korea. . . . We also have to answer the big question—what will this action achieve? There seems to be a larger hole in this than on anything. Most of the assessments from the US have assumed regime change as a means of eliminating Iraq's WMD threat. But none has satisfactorily answered how that regime change is to be secured, and how there can be any certainty that the replacement regime will be better. Iraq has had no history of democracy so no-one has this habit or experience."

For these and other reasons, the foreign minister warned Tony Blair, "[t]he rewards from your visit to Crawford will be few."[18]

JACK STRAW WAS NOT ENTIRELY CORRECT. TONY AND CHERIE BLAIR ARRIVED with their team in north-central Texas on the cold and rainy afternoon of April 5, 2002. While the American and British advisers ate a steak and Tex-Mex dinner in downtown Waco and Ambassador Meyer was fitted for cowboy boots,[19] Bush and the prime minister dined one-on-one at the ranch and discussed the Iraq problem. The president acknowledged that CENTCOM was drawing up war plans but insisted that this did not make war a fait accompli, that he was open to other approaches. That night as well as the following morning, Blair in turn assured Bush that the UK would stand "shoulder to shoulder" with America.

But there were two conditions for Blair's stated fidelity. One was that Bush reinsert himself in the Middle East peace process, despite his distrust of Arafat. The region, he argued, was "in transition." Showing leadership on this matter would signal to the Arab world that the United States was not simply settling old scores and throwing its weight around. The president saw the logic in Blair's argument.

The other was that Bush seek out a coalition through the UN—and, along the way, demand that Saddam let inspectors back into Iraq to assess whether the regime was continuing to violate WMD prohibitions. Such a route, the prime minister said, could achieve Saddam's disarmament and thereby forestall war altogether. Bush was less warm to this idea. As he would later write, "I didn't have a lot of faith in the UN. The Security Council had passed sixteen resolutions against Saddam to no avail." But Blair extracted from Bush the promise that he would consider it.[20]

Still, Jack Straw's pessimism was not entirely misplaced, for the Crawford summit did not produce any guarantees that Bush was committed to a multilateral path. Going the UN route, Blair's adviser Manning would later say, "is what we spent the rest of the year trying to do."[21] As for the Middle East peace process, on June 24 Bush announced from the Rose Garden that he would henceforth engage in negotiations only after the Palestinians elected "new leaders" and embraced democratic reforms.[22]

"Powell hated the June speech," recalled Elliott Abrams,[23] and the secretary had predicted in an NSC meeting that Bush would be seen by the Palestinians as telling them who their leaders could and could not be.[24] Reviewing the speech, Bill Burns had cautioned Powell, "Its tone is patronizing and preachy. No one—not even you—could sell this in the region."[25]

Indeed, the Arab world was infuriated by the Rose Garden speech. Egypt's president, Hosni Mubarak, had visited Camp David just two weeks earlier and had not been told that a speech of this sort was in the works; he bore a grudge against the Bush administration thereafter.[26]

The disconnect at work was not simply a reflection of Bush's unwillingness to let the outside world dictate U.S. policy. Instead, what Blair and others saw from the Bush White House was an inability to understand how the outside world viewed the United States. One of the more telling passages in the president's joint session speech began with his explanation for the roots of Islamic extremism: "Americans are asking, 'Why do they hate us?'" To Bush, the answer was plain: "They hate our freedoms—our freedom of religion, our freedom of speech, our freedom to vote and assemble and disagree with each other."[27]

In a way, the self-absorption and self-glorification reflected in Bush's assertion supplied a more accurate answer to his question than the one he gave. The possibility that the world did not accept America's innate goodness—and thus that an act of American military aggression in the Middle East might be viewed with cynicism—was a matter of bewilderment that extended to Bush's top advisers. "I think the basic problem was that they genuinely didn't understand anti-Americanism," Alastair Campbell would write in his diary following one visit to the White House. "They couldn't see how, given that in this instance they had been the victim, and given all the help they had tried to administer around the world, they were not more popular." When Campbell presented him with a poll showing how poorly some of Bush's remarks were registering with the British public, communications director Dan Bartlett "seemed surprised, even a little hurt."[28]

In fact, most of the world had reacted with grief and horror to the 9/11 attacks. Where it parted company with Bush was in the latter's Christian determination to find good in tragedy—to seek "opportunity," a word he would use repeatedly in the days and weeks following the attacks.[29] For Bush, "opportunity" had meant freedom from the Taliban in Afghanistan. The same could happen in Palestine, he said in the Rose Garden: "You deserve democracy and the rule of law." He then added, "This moment is both an opportunity and a test for all parties in the Middle East."[30]

It was Bush who insisted on dictating the terms, the timetable, and the stakes—and, for that matter, the "opportunity." But restoring the moral sphere and attempting to foist one anew were not just different propositions. They were contradictory, suggesting arrogance rather than idealism.

On the morning of August 1, five weeks after Bush's Rose Garden speech, the president welcomed King Abdullah II of Jordan to the Oval Office. Cheney, Powell, Rice, and U.S. Ambassador to Jordan Skip Gnehm were among those present, along with a coterie of royal advisers. Abdullah was forty and had been the country's ruler for less than three years. His father, King Hussein, had joined President Saleh of Yemen as the only two Arab leaders to side with Saddam Hussein during the Gulf War. Under Abdullah, Jordan continued to have an economic relationship with its neighbor. The son was not given to confrontation. But today he had a thorny issue to discuss with Bush.

"Mr. President, I want to talk about Iraq," Abdullah said in his impeccable English.

"Good," said Bush without hesitation. "Let's talk about Iraq."

In fact, the president was already aware that the Jordanian ruler had spent the previous days telling journalists that he would vigorously oppose any effort to topple Saddam. Bush listened to his concerns with welling impatience. Watching the contortions on the president's face, one attendee wrote down in his notepad: "Hyperventilation."

"Saddam is a bad guy," Bush snapped. "My opinion of him hasn't changed. We need to take him down."With exasperation he continued: "What will people say thirty years from now? I don't want them to say that the king and I backed away from a showdown—using whatever excuse we could find not to move forward."

Sitting beside the Jordanian ruler, leaning into his face, Bush's voice rose: "History has called us. We will affect how the world looks tomorrow!"

Composing himself, the president half apologized: "I'm passionate on the subject. I've dealt with the Europeans on this. All the excuses in the book. They don't get it." An unwillingness to act would send a disastrous message to adversaries around the world, he added, such as North Korea.

"When I said 'axis of evil,'" said Bush, "I meant it."[31]

On the flight back to Amman, Abdullah spoke to Ambassador Gnehm. In a resigned voice, the king said, "Skip, if he's going into Iraq, then I've got to do everything I can to see to it that he's successful. Because if he fails, I'm finished."[32]

THAT KING ABDULLAH WAS ACQUIESCENT ONLY MEANT THAT HE RECOGnized Bush's fixation on the "opportunity" in Iraq. Knowing that Jordanians were overwhelmingly opposed to war with their neighbor, Abdullah would continue to publicly voice objections as well. Military aggression, he predicted, "will form a catastrophe for the region and will increase instability and chaos."[33]

Abdullah, Blair, and other foreign leaders trusted the American president's sincerity of purpose. What they doubted was his grasp of what he viewed as the next great opportunity.

For, as the Syrian autocrat Bashar al-Assad warned a visiting British official, "Most Iraqis hate Saddam. *All* Iraqis hate America."[34]

CHAPTER SEVEN

═══

SECRET LUNCHES

I t's called coercive diplomacy," Condoleezza Rice said to Bush one day during the early summer of 2002. The national security adviser was explaining how the threat of military action could force Saddam Hussein to comply with the UN and ultimately turn over his WMD, as Tony Blair had been advocating.

"That's a nice phrase," the president said. "Where'd that come from?"

Smiling, Rice replied, "Political science."[1]

Bush rolled his eyes, to Condi Rice's complete lack of surprise. It was a kind of game the two had been playing since they first became close in early 1999: the brainy Stanford academic flinging shiny verbiage from the ivory tower into the dirt, where the Texan then poked at it with his cowboy boot and pronounced it horseshit. After that, the phrase would become his—though of course the president still reserved the right to chortle, as he often did, that something was a "political science" word or, worse still, a "Washington" word or, worst of all, a "poll-tested" or "focus-grouped" word. But just as Karl Rove had been Bush's indispensable political adviser, so too did he turn to Rice on matters of national security—and never so much as in the days and months after 9/11, when the ground had shifted beneath the Texas president's feet and he was now forced to consider, for the first time in his life, the fuzzy-headed notion of "geopolitics."

Rice was, by her estimation, in the Oval Office about seven times on the average each day during that period. No one else had such frequent and ongoing access to the president. Those who did gain access—Cheney, Rumsfeld, Powell—would invariably find Rice in the room as well.[2] So constantly was she by Bush's side, and so easy did their banter seem, that even members of her own staff found their closeness odd.[3] To some degree that viewpoint bespoke the contrast between her access and the staffers' own distance from Bush in a notably hierarchical administration, where meetings were kept small and formality was rigorously enforced by Chief of Staff Card.

But it was also true that Rice and Bush—who shared an affinity for hard workouts, sports metaphors, and ridiculous movies but whose life experiences could not have been more different—were now walking together in a terra incognita that neither had foreseen. All carefully composed assumptions about the world had gone down with the Twin Towers. They had to rethink everything on the fly.

Rice was far more candid than her male White House colleagues about the trauma. While Bush, Cheney, Rumsfeld, and others would describe the significance of 9/11 with clinical factuality, Condi Rice conveyed it experientially, sensually, right down to the smell of the smoke on her clothes after she visited the Pentagon. "I have always felt as if I operated in a kind of fog, a virtual state of shock, for two days after 9/11," she wrote in her memoir. She choked back tears in the beauty salon; she wept in her apartment at the Watergate, where she lived alone.[4] When Richard Clarke's chemical-and-biological-weapons specialist, Lisa Gordon-Hagerty, stepped in to brief Bush during the anthrax scare, Rice gladly withdrew, telling Clarke, "I didn't take this job to worry about homeland security."[5]

It was perhaps a joke. But for a single African American woman from Birmingham who had run up against forbidding odds all her life, confidence that she could do her job was the one thing Condoleezza Rice had always been able to count on. Now her job was part of the "everything" that 9/11 had changed.

Bush had not changed. As she watched him confront a new era, a post-9/11 presidency, "clarity" was the word that kept coming to Rice's mind. For those who had doubted his experience, Bush's sturdy purposefulness was what now mattered. "Nuance"—her word, never his—seemed less useful a device following an act of pure evil. For that matter, her encyclopedic mastery of super-power dynamics had receded in relevance. In the coming months, Rice would remain Bush's closest adviser. But her ability to steer his thinking would steadily dwindle.

Rice's peers on the National Security Council were all males. They were Washington's supermen. Their experience, far surpassing hers, was also intertwined—decades of shared power, the secret language of a fraternity from which women like her had long been excluded. That she owed *her* power to proximity to the ultimate power, George W. Bush, did not guarantee respect. In Donald Rumsfeld's case, it ensured resentment.[6]

At Principals Committee meetings, the defense secretary would ignore Rice "to the point of absolute rudeness," recalled Bill Burns.[7] Just as ignominiously, Bush's national security adviser was reduced to a woman's familiar role of officiating disputes between two titanic male egos, Rumsfeld and Powell. They bickered face-to-face. They carried their quarrels into bureaucratic back alleys. Rice's own power was drained in the process. "Even in the early days, you could see the dynamics of a very weak Condi Rice unable to manage these big guys around the table," recalled one NSC aide.[8] During a dinner in the late spring of 2002 with Tony Blair's communications director, Alastair Campbell, former secretary of state James Baker commented that Bush had let things get out of hand: "Powell and Rumsfeld were at odds the whole time," Campbell wrote in his diary of Baker's assessment, "whilst Condi was less a full time national security adviser to the president but instead a mediator between the two."[9]

Arguably, she was the one genius among them. A competitive ice skater, concert pianist, and Cold War scholar with a photographic memory—all of these attributes, present in any one human anywhere, would have qualified her as such. But Rice's brilliance had been forged during the church bombings and fire hose sprayings of the Jim Crow Deep South. That experience—"not to feel safe in your home, you know, to have your father out with a shotgun," as Rice recalled to her biographer, Elisabeth Bumiller—was utterly foreign to her NSC counterparts, including Powell, child of the Bronx that he was.[10]

But Rice's many talents did not ensure a well-run national security apparatus. Instead, the interagency process she oversaw quickly became one of deep and intractable disagreement, particularly between Powell and Rumsfeld. That the Departments of State and Defense would not see eye to eye was hardly a new development in American political life, as was attestable by those who witnessed the toxic discord between Reagan's top diplomat, George Shultz, and his two Pentagon chiefs, Alexander Haig and Caspar Weinberger. (One such witness was Reagan's last national security adviser, Colin Powell.)

What made the Powell-Rumsfeld disputes fatefully corrosive was that Bush was barely aware of them. Some of this stemmed from the president's apparent belief that, since those surrounding him in the West Wing—Card, Rove, Hughes, Bartlett, Fleischer, deputy chiefs of staff Josh Bolten and Joe Hagin—generally got along, it figured that others in the administration did, too. It was also the case that Powell and Rumsfeld tended to affect collegiality in front of the president, fooling no one except for their boss.

But it was also true that Rice actively sought to insulate Bush from such conflicts. It was her view that presidents did not want to spend their valuable time listening to secretaries debate.[11] But in fact, under Bush's predecessor, Bill Clinton, "different positions were aired, along with their rationales, and Clinton asked questions to help him decide," recalled Kenneth Pollack, Clinton's NSC director of Persian Gulf affairs.[12] As for Bush's successor, Barack Obama, Deputy National Security Adviser Ben Rhodes would say, "In almost all of the key decision meetings, there were cabinet secretaries with differing views. And all of those views were aired by the cabinet secretaries in front of Obama."[13]

Rice understood well her boss's inclinations. President Bush preferred short, orderly meetings, with minimal discursiveness, focused on a single recommendation that had been issued by the team arrayed before him. "He wanted people to do their jobs and come up with a policy," explained one of

Rice's senior staffers.[14] As Rice herself remarked during one Principals Committee meeting, "If I bring a gross disagreement between cabinet officers to the president, I've failed at my job."[15]

Rather than fail at her job, Bush's national security adviser sought to find commonality where oftentimes it did not exist—to blend the contrasting viewpoints into a muddled consensus. In one of Rumsfeld's memos to Rice expressing his myriad unsolicited thoughts on how the interagency process could stand improvement, he noted, "Papers should not aim at a homogenized consensus. It is useful to clearly and accurately present differences among agencies."[16]

The result of this "homogenized consensus" often meant that the prevailing argument, when there was one, was subject to everyone's interpretation. Both sides would thereby emerge as the self-appointed winner—or, as was often the case with Rumsfeld, "would continue to litigate the argument, long after it ceased being in the president's interest to do so," according to an NSC staffer.[17]

By early 2002, the subject of Iraq had become the text or subtext of nearly every Principals Committee meeting. The sides were understood by all participants. On one end, pushing for quick and aggressive action, sat the Office of the Secretary of Defense and the Office of the Vice President; disagreements between the two were practically nonexistent, and so the two bodies acted as one. On the other end, notably less gung-ho, sat the State Department and from time to time the CIA, which shared office space with the former in embassies and viewed the world in much the same way as Foreign Service officers. (Wedged uncomfortably in the middle were the Joint Chiefs, who of course took their orders from the Pentagon and therefore had reason to suppress their unease about its war ambitions.)

The Iraq issue, Rice would concede, brought the NSC process "nearly to the breaking point."[18] The rancor at times called to mind a Hatfield-McCoy interfamilial dispute, involving earlier unforgotten quarrels that went back to the Gulf War, when Powell was Cheney's reluctant warrior, ultimately pushing for an "overwhelming force" military posture that Rumsfeld now rejected as outmoded. Men who had known each other for decades, once lukewarmly, could no longer disguise their ill feelings. Or, when they attempted to do so, no one was fooled by it. At the beginning of one principals meeting, Powell's deputy, Richard Armitage, genially offered the vice president some coffee.

Armitage was awarded Cheney's asymmetrical quarter smile. "Rich," replied the vice president, "if you gave it to me, I'd have to have a taster."[19]

The joke might have been funnier had it been less poignant. As one NSC aide who had previously served in the Clinton administration recalled, "I think Condi and Steve [Hadley] were wasting a lot of energy, time, and intellectual capital basically trying to shepherd the unruly children who had not learned how to play nice in a sandbox. Rumsfeld and Cheney—they treated her like assholes."[20]

IN OTHER ADMINISTRATIONS, CLASHES BETWEEN PRINCIPALS WERE OFTEN preempted through negotiations between their corresponding deputies. Under the Bush administration, this was not possible. As one senior White House official would say, "You can talk about the principals. But with the deputies— Wolfowitz, Armitage—you had some serious personalities and agendas. If there's a place where the process completely broke down, it was there."[21]

Armitage was a policeman's son and graduate of the Naval Academy (where he played football with Hall of Fame quarterback Roger Staubach) who had served six years in Vietnam and who reportedly could bench-press four hundred pounds. He and Wolfowitz had worked together collegially in both the Reagan and elder Bush administrations. For that matter, when Armitage in the mid-1980s took legal action against an author he believed had libeled him, his attorney of record was I. Lewis "Scooter" Libby. He had been a petition signatory and an op-ed advocate of overthrowing Saddam throughout the nineties, much like Wolfowitz and Libby.[22]

But the razor-witted deputy secretary of state harbored disdain for civilian hawks who had "never fucking smelled cordite," as he put it to one friend.[23] He was extremely close to and protective of Powell—"a friend of the heart," as Powell would describe it in his memoir[24]—and he shared his boss's penchant for venting and gossiping to the media.

It was evident to Armitage immediately after 9/11 that both Wolfowitz and Feith were pushing for regime change in Iraq. When Armitage was asked on a Sunday TV show a month after the attacks whether the United States might extend its bombing campaign in Afghanistan into other countries, like perhaps Syria or Iraq, the deputy secretary responded that "this would be a matter for the coalition to discuss among themselves."[25]

When word of this reached the Pentagon, Rumsfeld immediately fired off a memo to Powell: "I think we have all agreed that there is not a single coalition, and that the mission will determine the coalition—not that the coalition would determine the mission. . . . I think we ought to try to all get our positions calibrated so we are all on the same sheet of music."[26]

In fact, Powell and Armitage had not agreed to this Rumsfeld's Rule, which they viewed as anathema to State's diplomatic mission. Thus, there would be no "same sheet of music." Far from it: at the Deputies Committee meetings, recalled one participant, "we became the Bickersons—couldn't sit down at the table without getting into a fight."[27]

The job of officiator fell to Rice's deputy national security adviser, Stephen Hadley. An intelligent, cautious, painstaking mediator, Hadley had worked for Defense Secretary Cheney in the elder Bush administration before entering the private sector as an international business attorney. His one client was now George W. Bush. Knowing the president's intense dislike of leaks, Hadley saw to it that official notes of NSC meetings were not taken, so that Bush could feel free to air whatever half-baked or intemperate thing was on his mind. He also knew that Bush preferred a policy recommendation over prolonged debate. Even more than Rice, Hadley "was very reluctant to push something up where there was disagreement," recalled one top NSC aide. "He would try to find consensus."[28]

But, as Hadley soon learned, consensus was nearly impossible to come by among the deputies. "I remember Steve telling me once that the deputies were just at each other's throats," recalled Ari Fleischer. "And that was prior to September 11. It was Wolfowitz and Armitage. Those two were at loggerheads."[29]

Because of Hadley's determination to resolve disputes, he would reconvene the deputies again and again, hoping for resolution. A State diplomat who had served in the first Bush administration recalled how during that earlier presidency "there weren't a lot of these Deputies Committees—only once every few weeks, if something really difficult had come up. Then I come back in 2001 and they're having these things all the time. And when the Iraq stuff started getting more active, it went crazy. All these nutty papers started getting injected into these meetings.

"My private term for it was the Reign of Shit."[30]

The Sisyphean futility of these Deputies Committee meetings owed to deep personal and policy differences. But another major factor concerned an individual who did not even attend the meetings: Donald Rumsfeld. The defense secretary had at one point argued to Rice in a memo, "We don't need a PC [Principals Committee]—we should have an NSC and the deputies should do the rest. We should energize the deputies."[31] This was a hilariously disingenuous proposal on Rumsfeld's part, since it was he who had decreed that deputies could not make decisions. "The way some principals operate with their deputies is 'I'm a very busy guy, and I don't want to be bothered with anything that can be resolved at a lower level, okay?'" recalled Feith. "That's a common attitude. That was absolutely not Rumsfeld's view. Rumsfeld's view was 'Anything of any significance, I want to decide.'"[32]

As a result, the Deputies Committee became little more than an acrimonious debating society. The chief perpetrator was Feith, whose windy, professorial manner—"like this was a goddamned Sunday talk show," in the words of one NSC staffer[33]—frustrated even his allies. (Recalled one of them, "I'd come into Deputies Committees and say, 'I'm going to agree with DOD on this one.' And thirty minutes in, Doug would convince me I'm not on his side.")[34]

Because of Rumsfeld, even those matters that the deputies could manage to agree on would not ultimately be agreed to. A day after a Deputies Committee meeting, Hadley's notetaker would send out a summary of conclusions, or SOC, to each participant. Invariably, Feith would contact Hadley to inform him that his boss had in fact agreed to no such things, and that therefore the SOC would have to be rewritten—which meant, of course, that the other participants would read the amended SOC and complain to Hadley that these were not what the group had agreed to. Sometimes Hadley would side with Feith. At other times the deputy national security adviser would sigh to the other deputies, "You'll have to sort it out with the Pentagon—I can't do it." That amounted to a dead end, since, as one attendee said of Feith, "the poor man got yelled at enough."[35]

For those who attended the Deputies Committee meetings as neutral participants, the spectacle was an appalling one. General Greg Newbold of the JCS would take in the sniping with "a rictus-like smile on his face, while everything he stood for was being gone against," said Armitage.[36] A CIA operative recalled seeing the deputy secretary of state glowering while Wolfowitz spoke and conspicuously rubbing his middle finger across his forehead.[37] Armitage's contempt for his Pentagon counterparts seemed to harden in direct proportion to the frequency of the meetings. He began referring to Wolfowitz and Feith variously as congregants at a Star Wars bar or as bats who spent much of the time hung upside down and then suddenly took wing.[38]

Even those who admired Armitage worried that his disdain for the "neocons" had become counterproductive. "Armitage used to talk about bureaucratic jujitsu—'We'll take their statement and use it against them,'" one colleague said. "It wasn't in keeping with his character."[39]

"We could be talking about easy things—Liberia, Panama—and every fricking subject became contentious," recalled one of the deputies. "Because we were playing out our antagonisms across the board. And nobody at any point called us in and said, 'What is the matter with you people? Don't you realize you work in an office where the American flag flies, and if a taxpayer was at these meetings they'd kill you?'"[40]

BY THE BEGINNING OF 2002, IT WAS CLEAR TO STEVE HADLEY THAT BUSH was seriously considering Iraq for what the president termed the next "theater" in the war on terror. Bush had ordered Rumsfeld to oversee new Iraq war plans with Tommy Franks in late November 2001. He had directed his speechwriters to devote inordinate attention in his January 2002 State of the Union address to the Iraqi threat. And in February, he had approved the covert deployment of CIA teams to northern Iraq.

Model of prudence that he was, Hadley recognized that the NSC would need to be armed with answers and plans, should the president elect to confront Saddam Hussein by force. At the same time, any news leak that senior officials of the Bush administration were already mapping out regime change in Iraq could set off a disastrous chain of events throughout the world. The deputy national security adviser therefore convened, with utmost secrecy, the first interagency group to discuss going to war in Iraq, gathering them for what would be known as the Deputies Lunches.

The meetings began in February, just after Bush's "axis of evil" speech. Like most Deputies Committee meetings, they took place in the White House Situation Room, over lunch. Unlike the former, where as many as two dozen administration staffers might convene, no more than eight invitees—from DOD, State, CIA, JCS, and NSC—were summoned to Hadley's secretive lunches. They were forbidden from telling their colleagues.[41] When Frank Miller, the NSC's director of defense planning, heard rumors from his Pentagon contacts about the lunches and inquired with Hadley as to whether he could be of use, the deputy national security adviser discreetly steered Miller back to his office, saying, "When the time comes, we'll get you."[42]

The purpose of the lunches was not to discuss whether to topple Saddam. That decision was Bush's alone. Rather, the lunches were intended to explore the issues that might arise should the president decide to go to war. "And yet," as CIA deputy director John McLaughlin would say, "you couldn't fail to understand that if we're spending this much time talking about a what-if, there's a pretty damn good chance we're going to do this."[43]

At the lunches, topics ranged from the strength of the Baath Party to proposals for a new Iraqi currency. Many of the speculated issues bore a whiff of déjà vu, redolent of the Gulf War: What if Saddam blew up his dams, set his oil fields aflame, or launched missiles at Israel? What if a humanitarian disaster ensued? The tendency to refight the previous war rather than discern the upcoming one was evident in the lunches.[44]

The inconclusiveness and ill feelings of other Deputies Committee meetings spilled over into the lunches. "They got to be kind of maddening," recalled McLaughlin. Before long, the CIA deputy director began to send the deputy director for intelligence, Jami Miscik, in his place, just as Wolfowitz would deputize Feith and Armitage would dispatch Marc Grossman.[45]

It had been Armitage's initial hope that the meetings would serve a constructive purpose. Everyone, he dared to think, would see the steepness of the mountain that invading Iraq would represent and soon back away.[46] Instead, the opposite occurred. By institutionalizing such discussions, Hadley had—unintentionally, for he was never one of the administration's vigorous proponents of war—created bureaucratic locomotion for a policy that had yet to be debated, and in fact never would be.

By the spring of 2002, with the president still officially undecided, his administration was focused on a single pathway. It led to Baghdad, not away from it.

IN ONE OF THE EARLIEST DEPUTIES LUNCHES, PROBABLY IN FEBRUARY 2002, Scooter Libby floated what seemed like an innocuous proposition. Why not organize a conference of leading Iraqi exiles to begin making the case for regime change and a post-Saddam future?

But it was not a straightforward and easily ratified notion. For as Cheney's chief of staff well knew, any discussion about Iraqi opposition figures necessarily led to the irksome subject of Ahmad Chalabi.[47]

The fifty-seven-year-old head of the Iraqi National Congress—a coalition of anti-Baath exiles and Kurdish oppositionists founded in 1992—had equal numbers of friends and foes in the Situation Room that afternoon. But he did not trust any of them, and even many of his allies would come to distrust him in return. For longer than any of them, Chalabi had been agitating for Saddam's removal. Along the way he had cultivated ties with Wolfowitz, Cheney, Libby, Feith, Hannah, and many others in the U.S. government. His gabby conviviality masked a ruthless pragmatism. As Chalabi told friends in confidence, Americans kept promises only to each other, not to foreigners.

Toppling Saddam would occur only if it became official U.S. policy and not simply a fuzzy-headed ideal of a few dozen Iraqi expatriates.

The CIA had discovered Chalabi not long after the Gulf War, in December 1990. His family had fled Iraq in 1958, when he was a teenager, after the emperor installed by the British had been deposed in a military coup and Shia elites like Chalabi's father were no longer welcome. Another forty-five years would pass before he saw Baghdad again. In the meantime, Chalabi obtained a PhD in mathematics at the University of Chicago, three years before Wolfowitz also earned a doctorate there. In Jordan, he founded the Petra Bank, amassed a fortune, and achieved high-society status. When the bank failed in 1989, the Jordanian government indicted Chalabi for fraud. He snuck out of the country. A year later, when the CIA was seeking opposition leaders to help sow dissent against the Iraqi dictator, they learned of Chalabi and commissioned an American lobbying firm, the Rendon Group, to set up a support office for him in London.[48]

Very soon, it became apparent to the agency that they could not control Chalabi. He made little secret of his ties to the Iranian Shiites who shared his hatred of Saddam. (This hardly made him their instrument; as one of Chalabi's top aides, Zaab Sethna, would point out, "He was equally out of control for the Iranians.") Chalabi was a secularist, but he was also a sectarian: the restoration of his father's Shia aristocracy in Iraq was his apparent endgame. The elder Bush administration's hope for Iraq was far less grandiose. The Americans would be content to see a friendlier strongman in Saddam's place.

Chalabi, by contrast, would settle for nothing less than the end of Baathist authoritarianism. He despised the Scowcroft "realists" and was delighted when Clinton beat the elder Bush in 1992. Quickly, Chalabi and his Iraqi National Congress made inroads with the new administration, especially Vice President Al Gore. In September 1994, a CIA operative named Bob Baer indicated to Chalabi that the U.S. government would back an Iraqi-led insurrection against Saddam. The coup fizzled six months later when Clinton's national security adviser, Anthony Lake, informed Baer and Chalabi at the eleventh hour that the administration would not support such an effort.[49] A year later, when a Kurdish coup attempt against Saddam failed, the CIA suspected (without any solid supporting evidence) that Chalabi had played a role in its unraveling. Their relationship was terminated in 1996.

Chalabi was undeterred. With help from the American lobbyist Francis Brooke, he began to accumulate important friends. In the American media, they included ABC anchor Peter Jennings, *New York Times* columnist William Safire, *Washington Post* columnist James Hoagland, and journalist/agitator Christopher Hitchens. Conservative opinion makers like Bernard Lewis, Fouad Ajami, and Richard Perle fell under his sway. On the Hill, his allies were as myriad as his messages. To Republican senators Jesse Helms and Trent Lott, Chalabi emphasized Saddam's menace. To Democratic congressman Stephen Solarz, the INC leader was emphatic that a post-Saddam Iraq "would be friendly to Israel," as Solarz recalled to Chalabi biographer Richard Bonin. ("Such was his regard for the Iraqi," Bonin wrote, "that Solarz invited Chalabi to celebrate a Passover seder at his house.")[50] To Democratic senator and war veteran Bob Kerrey, backing Chalabi's goal of removing Saddam meant being forthright with the American people about U.S. policy—"bringing our clandestine objective out in the open," as he would put it.[51]

And to those from both parties who were reluctant to see American troops get bogged down in a Middle East quagmire, Chalabi offered the magic words: "I want to emphasize that the INC does not request any U.S. occupying force." Echoing his friend Paul Wolfowitz, Chalabi conjured up an Iraqi-led opposition that would attack Saddam from an enclave in the Shiite-dominated south. The concept of an indigenous fighting force was itself appealing to the staff director of the House Foreign Affairs Committee, Stephen Rademaker, who had worked with the Nicaraguan rebel group known as the Contras during the Reagan administration and who would ultimately become the author of the Iraq Liberation Act.[52]

"Best of all," Chalabi assured the Senate Foreign Relations Committee in 1998, with a traveling salesman's verve, "the INC will do all this for free."[53] His promises struck many as fantastical. How could the INC lead a resistance in a country that had never heard of Ahmad Chalabi? How could it

possibly succeed in toppling Saddam where the Iranians and two coup attempts had already failed? Why should Israel trust that a post-Saddam, Shia-
majority Iraq would offer a rosy ecumenical welcome? Why should anyone
trust Ahmad Chalabi, whose gift for making enemies matched his facility
for telling disparate Americans whatever each of them wished to hear?

Chalabi's relentless lobbying helped secure passage of the Iraq Liberation Act in 1998. The bill pledged $97 million in support. But to whom?
Chalabi's INC was openly feuding with the group of Baathist military defectors known as the Iraqi National Accord, whose leader, Ayad Allawi, now
had the CIA's backing. President Clinton departed office with regime change
unfulfilled. Chalabi eyed the new Bush administration warily. Cheney,
Libby, Wolfowitz, Feith, Hannah, and a few other allies were there. But so
was a Scowcroft protégé, Condi Rice, and, even worse, George Tenet at the
CIA, who had been its deputy director when the agency washed its hands of
him. The State Department, which was the designated custodian for the $97
million in opposition grant money, was loaded with antagonists—among
them Assistant Secretary of State for Policy Planning Richard Haass, who,
when Chalabi first met him in 1991, in the previous Bush administration, had
his shoes up on his desk, a sign of disrespect in the Arab world.

On the morning of September 11, 2001, Ahmad Chalabi and his aide
Zaab Sethna woke up in Santa Monica (where Chalabi was scheduled to give
a talk at the RAND Corporation) to find that the United States had been
attacked. A week had passed before they managed to get a flight back to
Washington. During that time, word reached them that Wolfowitz and others in the Bush administration were scrambling to determine the extent of
Saddam's involvement in terrorist activity. Chalabi began to assist this effort,
recalled Sethna, "the day we got in from L.A."

About two weeks after Chalabi's return, the INC leader received a request from Cheney's Middle East specialist, John Hannah. The two met at
a Starbucks a few blocks from the White House. "The administration is
looking for people who know about Iraq's weapons of mass destruction,
Iraqis who know about these weapons firsthand," Hannah said to Chalabi.
"Can you introduce us to any?"[54]

Up until that point, Chalabi's focus had been on Saddam's murderous treatment of his own people—and then, at the Bush administration's request, on any ties between Iraq and Al Qaeda. The INC had scant knowledge of the dictator's weapons systems, apart from what he had helped an UNSCOM inspector named Scott Ritter leak to Chalabi's friend Jim Hoagland at *The Washington Post* three years earlier.[55] Still, in Chalabi's ongoing war against the regime, a new front had presented itself. If the U.S. government now saw Saddam Hussein's WMD arsenal as the most appealing case for regime change, then Ahmad Chalabi was going to do everything in his power to assist it.

But, as Chalabi soon learned, not everyone in the Bush administration was on the same page. On November 14, 2001, Under Secretary of State for Political Affairs Marc Grossman and UN Ambassador John Negroponte met with four members of the INC at the Waldorf Astoria in New York. Knowing his unpopularity at State, Chalabi had dispatched the others in his stead. One of them, Sharif Ali bin al-Hussein, stressed the INC's "total support" in America's war on terror—though, according to a cable written two days later by Grossman's deputy, Tom Krajeski, he went a step further: "Ali said that the INC was convinced that Saddam Hussein and the Iraqi regime had been involved in the 9/11 attacks, and perhaps even in the recent anthrax episode." For this reason, Ali argued, the INC and the Bush administration should work together to "help liberate Iraq." The first step would be for the State Department to provide financial support for the INC to move surreptitiously into Iraq—the better to learn more "about the Iraqi regime's WMD programs and its support for terrorism," Ali said.

Grossman's answer was not what Chalabi's representatives wanted to hear. "There is unfinished business in Iraq and the U.S. will address it, but on its own timetable, not on anyone else's, and in its own way," the State official replied. The U.S. government could not fund dissident action inside Iraq. Grossman recommended that the INC spend its money on broadening its outreach "to include all Iraqi opposition groups."[56]

The news soon got worse for Chalabi. Rich Armitage had ordered an audit of the INC's spending practices in the middle of 2001. While conducting the audit, the State Department's inspector general, Clark Kent Ervin, was contacted by Vice President Cheney, who asked to be briefed on the matter. Ervin also received an invitation by White House speechwriter David Frum to meet Chalabi in person, at the residence of Christopher Hitchens. (He agreed to the former but declined the latter.)[57] The audit nonetheless found "serious financial management and internal control weaknesses."[58] Armitage, who had long distrusted Chalabi and his "siren's song,"[59] recommended that funding for the INC be slashed, a fact that immediately found its way into *The New York Times*.[60]

The news leak outraged Chalabi, who met with Grossman later that month and complained that it had severely undermined the INC's credibility. "We have no intention of putting pressure on you," Chalabi told the State Department official.[61] But Grossman had reason to doubt this: just after the *Times* story was published, Wolfowitz complained about State's punitiveness to Rumsfeld, who brought up the matter to Powell when the two had lunch a few days later. Powell told Rumsfeld that Chalabi's group was being sketchy about how it was spending its money. Later that day, Rumsfeld wrote to Wolfowitz, "You ought to get the Deputies back on this subject, I would think."[62]

It was in this context that Scooter Libby floated, during a Deputies Lunch, the not-so-innocent proposal of sponsoring a conference of Iraqi exiles. A new clash among the deputies would ensue, inviting new headaches for Steve Hadley. As he would later reflect, "There were two banes of my existence. One was the split over Ahmad Chalabi between the DOD, on one hand, and the agency and State on the other. I tried many times to find a way forward."

The second bane for Hadley, he would recall, "was this whole dispute between the Office of the Vice President and the intelligence community on that supposed link between Saddam and Al Qaeda. The vice president would get raw intelligence that would give basis for that linkage. And his concern was that the agency wasn't taking it seriously—that it had a bias and was sweeping it under the rug. I didn't know the answer."[63]

But the strain on the deputy national security adviser to find consensus across so stark a divide was evident to Deputy Assistant Secretary of State for Near Eastern Affairs Ryan Crocker. During one Deputies Committee meeting in the early summer of 2002 to discuss the link between Al Qaeda and Saddam, Crocker—who had served in the region for numerous years and had attended the wrestling tournament in Baghdad in 1979—raised his hand. "There isn't any," he said.

The mild-mannered Hadley became livid. He proceeded to denounce the Middle East diplomat's ignorance. Crocker left the meeting convinced not of Saddam's link to terror but of something else: *If someone as solid as Hadley has adopted that point of view, we are totally fucked.*[64]

CHAPTER EIGHT

THE MURKY PAPER

O ne day in the late spring of 2002, CIA director George Tenet hosted a town hall for his employees in the Awards Suite of the agency's Original Headquarters Building. The event was a show of inclusiveness in keeping with Tenet's reputation as an accessible, gregarious boss who ate in the employee cafeteria and worked out in the campus gym with the GS-12 careerists. It was also the director's way of acknowledging that morale had plummeted after 9/11 and now, as the Bush administration began pressing its case against Saddam Hussein, was falling through the floorboards.

A counterterrorism analyst named Susan Hasler raised her hand. The concern on her mind did not pertain to Tenet's management of the agency. Rather, what dismayed Hasler was the director's inability to ward off the unreasonable demands of the Bush administration.

"People here are being tasked on the same question over and over," she said. All of them had been putting in excruciating hours trying to thwart the next attack. But that crucial work was competing for time with seemingly pointless inquiries that had already been answered, time and again. "And frankly," Hasler concluded, "it's wearing people down."[1]

Everyone in the room, including Tenet, knew what the analyst was referring to. For months now, Paul Wolfowitz had been on a tear, with support from Scooter Libby. The subject of their taskings was 9/11 hijacker Mohamed Atta. Six weeks after the attacks, Czech authorities dropped a bombshell: on April 9, 2001, Atta had met with an Iraqi diplomat and former intelligence officer named Ahmad Khalil Ibrahim Samir al-Ani at the Iraqi embassy in Prague. Here, it appeared, was a seemingly irrefutable connection between Saddam and Al Qaeda's hijackers. "If you could establish that," CIA Deputy Director John McLaughlin would say of the alleged Atta meeting in Prague, "then going after Iraq made all the sense in the world."[2]

There were several reasons to doubt the report, however. First, it relied on a single unnamed informant who was shown a newspaper photo of Atta and asserted that this was the man he had witnessed with al-Ani. Czech officials said that the informant was "70 percent sure." Moreover, FBI records showed that Atta had been in Virginia and Florida immediately before and after the alleged meeting, with no evidence of an international flight between the two continents. (Al-Ani, it would later be learned, was himself seventy miles away from Prague during the time of the alleged encounter.)[3]

But a fundamental illogic also pervaded the Prague scenario. One of the CIA analysts saddled with responding to more than ten of Wolfowitz's repeated queries on the subject described it this way in a personal journal he kept: "As for Atta's motive for taking this travel, which probably didn't occur, I lay out our case for why we find such reporting problematic. What did a simple, but well-orchestrated plot, that relied on box cutters, Internet access and easy ingress into U.S. society need from Iraq alone to ensure success? What crucial ingredient was so uniquely in Iraqi possession as to lead Atta and his Al Qaida bosses to undertake the substantial risk of contacting Iraqi officialdom to obtain?"

Still, the taskings kept coming from Wolfowitz, whom the analyst referred to in his journal as "this obsessive fanatic."[4] Wolfowitz's daily briefer at the agency kept notebooks filled with pages of Atta barrages, each question varying from the other by only a word or two.[5]

But the deputy secretary of defense was not the only inquisitor on the subject. Cheney, said a second analyst who had briefed the vice president on the subject, "had a hard-on for the Atta meeting."[6] Cheney's Middle East specialist, John Hannah, "couldn't be dissuaded" from the Atta-Iraq connection, said a different analyst who briefed him on the matter.[7] Scooter Libby more than once called a top CIA official he knew to say, with exasperation, "Look, the Prague meeting took place!"[8] The repeated hammering on the subject compelled one exhausted CIA analyst to react to an Atta tasking with a three-word reply: "He's still dead."[9]

Tenet knew about the maddening reiterations. Still, his answer to Susan Hasler at the town hall was the dutiful reply of the Bush administration's intelligence chief. *You have the unique privilege,* Tenet reminded her and the others present, *of writing memos for the president of the United States.*[10] The convening of the town hall was Tenet's implicit message of sympathy. Beyond that, he was not about to say anything that might, if it leaked, make the CIA's precarious standing in the Bush administration any worse than it already was.

What could George Tenet say, after all? The Central Intelligence Agency, founded in 1947, had implicitly been created to avert another Pearl Harbor. It could be said that the agency had failed in this mission on September 11, 2001. Yes, Tenet and his subordinates had issued repeated warnings to the new administration about bin Laden's fatwa against America, about the "system blinking red." But, as Henry Kissinger was said to have admonished one of the agency's top analysts in 1973, after the outbreak of the Yom Kippur war, "You warned me. But you did not persuade me."[11]

After 9/11, the agency's rank and file rallied around Tenet, cognizant that their boss would be viewed as an obliging scapegoat. After all, he had been a holdover from the Clinton administration, kept on only because Bush's other choice for CIA director, Donald Rumsfeld, was moved over to Defense when the top two candidates for that post, Wolfowitz and Dan Coats, failed to impress the president-elect.

In fact, Tenet's loyalists need not have worried. For Bush to fire his CIA director on the heels of the 9/11 attacks would have suggested a tacit admission of poor hiring judgment on his own part—the kind of mea culpa he

typically went to great lengths to avoid. It was also a mistake to underesti-
mate George Tenet's political agility.[12] The son of a Greek restaurateur had
been imbued with the importance of customer service well before he became
a Capitol Hill staffer and then the chief intelligence adviser on Clinton's
National Security Council. He was also temperamentally Bush's kin: visceral, gabby, a snapper of towels and hurler of profanities who nonetheless
respected decorum and hierarchy.

Tenet was aware, of course, that the new president was the son of a former CIA director (whose name had adorned the agency's headquarters since
April 1999). The years immediately preceding the younger Bush's inauguration had been fallow ones for the agency. In 1996, while Tenet served as
deputy director, the agency brought in the smallest recruiting class in its
history. But drastic budget cuts resulting from the post–Cold War "peace
dividend" were only one sign of the CIA's waning relevancy. President Clinton seldom took face-to-face briefings. Scrambling to accommodate him, the
agency under Tenet overhauled the Presidential Daily Brief as part of an
effort to give the "First Customer" what he wanted. But the real remedy
proved to be a new president—who, after finally attaining victory following
the conclusion of *Bush v. Gore* in December 2000, told his briefer that upon
being sworn in he expected the agency would now be sharing with him "the
good stuff."

The good stuff? Tenet, his deputy John McLaughlin, and Bush's briefer
Michael Morell had been put on notice: there was a new First Customer in
town, one who would be as demanding as the previous one had been seemingly disengaged.[13] Bush would take his briefing at eight in the morning, six
days a week. ("It never even crossed our minds that we could get the PDB
later in the day, like Trump does, or that it'd be handed to him in writing,"
recalled Dan Bartlett. "I mean, this was sacred, it really was.")[14] The new
president added an unusual stipulation: he also wanted the CIA director
present at the daily briefings. The inconvenience of Tenet having to begin
each morning "downtown" (in the agency's parlance) was more than compensated for by being the one federal agency chief to meet with the president
first thing every morning. That such proximity might imperil the CIA's stolid

neutrality on matters of policymaking was a happy challenge that, to George Tenet, beat the hell out of the alternative.[15]

He understood that politics is a feat of the personal touch as much as of substance. The director would sometimes stick around the West Wing after the briefing to offer Bartlett a preview of what was likely to drive the news that day. While protective of his subordinates, Tenet was savvy enough to imply some distance from them as well. "The building thinks this," he would say to Cheney or Libby—the director's way of also saying, *That's them, not me—and I know you see things another way, and we're gonna keep an open mind, take it to the bank.*

Above all, Tenet went the extra yard to maintain First Customer satisfaction. Until Bush, daily briefings had been conducted by an analyst from the Directorate of Intelligence (DI). But Bush, like Tenet, was "action oriented." He relished "the operational details, the dead drops, how people met." At times he would ask, "Who's the source?" Against long-standing CIA tradition, Tenet and his officers would divulge such highly sensitive sourcing details to the president. The director also frequently brought into the Oval Office visiting case officers from the Directorate of Operations (DO)—the overseas spies—who invariably offered more flamboyant testimonials than the dry, caveated monologues of the analyst briefers.[16]

It was never hard for Tenet to tell when he was losing the First Customer during a briefing. Bush would begin "screwing his face up" or fidget in his chair or look sidelong at Rice, Cheney, and Card, the daily Greek chorus for whom Tenet and Morell were also performing. The president's interjections began before Morell had gone through the first paragraph. "I've heard this already," Bush would snap—or simply, "Duh!" The First Customer was always right, of course. Sometimes Tenet would anticipate Bush's discontent, angrily discard the PDB before walking into the Oval, and tell the accompanying case officer to improvise. Other times he weathered the First Customer's negative reaction to the fare, then returned to "the building" across the river in Langley, Virginia, and barked at Jami Miscik, the deputy director for intelligence, "Don't give me any more shit in the morning!"[17]

Tenet kept one eye on Cheney during the briefings. The vice president was always cordial to the CIA director, not to mention an unwavering ally on budgetary matters. He said very little in the Oval. But Cheney was acutely inquisitive during his one-on-one briefing with CIA analyst David Terry, as was Libby during his own daily briefing. Through these and other channels, the director was made aware that the Office of the Vice President did not intend to defer to the agency's judgments.[18]

Shortly after Czech officials disclosed that Mohamed Atta may have met with an Iraqi intelligence official in Prague, Cheney and Wolfowitz tasked a full paper on the subject. About three weeks later, the World Trade Center Branch—which Tenet had set up after 9/11 to deconstruct the attacks— produced a four-page paper. Tenet found it too dense and ordered it to be rewritten. The second version consisted of a chart. One column listed the numerous data points, furnished by the FBI and foreign intelligence services, that cast doubt on such a meeting. The other column listed the evidence favoring such an encounter, which comprised one item: the eyewitness with his 70 percent certainty. Cheney and Wolfowitz "did not like it," said the paper's supervisor, but Tenet nonetheless stood by the team's findings.[19]

In doing so, Tenet "met with incredible resistance, because the absurdity around Atta continued," recalled another senior CIA official.[20] The director had been around Washington long enough to know how vulnerable his agency was. He oversaw a $10 billion bureaucracy of twenty thousand employees— too small to compete with the Defense Department, but far too big to reinvent itself quickly enough to please the critics. Like any other federal agency, the CIA's top talent chafed against the building's ecosystem of inertia and often departed for other jobs, leaving "the B team, which hires the unthreatening C's, which then hires D's," as one veteran analyst put it.[21] It could be, in the manner of any government entity, small-minded, territorial, self-absorbed, and prone to groupthink. George Tenet knew all this. He also knew that veteran Washington warriors like Cheney, Rumsfeld, Wolfowitz, and Libby each carried with them vivid memories of when the CIA had been wrong.

Were they wrong now about Atta? Cheney obviously thought so: on December 9, 2001, he told Tim Russert on *Meet the Press* that Atta's meeting in Prague was "pretty well established," a month after the CIA paper had strongly suggested otherwise.[22] The larger question was whether, the Atta meeting aside, there existed a meaningful connection between Saddam's regime and Al Qaeda. Tenet's building insisted that there was not. They suspected that Cheney, Wolfowitz, and other hawks in the Bush administration were simply using 9/11 as an opportunity to settle unfinished business with Saddam. The analysts were being used, one of them would say, "like a drunk uses a lamppost: more for support than for illumination."[23]

But some in the building went a step beyond doubting the suggestions of a connection between bin Laden and Saddam. They argued that there *could never be* such a connection, given that Saddam was a secular megalomaniac unlikely to confederate with an Islamist leader beyond his control. This itself suggested bias of a sort ably refuted by history: Roosevelt and Stalin, after all, had only an enemy in common.

The lawyer in Scooter Libby lived to carve up fatuous assertions of this sort. Cheney's chief of staff "would ask the same question seven consecutive days," recalled another CIA senior official who fielded Libby's inquiries. "Then he'd say, 'On Tuesday you said this, but now your language is different.' It was just killing me."[24]

"We may have overreacted," one of Libby's colleagues in OVP would later reflect. "We may have been so angry that they were poo-pooing everything that we put more emphasis than we should have on some of this stuff."[25] But in probing the CIA analysts, the hawks also did not bother to hide their sense of intellectual superiority. Wolfowitz "believed he was smarter than the agency," a DOD colleague would recall.[26] And it showed: "Wolfowitz asked the same question different ways," recalled a senior agency analyst who respected the deputy secretary, "partially because we weren't giving him the answer he wanted—but also partly to prove that we were idiots."[27]

Intellectually as well as emotionally, Tenet's inclination was to side with the building. When the CIA director had briefed the incoming president Bush on worldwide threats, Al Qaeda, China, and nuclear proliferation were at the top of Tenet's list, but Iraq was not. Throughout the nineties, the State Department's annual "Patterns of Global Terrorism" report described the activities of both Iraq and Al Qaeda—never, however, in conjunction with each other. Given that bin Laden had openly declared a holy war against the United States in 1996, why hadn't Saddam already joined that war by providing Al Qaeda with weapons of mass destruction? Why, instead, had the 9/11 hijackers boarded the planes armed only with box cutters? And though Tenet had not expected nineteen Al Qaeda hijackers to use four commercial airplanes as deadly weapons, he was convinced by the foiled 1995 "Bojinka" plot—in which Ramzi Yousef hoped to seize several planes in Manila and then explode them while airborne—that Islamic jihadists did not require the assistance of a state sponsor to hatch such a scheme.

In the wake of 9/11, Tenet—whose stress level could be determined by the length of the cigar he habitually chewed on (and, at times of maximum stress, swallowed)—found the system blinking red again. Domestic threats continued to pour in; the second wave, he somberly predicted, "will happen." The godfather of Pakistan's nuclear program, Abdul Qadeer Khan, was found to be selling nuclear materials on the black market. And then, by early 2002, Ibn al-Shaykh al-Libi, Al Qaeda's senior military trainer, was telling his Egyptian interrogators that bin Laden's group was sending militants to Iraq to receive WMD training—the very confederation that George Tenet's analysts in the building had assured him did not exist.

What to believe?

"THE THING ABOUT INTELLIGENCE," THE AGENCY'S FORMER IRAQ GROUP chief Hal Rooks would say, "is that you can always find what you want somewhere on the spectrum."[28] But even that full spectrum of intelligence data—conflicting statements, unverified sightings, ambiguous imagery, and overheard innuendo—had begun to lose its primacy after 9/11. The CIA now confronted the specter of a post-intelligence era. Rather than make sense of the unfathomable, policymakers fell prey to "allowing their imagination to serve as a substitute for information," according to the British sociologist Frank Furedi. Or, worse, they might even choose the fantastical over the factual.

In the face of inconclusive intelligence, wrote Furedi, policymakers took license in "promiscuous speculation" and "the institutionalization of 'thinking outside the box,' which is another way of saying, 'more imagination.'"[29]

Tenet responded to this compulsion by indulging it. Late on the evening of September 12, 2001, he and Jami Miscik decided to create a group whose job would be to think (as he would later write) "so far outside the box they would be in a different zip code."[30] Tenet termed the group the Red Cell, a moniker he found agreeably subversive. The next morning, Miscik summoned two analysts—a China specialist named Paul Frandano and Robert Ovelmen, an expert on European issues—and told them, "Your lives are about to change." She instructed them to find another half-dozen colleagues in the building who were not entrenched in the Middle East or counterterrorism. The deputy director for intelligence then said, "We'll give you access to the most sensitive raw intelligence we have. And you'll give us ideas for things you think policymakers ought to be worried about related to terrorism."[31]

The Red Cell's very first topics seemed designed to invite paranoia. What if the 9/11 hijackers' names were in fact aliases and their true identities a mystery? What if future hijackers looked identical to average Americans? "We did a lot of Red Cell papers thinking of all kinds of ways we could be attacked," said a team analyst. "And the president saw just about all of those."

"Oh, this is very good," murmured Tenet as he thumbed through the earliest papers. "You've got to keep doing this." During its first week, the Red Cell produced a document for the Principals Committee speculating about Saddam's involvement in 9/11. Departing from the standard CIA treatment, the Red Cell paper acknowledged "unanswered questions" and "tried to develop the strongest case for Iraqi involvement," recalled a Cell member.

Very quickly, the Red Cell's work product became a hit within the Bush administration. Their papers were punchy (no more than three pages) and irreverently written. Because Frandano and Ovelmen sat in on the morning postmortem sessions with PDB briefers, they could discern what was of interest to Bush, Cheney, and the rest. "I'd like to meet the guys from the Red Cell," Wolfowitz said one day to Tenet—and, upon doing so, the deputy secretary of defense eagerly inquired how they came up with their ideas and whether any of them were alumni of Johns Hopkins SAIS, where he had once been dean. Red Cell members were invited to Principals Committee meetings to brainstorm. On at least one occasion, Cheney flourished a Red Cell paper to Deputy Director McLaughlin to buttress a point—when, as one of the team members would say, "our goal was plausibility, not anybody's notion of truth."

In practicing flights of fancy, the Red Cell team was not deliberately seeking to ingratiate themselves with the Bush administration. Like others in the agency, they were asked repeatedly to examine Mohamed Atta's supposed sojourn in Prague. ("Wolfowitz would have loved it if we had changed our view," said one. "But we didn't.") They imagined the case for going to war later rather than sooner. They contemplated the international implications of America's invading an Arab country preemptively. They waited hopefully for a policymaker to ask whether Iraq's sponsorship of terrorists was as great as Saudi Arabia's. They also wondered among themselves whether it had occurred to the Bush White House that, as one of them said, "You probably ought to go to war based on probabilities, not plausibilities."

Still, as the same member of the Red Cell observed, "Why were we getting so many taskings? Why did the policymakers keep liking us and agreeing with us? The obvious answer is we were scratching a policymaker itch that the mainline analysis wasn't doing." In practical terms, the Red Cell musings offered permission to cast doubt on the agency's "mainline analysis." At the bottom of this slippery slope was what Furedi would term "the enthronement of ignorance," in which intelligence could be discarded altogether and the American public could be exhorted "to take what we don't know as seriously as what we do."[32]

Not surprisingly, the Red Cell churned out numerous papers on the Iraqi leader, with most of the topics being generated from "downtown." How might Saddam attempt to slow down the United States' war timetable? What tactics could he employ to discredit the case against him? How would he fight a second war with U.S. troops? How would he mobilize terrorist groups to assist him? What would he do if offered a huge sum of money to vacate Iraq?

Yet for all its remarkable exertions, there was one scenario the Red Cell never imagined, and thus never wrote about—an omission that one of its members would later describe as "a cause of great concern to me."

The unimagined possibility was: What if Saddam Hussein did *not* possess weapons of mass destruction?

AFTER THE ATTACKS ON AMERICA, A POLICYMAKER COULD PART WAYS WITH the CIA's mainline analysis and lie down in the darkness of what Furedi termed "the catastrophist imagination."[33] But there was another alternative after 9/11: to ferret through the reams upon reams of raw information now pouring into the intelligence community and thereby find any nightmare scenario conceivable.

In the CIA's station in Amman, Jordan, the traffic of walk-in informants shot up after 9/11, from about two a week to seven a day. One of these, a self-proclaimed Iraqi microbiologist, told agency personnel that he was receiving death threat notices from the Iraqi regime—which, intelligence officials later determined, he had written himself.[34]

In Ankara, Turkey, a man who claimed to be an Iraqi general presented himself to Turkish intelligence agents with information about a camp in Salman Pak where Iraqis had been trained to hijack planes. The general said that he had fled Iraq after associates of Saddam's son Uday had tortured him by smashing his testicles with a hammer. Officials from the DIA, CIA, and Turkey examined the man and found no physical damage. They sent him away.

On the flight back from Ankara, one of the American agents was surprised to see an op-ed about the informant in *The Washington Post*.[35] It said that he had been "treated dismissively by CIA officers in Ankara this week. They reportedly showed no interest in pursuing a possible Iraq connection to Sept. 11."[36]

The agent did not know that the author of the piece, renowned columnist Jim Hoagland, was a close friend of Ahmad Chalabi's. Subsequently, however, the agent learned from Turkish intelligence officials that the phone records of the Iraqi "general" showed several calls to Chalabi before and after his debriefing with them. The Salman Pak story was later picked up by numerous news outlets, from *The New York Times* to *Vanity Fair*, even as the CIA was coming to learn the likeliest purpose of the facility: training Iraqi soldiers to *thwart* hijackers, not to become them.[37]

Practically overnight, Chalabi's Iraqi National Congress, through its Information Collection Program, bankrolled by the State Department, had become the preeminent matchmaking service between Iraqi defectors and intelligence seekers. Some of the information it provided, pertaining to generals in Saddam's Military Industrial Commission, was useful.[38] Some of it reflected the challenges of intelligence collection in an authoritarian regime, such as its information on the Iraqi military's positioning—which, said an agency analyst, "was three years out of date."[39]

In other cases, the INC would present a defector to intelligence officials and essentially offer a disclaimer: *This man has an interesting story to tell. As to whether or not it's true—well, you're the experts at source validation, not us.*[40] In one such case, CIA and DIA officers were dispatched to Turkey to interview an INC-sponsored defector who represented himself as an Iraqi nuclear physicist. The informant repeatedly excused himself to visit the restroom. Finally, one of the officers followed the defector into the bathroom. He saw the man roll up his sleeves and consult the handwriting covering his forearms.[41]

In the case of this bogus scientist, the CIA could only speculate that he had been coached by the INC. In other cases, the group's active participation in conveying false information was impossible to miss. During the late summer of 2002, a fifty-four-year-old woman of Greek extraction named Parisoula Lampsos began making the rounds in the United States, courtesy of Chalabi's group.[42] Lampsos purported to have been Saddam's lover. But her elaborate narrative included one gold nugget that fell squarely under the too-good-to-fact-check category: during a visit to one of the dictator's palaces in the 1980s, she claimed to have seen a tall, bearded man whom Uday Hussein identified to her as Osama bin Laden.[43]

The Lampsos story attracted interest from Wolfowitz and Cheney's office, which obligated the CIA to include the item in Bush's PDB. The item mentioned that Lampsos was being sponsored by Chalabi's INC. Deputy Director for Intelligence Jami Miscik had the sourcing removed.[44] Her motive for doing so was evident. As one senior CIA official explained, "Tenet was concerned that we had such an anti-Chalabi, anti-INC view that we had discredited ourselves with the administration on that subject."[45]

Tenet and his lieutenants were faced with a frustrating conundrum. On the one hand, they feared the prospect of President Bush being spoon-fed a bouillabaisse of truths, unverified stories presented as truths, and likely falsehoods. On the other hand, the agency stood to lose its role in helping separate fact from fiction if it appeared to be closed-minded. And so when the chief of the Iraq Operations Group, Luis Rueda, refused to fulfill a request by Cheney's office to interview a Vienna walk-in who was known to be a fabricator, Miscik angrily stormed into his office, saying, "You're not supporting the consumer!"

Rueda replied that the agency was paying him to supply his operational judgment—and that his judgment was that the walk-in was a known liar. Miscik backed down.[46] But she continued to remind the analysts that, as one of her subordinates would recall, "it's very important to maintain contact, for them to continue to rely on us. As soon as they say 'To hell with you all,' you're lost. That was a really big deal for her."[47]

It was also a big deal for Deputy Director McLaughlin, who continually reminded his colleagues of how important it was for the agency to maintain a "seat at the table."[48] Most of all, relevancy was George Tenet's raison d'être, after the ignominy of the Clinton years. "Here we had this precious access," recalled one senior analyst, "and he didn't want to blow it."[49]

But Tenet's dilemma—how to preserve the agency's access while remaining true to the intelligence—could also be viewed conversely: just how true to its mission could the CIA be while maintaining so subservient a posture of "customer support"? The CIA's great ur-director Richard Helms was known to solemnly leave any White House meeting the moment a policy matter came up.[50] Another former director, William Colby, was said to have described the CIA's duty as being "the skunk at the garden party," and resisted the temptation to tell policymakers what they wished to hear. The balancing act, as one analyst would say, was to "get in bed with the policy-maker and somehow retain your virtue."[51]

Tenet's tightrope act was, to his subordinates, a valiant but at times un-nerving spectacle. Frequently he met with legislators on the Hill. Some of them had heard Bush administration officials speak with certainty about Saddam's ties to Al Qaeda and wanted to know what the CIA had to say on the subject. Tenet did not ask for a firm position from his analysts. Instead, recalled one, "he'd come up and say, 'Can we say these three things? There were some contacts. There was possibly some training. There was some haven.'

"I'd say, 'Yeah, you can say that. But you should put it in context that these three things add up to zero.'"[52]

Tenet did not say whether he agreed with the analyst, who had already seen the director and his agency undergo painful contortions during the tortured exercise known internally as the Murky Paper.

PERHAPS APPROPRIATELY, NO ONE WOULD SEEM TO REMEMBER THE MURKY Paper's origins—whether it was tasked by Cheney's office or by Wolfowitz, whether it arose from a discussion during an NSC Deputies Lunch, or whether Tenet and his intelligence deputy, Jami Miscik, commissioned the document proactively. What is clear is that its genesis during the early months of 2002 coincided with the emergence in Iraq of a Jordanian militant named Abu Musab al-Zarqawi.

The jihadist had been operating a terrorist training camp in western Afghanistan until the arrival of coalition troops. Wounded by an air strike, Zarqawi and several of his confederates fled to northern Iraq. (Intelligence reports suggesting that Zarqawi first had his leg amputated in a Baghdad hospital were at least half wrong, as he would later be seen walking on his natural limbs.)[53] There they took refuge near the Iran border, under the pro-tection of the Islamic extremist group Ansar al-Islam.

"We have noted an increased al-Qaida presence in Iraq in recent weeks," wrote a State Department intelligence official in a classified memo during the spring of 2002. She went on to write, "Zarqawi's presence in Iraq may indicate an effort to strengthen operational capacity there."[54]

There were several problems with this analytical judgment. First, Zarqawi was not a member of Al Qaeda (though two years later he would be). Second, northern Iraq, or Kurdistan, was not under Saddam's control. Third, the founding members of Zarqawi's host, Ansar al-Islam, were hardly confederates of the regime; rather, they were Kurdish jihadists who had sworn vengeance against Saddam for the chemical weapons attack at Halabja in 1988.[55]

But the most significant error was one that would prove fundamental to the Bush administration's "promiscuous speculation" when it came to their supervillain in Baghdad. A CIA analyst would describe it as "this assumption that totalitarian regimes have such pervasive intelligence services, and are so good at knowing what's going on, that there's no way a bad actor could be running around without them being complicit. That critical assumption was wrong. It's almost always wrong. Because it gives those services far more credit than they deserve. Zarqawi was in Iraq because it's an easy place to hide. And there are a bazillion Jordanians there—many to get medical treatment, because the facilities in Iraq are relatively good. That a Jordanian might show up in an Iraq hospital means nothing."[56]

At the time, however, the reductive view of Zarqawi—a known terrorist relocating from the refuge of Al Qaeda to Iraq—demanded close examination. Responding to "senior policymaker interest," Deputy Director for Intelligence Miscik commissioned "a comprehensive assessment of Iraqi regime links to al-Qa'ida," as the paper would later say—one that would be "purposefully aggressive in seeking to draw connections, on the assumption that any indication of a relationship between these two hostile elements could carry great dangers to the United States."[57]

Miscik was essentially instructing her mainline analysts to conduct themselves as the Red Cell group would: *Lean forward, imagine away, engage in an exercise of the possibilistic.* Those marching orders did not sit well with the Iraq specialists in the Office of Near Eastern and South Asian Analysis (NESA). Their view since well before 9/11 was that Saddam and bin Laden were never going to be allies. As NESA's Iraq group chief, Jane Green, would put it, "Saddam trusted no one outside his inner circle of family and friends, and he certainly wouldn't trust UBL, who had called for his overthrow and was trying to foster a type of Islam that would undermine Saddam's largely godless regime."[58]

The NESA analysts were all too aware that Cheney, Wolfowitz, and others in the Bush administration were convinced that such a relationship existed. To those analysts, the Murky Paper project reeked of First Customer service at its most obsequious. Objecting to the assignment, analyst Ben Bonk—who had been NESA's national intelligence officer—told a senior agency official, "I don't want to put anything out there that gives them the pretext to go to war."[59]

It took several months for Green's group to complete the paper. When Scooter Libby asked Tenet what was holding things up, the director sighed. "There's a disagreement in the building on this," he said.

Tenet was referring to the fact that NESA had a coauthor on the paper: the Office of Terrorism Analysis, or OTA. Newly organized after the 9/11 attacks, OTA's implicit mission was to not miss again the dots that had gone unconnected before September 11. Its analysts lived in manic pursuit of the next attackers. In that quest, no possibility could be rejected out of hand. Just as the NESA analysts were disciples of history, the worst-case scenario was OTA's golden calf.

"Then why don't you just publish two papers and let us see them both?" Cheney's chief of staff suggested.

Tenet knew what that would lead to. Libby and the other Iraq hawks would choose the paper they preferred—OTA's—and then claim that this was the CIA's official position. The director was determined that the matter be resolved internally. Jami Miscik therefore ordered that the OTA analysts write a single final version.

Iraq and al-Qa'ida: Interpreting a Murky Relationship was published on June 21, 2002. Green's group was given a couple of hours to review the paper before it went out to the policymakers. They were appalled. As one of them would say, "It pretty much used every scrap of poorly sourced reporting—stuff that people who walked into a U.S. embassy off the street would say in order to get some money from Uncle Sam by telling the CIA something they thought the agency wanted to hear."[60]

The NESA analysts registered their dissent in a "scope note" appended to the Murky Paper, arguing that "the available signs support a conclusion that Iraq has had sporadic, wary contacts with al-Qa'ida since the mid-1990s, rather than a relationship with al-Qa'ida that developed over time. These analysts would contend that mistrust and conflicting ideologies and goals probably tempered these contacts and severely limited the opportunities for cooperation."[61] Still, OTA's analysts had carried the day. Scooter Libby's CIA briefer took a copy of the Murky Paper and delivered it to him that afternoon.

President Bush was in Orlando that afternoon, campaigning for the reelection of Florida's governor, Jeb Bush—though even stumping for his brother provided an occasion to declare to an audience, "We're chasing down every single lead. If there is a hint that somebody might try to do something to America, we're on them."[62] Bush's early departure from the White House that day meant that Libby was spending the afternoon at his home in McLean, Virginia. He greeted the briefer on his porch. She placed the paper beside him. A bird flying overhead promptly relieved itself all over the cover page.

Removing the page, the analyst said, "How about if I take this back and say, 'Here's his reaction?'"

As it turned out, she and the bird were prescient. Libby, Cheney, and Wolfowitz "were wildly disappointed" with the Murky Paper, one of its authors remembered. "They were frustrated that it didn't go as far as it should go."[63] Even the CIA's most fevered authors had refrained from unequivocally linking Zarqawi to Saddam, placing Mohamed Atta in Prague, or bringing alarming clarity to a "murky relationship."

It was time for Doug Feith's intelligence analysis team to emerge from the basement and shed its own harsh light.

————

FEITH HAD FORMED HIS TWO-PERSON "TEAM B" TWO MONTHS AFTER 9/11, with Wolfowitz's approval. The undersecretary's stated view was that it was important to understand "what is known about Al-Qaida's worldwide terrorist network, its suppliers and relationship to states and other international terrorist organizations, including their acquisition networks."[64] But the focus of Feith's so-called Policy Counter Terrorism Evaluation Group was best represented by the scroll created by founding member David Wurmser. On one end of the large sheet of butcher paper was the name Osama bin Laden. On the other end was Saddam Hussein. Between the two was a long, tangled web of connecting lines, with names and dates in tiny handwriting. Witnesses in the Pentagon dubbed it the "Beautiful Mind" document, after the movie about the Nobel Prize–winning mathematician and paranoid schizophrenic John Nash.[65]

The document and PCTEG itself grew out of Wolfowitz's frustration that the intelligence community was dismissing the Saddam–Al Qaeda connection outright. After tasking and re-tasking analysts on the subject, the deputy secretary had concluded that no one at the CIA had an open mind.[66] Wolfowitz went so far as to reach out to the UK's permanent secretary at the Ministry of Defence, Kevin Tebbit. "Surely your intelligence people have got stuff on this," he pleaded. (Tebbit apologetically replied that they did not.)[67]

By February 2002, Wurmser had departed. But he left behind the Beautiful Mind scroll for his successor, a naval intelligence officer named Christopher Carney. Carney and another Navy reservist, Jack Moran, worked in a windowless twelve-by-twelve-foot room in the Pentagon basement. Hired, as Wurmser would tell them, "to look for links between Iraq and Al Qaeda," they combed through obscure cables collected by the DIA and CIA years earlier.

Nearly every day, Wolfowitz asked for a briefing from Carney, wanting to know if any new connection had been unearthed. To the Iraq hawks, PCTEG's labors were nothing short of heroic. Harold Rhode, from the DOD's Office of Net Assessment, invited Carney to his home, where he introduced him in glowing terms to another house guest, Ahmad Chalabi—

who struck the naval intelligence officer as a bullshit artist. Carney did not share that view with Wolfowitz, or his personal doubts about the stacks of data he had been sifting through. "He'd leave his windowless office and come into mine," recalled another Pentagon official, "and commiserate with me over how crazy this shit was."[68]

But by the late spring of 2002, Moran had completed his deployment and Feith's office had acquired a decidedly gung-ho DIA specialist on Soviet intelligence named Christina Shelton. Without anyone's direction, Shelton had spent months digging through raw CIA reports from the 1990s in search of links between Iraq's intelligence service and Al Qaeda. Nothing she found suggested either an operational relationship or any indication that Saddam's regime had been involved in 9/11—or, for that matter, any communications after 9/11. Still, the scattered associations seemed to her worthy of examination, and it bothered Shelton when a DIA superior told her not to make too much of such incidents because "it just gives Wolfowitz more ammunition."[69] After the CIA's Murky Paper had failed to animate the Iraq hawks, Shelton advised Wolfowitz and Feith in a memo that the agency's "interpretation ought to be ignored."[70] She had her own non-Murky alternative.

On August 8, 2002, Shelton presented her brief—"Assessing the Relationship Between Iraq and al Qaida"—to Rumsfeld, Wolfowitz, and Feith. It was, indeed, a contrast. In Shelton's version, to which others in Feith's office had added their own contributions, Iraq *was* providing safe haven to (as opposed to imprisoning) 1993 World Trade Center conspirator Abdul Rahman Yasin. Zarqawi *was* "a leading advocate of al Qaida relations with Iraq." Saddam *did* control Kurdistan, where bin Laden had set up training camps. And—in a briefing slide that one of Feith's team had added, but that Shelton herself did not agree with—Mohamed Atta *had* gone to Prague to meet with an Iraqi intelligence officer.

An additional slide that had been added by someone on Feith's team other than Shelton[71] seemed customized to win Rumsfeld's heart. It chided the CIA for failing to recognize that the "absence of evidence is not evidence of absence." This was in fact one of Rumsfeld's Rules (though of course the secretary did not invent the adage).[72] More important, the phrase granted permission to rely on imagination, to assume that crucial associations would be a "closely guarded secret," and, in essence, to place suspicion on par with knowledge.[73]

"This was an excellent briefing," gushed Wolfowitz that afternoon in an email to Shelton. "The Secretary was very impressed."[74] At Rumsfeld's urging, Doug Feith contacted George Tenet, offering to show the same brief to the CIA.

Tenet was not a fan of the loquacious ideologue Feith. ("He made George's skin crawl," said one colleague.)[75] Moreover, the very existence of an "alternative intelligence analysis" unit inside the DOD was something of an affront to the director of central intelligence—and perhaps even more so to DIA director Lowell "Jake" Jacoby. Still, both men agreed to receive Feith and his team at CIA headquarters on the morning of August 15, 2002.

On the drive from the Pentagon to Langley, Feith emphasized to his team, without apparent irony, "Tone is important. When you criticize, you want to do it in a respectful way, not an arrogant, offensive way."[76] But this was not destined to be a collegial encounter; as one of them would say, "One of the causes of the meeting was the political heat the CIA was taking at the time."[77]

Tenet had assembled close to two dozen of his analysts and senior staffers. "The attitude going in was 'This is bullshit—we already know what they're going to say,'" said one of the latter.[78] And from Feith's opening remarks, their suspicion was confirmed. "This is *your* intelligence," the undersecretary said, presumably to assure the analysts that he was not insulting them by bringing in something that their case officers had failed to collect. Instead, however, he was insulting them by saying, in effect: *This is your intelligence that you're too stupid to understand the value of.*[79]

Christina Shelton then took the floor. She introduced each briefing slide by saying, "According to CIA reporting," which did not endear her to the others in the room. To the analysts gathered, Shelton's twenty-minute elucidation of Iraqi involvement in Al Qaeda's activities, followed by Chris Carney's ten-minute presentation on terroristic activity in northern Iraq, amounted to amateur hour. "They were taking raw traffic completely out of context, without the knowledge of a regional analyst, but simply with the determination to make the case," said one Middle East analyst.[80] "They were connecting dots that weren't even there—things we'd dismissed and which, in hindsight, never took place," said a second analyst.[81] Recalled another senior official of the spurious connections, "It was one percent. It was moons away. It was six degrees of Kevin Bacon's *mom*."[82]

Tenet asked Feith to join him in stepping out of the meeting—leaving the latter's subordinates across the table from the former's, "all of us just looking at each other," a CIA senior staffer recalled.[83] In his memoir, Tenet did not mention this moment. Feith, in his, recalled a cordial exchange, with the director acknowledging some disagreements within the agency. Both men were smiling when they returned, and Tenet announced a compromise: the CIA, the DIA, and Feith's group would work together to produce a paper that all of them could agree on.[84]

Of course, this was Tenet playing the political angles and buying time. No such compromise document was achievable. Shelton and Carney attended a single additional discussion at the agency, then saw the fruitlessness of doing so and, without fanfare, simply stopped showing up.[85] Thus unfettered from Feith and Wolfowitz's convictions, the CIA was now permitted to write the assessment "we really believed," as one of the analysts put it.[86]

The paper, *Iraqi Support for Terrorism*, authored by senior Iraq political analyst Colin Winston, proceeded to walk back the Murky Paper that Shelton and Carney had already found to be so equivocating. The intelligence "casts doubt" on the supposed Atta meeting in Prague, it said. "There have been fewer reports" of Al Qaeda training in Iraq since 1996.[87] The paper drew a crisp distinction between Saddam's unassailable ties to Palestinian rejectionist groups and the sketchier associations with Al Qaeda.

Libby was infuriated by the *Iraqi Support* paper, demanding modification after modification—to the point that Jami Miscik threatened to quit if Tenet continued to allow such intrusions.[88]

"We're done here," Tenet informed Steve Hadley. But the director was only referring to the paper. The debate, if it was indeed done, had not left a clear winner. Cheney continued to talk about Saddam's associations with Al Qaeda. So, for that matter, did the First Customer. The arguments of the CIA's premier analysts had been swept aside. The agency teetered on irrelevancy.

Unlike Rumsfeld, Tenet had always been viewed by his subordinates as approachable—which, unfortunately for him, made him the recipient of all sorts of unsolicited advice. One of the agency's legendary deputy directors for operations, Tom Twetten, dropped by the office during the summer of 2002 and, during a brief visit with the director, warned that an invasion of Iraq would be catastrophic. "Wolfowitz has got to be fired," Twetten said.

Tenet laughed ruefully. "That's not going to happen," he said.[89]

The director also received numerous "issue manager memos" from Hal Rooks, the agency's preeminent Saudi Arabia analyst, who also headed the Iraq analytical group for much of 2001 and 2002. Rooks did not bother to hide his dismay with the Bush administration's seeming determination to topple Saddam. Doing so, Rooks warned in his memos, "will create more terrorism, not less." After one meeting in which Wolfowitz's advocacy of Ahmad Chalabi was discussed, an exasperated Rooks said to Tenet, "Don't they know that if you put a Shia regime in power, that's going to work to Iran's advantage?"

"Yeah, I know," Tenet muttered in a fatigued voice—an admission, it seemed, that neither his opinion nor that of his senior analyst mattered in the end. Rooks's increasingly vocal opposition to invading Iraq only meant fewer invitations to such discussions. He took early retirement from the agency in the summer of 2002.[90]

Rooks believed that Tenet got it. Others in the building, including those who were fond of George Tenet, worried that what the director got most of all was the thinness of the ice underneath him. Wedged between conflicting certitudes, it was Tenet who occupied the murky middle. At one meeting to discuss Libby's continued objections to the *Iraqi Support for Terrorism* paper, the CIA director listened to his analysts make their case that any meaningful connection was a fiction.

Then he murmured, more in befuddlement than in certainty, "Where there's smoke, there's fire."[91]

IN SEPTEMBER 2002, CHENEY AND LIBBY VISITED CIA HEADQUARTERS TO discuss the Saddam–Al Qaeda connection. Leading the briefing from the agency was Philip Mudd, a well-liked senior staffer who also was skilled in the art of interagency politics (and who would later enjoy a successful second career as a CNN commentator). But Mudd was a poor choice to debate the minutiae of intel data from years past. Calmly, politely, the vice president and his chief of staff eviscerated Mudd.[92]

After the meeting had concluded and Cheney and Libby had departed for downtown, Miscik—who had sat throughout the horror show, fixing Mudd with what one participant would term "a death stare"[93]—stormed into the office of Mudd's supervisor, Pattie Kindsvater. "You're losing the policy-maker," the deputy director for intelligence told Kindsvater.[94]

The agency scrambled to fashion a redo. They invited the vice president to return. They assembled "murder boards" of evidence and spent days rehearsing the data. Cheney and Libby listened, asked more questions, and were not placated.[95] By the fall of 2002, the argument over the Saddam–Al Qaeda connection would be supplanted by fervent assertions relating to the Iraqi regime's weapons program. To some, this was proof that the CIA had held fast to its analytical assessments and ultimately carried the day.

But in October 2002, when asked by Senate Select Committee on Intelligence chairman Bob Graham to address the alleged links between Saddam Hussein and Osama bin Laden, Director Tenet issued a reply that Cheney, Libby, Wolfowitz, and Feith could only have dreamed of:

> Our understanding of the relationship between Iraq and al-Qa'ida is evolving and is based on sources of varying reliability. . . . We have solid reporting of senior-level contacts between Iraq and al-Qa'ida going back a decade. . . . We have credible reporting that al-Qa'ida leaders sought contacts in Iraq who could help them acquire WMD

capabilities. The reporting also stated that Iraq has provided training to al-Qa'ida members in the areas of poisons and gases and making conventional bombs. . . . Iraq's increasing support to extremist Palestinians, coupled with growing indications of a relationship with al-Qa'ida, suggest that Baghdad's links to terrorists will increase, even absent U.S. military action.[96]

The director had walked back his agency's walk-back. Tenet loved the building. But as his deputy, Jami Miscik, had said, "losing the policymaker" was untenable. Without its customers, the building was only a building.

==≡==

CHAPTER NINE

THE UGLY DUCKLING

L isten, we need to answer Rumsfeld's snowflakes immediately," Marc Grossman said to the secretary of state one day during the summer of 2002.

Powell looked up from his desk at his undersecretary for political affairs. "Why?" he said, with evident annoyance.

Because, Grossman said, Rumsfeld was having his way with things. His ceaseless lecturing, power hoarding, and disingenuous memos might well be shaping the president's thinking. Bush needed to be aware of where State stood on these matters. "I'll take one of the people off my staff," Grossman added, "and you should just shoot an answer back every day."

Powell's reply left no room for argument. He wasn't going to get into some kind of never-ending snowflake debate with Rumsfeld. He was above that kind of behavior. "I am who I am," the secretary told Grossman. "And I'm going to deal with this my way. And I'm the secretary of state."[1]

Grossman retreated, chastened if not thoroughly convinced. The episode served to remind the assistant secretary why he and so many others revered Colin Powell. He was always measured, appropriate to the occasion, the adult in the room. It also reminded Grossman why Powell's diminished stature in the Bush administration was a compounded tragedy.

Of late, Powell had been testier than usual. He privately spoke of quitting, though no one believed that he would ever do so.[2] At Principals Committee meetings to discuss Iraq, the secretary of state's learned counsel—as the only one among them who had served on the battlefield, the only one who had designed battlefield plans—was wholly disregarded by Rumsfeld and Cheney. A senior aide who had back-benched one of these meetings said to him as they drove together back to Foggy Bottom, "Mr. Secretary, how can you stand the way they treat you?"

Smirking, Powell replied, "They thought they were getting a black guy who could help them out at the polls. They forgot that I might know something."[3]

In his memoir, Colin Powell wrote, "I am capable of self-pity. But not for long."[4] He had prevailed over racism, hard-ass generals in the Army, and right-wingers who found him insufficiently hawkish. Still, this was a novel challenge for a man who had amassed such prestige and influence in Washington—a man who had become not just a leader but a great one. After the Iran-Contra mess, the Reagan administration had tapped General Powell as national security adviser to restore order and, more important, dignity. He had done so. The decision by President George H. W. Bush and Secretary of Defense Dick Cheney to elevate Powell to chairman of the Joint Chiefs—leapfrogging him over several longer-tenured four-stars—turned out to be a stroke of genius, never more so than during the Gulf War, when the televised image of his poise and resolve served as a comfort to Americans whose last memory of war was the endless debacle in Vietnam.

The careerists at State who had trouble envisioning an Army man as America's top diplomat were instantly charmed. "You are my team, and I am your leader," he told his assembled staffers during his first day on the job in January 2001—adding, with an emcee's aplomb, "But remember that I'm a military man, and if you play in the ballpark, no problem; but if you don't, you *will* do push-ups."[5] Powell viewed the ambassadors as his field generals (rather than glorified travel guides to visiting American elites) and gave them a long leash.[6] He preached that leadership required knowing what those being led were thinking; accessibility was therefore compulsory, from the secretary on down.[7] Correspondingly, Powell's deputy, Rich Armitage, encouraged the senior staff to be accessible to reporters and legislators: "The only complaint I want to hear from anyone on the Hill," Armitage would say, "is that we're offering too *many* briefings."[8]

But Powell and Armitage now worked in an administration that regarded such engagement as preening. Cheney, having seen how memos and tapes had brought down the Nixon administration, proudly made it his business not "to leave a lot of tracks around," as he would put it.[9] As defense secretary, Cheney watched attentively as his JCS chief hoovered up publicity. That was one thing—and, for the Defense Department, a useful thing, up to a point. But for Powell to offer unsolicited policymaking advice to the White House and off-the-cuff troop-downsizing estimates to the press—both of which he did—confirmed to the elder Bush's defense secretary, whose Secret Service code name was Back Seat, that Colin Powell was playing for Colin Powell.[10]

Armitage anticipated that they might have problems with Cheney, despite the latter's daughter Liz's having worked for Armitage. On December 16, 2000, he watched on television as his friend, the newly nominated secretary of state, stood behind a podium at Bush's Texas ranch and promptly stole the show from the president-elect, while the VP-elect stood off to the side, noticeably unamused. Powell later asked Armitage how he had done and was distressed when his new deputy said, "We are fucked. Not because of the president. It's Cheney. I saw his face. We are fucked."[11]

What Armitage and Powell failed to foresee was the difficulty of winning over the commander in chief. Bush was not at all like his father, whom Powell had greatly admired. The new president was far more conservative, far less reverential of international alliances. State's world of half-a-loaf realpolitik, of treading gingerly across a trap-laden world—a world "where we give you 150 reasons not to do something"—did not comport with the younger Bush's notion of American primacy.[12] He held Congress in only slightly higher regard than the Washington press corps. To Powell's brain trust, Bush "tended to try to make up for in principle what he lacked in knowledge," one of them would say. "Like 'You're either with us or you're with the terrorists.'

He sometimes didn't understand the implications of what he was saying. And he didn't want to hear anyone explain the implications to him.

"That was more our thoughts than Powell's. Powell's were more 'He comes from a good family, and he knows what's right and what's wrong, and that's good. And I can help educate him on the rest.'"[13]

But Powell's difficulty with the president was only partly explained by differences in ideology or temperament. As a shrewd politician, Bush understood the power that Powell's popularity conferred on him. Like Cheney, Powell had thought once about running for president, then decided against it. Unlike Cheney (with his heart troubles and unenviable approval rating), Powell could change his mind anytime he wished. Just as there were those at State who believed without any evidence that Karl Rove was whispering in his boss's ear, *We can't give Powell any path to a 2004 challenge,*[14] there were also those in the West Wing who viewed State, somewhat hyperbolically, as an ever-leaking rival campaign shop.[15]

Though Bush paid almost no attention to how his principals interacted with one another, his antennae were well attuned to how they interacted with the press. Joining the Bush administration meant signing on to the proposition that the president's reputation came before anyone else's. "The White House has a level of paranoia that could've contributed to this—but, yeah, it looked like State had their own rules, and Armitage got on everybody's radar screen early," recalled one of the president's top advisers. "The president had much more reason to be hesitant about Tenet than Powell. But Tenet knew his boss—he was a good player. With Powell, the question was, can he click it down and be a staffer?"[16]

Powell and Armitage believed that you were a good staffer if you scored some wins for your boss. And this was what they had done early, when, after the downing of an EP-3 spy plane in Chinese territory, State officials fed to journalists a timeline of events that played up Bush's hands-on management of the episode.[17] Such backstage connivances, long a hallmark of what one State admirer termed Powell's "diabolical brilliance,"[18] were nonetheless defiant of process and hierarchy, revered traits in Bush World. Only Rove, the president's indispensable political strategist, was permitted such trespasses.

It might have helped if, like Tenet, Powell knew how to appeal to Bush's rough-hewn side. Alas, Powell's many skills did not include affecting a good ol' boy swagger. When visiting Crawford, he could not pretend that the scruffy charms of rural Texas spoke to him, and he did not wear cowboy boots.[19] His occasional attempts to talk baseball with Bush fell embarrassingly flat.[20] "Rich, he's gotta go locker room," a close Bush associate implored to Armitage.[21]

Powell, a sixty-five-year-old icon, was not about to debase himself with frat-house supplication. Still, when the secretary told his staff, as he often did, that Bush tended to make a decision "based on the last person left in the room with him,"[22] it was his glum way of admitting that, as one who never lingered with Bush, he was unlikely to get his way.

When tasked with a mission, Bush's secretary of state frequently succeeded: managing the United States' withdrawal from the ABM treaty, negotiating a new arms reduction treaty with Putin, siccing Armitage on the Pakistanis to secure an alliance against Al Qaeda after 9/11, and beginning back-channel talks with the regime of Muammar Qaddafi that would culminate in the end of Libya's nuclear weapons program. But when it came to policy in the Middle East, Powell was not where the rest of Bush's team was. He was, as a top NSC staffer who greatly admired Powell would recall, "more of a dissident, who would say, 'I'm fighting a rearguard action against these fucking crazies.'"[23]

That he, a four-star general, could somehow be viewed as a figure of lesser relevance in a wartime presidency was a narrative that the State Department endeavored to combat. This became evident to White House press secretary Ari Fleischer one day when Powell's spokesman, Richard Boucher, called to lodge an unusual complaint. It seemed that, in reading out the president's daily schedule to the White House press corps, Fleischer had failed to mention that Bush and Powell were having a one-on-one meeting. Reminding Fleischer that he never failed to mention Rumsfeld's weekly get-together in the Oval Office, Boucher said, "You need to be reporting when the secretary and the president meet."

"Okay, fine," Fleischer said, thinking, *Who the hell cares?* Only later did it dawn on Bush's spokesman: *My God. They're counting meetings—"He got his. Now I need mine."*[24]

————

TO POWELL, THE WOLFOWITZIAN FEVER DREAM OF INVADING IRAQ DIRECTLY
on the heels of the 9/11 attacks *was* crazy—and surely, he figured, the president would come to see that. Before the attacks, Bush had not seemed particularly fazed by the many briefings on military options for Iraq—largely
related to enforcing no-fly zones—that the Pentagon was giving him. "I'm
not getting ready to invade a country," he had assured Powell.[25]

After 9/11, Powell could see that the calculus had changed overnight.
Still, as one of his subordinates put it, "The secretary and Armitage thought
we could get by with a rope-a-dope approach: *Let's play along, let them hang
themselves. Because this idea is so cockamamie, it'll never happen.*"[26] Of Saddam,
"Powell kept saying, 'He's a bad guy in a box, so let's keep building the box,'"
one of his deputies recalled. "And he hoped that, over time, the president
might say, 'Ah, okay, I get it. The box is good.'"[27] After all, Reagan—the
closest thing Bush had to a political role model—won the Cold War relying
on the same theory of containment, confident that a boxed-in Soviet empire
would drown in its own ideological toxins.

Then again, the homeland had never been attacked on Reagan's watch.
The Soviets respected mutually assured destruction. Bin Laden did not. Did
Saddam? The question itself presumed that the dictator had malevolent de-
signs on the United States—a belief that, before September 11, very few in
the Bush administration espoused, certainly not Powell. Now a different
formulation was embraced. It was Saddam's burden to prove his harmless-
ness. And it was Colin Powell's burden to prove that diplomacy, rather than
war, was the answer. In this perverse manner were the secretary and the
dictator joined as partners in peace.

Self-assured and optimistic even by military standards, Powell did not
immediately appreciate the odds against his sales pitch. "We were competing
against the Beautiful Vision," recalled one of his deputies. "*We'll overthrow
this brutal dictator. We'll create this provisional government of exiles. They'll be
welcomed, and we'll leave them to their economic prosperity and representative*

government. All these other awful regimes in the region will fall like dominoes. The whole place becomes better for Israel. Beautiful picture!

"Ours was ugly. *If we go in, it won't be easy and it won't be cheap, and there's not going to be a quick departure.* And for the first half of 2002, it was a tug-of-war between the Beautiful Vision and the Ugly Duckling."[28]

The duckling had its fine qualities. In a sense, State's argument—as Assistant Secretary Burns summarized it, "Let's take advantage of this moment, once we've knocked the Taliban off, to mobilize coalitions of countries so we can get at states harboring terrorists and squeeze the Libyans, Syrians, and Iranians, but not through another armed conflict in the Middle East"—was far less stark than the outlook promoted by Cheney.[29] The problem was that this approach hewed closely to the status quo: Make the sanctions against Saddam smarter: more limiting of his militaristic aims, more humane toward the Iraqi people. Remind the world (as Powell did in Senate testimony two weeks after Bush's "axis of evil" speech) that regime change had been official U.S. policy since 1998. Cast the administration's tough rhetoric as a diplomatic tool designed to show Saddam that the United States was serious. And, in the meantime, strengthen alliances in the Arab world, with the aim of making Saddam the unsympathetic party.

State's vision was, like most practical remedies, aesthetically unsatisfying. But its greatest flaw was that it was never articulated *as* a vision—leaving State's adversaries at the Pentagon and the vice president's office to conclude that Powell's team had no coherent argument to make and was instead bent on slowing the war train to a crawl, in hopes that Bush would eventually turn his attention to immigration reform or Social Security privatization.

That was, in fact, exactly what State was up to. Inside headquarters at Foggy Bottom, Powell's deputies spoke variously of "slowing down the train," of playing "judo" or "jujitsu" against Wolfowitz and Libby.[30] "Powell's strategy," recalled one of them, "was: *Keep talking to the others, participate in the meetings, chop down the really dumb ideas, and we'll win in the end.*"[31]

But by the summer of 2002, it had become evident to Colin Powell that State was not winning. Whether out of bewilderment from Rumsfeld's

riddle-speak or dismay that Wolfowitz's once quixotic scheme to depose
Saddam had become the administration's majority view, the secretary became a subdued presence at principals meetings. As one senior CIA official
who participated in the meetings recalled, "I never saw him pushing back
against Rumsfeld and the others. He could've been a great, great counterbal-
ance. But 9/11 started a tidal wave that Rumsfeld, Cheney, Libby, Wolfowitz,
and Feith rode. And Powell didn't stop it."[32]

It was not in Powell's nature to be a dissenter. Though never shy about
voicing his opinions, and skilled at finding back channels through which
such opinions might gain traction, Powell in the end had earned his four stars
through deference rather than defiance. That fact had been discerned by a
former colleague during the first Bush administration, Secretary of State Jim
Baker, who had predicted to an acquaintance just as the younger Bush was
taking office, "Those neocons are going to eat George W. alive. The only one
who could protect him would be Powell. But Powell doesn't know his own
strength. He's the good soldier."[33]

"It's ironic," one of his deputies would reflect. "Powell was a very political
general when he was at the Pentagon. He was a military general when he was
at State. He had reservations about going into Iraq. But at the end of the day,
you do what you're told."[34]

ONE MORNING DURING THE SUMMER OF 2002, MARC GROSSMAN CALLED
Scooter Libby's deputy, Eric Edelman. The two men had traveled in the same
foreign policy circles for decades. Before Bush took office, Grossman had
been the ambassador to Turkey; in 2003, Edelman would hold the same post.
For the moment, however, their long-standing collegiality had begun to fray
over Iraq. At the Deputies Lunches chaired by Steve Hadley, the two consistently took opposite positions. And so it was something of a surprise to
Edelman when Powell's undersecretary for political affairs said, "I'd like to
meet with you on some kind of neutral territory."

They chose the coffee shop in the basement of the Corcoran Gallery.

Grossman got right to the point once they were seated. "Eric," he asked, "has the president already decided to go to war, and we're just in this interagency circle jerk?"

That Grossman was asking one of Cheney's deputies what was going on inside Bush's head was itself a reflection of State's diminished standing. "I don't think the president has decided to go to war," Edelman replied. "But I do think the president has decided the problem Saddam presents can't just drag on forever."[35]

Tacitly expressed in Edelman's reply was: *You guys at State want to drag this on forever.* Grossman happened to be more receptive to the Iraq hawks than his other compatriots were. Where his sympathy ended was at their suggestion that war in the Middle East would be a quick and straightforward proposition. If Powell's team appeared intransigent, it was not out of bureaucratic inertia. Their fretfulness was genuine and grounded in the hard realities of the region.

"We'd have these hand-wringing sessions," one of State's Iraq specialists would recall, "because each of us knew different parts of what we covered and could see what was coming down the road and were concerned about it. We were talking about the lack of planning of the political process, lack of a meaningful Sunni component. There was a lot we were anxious about."[36]

One July afternoon, a hand-wringing session in Bill Burns's office became particularly morose. "What if the whole Iraq team just resigned in protest?" one of the team members said.

A few murmured their assent. It fell to one of the veteran officers, Ryan Crocker, to provide the reality check. "You could do that," he said. "And it'll be a one-day newspaper story. Then everyone will say, 'Who cares about a bunch of whiners at State?' If you really want to have an impact, stay and do what good you can."[37]

Following the meeting, Burns approached one of the attendees, David Pearce, State's director of the Office of Northern Gulf Affairs. The assistant secretary asked Pearce to compile the group's concerns into a single memo.

Pearce shut his door and in one sitting produced a ten-page stream-of-consciousness expression of agency-wide perturbation. "Thoughts on Iraq," he entitled the memo. Burns edited the opening and closing passages, changed the title to "The Perfect Storm," and sent it to Secretary Powell.[38]

The memo was the State Department's contribution to the Bush administration's growing reliance on imagination over evidence. "The Perfect Storm" conjured up a Hieronymus Bosch–like specter of attacks on U.S. embassies, assassinations of Iraqi exiles, terror attacks on the Kurds, plunging markets, a side war between Israel and Hezbollah, nighttime bloodlettings on the streets of Baghdad, and the exaltation of an Iraqi colonel who shoots Saddam, only to become the country's new despot.[39] Like another Iraq memo written two months later by Rumsfeld—a list of twenty-nine worrisome consequences dubbed the "parade of horribles" by Feith[40]—the items ranged from the fantastical to the prescient, with no degree of probability assigned to them. Pearce's and Rumsfeld's Iraq memos had another thing in common: both would go undiscussed at any NSC meeting in the run-up to war.

But far more of the enumerated concerns in "The Perfect Storm" emanated from Wolfowitz's preferred scenario—that of U.S. troops quickly handing over postwar administration to a group of Iraqi exiles such as Ahmad Chalabi—than from what Pearce and his colleagues believed to be the more realistic eventuality: "a long-term civil and military presence to contain Iraqi factionalism and deter external intervention." Even if the latter were to occur, Pearce's memo warned, "this is a five- or ten-year job, not a fast in and out. It is MacArthur and Japan, not Oakley and Somalia."[41]

Burns forwarded the memo to his boss with the awareness that Powell, in turn, might see fit to share it with the president. Because of this, the veteran diplomat reframed the opening passage to emphasize that State intended to be a team player: "We all seek a process of regime change in Iraq that leads to a democratic, representative government and security in the region. It could be a historic turning point in the Middle East, and for U.S. interests."[42]

Burns would later write, after retiring from State in 2014, that failing to express his unambiguous opposition to the war "remains my biggest professional regret."[43]

AS IT TURNED OUT, POWELL NEVER SHOWED "THE PERFECT STORM" TO BUSH, just as Rumsfeld never provided the president with a copy of his "parade of horribles." Pearce's memo nonetheless became the intellectual framework for the monologue Powell delivered to Bush a few days later.

The secretary reached out to Condi Rice and told her that he needed private time with the president. The national security adviser arranged for the three of them to have dinner at the White House residence on Monday, August 5. Coincidentally, it was the same day that General Franks briefed Bush on what would become the final war plan for invading Iraq. It was also the president's last day in Washington before flying to Texas for his summer vacation.[44]

Rice sat silently while Powell, over the course of two hours, proceeded to do what no one else in the Bush administration had done or would do: tell the president to his face that things in Iraq could go horribly wrong. "If you break it, you own it," he famously told Bush.[45] Postwar governance would be an expensive and dreary slog. It would swallow whole his agenda. "This will become your first term," he warned the president.

Powell could see that the last remark registered with Bush. "What should I do?" the president asked.

Go to the United Nations, Powell advised him. After all, Saddam had repeatedly violated the UN's resolutions. They were the aggrieved party. *But if you do so,* Powell added, *there is a chance that the dictator will surrender his weapons and become compliant.* Bush would have to accept a "changed regime" as a substitute for "regime change."[46]

It was arguably the most important message that George W. Bush would hear from any of his subordinates in his entire presidency. But it changed nothing. After all, just four days earlier, the president had declared emphatically to the king of Jordan that "Saddam is a bad guy" and that "we need to take him down." The notion of leaving even a defanged Saddam Hussein in power was no longer among Bush's options.

And, though much of Powell's monologue had focused on unanticipated outcomes of invading Iraq, the dinner itself would lead to an unintended consequence. When Bush asked, "What should I do?" his secretary of state saw the opportunity to say "Don't invade Iraq" and passed on it. Like his fellow reluctant warriors at State, Colin Powell had declined to articulate his conviction that going to war against Saddam under the present circumstances could *only* invite a perfect storm.

Instead, by advising Bush to go to the UN, Powell had provided the president with the only politically feasible pathway to war.

"I TOLD HIM, 'REMOVING SADDAM IS THE EASY PART,'" POWELL SAID TO HIS friend Jack Straw, the foreign minister of Prime Minister Tony Blair. "I said, 'You'll be the proud owner of twenty-five million Iraqis in eighteen fractious provinces.'"

The two men and Straw's private secretary, Simon McDonald, sat on the veranda of the Hamptons beach house owned by Powell's good friend the billionaire Ronald Lauder. The secretary was spending most of his August here with his wife, Alma. On the property was a small church that the State Department had retrofitted as an operations room, filled with close to two dozen staffers. Straw and McDonald, for their part, had flown in on a Concorde that morning with two bodyguards and would be returning to the UK that evening.

The foreign minister and the secretary of state had become extraordinarily close over the past year. Powell's customary 11 p.m. calls to the Straw household had prompted his wife, Alice Perkins, to refer to him as "the other man in my life." Still, the August meeting at the Lauder residence was not about pleasantries. Instead, as Powell would later say, it was an attempt to solve a riddle: "Could we both stop a war?"

They sat on the veranda and talked for three hours. Powell spoke ruefully of Cheney and Rumsfeld. Both men had changed, he told Straw, and not for the better. Wolfowitz, Feith, Cheney, and Libby were hopelessly smitten with Chalabi and his assurances of a post-Saddam utopia. "You wouldn't believe how much this guy is shaping our policy," he told the two Brits.

Still, Powell was more upbeat than Straw. Blair professed a commitment to a regime change that was orderly and supported by other countries in the West as well as in the Arab world. But his attempts to deliver hard truths to Bush were not getting through, in part because the prime minister was not terribly forceful in delivering them. Straw was plainly frustrated with his boss, who he feared was becoming Bush's enabler.

"You've got to get Tony to convince the president to go to the UN," Powell said. The secretary had already made his pitch on the subject to Bush over dinner. But he had come away from the White House without a commitment, and with Cheney and Rumsfeld sure to advise the opposite course.

The men wrapped up their afternoon with a drive along the country roads in a vintage sedan owned by Lauder that had once been FDR's. That evening, on the flight back to London, the two Brits marveled at Powell's optimism. Perhaps it was his military disinclination to show doubt. Perhaps it was the beach weather. Or perhaps Powell was whistling past the graveyard.

But Jack Straw did not project sunniness when he warned Blair the next day that the prospect of Bush taking the Iraq matter to the UN was far from assured. "You have to take this seriously," he told the prime minister. "There are contrary voices. We haven't landed this yet."[47]

SHORTLY AFTER POWELL RETURNED FROM THE HAMPTONS AT THE END OF August, Skip Gnehm, the ambassador to Jordan, flew into Washington for his own vacation and decided to drop by Foggy Bottom. Having sat in on the Oval Office encounter between Bush and King Abdullah earlier that month, Gnehm suspected that war was a foregone conclusion. But, having previously served as the ambassador to Kuwait during the Gulf War, he had unique insight into postwar challenges.

Walking into Rich Armitage's office, Gnehm offered to draw up a list of what the previous Bush administration had done right after Desert Storm and where they had fallen short. The deputy secretary's immense bald head was motionless for a time.

Then he said, "Don't bother."

"It's not a bother," the ambassador insisted. "It might be helpful if—"

"It won't be helpful," Armitage said flatly.

At the first syllable of Gnehm's protestations, the deputy secretary said loudly, "Don't you understand English? Nobody is going to listen to what you have to say."

Shaken by Armitage's vehemence, Gnehm nonetheless brought up his offer to Powell the next day. The secretary was genial but firm. "Skip, Rich was right," he said. Referring to the Pentagon, he went on, "If you go across that bridge, you're going to be burned, and you'll be of no use to me in the future. And I'm going to need you more in the next six to eight months than ever. So do as Rich says: Forget it."

Gnehm flew back to Amman and did what he could to forget.[48]

CHAPTER TEN

THE DECIDER, DECIDING

Had Powell gotten through to Bush?

In their executive deliberations, presidents are frequently loath to show their hand. Abraham Lincoln's private anguish over whether to emancipate all slaves in the United States kept even his closest aides guessing throughout 1862. As attested by audiotapes during the 1962 Cuban Missile Crisis, John F. Kennedy remained largely silent while his advisers debated whether to conduct air strikes or a naval blockade on the Soviet-allied country. For that matter, Republicans did not see coming the announcement by President George H. W. Bush, in June 1990, that, after numerous meetings on the Hill and in the White House, he had decided to break his campaign pledge and raise income taxes.

The younger Bush had himself spent several weeks in the first year of his presidency wrestling with whether to approve federal funding for embryonic stem cell research. (He ultimately did so, though not for new embryos.) But that decision had been an elaborately, even theatrically transparent one, with Karen Hughes and Dan Bartlett proactively disseminating to the media the multitude of consultations their boss had received.

On the matter of Iraq, the self-proclaimed "decider" had been cipher-like. After blurting out to a British reporter in April 2002, "I've made up my mind that Saddam needs to go,"[1] he retreated into literalistic formulations such as "There are no plans on my desk right now."[2] (Those plans rested on the desk of General Tommy Franks, in CENTCOM headquarters in Tampa.)

Bush had certainly heard Powell's note of caution, just as he had heard the concerns of Jordan's King Abdullah—and, in the White House residence, the protestations of his twenty-year-old twin daughters, Jenna and Barbara, who opposed going to war in Iraq.[3] But for George W. Bush, the information he received was not always as important as how he received it, through the narrow-mesh filters of his human experience.

Beginning with his first campaign for Congress, in 1978, the abiding political through line for the Texas oilman had been his embrace of individual liberty. He repeatedly cited freedom as God's gift to all humanity. In a well-publicized campaign speech at the Reagan Presidential Library on November 19, 1999, then-Governor Bush mentioned the word "free" or "freedom" twenty-seven times. The candidate dared his audience to imagine a free China, a free Russia. He ticked off the intoxicating effect of free markets, free trade, free elections; of the freedom to worship; of whole regions one day giddy with the contagion of freedom.[4]

Bush's deeply held views were rooted in faith and conservatism, but also in a life of privilege. He had no experience in countries racked with poverty and violence where the daily struggle to survive trumped any abstract yearning for participatory democracy or unregulated markets. In Bush's distinctly indigenous frame of reference, what America's adversaries detested about America was its constitutionally enshrined attributes. Al Qaeda were "enemies of freedom"; the destruction of the Twin Towers signaled to him that "freedom is under attack."[5]

The Bush family, of course, had been under attack when Saddam's intelligence service apparently orchestrated the failed assassination attempt in 1993. "There's no doubt his hatred is mainly directed at us," Bush would tell a roomful of Texas donors in 2002. "There's no doubt he can't stand us. After all, this is the guy that tried to kill my dad at one time."[6] But alongside family animus, Bush had now begun to levy a new charge against the dictator: "This is a man who cannot stand what we stand for. He hates the fact, like Al Qaeda does, that we love freedom."[7]

This sweeping notion of Saddam, as a despiser not only of Bushes and Israelis but of freedom itself, had crystallized in him at some point in 2002. The president was not yet espousing the removal of Saddam as a critical first step in the democratization of the Middle East. But Bush was nonetheless affronted by Saddam's swaggering tyranny—and, perhaps as much, by the suggestion by some that totalitarianism was the best Iraqis could hope for. "He would really bristle at that," a White House aide would recall. "He'd say, 'That's bullshit. Everyone deserves freedom.'"[8]

Accompanying his deliberations on Iraq was a series of not entirely fact-propelled leaps of logic. The terrorists' primary objective was to destroy America's freedom. Saddam hated America. Therefore, he hated freedom. Therefore, Saddam was himself a terrorist, bent on destroying America and its freedom. How, under those grim circumstances, could Bush accept a "changed regime"? Or, as the previous President Bush had rhetorically asked of the dictator a dozen years earlier, "Can a leopard really change his spots?"

"We love everything about freedom—and we're not changing," the younger Bush would declare in the fall of 2002.[9] He and Saddam were thereby placed on an unalterable collision course: the unflagging defender of freedom pitted against freedom's aspiring destroyer.

Given these colossal stakes, did the details matter? Did evidence? In his morning intelligence briefings, the president continued to interrupt the CIA analysts, peppering them with questions. But when it came to intelligence that attested to Saddam's evil—his connections to terrorists, his suspected amassing of weapons—Bush seldom, if ever, raised a note of skepticism.[10] When, for that matter, Tenet clashed with Cheney over whether the 9/11 hijacker Mohamed Atta had met with an Iraqi agent in Prague, Bush did not share his own opinion. By the early summer of 2002, the CIA director had concluded that the Prague meeting had not occurred, "and the president left it alone," recalled John McLaughlin.[11] Yet the vice president continued to assert publicly that Atta had in fact met with the Iraqi agent.[12] Bush left Cheney alone as well.

Was the president unconcerned by such disagreements? Was any further proof of Saddam's malevolence deemed by him superfluous? In the coming months, Bush would speak repeatedly and with unchecked self-confidence about the mind and motives of a man he had never met but who had come to garish light in his imagination: "Saddam Hussein would like nothing more than to use a terrorist network to attack and to kill and leave no fingerprints behind."[13]

His increasingly bellicose rhetoric reflected a wartime president who was no longer tethered to anything other than his own convictions. He had dispensed with his post-9/11 Tuesday morning breakfast with leaders from both parties—conferring thereafter chiefly with Republicans and the occasional reliably acquiescent Democrat.[14] Correspondingly, his approval rating among Democrats settled to earth, falling from 84 after his joint session speech in September 2001 to 48 a year later.[15] Bush's support had begun to plummet among Arab Americans, who felt intimidated by the sweeping surveillance powers given to the FBI by the Patriot Act and were outraged by the "special registration" program that resulted in deportation proceedings against fourteen thousand Muslims.[16]

The degree to which Bush had become his own man surprised many in his administration who had observed his tentativeness in the early months. During one intelligence briefing in the Situation Room, a CIA official began to explain to the president the challenges in recruiting support inside Iraq. The briefer stammered a bit when describing to Bush how the uprising by Shiites in 1991 had been undercut by his father's failure to provide support in southern Iraq after first encouraging them to revolt.

To the CIA official's surprise, Bush did not hesitate. "Absolutely," the president said. "That was a huge mistake."[17]

Bush's self-assuredness was buttressed by the recognition that he was not, in the end, the least bit on his own. He could rest assured that he had the support of his father, though they did not discuss Iraq: "He knows, as an ex-president, he doesn't have nearly the amount of knowledge I've got on current things," he would later tell this author.[18] His wife, Laura, was there as well. So was God. And so were the pantheon of war leaders like Lincoln and Washington hanging on the walls of the Oval Office, reminders that even the heaviest of burdens could be borne.

Early in Bush's presidency, Tony Blair had loaned him a bust of Churchill to keep in the Oval Office. "He stood on principle," Bush said of the legendary Tory upon receiving the bust—adding, as the ultimate compliment, that Churchill "seemed like a Texan to me."[19] The prime minister would remain a source of inspiration throughout Bush's presidency. (And post-presidency: he would follow Churchill's lead and take up painting. Among Bush's portraits were three of the British leader.)[20] At Karl Rove's recommendation, he read *Troublesome Young Men,* an account of Churchill's rise to power during the disastrous final years of Prime Minister Neville Chamberlain. Bush and Rove were both enraptured by author Lynne Olson's portrayal of Churchill.[21] Olson found this interesting: in her reading of her own book, Bush far more closely resembled the press-baiting, self-certain Chamberlain.[22]

Still, Bush's quiet deliberations throughout the middle months of 2002 suggested a man in continued search for more answers than he currently possessed—perhaps realizing, as Churchill had written in 1930 of wartime leadership, that "once the signal is given, he is no longer the master of policy but the slave of unforeseeable and uncontrollable events."[23]

FOR THE FORTY OR SO FOREIGN POLICY EMINENCES GATHERED AT THE AN-nual Aspen Strategy Group forum, August 4 to 8, 2002, the previously designated topic, "Biological Security and Global Public Health," had effectively been superseded. The chief preoccupation instead was the Bush administration's seeming determination to go to war in Iraq.

No one among the group was more fretful than Brent Scowcroft. He had been the elder Bush's national security adviser during the Gulf War. Scowcroft had also been a mentor to Condi Rice, who endeavored to model her NSC after his and who also convinced the younger Bush to put Scowcroft in charge of the President's Foreign Intelligence Advisory Board. But the White House was now closing ranks. The president and Rice were not soliciting views about Iraq from Scowcroft or anyone else from the first Bush administration.

The White House's talk was not idle, Scowcroft warned others at the gathering. "Brent was worried about this—so much so that I wondered if he was being alarmist," recalled the Aspen group's director that year, Philip Zelikow.[24] Some in the group were enthused by the prospect of war. But, said another attendee, Senator Jack Reed of Rhode Island, "Scowcroft had more experience on Iraq than anyone else there. And now he was taking a very strong stand against attacking Iraq. He was asking them very probing questions about what the next steps would be. I thought it was an extraordinary effort on his part."[25]

But Scowcroft was not content to confine his worries to the Aspen Strategy Group. While in Colorado, he appeared on *Face the Nation* and predicted that invading Iraq "could turn the whole region into a cauldron and, thus, destroy the war on terrorism."[26] Then, on August 15, *The Wall Street Journal* published an op-ed written by Scowcroft. "Don't Attack Saddam" was its title. It was, if anything, more emphatic than Scowcroft's televised comments, warning that Bush would be "unleashing an Armageddon in the Middle East."[27]

The Scowcroft column "was a big stick of dynamite," said Antony Blinken, the foreign policy adviser to Senate Foreign Relations Committee chairman Joe Biden, who convened hearings to examine what might happen if Bush were to wage war on Iraq. "Here's a guy with extraordinary credibility on both sides of the aisle—the closest thing to Bush's father, after maybe Jim Baker."[28]

That was precisely why Bush, reading the column at his ranch in Crawford, was so livid. He promptly called Rice as well as Card (who had worked with Scowcroft while serving as the elder Bush's deputy chief of staff). "I know my dad," he fumed. "If he wanted me to know something, he'd pick up a phone and let me know!"[29]

Bush was being disingenuous. He knew that his father was as reluctant to dispense unsolicited advice to a sitting president as the son was to receive such advice. It would be another four months before the subject of Iraq would at last come up in their conversations.[30]

As it happened, Scowcroft had received permission in advance from the elder Bush to express his concerns in writing and had sent a courtesy copy of the op-ed to the latter's home. Scowcroft was confident that his views reflected those of his former boss. The younger Bush no doubt also suspected this was true.

"He didn't do us any favors, Dad!" he later said to his father. To Card he hollered, "He's in my administration, and he communicates to me through an op-ed piece?" Bush was clearly embarrassed that he was being publicly taken to task by surrogates of his father. But it also offended him that a supposed loyalist had refused to keep things inside the family, as devotees of the Bushes were expected to do, and had instead heaved a carcass out on the White House lawn for the carrion in the media to pick apart.

Years later, the president would describe Scowcroft's talking out of school as emblematic of "how it works inside the Beltway."[31] What the president did not seem to appreciate was how, after long boasting that he was a product of Texas rather than the "bubble" of Washington, he was now in his own impermeable ecosystem, sealed off from the impurity of dissent.

The day after Scowcroft's piece ran, Rice flew down to Texas. The national security adviser huddled over dinner with press secretary Ari Fleischer at the Waco steakhouse Diamondback's. Members of the traveling White House press sat three tables way, so the two kept their voices low. "So what's he going to say at the UN?" Fleischer asked.

He was referring to the first major speech on the president's schedule after his August vacation, to be delivered in New York at the United Nations on September 12. "Probably the Middle East peace process," Rice said.

Fleischer then brought up the Scowcroft op-ed. "You'd probably better make it about Iraq," he said. "Just confront it. Deal directly with the issue. Because it's all the press is going to want to talk about anyway."[32]

Fleischer had another reason for recommending Iraq as the central topic of Bush's upcoming UN speech. Throughout August, he and Rice had been secretly discussing the subject with a few other administration officials. As with the Deputies Lunches, the activities of the White House Iraq Group, as it was called, were confined to the Situation Room. And though the president had not requested it, the group, like the Deputies Lunches, had nonetheless been formed (in this case by Card) in anticipation of a decision—going to war with Saddam Hussein—that had not been formally made or even debated.

But where Hadley's deputies hashed out policy, Card's group convened to orchestrate a communications strategy for selling the threat of Saddam to a skeptical public and Congress. Because it was a political operation and because such strategizing did not require high-level security clearance, its membership included Karl Rove, who, until its formation, had been deliberately walled off from what would be the most consequential decision of the Bush presidency. (By contrast, Scooter Libby was a member of both groups and, unlike Rove, had clearance to read classified information.) Within the White House Iraq Group, there had already been debate about whether to begin pushing out a messaging campaign in August. Now, with Scowcroft issuing a preemptive strike, Fleischer argued to Rice that it made even more sense for the president's UN speech to be a centerpiece of their Iraq communications strategy.[33]

"And then," recalled one member of the group, "the vice president jumped the gun."[34]

JUST TWO YEARS BEFORE THIS, IN MARCH 2000, CHENEY HAD BEEN AMONG the longtime friends who threw Brent Scowcroft a surprise party in honor of his seventy-fifth birthday.[35] Their closeness masked deep ideological differences that had largely gone unnoticed during the first Bush presidency. In that administration, George H. W. Bush and Scowcroft, his close friend and national security adviser, were consistently in lockstep, with Defense Secretary Cheney the odd man out.

But now it was Scowcroft at a remove and Cheney who had the president's ear. While vacationing at his ranch in Wyoming, the VP read his old friend's August 15 op-ed. After letting "Don't Attack Saddam" settle in his thoughts, he looked on his calendar to an event eleven days from then that had long been on the books: a speech he was to deliver to the Nashville chapter of the Veterans of Foreign Wars. Cheney received the president's permission to devote that speech to national security. He then notified his team—Libby (who was already at Cheney's ranch), Eric Edelman, John Hannah, and speechwriter John McConnell—that he intended to give a big speech on the Iraq threat.

While Libby had thrown much of his energy into the debate over Saddam's association with Al Qaeda, Hannah had immersed himself in intelligence relating to the dictator's WMD. He and Cheney were both confident that Saddam possessed such weapons, and the OVP vaults contained plenty of reporting to buttress that belief. What there had not been was a White House messenger to definitively spell out the case for war. Cheney was about to change that.[36]

"Intelligence is an uncertain business," the vice president told the Nashville crowd on August 26. He cited the pre–Gulf War belief that Saddam was at least five years away from developing a nuclear weapon—an estimate that was revised after the war, he said, when the intelligence community came to learn that the dictator was "perhaps within a year of acquiring such a weapon." The latter statement was inaccurate. But, having granted himself permission to depart altogether from intelligence's uncertainties, Cheney spelled out the truth as he saw it: "Simply stated, there is no doubt that Saddam Hussein now has weapons of mass destruction; there is no doubt that he is amassing them to use against our friends, against our allies, and against us."

Cheney concluded his fiery speech on a joltingly upbeat note. Quoting one of the several conservative foreign policy thinkers who had visited his office in recent months, he said, "As for the reaction in the Arab street, the Middle East expert, professor Fouad Ajami, predicts that after liberation, the streets in Basra and Baghdad are sure to erupt in joy in the same way throngs in Kabul greeted the Americans."[37] That rosy assessment of post-Saddam Iraq, so often espoused by Paul Wolfowitz and scholar Kanan Makiya, would receive considerable media attention later. For now, it was Cheney's apocalyptic evocation of Saddam that provoked comment worldwide, and caused one of the CIA's top weapons analysts to murmur to himself, while watching the VP's televised speech, "Did he just declare war on Iraq?"[38]

But Cheney's speech was also dismissive of UN weapons inspectors, saying that they were no match for Saddam's deceptions. Powell promptly called Rice and told her, "This is *not* what the president agreed to."[39]

"Bush was not pleased," Fleischer recalled. "It was not the administration's position."[40] The president told Rice to talk to Cheney. She did so. The vice president left Rice with the impression that he would walk back his comments in a speech he was delivering three days after the VFW speech, to a Korean War veterans audience in San Antonio.

Cheney indeed delivered a different speech three days later: he instructed McConnell to cut it by about 20 percent. The lines about Saddam without any doubt possessing WMD, UN inspectors not being up to the task, and liberated Iraqis erupting in joy all stayed in.[41]

No one in the White House admonished the vice president for the San Antonio speech.[42]

WHILE CHENEY WAS PULLING BUSH TOWARD WAR, TONY BLAIR WAS TUGGING as well, though not quite in the opposite direction.

The two heads of state spoke by phone just after Cheney's incendiary Nashville speech—which, a senior White House official would say, "hurt Blair. Cheney pissing on inspections—I mean, that was problematic for several weeks."[43] Bush acknowledged to the prime minister that the vice president had gone overboard with his rhetoric—though, he added defensively, Cheney's comments had come in reaction to Brent Scowcroft's unhelpful column. Blair's senior foreign policy adviser, David Manning, had also been summoned to the Oval Office recently. Much as he had told King Abdullah of Jordan on August 1, Bush described himself to Manning as "evangelical" on the matter of toppling Saddam—adding that he saw himself as a "good versus evil guy."[44]

"There was a battle for the president's attention," Manning would later say. "There were those advocating an early resort to force. But I concluded, after my visit to the United States and my conversation with the president, that his mind was not made up."[45]

Blair was in a position to wield meaningful influence over Bush. Five years into his tenure, the forty-nine-year-old prime minister was at the zenith of his power at home and enormously popular in the States. He was also a Christian, like Bush, and similarly prone to seeing the world in moralistic and optimistic terms. The two leaders spoke frequently, and it was evident to each man's advisers that Bush valued Blair's advice. As the senior White House official would reflect, "Blair could've been very persuasive. Had he come to the president directly and said, 'I've looked at all of this and I don't think there's a threat,' he could've had a real impact."[46]

But Blair did not advance that argument, for two reasons. First, he genuinely believed that Saddam constituted a threat. And second, for all his concerns about the Bush administration's headlong gallop into the unknown of war, Blair was unswervingly committed to the British-American alliance. "I will be with you, whatever," he had written in the first sentence of a note to the president on July 28. The next sentence—"But this is the moment to assess bluntly the difficulties"—was of lesser consequence.[47]

Blair and his team flew across the Atlantic on September 7. By the time they arrived at Camp David that afternoon, the prime minister had already learned that Cheney would be there as well.[48] So would Rice, but not Powell. Three days prior, in a CNN interview, the secretary had offered up soothing words about reported internal strife on the Iraq issue: "We're all good friends. There are no wars going on within the administration; there's good debate."[49] Blair's team knew better. They also knew that it would now fall to the prime minister to parry Cheney.

The vice president professed to have nothing against coalitions. After all, as the elder Bush's defense secretary during Operation Desert Storm, he had helped assemble one of the most awe-inspiring coalitions in modern history. But Cheney "just didn't like the UN," Rice would later say. "I think it's that simple."[50] In the vice president's view, the imminent threat posed by Saddam had provided the commander in chief with all the legal authority he needed to declare war.[51] Requesting the permission of an international body to protect

America's safety was not just wrongheaded; it also risked the country being dragged into endless debates and stalling on the part of France, Russia, Germany, and other nations that, for various reasons, did not want to see the United States invade Iraq. In the meantime, with American troops already being deployed to Kuwait, "bureaucratic logic was going to take over," one of Cheney's aides would say. "How long can you keep them deployed? And at what cost?"[52]

Bush himself had mixed feelings on the subject. On the one hand, his father had been the U.S. ambassador to the UN from 1971 to 1973. "International relations matter, alliances matter—he's his father's son," Fleischer would observe. That said, his appreciation for the body did not equate to reverence. When talking to foreign leaders, Bush often referred to the UN as a "quagmire."[53] Blair had heard the president's skepticism on this subject.[54]

What the prime minister did not know, heading to Camp David, was that Bush had already made up his mind to agree to UN inspections as a precondition for invading Iraq. That morning at Camp David, he had informed his national security team of this—adding unambiguously, "Either he will come clean about his weapons, or there will be war."[55]

Blair arrived with a message of his own. He wanted Bush to seek a new resolution from the UN, one that would codify a tough inspections regimen. If Saddam were to violate it, then the UK would commit to joining the United States in war. It would be, at minimum, a coalition of two.

Bush's relief was palpable. "Your man has got *cojones*," he told Alastair Campbell.[56] The president then supplied the translation: "balls." He added, "But it's the right thing to do, and future generations will surely thank us."

Cheney was visibly displeased by the president's decision.[57] But the battle was not over. The agreement was that Bush would discuss Iraq at the UN five days later, on September 12. Exactly what he would say there was still up for debate.

For Blair and Powell, the purpose of the speech could be only one thing. "There's no point going to the UN if you're not asking for action, which is a UN resolution," the secretary told Bush. Of course, as Powell reminded the president, "If it works, and we can get him to fess up and turn everything over, we might solve the problem of WMD—but he might still be there. Can you live with that?"[58]

This "changed regime" scenario was unpalatable to Cheney. But even if he accepted it, the vice president considered a new resolution a foolish way to bring it about. What if the UN members failed to pass it? Besides, UN resolutions prohibiting Saddam from retaining a WMD program had already been agreed to in the wake of the Gulf War. Instead, Cheney argued, Bush should go to the UN and demand one thing: a full weapons declaration from Saddam. If the dictator didn't hand over his weapons, that would be sufficient cause to take them from him by military force.

Speech drafts flew back and forth. Blair's advisers heard from the State Department that Rich Armitage and Scooter Libby were taking turns inserting and deleting "resolution" from the text.[59] On September 11, 2002—the first anniversary of the 9/11 attacks, and also the day before Bush was to deliver his speech—Blair's team reviewed what was said to be the final version. No mention was made of a UN resolution. After a few phone exchanges, Rice assured them that it would be included.[60]

The next morning in New York, the president stood before the UN General Assembly and delivered perhaps the most confident prepared speech he had uttered to date. "All the world now faces a test," he told them, "and the United Nations a difficult and defining moment. Are Security Council resolutions to be honored and enforced, or cast aside without consequence? Will the United Nations serve the purpose of its founding, or will it be irrelevant?"[61]

Though Bush would later claim to one of Blair's attendees, foreign minister Jack Straw, that "I picked your face out to look at, since it was your government that convinced me to go there,"[62] in fact Bush made a point of surveying the scowls of all the delegates, who clapped only once during his twenty-five-minute speech. They did not even applaud when he declared, "We will work with the UN Security Council for the necessary resolutions"—an unintended pluralization, but forgivable, given that Bush had ad-libbed the line, as mention of a "resolution" had once again mysteriously fallen out of the speech.[63]

Bush did not particularly care whether the speech had garnered him any admirers. He had fulfilled his obligations by being there and agreeing to a process. As Ari Fleischer would observe, "Bush almost always agreed with Rumsfeld and Cheney's hawkish objective of what to accomplish. He almost always agreed with Powell and Condi's tactics for how to get there. *Go to the UN. Ask for a resolution. Put the inspectors back.* Cheney and Rummy didn't support any of those."[64]

"We argued up to the night before the speech," Powell would later say. "We argued with everybody."[65] That Bush had at last sided with him and Blair felt, for the moment, like a satisfying victory. It thus unnerved the secretary when, shortly after Bush's UN speech, word reached him from a highly regarded individual in foreign policy circles: *Every time this adminis-tration gets in a jam, Powell dutifully tries to clean it up. Like in an alcoholic family. He's an enabler.*[66]

On top of which, Powell had not won anyway.

===

CHAPTER ELEVEN

DRUMBEATS

B y August 2002, Quonset huts were arrayed throughout the Kuwaiti desert at Camp Doha, in preparation for a war that the president had yet to declare.[1] The first deployments would arrive in September, under the guise of previously scheduled military exercises. But the appointment of the widely respected Lieutenant General David McKiernan, on September 4, to oversee the Coalition Forces Land Component Command (CFLCC) was an early shot fired—a clear signal to the U.S. military that, as an Army War College analysis would later state, "an invasion of Iraq was near certain to occur."[2]

To CENTCOM's war planners, one triumph had already been accomplished. From Bush's first briefing at Crawford on December 28, 2001, it had been evident that he, Rumsfeld, and others in the administration wanted the option to take the battle to Saddam immediately after deposing the Taliban. General Franks saw the futility of protesting. "His briefing approach," said one of the planners, "was that telling people like Rumsfeld no only hardens their resolve to go forward. So the brief would be 'Okay, Mr. Secretary, we took your guidance. Here's what everybody needs to do to make this happen.' There'd be twenty tasks on a slide. Four would be CENTCOM's. Six would be the services'. The rest would be State's. And we'd say, 'We're on our tasks.' We'd build it, hoping they'd see the light."

After Cheney's trip to the Middle East in March, the light became more difficult to ignore. A coalition, if Bush wanted one, would take time to assemble. Meanwhile, service leaders nervously signaled that their troops were far from ready. By June, the desert temperatures in Iraq had begun to hit triple digits. The first window for invasion had seemingly closed—thankfully, the planner recalled: "I think it's a victory that we didn't go in during the spring of 2002."[3]

Even so, the tenacious Paul Wolfowitz was not ready to let a little summer heat prevent action. In June 2002, the deputy secretary sent a snowflake of his own to the Third Army headquarters, stationed at Camp Arifjan, Kuwait. The note was succinct: "We have a brigade on the ground. Why can't we go now?"[4]

But another military option presented itself during the summer of 2002. In July, eight CIA case officers traveled to Kurdistan to interrogate several detained members of the terrorist group Ansar al-Islam who had previously been interviewed by Jeffrey Goldberg of *The New Yorker*. According to Goldberg's article, the detainees admitted that they had used chemical weapons in Afghanistan that had been produced in the northern Iraq city of Khurmal, near the Iran border.[5]

No physical evidence existed that such production was taking place. Still, the basis for conducting air strikes on Khurmal was compelling to many inside the Pentagon. The CIA interrogators were told that cyanide had been produced and tested on live animals (and possibly the terrorists' own associates).[6] Though there had been debate over whether one of the terrorists in Khurmal, Abu Musab al-Zarqawi, had any ties to Saddam, his affiliation with Al Qaeda was beyond dispute. An assessment in early July by the State Department's intelligence bureau, INR, determined that bombing Khurmal "would cause concern in Tehran but probably would not prompt an Iranian military response."[7]

Rumsfeld and Cheney both argued in favor of a Tomahawk missile strike, followed by a boots-on-the-ground military investigation of the Khurmal facility. The Joint Chiefs unanimously concurred, as did Tenet. But Powell maintained that bombing Khurmal would collapse his coalition-building efforts. Any chance of enlisting support from the Turks would be undone, he predicted. Alone with Bush in the Oval Office, Rice told him that she agreed with Powell. Persuaded by her and Powell, Bush "decided to wait and let the larger Iraq strategy play out over the following months," Rice later wrote.[8]

That President Bush had elected to let the alleged WMD activities in northern Iraq go unpunished was a dismaying turn of events for JCS director of operations General Gregory Newbold. It was also a rare moment when he happened to agree with Rumsfeld and Cheney. After all, Newbold thought, hadn't the president pledged to the American public that the administration would hunt down terrorists seeking to do America harm and bring them to justice? Well, here they were: tracked from Afghanistan all the way to northern Iraq, and now assembling weapons that they intended to use against the United States. What was the war on terror about, if not this?

Newbold suspected he knew the answer. The president was more interested in what Rice would term "the larger Iraq strategy" than in actually killing terrorists. Taking down Saddam, the suspected enemy of America, took precedence over systematically destroying the known enemy, Al Qaeda.

The JCS director of operations saw evidence to support this suspicion. By early 2002, the two crucial elements in hunting down Al Qaeda—reconnaissance and strike drones and special operations forces—had been taken out of Afghanistan and reassigned to Iraq.

Along with many of his fellow generals, Greg Newbold had high hopes for the Bush administration. He had not approved of Clinton's equivocating foreign policy. He revered former JCS chairman Powell. He regarded Cheney and Rumsfeld as capable and experienced men. And, as a former Marine lieutenant during the disaster of Vietnam, the three-star general believed that the execution and restraint shown in Operation Desert Storm by the first President Bush had restored America to "the pinnacle of respect."

But disillusionment was soon to creep in as the new DOD team began derisively referring to the JCS staff as the "Clinton generals." At Principals

Committee meetings, Newbold saw the cutting disdain Rumsfeld showed for Powell and George Tenet. He experienced that same behavior a month after 9/11, when Rumsfeld publicly belittled Newbold for remarking that the Taliban had been "eviscerated" in battle.

Most egregious, however, was the administration's inexplicable blood-lust for Saddam. In Newbold's view, the dictator was a contemptible brute. But the Bush White House had somehow succeeded in elevating a petty despot to an international powerhouse.

Early in 2002, Paul Wolfowitz had invited him into his office. The deputy secretary asked, "What do you think about just striking and seizing the southern oil fields?"

Not knowing that this was Wolfowitz's cause célèbre, the general replied, "I think that's a crazy idea. It's counterproductive. You don't achieve any of the objectives—you certainly won't overthrow Saddam Hussein, because he could care less. He doesn't suffer a loss of money. He doesn't starve like the people would. He just gains an enormous victory internationally, because it reinforces all the negative stereotypes that the U.S. is only after oil."

The deputy secretary simply listened, then thanked Newbold. At least Wolfowitz seemed gentlemanly, unlike his boss, and intellectually open, unlike Wolfowitz's subordinate Doug Feith. During the spring of 2002, as the Pentagon began discreetly moving scarce intelligence assets from Afghanistan into the Middle East, Newbold happened to be standing next to the undersecretary before a meeting. "Doug," he said, "we're working on establishing basing rights for the assets we're moving over there."

Newbold cited countries like Oman and Kuwait as having been willing negotiators. He added, "We think it's going to be successful."

Feith replied dismissively, "You don't understand Arabs. You need to *tell* them what we're doing. They respect strength."

In May 2002, Greg Newbold informed James Jones, the commandant of the Marine Corps, that he could see the inevitability of war and thought it was a serious mistake. "Look, I'm willing to resign, put my stars on the table to help you and others to make the point this thing is flawed," he told Jones.

In effect, he was giving Jones the opportunity to go to President Bush and say that a top general was quitting in protest of Iraq policy. It could be, if Jones wished it, "a precipitating action."

Jones fell silent. Then he thanked Newbold, to whom it was evident that the Marine commandant preferred not to start a brush fire.

In early September, after Greg Newbold's resignation had been announced, the JCS senior staff held a routine meeting presided over by Vice Chairman Peter Pace. After various routine items were discussed, the director of operations asked to speak.

Newbold got straight to the point. Going to war in Iraq was a huge mistake. "We're using three reasons for going to war: he's disruptive in the Middle East, he's supportive of terrorism, and he's got WMD," Newbold said. On the first point, no one in the region feared Saddam anymore—not Kuwait, not Jordan, not Iran, not Israel. On the second, giving money to the families of Palestinian suicide bombers did not constitute a threat to America.

"And I don't doubt he has WMD," Newbold continued. "But among the nations that have WMD that pose a threat to the U.S., where does Iraq rank? Somewhere after Iran, Syria, and Pakistan."

After Newbold had finished, Pace looked at the other senior staff. "What do you think?" he asked.

A few nodded their assent. Only one, General George Casey, offered the slightest rebuttal. "I do think we have to overthrow Saddam," Casey said. "I just don't know why we have to do it now."[9]

The following evening, one of the meeting attendees, General Mark Hertling, the chief of war plans for the JCS, walked into the office of General John Abizaid, who had not been at the meeting chaired by Pace.

"You know, we had this session where all of us kind of voted on what we were doing," Hertling said. "I'd just like to be a little bit more adamant in my approach. I really think we're setting ourselves up for a disaster." Based on the war plans he had seen, Hertling worried that CENTCOM was not adequately prepared for urban warfare in Baghdad. "And I wouldn't feel right unless I expressed that to you," he finished.

Casey walked in. Abizaid told him, "I'm just talking to Mark here, and he says he thinks this is a big mistake. He's elaborating on the things everyone said in the meeting the other day."

The JCS director of strategy glared at Hertling. "So a newly minted one-star general is going to tell us what's strategically correct or not, huh?" he observed.

Hertling protested that he was only raising tactical concerns. Abizaid decided that it was time to head out for the evening.

The next day, however, Abizaid visited Hertling's office. He closed the door. "I got it," he said quietly. "I understand what you're saying. The momentum may be too great to stop. But I appreciate your courage."[10]

Greg Newbold's announced resignation and speech to his JCS colleagues had not fomented a "precipitating moment." The generals were cowed. The deployments continued, creating a locomotion with its own irresistible dynamic: billions spent, unique assets coalescing, tens of thousands of American soldiers on a desert stage with the clock ticking ever faster.

THE RUMORS WAFTING OVER THE PENTAGON THAT GENERALS LIKE GREG Newbold and Mark Hertling had reservations about invading Iraq did not surprise Wolfowitz. It had long been his experience that the military bureaucracy tended to undermine any idea that was not its own.

A student of the Civil War as well as a policy bureaucrat during the Cold War, the deputy secretary "had this outsize view of his military understanding and qualifications," recalled one of his aides. "But he'd never lived in the culture of the Pentagon. He thought he could just tell people what to do and it would happen."[11]

By the summer of 2002, Wolfowitz was cognizant of war's dangers. Saddam could use chemical weapons on American troops. He could massacre civilian foes, real and perceived. A Scud missile attack by Saddam on Israel could draw the latter country into the fight, and thus fracture support from Arab allies.

"I think the getting in is the dangerous part," he told *New York Times* writer and editor Bill Keller that summer. But once Saddam's army surrendered, Wolfowitz believed, a miraculous tableau would unfold. Iraq might well become "the first Arab democracy." Was this so wild a dream? The Afghans—poor, illiterate, wholly unaccustomed to republican governance—now had one of their own, Hamid Karzai, as a leader. By comparison, Iraq's population was relatively well educated, its bureaucrats were talented, and its oil economy was self-sustaining.

For years now, Wolfowitz had been promoting the idea that Iraqis would, if given a chance, lunge at the opportunity for democracy. Now that belief was embedded in CENTCOM's war plans.[12] It was embedded in the president, who would tell a group of conservative commentators in the Oval Office, "It's important for the world to see that first of all, Iraq is a sophisticated society with about $16 billion of income. The degree of difficulty compared to Afghanistan in terms of the reconstruction effort, or emerging from dictatorship, is, like, infinitesimal. I mean, Afghanistan has *zero*."[13]

Wolfowitz had no firsthand knowledge of how Iraqis would receive American troops. Though his experiences as ambassador to Indonesia supported the view that Muslim nations were capable of religious tolerance, Iraq was a country beset by altogether different factors. And though Kanan Makiya had, in *Republic of Fear*, laid out a powerful case for the wholesale suffering of Iraqis under the yoke of a Baathist dictatorship, Makiya himself had not visited Iraq in decades.

Remembered Wolfowitz's aide, "The parade of people coming to see him and saying 'They just want to be liberated' were mostly Iraqi expats who were looking to burrow in after the invasion."[14] Chief among the visiting burrowers-to-be was Ahmad Chalabi, who himself had not seen Baghdad in nearly a half century. Late one evening during the summer of 2002, Wolfowitz met with a friendly British journalist, David Rose, of *The Observer* and *Vanity Fair*, on the garden patio of Washington's Fairmont Hotel. The deputy secretary had brought along his daughter, Rachel, an aspiring journalist. His eyes were bright as he recounted what Chalabi had told him: *If you can solve Iraq, you can solve Israel–Palestine. The real motor of the continuing conflict is Saddam. If you lose Saddam, you can have peace throughout the region.*

"This could be so huge," murmured Wolfowitz. His emotional investment in overthrowing Saddam, Rose could see, was anything but feigned.[15]

One afternoon in his office, Wolfowitz asked a CIA case officer named
John Maguire, the deputy chief of the Iraq Operations Group, "Why do you
hate Chalabi?"

"I don't," protested Maguire. "One of the most intelligent men I've ever
met. I really admire him. He's survived in one of the biggest shark tanks in
the world. But he has his own agenda, and he can hurt the U.S. And we've
caught him lying, and as an agency officer we have a duty to spend taxpayer
money judiciously and get results."[16]

To Wolfowitz, this small-minded thinking was emblematic of the agency's ineptness. So what if Chalabi lied and stole? So what if he had an agenda?
One did not "survive in one of the biggest shark tanks in the world" by behav-
ing like a guppy.

Besides, Chalabi had more than an agenda. He had a plan. It was, in
fact, the scheme Wolfowitz had been touting for years, the one he had hinted
at to President Bush at Camp David: the so-called Downing Plan, devised
by Chalabi and a former U.S. Special Forces commander, General Wayne A.
Downing, that would use American air power to establish an enclave in
southern Iraq from which a rebel Iraqi fighting force could be mustered to
march northward and seize Baghdad. It was the same plan that Chalabi
claimed, in his 1998 congressional testimony, would cost the American taxpayer nothing. In reality, as Chalabi conceded when showing the plan to
weapons inspector Scott Ritter that same year, a greater U.S. military commitment would be necessary—but, he added, "we don't have to highlight it
at this time."[17]

After 9/11, and particularly after the anthrax scare, Wolfowitz had become convinced that the threat posed by Saddam was too severe to settle for
a low-cost, indigenous remedy. Nothing less than a full U.S. military invasion would do. But, he thought, what if the invasion were led by Iraqis?
Recruiting such a brigade as the tip of the spear would reinforce the argument that this was about liberation, rather than the malign impulse of oil-
thirsty Western occupiers.

The so-called Free Iraqi Forces idea "was very much Wolfowitz," recalled a senior Pentagon official.[18] To promote the FIF within CENTCOM, he deputized Feith, who had already dispatched two of his aides, Abram Shulsky and Bill Bruner, to Tampa with the express purpose of "arguing the importance of working with the [Iraqi] externals," as Feith would later say.[19]

Later in the spring of 2002, a group of about ten exiles, including Chalabi, were summoned to Feith's office. An NSC aide and retired Marine colonel named Tom Greenwood was dispatched by his boss at the NSC, Senior Director of Defense Policy Frank Miller, to sit in on the meeting. Feith did not let Greenwood inside. He nonetheless marveled in the anteroom at the expensive suits worn by the Iraqis. Shaking their smooth hands, the Marine thought, "These are not war fighters."[20]

Feith believed that could be remedied easily enough. His assistant secretary for international security affairs, a Kissinger protégé named Peter Rodman, fired off a memo on May 9 arguing, "Regional leaders seem to be of the view that Iraqis need to be seen as participating in the liberation of their country."

Anticipating that some might scoff at the idea, Rodman then pointed out that Roosevelt and Churchill had planned to occupy postwar France, rather than entrust that responsibility to the leader of the French Resistance, Charles de Gaulle. "They considered de Gaulle a phoney," Rodman wrote. "Only when de Gaulle was greeted by millions of cheering Frenchmen in June 1944 did they conclude that he indeed represented free France."[21]

Intentionally or not, Rodman and Feith were inviting comparisons between the legendary army officer de Gaulle and Ahmad Chalabi. The undersecretary sent Rodman's memo to Rumsfeld, who liked it enough to recommend that the information in it be transmitted to the NSC. Delighted by the secretary's reaction, Feith dashed off a note to Rodman: "This shd go out on Monday 5/20. Glad that SD [the secretary of defense] liked your memo. Do it as a memo from SD to Principals (VP, Powell, Rice, Tenet)."[22]

By refashioning Rodman's memo so that the idea bore Rumsfeld's letterhead,[23] Feith was hoping that the secretary would then throw his wholehearted support behind the Free Iraqi Forces. The undersecretary was somewhat chagrined, then, when Rumsfeld elected not to personally brief the planners at CENTCOM on the matter but to have Feith do it instead.

Feith did so, in July 2002. General Franks, recognizing that Rumsfeld was implicitly distancing himself from the FIF, made no attempt to disguise his low opinion of the idea. Franks's team regarded the Chalabi exiles as "Gucci Iraqis."[24] Franks himself coined a unique epithet for the Free Iraqi Forces: he referred to them as "fin-stabilized buttfuckers."[25] The CENT-COM commander later told Feith, after sitting through another briefing on the subject that Rumsfeld had also attended, "Doug, I don't have time for this fucking bullshit."[26]

But Feith already had Rumsfeld's signature, if not his enthusiasm. To keep the program on track, the undersecretary threw it over to his deputy undersecretary of defense for Near Eastern and South Asian affairs, William Luti, a retired Navy captain and *Drudge Report*–reading ideologue whose duties were notably wide-ranging.[27] In late April 2002, Feith had requested that Luti be promoted to assistant secretary for "special plans"—a moniker that would later launch a thousand conspiracy theories but simply meant that Bill Luti was Feith's point man for Iraq.

Luti, who had flown combat missions during the Gulf War, had the proper zeal for the job. Months before 9/11, he had informed an associate at the Pentagon, "They brought me here to take out Saddam."[28] During a briefing in August 2001 with Luis Rueda, the CIA's chief of the Iraq Operations Group, Luti volunteered his view, while Wolfowitz looked on approvingly, that the Downing Plan could easily trounce the Iraqi army: "One squadron of F-18s will take out the entire military in an afternoon, and we're done."

After the meeting, a JCS senior staffer took Rueda aside. "You have to understand," the general said quietly, looking over at Luti, "he doesn't speak for us." After that, Rueda instructed his deputies to refer any calls or memos from Luti to someone other than himself.[29]

Luti was effusively supportive of Chalabi's Iraqi National Congress.[30] "Chalabi could have told Luti that the sun came up at midnight and he'd have his sunglasses on," recalled one Pentagon aide.[31] And as someone who shared Wolfowitz's dim view of the CIA and State, the special plans overseer often played to the deputy secretary's fears that those institutions were colluding in an effort to slow down the march to war. "Luti would barge into his office," the Wolfowitz aide would recall, "and the common refrain was 'Paul, it's a fucking conspiracy.'"[32]

But it soon became apparent that recruiting and vetting potential members of the Free Iraqi Forces was a full-time job, one that would require more time than the intrepid Luti could devote to it. To that end, in the summer of 2002, Feith hired Christopher Straub, a much-respected former staff director for the Senate Select Committee on Intelligence. Though Straub's boss on the committee had been a Democrat, this was not a disqualifier. The Democrat in question was Senator Bob Kerrey, a fervent supporter of overthrowing Saddam Hussein. Straub shared with Kerrey a deep abhorrence of Saddam's brutal treatment of the Iraqi people. As someone who served twenty-two years in the Army, Straub commanded a level of respect from CENTCOM that Feith did not. And as a bonus, Straub had known Chalabi since 1989 and was an unabashed supporter of the Iraqi National Congress.

Straub's first task was to assemble a list of potential FIF recruits. For this he turned to Chalabi. The INC produced a list of several thousand names, mostly from the United States and Europe.

Straub then approached commanders of the Army, valiantly endeavoring to pitch the notion of overweight and soft-faced expatriates being converted into combat-capable additions to the U.S. Army. "They thought it was a political stunt," he recalled. It did not help Straub's cause that Chalabi was seen by the commanders as the not-so-silent hand behind the FIF, one who fancied himself an Iraqi de Gaulle, though without the military bona fides to show for it. ("We didn't have a lot of confidence in Chalabi from a military perspective," one of the CENTCOM planners acknowledged. "We saw him as a political and not a fricking war fighter. You don't need a bunch of politicals on the battlefield.")[33]

The agency's low regard for the FIF—shared by State, by Rice, and above all by CENTCOM—was more a judgment of the concept's authors than of the idea itself. None of the principals in the Bush administration— including Tenet and Powell—believed that a Western occupying force would play well in the Middle East. When the concept was briefed by Luti at a Deputies Lunch on August 20, 2002, all of them seemed to find virtue in having Iraqi liaisons, interpreters, scouts, and prison guards accompany U.S. forces.[34] Later, Luti proposed that some fifteen hundred to two thousand Iraqi expats be embedded as military police.[35]

But, as Hadley would later say, "this whole issue of the role of an Iraqi force was very tied up with Chalabi. And that made it controversial. State didn't think much of it. And the agency certainly didn't think much of Chalabi. My view was 'Look, let's try everything.' But, you know, Chalabi promised all kinds of numbers of people. Never delivered."[36]

In truth, Chalabi did deliver thousands of names. But the men belonging to those names did not interpret the "Free" in FIF's name to signify that they would be risking their lives as unpaid volunteers. Straub consulted with the Army's legal staff. The lawyers informed him that if the recruits received more than the U.S. military's lowest-grade private ranking, they would legally qualify as mercenaries. A team of mercenaries invading Iraq would not be regarded as liberators. This meant that the recruits would have to be paid less: about $1,200 a month. Suddenly, the prospect of getting shot at by Saddam's army in return for a minimum wage—and only after an invasive background check—considerably lessened the romantic appeal of the Free Iraqi Forces.

"Thousands of names," Straub would lament. "But I could not get those people to come, for all kinds of reasons. Some of them probably didn't exist. But in any event, they didn't show up."[37]

EVEN AS IT WAS BECOMING APPARENT THAT GEORGE W. BUSH HAD SETTLED on a path of diplomacy—taking matters to the United Nations and giving Saddam Hussein one last chance to comply with international law—Feith and Wolfowitz were aggressively mounting a case for war.

In late August, while the war council had scattered for the summer break—Bush and Rice in Texas, Cheney and Libby in Wyoming, Rumsfeld in New Mexico, and Powell in the Hamptons—Feith was doggedly at work on a memo he entitled "The Case Against Iraq." Condi Rice had just recently circulated an NSC paper called "Iraq: Goals, Objectives, Strategy,"[38] but that memo was largely intended to get the principals on the same page when publicly discussing aspirations for a new Iraq. Feith's paper, by contrast, was intended only for Secretary Rumsfeld's office, as well as for fellow hard-liners such as Libby and John Hannah.

The document had three sections. The first consisted of four arguments for regime change: Saddam's WMD program, his "direct involvement in terrorism" (including, Feith asserted, support for Al Qaeda), his prior invasions of Kuwait and Iran well over a decade earlier, and the repressiveness of his regime. Then Feith offered two legal justifications for war: Saddam's violation of UN resolutions and a concept known as "anticipatory self-defense," legalese for Bush's resolve to take preemptive action against perceived threats to America. Finally, Feith ticked off a "vision for Iraq's future," which emphasized building democratic institutions and "working with Iraqi opposition groups to plan for the post-Saddam regime."[39]

On September 12, 2002, the very day that Bush publicly exhorted the UN to hold Saddam's feet to the fire, Feith produced a second internal memo arguing that it was time to throw the dictator into the fire altogether. Entitled "The Case for Action," the memo elaborately laid out Feith and Wolfowitz's argument for going to war. Leaning heavily on the 9/11 experience, the undersecretary wrote, "We have more information *now* about what Iraq might do than we had *last year* about [what] al Qaida might do."

Feith devoted no space in this ten-page document to elaborating on exactly what Saddam "might do." He did, however, broadly describe the dictator as "a megalomaniac tyrant" with "tremendous geopolitical ambition." Feith devoted three pages to how "Iraq's pursuit of WMD has been continuing" while warning, "Experience tells us that what we have found is only a small part of what actually is there." Then, in enumerating "Iraq's ties to al Qaida," Feith relied on the raw intelligence that Christina Shelton and Christopher Carney had assembled and presented to a roomful of skeptical CIA analysts a month earlier.

Feith's memo revealed some contradictions inherent in the Iraq hawks' thinking. In anticipating the objection *Why Iraq rather than North Korea or*

Iran?, Feith quoted Lincoln's "one war at a time" doctrine—thereby neglecting to acknowledge his and Wolfowitz's stated desires to wage war on Iraq and Afghanistan simultaneously after 9/11. Unlike the previous memo, "The Case for Action" did not discuss democracy as a paramount objective. On the contrary, Feith unironically argued that, while an invasion might create turmoil in the region, "Arab regimes tend to be good at handling the 'street.'" The undersecretary also claimed in the memo that toppling Saddam "will help convince Palestinians that there is no alternative to peace." Yet he also observed that after Afghanistan, certain state sponsors of terror—Feith did not specify which ones—had "started to indicate willingness to cooperate with us" but that this show of good behavior "has begun to wear off." Hypothesized Feith, "Success in Iraq will reinvigorate it."[40]

Feith's reasoning may have been questionable. But his fervor had gathered locomotion in the NSC, where the ever-cautious Steve Hadley had decided that even if the president elected not to depose Saddam, the deputies had better be ready with an argument for why he should do so, just in case. Two days after Bush's UN speech and Feith's "Case for Action" memo, on Saturday, September 14, Hadley convened an emergency meeting of the deputies in the Situation Room. Hadley had entitled the agenda "Why Iraq Now?"

Attending for the CIA were two analysts and Bob Walpole, the agency's national intelligence officer for strategic programs. Walpole, a longtime weapons expert in the intelligence bureaucracy, had known Hadley going back to the first Bush administration. Unaware of the months of rancorous debate over Iraq that had preceded this meeting, he said, "Steve, I wouldn't do this."

Referring to nuclear capabilities, he went on, "Iraq is behind North Korea. Why are you worried about a country that *might* be working on nuclear weapons, as opposed to a country that's working on a means to deliver it? I mean, when North Korea's covert uranium program becomes public, you're going to have a devil of a time explaining why you're focused on Iraq."

Scooter Libby turned to Feith, who was seated next to him. Loud enough for others to hear, he asked with exasperation, "Who is this guy?"

Feith spoke up. Iraq's support for terror made Saddam a greater threat than North Korea, he argued. One of the analysts then said that if this was the concern, they should all be talking about Iran, not Iraq.

By the time the meeting adjourned, it was evident to Bob Walpole that his warning had not been absorbed by Hadley. They had their case for war, and they were sticking to it. Walpole reported his concerns to Tenet.[41]

The CIA director was hardly surprised. He himself had been preparing his agency for war for months now. In July, the first eight CIA operatives had set up camp in northern Iraq, only a few miles from the alleged chemical weapons laboratory in Khurmal. Their mission was to penetrate the Iraqi military and intelligence apparatuses—something the agency had tried and failed to do for more than a decade. In recruiting Iraqi assets, one of the operatives recalled, "We used this a lot: 'You guys don't understand. This is personal. You tried to kill his father, and now he's going to try to kill you all!' And they understood the blood feud."[42]

That same month, the CIA hosted a "peace game" at the Army War College, in Carlisle, Pennsylvania. The exercise presupposed that U.S. and UK forces had successfully toppled the regime in six weeks' time. Then, in keeping with the scenario envisioned in the State Department's "Perfect Storm" memo, a Sunni general murdered Saddam and assumed control of Baghdad. Meanwhile, the Kurds maintained autonomy in the north while various Shia elements fought among themselves in the south.[43] What quickly became evident in the simulation, according to one of the CIA participants, was that "there's nobody to replace Saddam. Every blade of grass that had stuck its head up had been chopped off by the regime."[44] Or, as another agency participant put it, "We didn't have any sense of how to fix what was broken. That's what was clear, and that's how we wrote it up, and I don't think much attention was paid to it at the time."[45]

A month later, in August, Tenet and his deputy director of operations, Jim Pavitt, met at Tenet's vacation home on the Jersey Shore. The director had also summoned his former chief of station in Islamabad, Bob Grenier. "I think we're going to be at war in Iraq," Tenet said grimly. "I don't have any inside information on it. They haven't given me a date. But I think this is going to happen, and it may happen as early as December."

Tenet then told Grenier to "get smart on Iraq," because he was going to be the agency's interagency point man on the subject thereafter.[46] Pavitt, in the meantime, dispatched associate deputy director for operations Steve Kappes and Iraq Operations Group chief Luis Rueda to London and Riyadh, to meet with two dozen CIA station chiefs who were posted in Europe and the Middle East. For months now, those chiefs had been hearing the rumors and had spent considerable time consoling their skittish intelligence counterparts in those countries: *No, America isn't going to invade Iraq. It's all just political posturing.*

To their astonishment, Kappes informed them otherwise: "Get your stations in gear. We are going to war, and we need you to bust your asses to support this. We expect you to recruit targets."[47]

BILL LUTI WAS ALSO MAKING THE ROUNDS IN THE LATE SUMMER OF 2002. Luti happened to be in Cairo when the U.S. ambassador to Egypt, David Welch, was hosting a reception. Standing in the garden, the assistant secretary for special plans proceeded to describe to the other guests the unique threat posed by Saddam Hussein. Among other things, Luti told them, "Saddam has nuclear weapons."

Ambassador Welch was startled to hear so bold a statement. "Bill," he said, "I appreciate you evaluating the risk here. But have you commissioned a NIE on this?"

Welch was referring to a National Intelligence Estimate, which represented the intelligence community's combined assessment of a particular country's threat capability. Luti confidently waved him off.

"We don't need one," he declared. "We already know it."[48]

CHAPTER TWELVE

===

BALLPARK ESTIMATES

As it became increasingly apparent to George Tenet during the summer of 2002 that the Bush administration was intent on going to war in Iraq, a CIA senior Iraq analyst named Colin Winston was dispatched from Langley to London, Berlin, and Ankara to brief the agency's counterparts in those countries on the threat posed by Saddam Hussein's WMD program. Winston's briefings with the British and Turkish liaison services went well. The Germans were less convinced. Much of the satellite imagery appeared inconclusive—an unidentified building, trucks driving in and out—and Winston's monologue was laced with "mights" and "coulds." The Germans traded bored stares; one of them fell asleep.

Winston's final stop was in Brussels, at NATO headquarters, with General Joseph Ralston, NATO's supreme allied commander. The analyst had already briefed the NATO intelligence specialists, who seemed impressed. Winston had every reason to believe that Ralston—who had no particular expertise in illicit weapons systems but had directed the no-fly-zone enforcement over Kurdish territory in northern Iraq—would be similarly appreciative.

Instead, the NATO commander glared at the briefing slides with palpable skepticism. "What did you say that factory is for?" he asked.

"It's used to make chlorine," Winston said, referring to the image of a sixty-eight-acre facility in Fallujah protected by walls and guard towers.

"So?"

The chlorine, Winston explained, could be used to manufacture mustard gas, or perhaps nerve gases like sarin and tabun.

"You can't make that leap," the general argued. Gesturing to the aerial image of the long, seemingly unremarkable building, Ralston continued, "This doesn't prove anything. It's not illegal to make chlorine. You need chlorine to clean water."

"Well, he's making more than he needs for that," Winston insisted.

"Well, how much does he need?"

Winston didn't know. Ralston informed the analyst that his case was "less than compelling" and showed him the door.

Once outside, a NATO colonel consoled Winston. "He's never satisfied," the colonel said.

The CIA analyst left NATO headquarters with a different reaction: *Ralston asked all the right questions. The questions no one else was asking me.*[1]

DONALD RUMSFELD WAS ASKING THE RIGHT QUESTIONS, TOO.

"You intel guys are all alike," he said one day in late August 2002 to Major General Glen Shaffer, the Joint Chiefs director of intelligence. "You just tell me what you know about Iraqi WMD. I want you to tell me what you *don't* know about it."

Shaffer and the other staffers in the room looked at one another, unsure how to respond. More emphatically, the secretary said, "Tell me what it is you think you know but you don't know for sure." In other words, the "known unknowns." With that, Rumsfeld concluded the meeting.

Shaffer sought out one of his best DIA desk analysts and transmitted the secretary's marching orders.[2] The analyst spent about two weeks reorganizing and studying the intelligence community's WMD information relating to Iraq. On September 5, Shaffer sent the results over to Rumsfeld in the form of six briefing slides with a cover page. "Iraq: Status of WMD Programs," it read.

"We assess Iraq is making significant progress in WMD programs," the memo began. Then followed a cascade of caveats: "Our assessments rely heavily on analytic assumptions and judgment rather than hard evidence. . . . We don't know with any precision how much we don't know.

"Our knowledge of the Iraqi nuclear weapons program is based largely— perhaps 90%—on analysis of imprecise intelligence," it went on. Regarding Saddam's biological weapons program, "our knowledge of how and where they are produced is probably up to 90% incomplete." The chemical weapons intel was "60–70% incomplete." For ballistic missile production, the knowledge base "is about half complete."

In other words, the intelligence community knew little to nothing about Saddam's weapons program. Its beliefs rested on a wafer-thin mattress of evidence.

"Please take a look at this material as to what we don't know about WMD," Rumsfeld wrote to JCS chairman Myers four days later. "It is big."[3]

But as was so often the case with the secretary of defense, the intellectual exercise of finding fault with another government agency seemed more important to him than the follow-through. Rumsfeld did not request that General Shaffer brief the CIA on its overconfidence about WMD, as he had urged Doug Feith to brief the agency on its underconfidence about Saddam's connections to Al Qaeda a month earlier. In fact, Rumsfeld did not follow up on the memo and its "big" findings with Shaffer, with the NSC, or with the president.

To be fair, it was a busy time. The Pentagon was preparing for war against a dangerous foe, which Rumsfeld described in this manner on *Fox News Sunday*, less than one hour before he sent Myers the sobering Shaffer memo with its findings as to "what we don't know about WMD":

"They have an appetite for weapons of mass destruction. They have been, every period since they've been able to get the inspectors out of there, working diligently to increase their capabilities in every aspect of weapons of mass destruction and ballistic missile technology. And as they get somewhat stronger, the problem gets somewhat greater."[4]

SADDAM'S POSSESSING WEAPONS OF MASS DESTRUCTION WAS "THE WHOLE ball of wax," Tony Blair confided to one of his top national security advisers— meaning that it offered the clearest, least controversial justification for war.[5] Blair himself wanted to see Saddam overthrown (albeit under the right circumstances), even if the dictator did not possess such weapons, as he would disclose years later in an interview while also admitting, "I mean, obviously you would have had to use and deploy different arguments about the nature of the threat."[6] Among the available "different arguments" to deploy, the British intelligence community rejected wholesale the claim by Cheney, Wolfowitz, and others that the Iraqi dictator had meaningful ties to Al Qaeda. One could even debate whether Saddam intended to do harm to the West, to Israel, or to his neighbors.

But here were incontrovertible facts: Saddam had possessed and used WMD in the past. He was proscribed by international law from having such weapons now. His regime had repeatedly lied to UN inspectors in an effort to conceal its past weapons program. And Iraq had not fully accounted for those weapons it now claimed were destroyed. Based on those facts, the overwhelming consensus within the intelligence community was that Saddam still retained some weapons, had retained the ability to produce more, and had ambitions of doing exactly that. It was, as Paul Wolfowitz famously told the journalist Sam Tanenhaus in *Vanity Fair*, "the one issue that everyone could agree on."[7]

Agreement about WMD became a seductive force of its own, a panacea to months of rancor and dysfunction. The consensus felt not only welcome but sensible, a moment of great minds thinking alike (at last). But, as in the case of most seductions, "thinking" lost the upper hand. For what everyone was agreeing on was little more than a series of hunches. The hunches were based on information that was badly outdated, almost completely circumstantial, and often fabricated.

The providers of the information frequently were individuals who had a vested interest in Saddam's removal. And the recipients were intelligence officials who also lacked dispassion. From their knowledge base, they had seen much to despise about Saddam and had been antagonized over the years by his maddening deceptions. Perhaps more to the point, the intelligence community had, in the past, gotten it wrong about Saddam's nuclear weapons program, a fact that Cheney and Wolfowitz never tired of pointing out. After 9/11, underestimating threats had become, in intelligence circles, the one unpardonable sin.

The CIA had learned this the hard way years before the September 11 attacks. In 1998, the ballistic missile commission chaired by Donald Rumsfeld condemned the National Intelligence Estimate published by the intelligence community in 1995. That assessment, like others before it, focused on likely ballistic missile threats to the United States. The NIE predicted—accurately, as it would later turn out—that Iran, North Korea, and Iraq would not produce intercontinental ballistic missiles before 2010. A panel headed by former CIA director Robert Gates agreed with that finding in 1996.

But national security hawks who had long been pushing for a strategic defense missile system were offended by such breezy estimations. The Rumsfeld Commission was thereby empaneled, providing Rumsfeld, Wolfowitz, and others with a forum to chastise the CIA for its shortsightedness. Faulting intelligence officials for focusing solely on what was *likely* to happen, and ignoring what *could* happen, the commission report argued that the threats posed by North Korea, Iran, and Iraq were far greater than the 1995 NIE had depicted. Its section pertaining to the Iraq threat offered a how-to on speculative threat assessment (with emphases added by this author): "Once UN-imposed controls are lifted, Iraq *could* mount a determined effort to acquire needed plant and equipment. . . . Iraq *could* develop a shorter range, covert, ship-launched missile threat that *could* threaten the United States in a very short time. . . . Prior to the invasion of Kuwait in 1990, Iraq *could* have had nuclear weapons in the 1993–1995 time frame, although it still had technical hurdles to overcome. . . . Knowledge, personnel, and equipment related to WMD remain in Iraq, so that it *could* reconstitute these programs rapidly following the end of sanctions."[8]

The commission issued its doomful forecasts confident in the knowledge that when it comes to national security, such dark soothsaying, once disproven over time, typically goes unpunished. By contrast, when, in October 1998, North Korea completed the successful third stage of the Taepodong-1 ballistic missile test—something that the 1995 NIE had failed to anticipate—the Rumsfeld Commission gleefully declared it an aha moment. Chastened, the CIA announced that the next NIE, published in 2000, would include "coulds" as well as "likelys."[9] In an additional act of subservience, that NIE's author requested that Rumsfeld serve as an outside adviser.[10]

To some, this capitulation smacked of politicization, auguring a sci-fi approach to threat assessments. "There were those of us who argued, *That's not analysis, that's imagination*," recalled Tom Fingar, the deputy director of the State Department's Bureau of Intelligence and Research. "You know: *Let's stop spending money on intelligence when you've got a bunch of clever guys who can make stuff up*."[11]

BECAUSE THERE WAS SUCH WIDESPREAD AGREEMENT IN THE BUSH ADMINistration that Saddam had some sort of prohibited weapons program, George Tenet was not prepared for the request made by Senator Dick Durbin during the first week of September 2002. Durbin's request was a basic one: *Where is your current National Intelligence Estimate on Iraq?*

Tenet didn't have such an estimate. Upon learning this, Durbin said the following week on the Senate floor, "I was stunned. . . . What is incredible, with all of the statements made by members of this administration about those weapons, is the fact that the intelligence community has not been brought together." The Illinois Democrat then proceeded to throw down the gauntlet: "It is time for the administration to rise to the occasion, to produce this evidence, as has been asked for and been produced so many times in the past when America's national security was at risk. We cannot accept anything less than that before any member of the House or the Senate is asked to vote on this critical question of going to war."[12]

Durbin was essentially telling the Bush administration: *If Congress doesn't give the president authorization to go to war, don't blame us. Blame your CIA director.* He was putting the onus on Tenet—who, thanks to Cheney, Libby, Wolfowitz, and Feith, already had enough headaches to contend with.

At the same time, Tenet could do the math. Durbin had issued his ultimatum on the 10th of September. By the looks of things, Congress would be voting on whether to authorize military force in early October. Ordinarily, a NIE—which represents the consensus opinion of the entire U.S. intelligence community—requires a bare minimum of four months to be produced and often takes as long as a year.[13] On September 12, Tenet gave his orders: he wanted an NIE ready in nineteen days, by October 1.

This absurd deadline all but guaranteed that the NIE would be a grossly inferior product. The CIA director believed—understandably but erroneously— that a gravely flawed product was better than no product at all. As one of the individuals involved in the production of the NIE would lament, "We had to do the best we could. The problem was, the best we could do sucked."[14]

The designated supervisor of the NIE was Bob Walpole, the national intelligence officer for strategic programs. Walpole happened to be the same CIA official who, two days after receiving this new assignment, would also be present during the NSC's "Why Iraq Now?" meeting and would express befuddlement as to why Iraq was the focus—as opposed to, say, North Korea. In his view, Saddam probably had chemical and biological weapons, as did other countries in the region, but this did not make the dictator a threat to America.

But Walpole was also the author of the 2000 NIE who had invited Rumsfeld to be its adviser. He had frequently testified before congressional committees. Walpole was not a naïf. He understood that what he was being asked to produce was a political document packaged as an intelligence assessment. He also understood that nineteen days gave him and his coauthors enough time only to summarize the existing views on Saddam's WMD program, not to carefully reexamine those views.[15] The evidentiary basis for going to war would thus be handed down in the manner of family lore, tall tales that tended to grow in the telling. And the bar for such evidence would be low—very low. "The basic tasking was 'Give me everything you've got,'" said one of the authors. "As opposed to 'What's credible? What levels of confidence have you got in this stuff?'"[16]

Accompanying the harried timetable were two baseline assessments that would prove oddly consoling to the NIE authors. The first was that they could hardly go wrong in assuming the very worst about the Iraqi regime. As one of the officials who helped supervise the NIE put it, "We knew Saddam was a liar. So there wasn't any point being generous."[17]

The second, perversely reassuring assumption was that President Bush was going to war anyway. Tenet had said as much in August to his new interagency point man Bob Grenier. The associate deputy director of operations, Steve Kappes, had issued the same prediction to his station chiefs in the Middle East and Europe. "We were making huge judgments on very little information," recalled Carl Ford, the State Department's INR director. "At least 70 percent was pure speculation, and no more than 5 percent hard evidence." Then again, if war was a fait accompli, then what difference did the scarceness of hard evidence make?

What these fatalistic assumptions set in motion was a high-stakes descent into circular reasoning. This was particularly evident as the NIE authors considered the matter of Iraq's chemical weapons program. Saddam's son-in-law Hussein Kamel had, upon defecting in 1995, flatly told his interrogators in Jordan, "All chemical weapons were destroyed."[18] For some reason, the CIA chose to believe most of Kamel's testimony but not this.[19]

The agency instead focused on the regime's failure to account for such weapons disposal in its records. It was also unmoved by Saddam's having heeded the admonition by James Baker before the Gulf War to refrain from using CWs or else. Nothing about Saddam's behavior since then had changed. It was the Bush administration's tolerance for risk that had been radically altered. The NIE authors thus figured that since war was inevitable, it was better to assume that Saddam possessed and would use CWs—as one senior intelligence official rhetorically asked, "You want to tell these soldiers that it's okay to leave their chemical suits at home?"[20]

"We knew where we were headed, and that was war," acknowledged another intelligence official. "Which ironically made it that much more difficult to change the analytic line that we'd stuck with for ten years. For ten years, it was our pretty strong judgment that Saddam had chemical capability. And with American soldiers about to go in, we weren't going to change our mind and say 'Never mind' as hundreds of thousands of GIs are gearing up, since the assessment of what chemical protection they'd bring was based on our judgment."[21]

But in fact, the "pretty strong judgment that Saddam had chemical capability" did get changed for the 2002 NIE. Shortly after Tenet instructed Walpole to begin work, the national intelligence author in charge of the paper's CW section, John Landry, called one of the agency's top analysts in that field, Loren "Larry" Fox.

"We need an estimate on the amount of chemical agents they have," Landry stated.

Fox was a systems analyst for the division of the CIA known as the Weapons Intelligence, Nonproliferation, and Arms Control Center, or WINPAC. One of the agency's last Soviet specialists, he tended to burrow for months or even years into research projects like Gulf War syndrome.

Now Landry was asking Fox to quantify an unknown. He thought for a moment. Saddam's previous CW stockpile had been thought to be about five hundred metric tons. Fox was almost certain that the dictator still had a stockpile. But he was not 100 percent certain. After all, the agency had no physical evidence that Iraq had *any* chemical weapons.

What the agency had was satellite photographs of so-called decontamination trucks traveling to and from a chemical plant known as Al Mussayib. The decontamination trucks were regarded by analysts as a "significant signature"—though the more innocuous explanation was that they were filled with water and used to hose down the factory floors.

Fox's analytical judgment proceeded step by dubious step. Step one: Saddam used to have five hundred metric tons (though this was never proven). Step two: As CWs tend to degrade over a year's time, his scientists were apparently now at work producing a new stockpile, attested to by the ubiquitous trucks (though the trucks in and of themselves proved nothing). Step three: Whatever the Iraqis were producing, it figured that they were intending a stockpile at least as big as their previous one (though this was only a guess).

"I'd say they have from zero to a thousand metric tons," Fox told Landry.

"*Zero?*" Landry sounded shaken. "What do you mean, *zero?* Our assessment is that he has *something.*"

"Yes," said Fox. "But there's a 10 percent chance he has none."

"That's not very helpful for an assessment that already says he has something," Landry pointed out. The national intelligence officer was sending the signal to Larry Fox that the "zero" should go. He seemed less concerned how it was that Fox had arrived at "a thousand" for his ceiling.

Seeing that his floor had been raised by Landry, Fox prudently lowered his ceiling.[22] Thus it was that the NIE came to include its most statistically precise line:

> Although we have little specific information on Iraq's CW stockpile, Saddam probably has stocked at least 100 metric tons (MT) and possibly as much as 500 MT of CW agents—much of it added in the last year.[23]

THERE WAS ANOTHER REASON WHY LARRY FOX AND OTHER WINPAC CHEMI-cal analysts believed that Saddam had a CW program. It was because their colleagues the biological analysts were supremely confident that Iraq had a BW program.[24]

That stratospheric confidence was based on assumptions that were strikingly similar to those embraced by Fox and the other CW analysts. Their logic proceeded from the known facts that Iraq's scientists at one time had a BW program and that they had lied about it to the UN inspectors, repeatedly and flagrantly.

What was not known to the CIA at the time was that in August 1991, three UN inspectors, led by chief biological weapons inspector David Kelly, had met with Iraq's biological weapons supervisor, Dr. Ahmad Murtadha Ahmad

Khalil. Asked if Saddam's regime had a biological weapons program, Ahmad responded, "Yes. A defensive and an offensive program." Ahmad offered to show them the main BW site at Al Hakam, where Iraq had produced approximately 500,000 liters of biological agents in the previous two years, under the supervision of the scientist who would later be nicknamed Dr. Germ.

In other words: Iraq had openly declared its entire biological weapons program within months after the end of the Gulf War. Inexplicably, however, Kelly did not take up the Iraqi weapons supervisor on his offer to lead them to the weapons facility at Al Hakam. The tapes of the interview were tossed into storage, untranscribed. Only in 2008, when UN inspector Kay Mareish was boxing up all of the Iraqi inspection material, did she come across the tapes, listen to them with fellow inspector Peter Prosser, and realize that Iraq's "denial and deception" of biological weapons was a fiction.[25]

Lacking this crucial information, the intelligence community embraced the conventional wisdom that Saddam's scientists continued to lie about the regime's BW program and had come clean only after Hussein Kamel's defection. Or had they come clean? Tons of "destroyed" anthrax had been left unaccounted for. And now, without inspectors or informants like Kamel, it followed that Saddam's BW plans would surely recommence. Didn't it?

Besides, the BW analysts had an ace in the hole. They had Curveball.

In September 1999, an Iraqi émigré in his early thirties named Rafid Ahmed Alwan al-Janabi showed up in Germany hoping for asylum. In return, he had information to offer. He claimed to have been a chemical engineer at a plant that had designed more than a half dozen mobile biological laboratories.

The CIA and the DIA first began reading German intelligence reports on the Iraqi chemical engineer code-named Curveball in February 2000. They were ecstatic. Here was the answer to the question *Why can't our satellite imagery locate any biological weapons facilities?* The facilities were on wheels! Clinton's national security adviser, Sandy Berger, pronounced Curveball's revelations a "gold standard" in Iraq intelligence gathering.[26] Following Berger's anointment, the DIA hosted an interagency meeting to brief other analysts on this remarkable discovery.

"The DIA guy who was running the meeting was so thrilled," recalled a CIA Iraq analyst who attended the meeting. "We'd been years without any reporting on WMD in Iraq. Now we finally have something new to chew on." But the Iraq analyst voiced his skepticism about the mobile BW vans Curveball had described. He pulled out a photocopy of a vehicle that appeared to fit the source's description. It was a field pharmaceutical van built by a Spanish company to use in disaster areas. The Iraq analyst had pulled it off the internet. Perhaps, he suggested, Curveball had done the same thing.

"We need to vet this guy," said the Iraq analyst, whose lack of enthusiasm would mean that he was no longer invited to the Curveball fan club meetings.[27] Still, American intelligence officials asked their German counterparts—the Bundesnachrichtendienst, or BND—for access to Curveball. They were rebuffed.

BND had refused because, by as early as the fall of 2000, after being coddled with cash and an apartment and a Mercedes, Curveball's story had begun to unravel. His former boss at Iraq's Military Industrial Commission told the Germans that everything Curveball had said about mobile BW vans was a lie. On September 8, 2001, BND terminated him as a source.

But WINPAC's BW team, led by a senior analyst with the first name of Beth, refused to let go of Curveball. His descriptions of places and procedures made perfect sense. They tracked with what the UN inspectors had conjectured in their final report—almost as if Curveball had read the open-source UNSCOM documents on the internet, as anyone could do if they wanted to tell intelligence officials exactly what they wished to hear.

In October 2001 alone—meaning after the Germans had cut him loose, but also after 9/11 and the outbreak of anthrax, when the Bush White House was overcome with anxiety about the "second wave" of terror attacks—the U.S. intelligence community disseminated no fewer than twenty-eight Information Intelligence Reports, or IIRs, based on Curveball's earlier claims. Not one of them warned that the only agency to conduct extensive interviews with him had already decided that he was not a reliable source.[28]

As a result, the October 2002 NIE included this definitive statement among its key judgments: "Baghdad has mobile facilities for producing bacterial and toxin BW agents; these facilities can evade detection and are highly survivable. Within three to six months these units probably could produce an amount of agent equal to the total that Iraq produced in the years prior to the Gulf War."[29]

OF COURSE, THE VERY WORST-CASE SCENARIO WAS THAT SADDAM HUSSEIN might come to possess nuclear weapons.

"The issue is that he has chemical weapons and he's used them," Vice President Cheney told CNN's Wolf Blitzer in March 2002. "The issue is that he's developing and has biological weapons. The issue is that he's pursuing nuclear weapons."[30]

All three of those statements would turn out to be untrue. At the time, however, Cheney had valid reason for concern. The previous month, he had learned from his CIA briefer that, according to an Italian intelligence report, the government of Niger had agreed to provide Iraq with five hundred tons of yellowcake uranium per year.[31]

The State Department's INR analysts were quick to throw cold water on the claim, arguing that Niger would not risk good relations with the United States by violating UN sanctions, that the French companies controlling the mines would have blocked the sale, and that trucking hundreds of tons across the blistering Sudanese desert was a near impossibility.[32] The CIA dispatched former U.S. ambassador Joe Wilson, the husband of Counter Proliferation Division case officer Valerie Plame, to Niger to look into the matter. Wilson also concluded from his interviews in Niger that the intelligence had no merit.[33]

Knowing that the Niger intelligence was at best hotly contested, NIE supervisor Bob Walpole was nonetheless in a box. The vice president continued to believe the story. In September, British intelligence officials released an unclassified "white paper" that referenced Iraq's seeking out "significant quantities of uranium from Africa."[34] That same month, the CIA had cleared language about Iraq's attempts to buy yellowcake for President Bush to use in an upcoming speech.[35]

Thus, for the sake of what one of the authors would term "completeness,"[36] the disputed story made its way into the NIE, albeit with equivocation: "As of early 2001, Niger and Iraq reportedly were still working out arrangements for this deal, which could be for up to 500 tons of yellowcake. We do not know the status of this arrangement."[37] (The supposed letter of agreement between Niger and Iraq was later determined to be a forgery.)[38]

But another strand of intelligence besides yellowcake pointed to Saddam's pursuit of nuclear weapons. In June 2001, a shipment from China containing thousands of carefully packed high-strength aluminum tubes was seized by intelligence officials in Jordan. The tubes were about a yard long and three inches in diameter. The intended recipient was a Baghdad trader working with Iraq's Military Industrial Commission. As the tubes had not been imported through the UN, the shipment was illegal.

The CIA's stated assessment was that the MIC expected to use them to build centrifuges for uranium enrichment.[39] Both Director Tenet and Deputy Director McLaughlin were told by their subordinates that this was the agency's consensus opinion.[40]

But it was not. The expert analysts working in the CIA's Counter Proliferation Division "recognized immediately that the physical characteristics of the aluminum tubes made them unsuitable for uranium enrichment," one of them would later say.[41] That expert judgment was stifled by CPD's Iraq branch managers—who, like everyone else at the agency, were aware that Cheney and Rice were evoking the specter of mushroom clouds, and that Tenet would be grateful for assistance in supplying the First Customer with evidence. It was also the case that the WINPAC analysts—whose expertise was considered paramount on such matters—had concurred that the tubes were likely for nuclear use. Employing bureaucratic logic, the Counter Proliferation Division managers could see that they had nothing to lose and everything to gain by signing on to the prevailing assessment, even if it was one that their own experts disagreed with.

The Department of Energy's experts took note of the CIA's opinion and disagreed with it. To them, the evidence seemed plain that the intended use for the tubes was the production of artillery rockets—and, further, that the composition of the tubes made them ill-suited for centrifuge operations. The DOE specialists co-wrote a rebuttal to the CIA assessment with the INR analysts at State. It read in part, "We find it unfortunate that CIA has energetically propounded its views without, in our view, taking adequate stock of the accumulating evidence."[42]

The DOE/INR report was referring to one very specific energetic propounder from the agency: a WINPAC analyst named Joe Turner who had worked at the Oak Ridge Laboratory's gas centrifuge team. Turner had given his pitch to the INR analysts. "He was passionate and had his arguments down," recalled Greg Thielmann, one of the INR's top weapons analysts, "but he wasn't convincing."[43]

Other experts found the silver-tongued Turner glib—"one of those technical people who was book-smart and had a great gift of gab but had never really built anything in his life," as one Department of Energy technician would put it. Turner's false claim that these aluminum tubes had in fact been used in Iraq's pre–Gulf War nuclear program had won him a stinging rebuke by a veteran Atomic Energy Agency inspector.[44] At Oak Ridge, there were technicians with far greater centrifuge experience who were lending their opinions to INR and DOE. The difference was that Joe Turner worked for the nation's preeminent intelligence service, the one that produced daily briefings for the president of the United States.

On September 8, 2002, Judith Miller and Michael Gordon of *The New York Times* divulged that Iraq had sought to acquire "specially designed aluminum tubes" as evidence that "Iraq has stepped up its quest for nuclear weapons." The front-page story quoted unnamed administration sources. That at least one of them resided in the NSC was tipped off by the authors' use of a memorable phrase[45] that Condoleezza Rice introduced to a TV audience that same morning. Speaking of Saddam's attempts to acquire aluminum tubes, Rice told Wolf Blitzer, "The problem here is that there will always be some uncertainty about how quickly he can acquire nuclear weapons. But we don't want the smoking gun to be a mushroom cloud."[46]

Neither Rice nor the authors of the *Times* piece were aware of the intense inter- and intra-agency disagreements surrounding the aluminum tubes. The matter remained unsettled until October 1, the day the CIA expected to

publish the classified NIE. That morning, members of the National Foreign
Intelligence Board convened to reach a consensus on the NIE's findings.
Among the outstanding issues slated for discussion was the question of the
aluminum tubes. To advocate for its position that the tubes were intended
for use in a nuclear centrifuge, the agency had sent Joe Turner to the NFIB
meeting.

The DOE, by contrast, did not send any of its Oak Ridge experts who
had convinced the INR analysts that Turner's arguments were flawed. Those
experts had been overruled by DOE's management team. The superiors included Linton Brooks, the DOE's chief of nonproliferation programs, who
had known vice president Cheney since the first Bush administration. Like
Cheney, the DOE managers were convinced that Iraq was purchasing tons of
uranium from Niger, a proposition that the department's own experts found
absurd. (To one of the latter, a DOE manager had sneeringly predicted, "Once
we go to war and find Iraq's nuclear plant, you're going to be looking for a new
job.")[47] As a result, the agency's representative at the NFIB meeting was
Thomas S. Ryder, DOE's acting intelligence director. Ryder had been on the
job only five months and possessed no technical expertise.[48]

CIA deputy director John McLaughlin presided over the aluminum
tubes discussion. Recalling McLaughlin's interrogation of the DOE rep, a
colleague said, "I just remember John tearing that guy apart."[49] As McLaughlin put it, Ryder was "an expert on something else, but not this subject. So in
this debate he gets clobbered by our analyst. It comes down to making your
case persuasively and in detail. And because we're in a big hurry, you don't
have the multiple meetings we might otherwise have had."[50]

But in fact the NFIB debate would have been meaningless even had the
Department of Energy sent one of its most highly conversant technicians
rather than Tom Ryder. After all, the chairman of the meeting was the CIA
director, George Tenet. The interrogator, McLaughlin, was the agency's
deputy director. Joe Turner was representing the agency's assessment, which
was unlikely to be reversed at the eleventh hour no matter how compelling
the DOE's arguments might be. "By the time it got to the NFIB, the game
was over," one of DOE's top technicians would later say. "That wasn't the

place to argue. We'd already lost, and so now we had to make nice and find a way to work together."[51]

The NFIB voted in favor of the CIA's assessment. The NIE was published that evening. It included this line among its key judgments:

> Most agencies believe that Saddam's personal interest in and Iraq's aggressive attempts to obtain high-strength aluminum tubes for centrifuge rotors—as well as Iraq's attempts to acquire magnets, high-speed balancing machines, and machine tools—provide compelling evidence that Saddam is reconstituting a uranium enrichment effort for Baghdad's nuclear weapons program.[52]

The document included a footnote detailing INR's reservations. The DOE's managers elected not to join in the footnote. Instead, they signed onto the assessment that Iraq's "reconstitution of the nuclear program is underway"—a position that DOE's experts at Oak Ridge did not support. Tom Ryder later apologized to at least one of them for having not heeded their views.[53]

"In retrospect," weapons inspector Charles Duelfer would lament, "we envisioned this whole nuclear program based on two wobbly data points."[54]

THE NATIONAL INTELLIGENCE ESTIMATE RAN TO NINETY-TWO PAGES. AS George Tenet, a former Hill staffer himself, could have predicted, few senators read the document in its entirety. For them, the NIE's summary sufficed. The summary was a merger of the NIE's "key judgments" and an unclassified paper that national intelligence officer Paul Pillar had written months earlier. Pillar's paper was intended to be released as a public document once the White House Iraq Group began pushing out its Saddam-must-go messaging. That time had now arrived. In the merging of the two documents, double caveats and other qualifiers fell by the wayside. The end product contained stark assertions that even some of the NIE's authors felt were not supported by the intelligence,[55] such as: "Baghdad has chemical and biological weapons as well as missiles with ranges in excess of UN restrictions; if left unchecked, it probably will have a nuclear weapon during this decade."[56]

Still, the entire document was leaden with doubt. The phrase "we don't know" appeared thirty times, and "we know" on only three occasions. Fully 40 percent of its assessments were made with "low confidence." Among the key judgments, three were listed as low confidence:

> When Saddam would use weapons of mass destruction.
> Whether Saddam would engage in clandestine attacks against the U.S. homeland.
> Whether in desperation Saddam would share chemical or biological weapons with Al Qaida.

Those three judgments formed the basis for war. The U.S. intelligence community had low confidence in each of them.[57]

But the tissue-thin foundation of facts was all the Bush administration would need in making its case for war. One week after the NIE was published, the president appeared before an audience at the Cincinnati Museum Theater. Bush was not his usual folksy self. After a few seconds' worth of thank-yous, he got right to the point: he was here "to discuss a grave threat to peace."

Hours before Bush took the stage, a just-released *New York Times*/CBS News poll revealed that most Americans disapproved of his handling of the economy and believed that his focus on Iraq was coming at the expense of domestic issues.[58] The president's mission that night was implicitly clear. He needed to put the fear of God in the American public. During his twenty-nine-minute address, Bush trotted out some of the NIE's most alarming revelations. Saddam was rebuilding his chemical weapons stockpile. He had developed "mobile weapons facilities to keep a step ahead of inspectors." He was trying to acquire aluminum tubes for the purpose of building a nuclear arsenal.

The president also revealed things about the regime that the NIE's authors had decided not to publish. He spoke of "one very senior al Qaeda member who received medical treatment in Baghdad this year and who has been associated with planning for chemical and biological attacks"—referring to Zarqawi, who was neither a "very senior member" of Al Qaeda nor an ally of Saddam. Bush also asserted that "Iraq has trained al Qaeda members in bomb-making and poisons and deadly gases"—information that the Egyptians had obtained from al-Libi through torture and that was subsequently recanted by him. (Bush had also planned to speak about Iraq's attempts to acquire yellowcake uranium from Niger, but Tenet convinced Steve Hadley to remove it from the speech.)[59]

But then Bush called and raised the NIE in a manner that would have done the 1998 Rumsfeld Commission proud. After quoting former weapons inspector Richard Butler, who had termed Saddam "a homicidal dictator who is addicted to weapons of mass destruction," the president enjoined the hushed audience to imagine what such a man *could* do: "Iraq could decide on any given day to provide a biological or chemical weapon to a terrorist group or individual terrorists. Alliance with terrorists could allow the Iraqi regime to attack America without leaving any fingerprints."

Gifted politician that he was, Bush used the very weakness of the WMD intelligence as an oratorical asset. "Many people have asked how close Saddam Hussein is to developing a nuclear weapon," he observed. "Well, we don't know, and that's the problem."

But it was a problem with an obvious solution. Arguing that "the risk is simply too great that he will use them, or provide them to a terror network," Bush then landed on his national security adviser's already famous rhetorical device: "Facing clear evidence of peril, we cannot wait for the final proof— the smoking gun—that could come in the form of a mushroom cloud."[60]

Bush would later register disappointment with how his Cincinnati address had been received, calling it "the speech nobody watched."[61] Still, he was proud of it, and with good reason: he had made his case, one that captured the Bush administration's post-9/11 catastrophist mind frame. To Daniel Patrick Moynihan's adage that "facts are stubborn things," there was now a corollary: sometimes facts were too stubborn to wait on.

≝≝

CHAPTER THIRTEEN

THE BLANK CHECK

As of September 9, 2002, when Senator Dick Durbin demanded that George Tenet produce a National Intelligence Estimate of what the intelligence community knew about Saddam's weapons program, it seemed far from certain that Congress would grant President Bush the authority to invade Iraq. The previous month had been dominated by the cautionary voices of Scowcroft in *The Wall Street Journal*, Henry Kissinger in *The Washington Post*, and Jim Baker in *The New York Times*.[1] As members of Congress learned from their constituents over summer recess, Americans were more concerned about the struggling economy than Iraq. Bush remained popular, with an approval rating in the low sixties, and the public was inclined to trust his judgment as commander in chief. But they also believed that Bush should first exhaust all diplomatic options before resorting to war, and that Congress needed to be consulted on the matter.[2]

The first briefings after summer recess did not go especially well. On the morning of September 4, Bush met in the Cabinet Room with twenty congressional leaders from both parties. To the relief of many in the room, the president made it clear that he would ask Congress for an authorization resolution—something that Cheney and a few others in the administration did not feel was either necessary or advisable. (As secretary of defense in the first Bush administration, the former Wyoming congressman had opposed going to Congress to receive authorization for Operation Desert Storm.)[3] Bush also insisted that his mind was not made up on the matter of war.

But the president's mind was not open when it came to Saddam, whom he described as "a serious threat to the United States, a serious threat to the world."[4] Beyond his rhetoric, many in the room were well aware that the war machine had been churning throughout the summer. "You really need to talk to a lot of the uniformed guys," Carl Levin, the Democratic chairman of the Senate Armed Services Committee, warned the president. "Not just the [JCS] chairman. I've heard a lot of skepticism from them. A lot of questions."[5]

After the meeting, Democratic congressman Ike Skelton—the ranking member of the House Armed Services Committee—spoke with one of Bush's legislative affairs aides, Dan Keniry. Like Levin, Skelton had been hearing from some of the generals that the administration was rushing headlong into war without having thought through the second- and third-order consequences. Nothing the president had said that morning had assuaged the Missouri congressman's concerns, which he conveyed to Keniry.

The Bush aide responded, "Well, Congressman, we really don't need your vote. We've got the votes."[6]

Things got worse that afternoon, when Donald Rumsfeld came to Capitol Hill. The bipartisan group of nearly seventy senators had been told that Rumsfeld would be providing a classified briefing on Iraq. But the secretary did not offer any new intelligence at all. Instead he treated the senators to an extended discourse on "known unknowns."

With evident exasperation, Senator Dianne Feinstein informed Rumsfeld that she had received a number of intelligence briefings over the past two weeks. The conclusion she had reached from them was that Saddam was not close to achieving nuclear capability and was therefore not an imminent threat to the United States. Going to war and killing innocents under such dubious pretenses struck Feinstein as foolish. A fellow Democrat, Senator Kent Conrad of South Dakota, stood and said that he agreed with everything Feinstein had said. Several others in the room seemed put off by Rumsfeld's flippancy. The White House legislative team viewed his performance as a disaster.[7]

In addition to harboring doubts about the Bush administration's case for war, Democratic legislators had reason to feel confident about their leverage. According to a Gallup poll conducted in October, 50 percent of Americans approved of Congress, a rating that was unheard of in modern times.[8] The November midterm elections historically tended to favor the opposition party, that much more so in a lagging economy. October 2002 therefore seemed an auspicious opportunity for Congress, including the Democratic-controlled Senate, to exercise significant influence over whether America waged war with Iraq. Declaring war was, in fact, the prerogative of the legislative branch under the U.S. Constitution.

But Congress did not step up. More than any other branch of government, it had been completely unprepared for the events of September 11, 2001. The Capitol's 535 officeholders organized their daily lives around fundraisers, committee hearings, and parochial fixations. Most of them had never given a thought to terrorism until the morning they were evacuated from their building amid rumors that one of the hijacked airplanes was headed their way. Their leaders were whisked off to undisclosed locations. The next morning, CIA deputy director John McLaughlin stood on the House floor for hours while saucer-eyed members deluged him with anxious questions.[9] A month later, envelopes containing anthrax arrived at the Senate offices of Tom Daschle and Patrick Leahy.

During the first week of October 2002, six individuals were shot in different locations throughout the Beltway by an unidentified sniper. Washington elites were palpably terrorized. The unimaginable had occurred, was occurring, might occur again. One could not assume otherwise. One could not rest on probabilities. As a Democratic leader's senior aide would recall, "Even the *possibility* that the worst weapons in the world could get in the hands of the worst people in the world was a driving concern for many. If this could happen and we didn't do something about it, the consequences would just be devastating. Even with the speculation that some of the intelligence wasn't accurate or fully vetted, that gnawing feeling was compelling for a lot of people."[10]

Briefing members on the Hill, intelligence officials could see their disengagement from the details in the NIE. (As one of the NIE coauthors put it, "If you read as far as the third sentence—and on a question of war and peace, maybe you can read that far—you would know there's dissent on a key judgment. Gee, wouldn't that elicit some curiosity, a request for 'Explain this to me?' And it didn't.")[11] Some of this seeming disinterest could be chalked up to the limited attention span for details that was not uncommon among politicians. But it was also likely, as one CIA briefer concluded, that "they didn't want to know, because 9/11 had rocked their world and all of this scared the shit out of them."[12]

Many of them were also politically scared. Defying President Bush on matters of national security was, in many quarters, deemed unpatriotic. A week after 9/11, Congress had voted to authorize the president to use force against anyone associated with the attacks. Only one member, California congresswoman Barbara Lee, voted against the authorization, on the grounds that Bush should not receive a blank check to retaliate on a whim. Lee received widespread vilification as well as death threats.[13]

The day after Bush hosted congressional leaders in the Cabinet Room, he hit the campaign trail on behalf of his fellow Republicans. His references to 9/11—"The enemy struck a great country"—stirred the vengefulness of the audience, thereby whetting the appetite for war against a wholly different foe, one "who hates America and hates freedom."[14]

The president had executed a deft rhetorical shift in recent months. After repeatedly invoking the name of Osama bin Laden in the wake of the attacks, by early 2002 Bush had ceased to make mention of the escaped terrorist altogether. Instead, even while continuing to remind audiences of 9/11, he now spoke of Saddam Hussein with increasing frequency—until, by September 2002, the president was mentioning Saddam more often than he had *ever* cited bin Laden. The new emphasis created a phenomenon by the fall of 2002 that, intended or not, would prove fortuitous to the politics of Bush's war campaign: according to several polls, a majority of Americans now believed that the Iraqi dictator was responsible for the 9/11 attacks.[15]

To most Americans, then, Bush was not changing the subject at all. This conflation of 9/11 and Saddam, never once explicitly made by the president himself, conferred a justness and a logic on invading Iraq that Democrats were at pains to refute. They were no match anyway for the supremely confident Bush, who, on the campaign trail, displayed remarkable skill in toggling between relatably rustic Dubya and sober war president. Most of all, he conveyed the conviction of his beliefs—a certitude that could be seen as moral clarity: "You know where I stand."

Many Democrats were far less sure of where they stood. But they would have to make up their minds in a hurry, as Bush had conveyed his preference on September 4 that Congress vote on the matter before it recessed on October 12. Senate Majority Leader Tom Daschle had injudiciously reminded the president that his father had held off *his* Iraq authorization until after the 1990 midterms—prompting the peeved reply "They're totally different circumstances. That was reactive. This is proactive. We need to act quickly."[16]

Bush did not explain to Daschle why he believed quick action was necessary. But, as another White House official would recall, "it was about getting the votes done in time to have the right weather—before it got too hot in Iraq. Absolutely, that was discussed internally."[17]

The hand-wringing over how to vote was especially intense among those in Congress—House Minority Leader Richard Gephardt and Senators Daschle, Joe Biden, Hillary Clinton, John Edwards, John Kerry, and Bob Graham—who were looking beyond the 2002 campaign to a presidential run two (or, failing that, six) years later. Looming in their memory was the experience of the 1991 authorization vote for the Gulf War. Most Senate Democrats had voted against that resolution, fearful that they would be affixing their signatures to another Vietnam.

Instead, Saddam was routed out of Kuwait in one hundred hours, and at least one presidential hopeful who had voted no, Georgia senator Sam Nunn, was thought to have ruined his chances thereafter. For the 2004 aspirants, recalled one intelligence analyst who had briefed several of them, "it was a combination of things. 'Saddam's a bad guy, I've been told that for years, so that inclines me to say we should do bad things to him.' 'We're after 9/11, and I don't want to be seen as not protecting the country.' And, 'I don't like that they're jamming this down my throat, making me out to be a traitor if I don't do this—that pisses me off—but I also don't want to be Sam Nunn, on the wrong side of a very popular war.'"[18]

THE ONE SENATOR WHO HAD STUDIED HIS DOG-EARED COPY OF THE NIE closely—who "knew it better than we did," in the words of one of its coauthors—was Carl Levin.[19]

The stooped and gravel-voiced Michigander had visited the smoldering Pentagon on September 11 with Republican senator John Warner, in a show of unity. But the tragedy and chaos of that day had not knocked Levin off-center as it had some of his colleagues. He found Bush to be decent but insecure. Cheney struck him as an ideologue, except worse: the vice president's admiration for Chalabi (whom Levin had met and whom he regarded as a "con artist") and his stubborn insistence that 9/11 hijacker Mohamed Atta had met with an Iraqi intelligence official in Prague made Levin question his judgment. Rice seemed far too intent on pleasing Bush. The only one in the administration whom Levin thoroughly admired was Colin Powell—though, the senator would later say, "he had credibility he didn't use. It was wasted."[20]

Throughout the summer and fall of 2002, Levin berated briefers from the Pentagon and the CIA for withholding information on war plans, for inferring rather than proving.[21] On October 2, during a closed hearing, Levin elicited from Deputy Director John McLaughlin the judgment, memorialized in the just published (but still classified) NIE, that Saddam would likely use his WMD against America only if first attacked by U.S. troops. Levin immediately moved to have that assessment declassified for public consumption.[22]

Condi Rice reacted with alarm to the newspaper stories that had resulted from Levin's exchange with McLaughlin. Saddam, if the CIA deputy director was to be believed, was *not* an imminent threat to the United States.

Rice called Tenet and instructed him to "clarify" the matter. To Levin's chagrin, the director dutifully issued a statement insisting that there was "no inconsistency between our view of Saddam's growing threat" and that of the president. Tenet would later acknowledge that in diminishing his deputy's testimony at the wishes of the Bush White House, "I gave the impression that I was a partisan player."[23]

Regardless, Levin now had all the confirmation he needed that war was not an urgent necessity. The Senate Armed Services Committee chairman proceeded to draft a war resolution that did not constitute a blank check. It would require the president to demonstrate that Iraq represented an imminent threat, which was the standard under international law for use of force. Levin's resolution also mandated that the president first seek an authorization resolution from the UN—and if the world body failed to grant him that authorization, Congress would promptly reconvene and Bush could then make his case for unilateral action.

Levin's approach, which emphasized the importance of multilateral support to any war effort, began to garner support from some of his colleagues. None of them, as it happened, were from among the group of legislators seeking higher office.

DICK GEPHARDT HAD BEEN THE CARL LEVIN OF 1991. THAT JANUARY, DURING the Gulf crisis, he and Congressman Lee Hamilton had drafted an alternative resolution that prescribed sanctions and diplomatic pressure rather than military force. The Hamilton-Gephardt measure failed,[24] Desert Storm marked a triumph for the elder Bush, and the Missouri Democrat decided a few months later not to challenge the incumbent president in 1992.[25]

A decade later, Gephardt's "most important validator" on Iraq was George Tenet, according to a top aide.[26] In mid-September, the House minority leader visited CIA headquarters at Langley. Tenet and a couple of analysts walked Gephardt through the intelligence, including the presence of Zarqawi in northern Iraq. The evidence was anything but conclusive. But Gephardt could see that Tenet, a former Democratic staffer on the Hill, was comfortable with the assessment that Saddam had reconstituted his weapons program. Even if this did not make Iraq an imminent threat, Gephardt figured that the possibility of the dictator turning his weapons over to Al Qaeda constituted an intolerable risk.[27]

On October 1, Bush rejected Levin's multilateral approach, as well as a less restrictive resolution drafted by Biden and Republican senator Richard Lugar that would require the president to return to Congress a second time and demonstrate that Saddam was an imminent threat before pursuing military action. "I don't want to get a resolution that ties my hands," Bush told reporters that morning.[28] And, thanks to Dick Gephardt, he would not need to.

At seven the following morning, Gephardt, Daschle, House Speaker Dennis Hastert, and Senate Minority Leader Trent Lott joined Bush and Cheney for breakfast in the president's private dining room. Daschle had not been aware that his friend Gephardt had spent much of the previous day on the phone with Bush, hammering out the language of a resolution that would give the president everything he wished. Several issues were discussed at the hour-long breakfast, but neither Gephardt nor Bush revealed his hand.[29]

Less than five hours later, Gephardt, Hastert, and Lott—but not Daschle—were back at the White House. This time, it was to announce that House leaders had agreed on a resolution, cosponsored by Democrat Joe Lieberman in the Senate. Daschle's chief of staff, Denis McDonough, was livid and yelled on the phone at one of Gephardt's top staffers.[30] Biden and his staff were "totally gobsmacked" by the secret deal, one of his senior aides recalled; Gephardt, the Delaware senator believed, had betrayed him.[31]

But Biden, who had voted against the 1991 Iraq resolution and whose presidential ambitions remained unfulfilled, decided to give Bush the benefit of the doubt. He announced that he would support the Lieberman-Gephardt bill, on the grounds that it would give the president leverage to make Saddam submit to weapons inspections. Biden convinced himself that in such a scenario, the likelihood of war would be decreased. "We never thought the fix was in," Biden's senior aide would lament.[32]

By contrast, Bob Graham was convinced that the fix was in. The Florida senator and chairman of the Senate Committee on Intelligence had not forgotten his conversation at CENTCOM with Tommy Franks in the spring of 2002 about how assets from Afghanistan were quietly being diverted to the Middle East. This was evidence, Graham would later say, "that the president had already made up his mind and was pretty deeply committed to war."[33]

Like Levin, Graham had studied the NIE carefully. He had also met with Polish and German intelligence officials who had cast doubt on Saddam's supposed weapons arsenal. Most of all, Graham was chagrined that the war on terror was taking a back seat to the Bush administration's fixation with Saddam. In his view, there remained unanswered questions about the 9/11 attacks—among them, the possibility that one or more hijackers had connections to the Saudi government. Iraq constituted a change of subject. Alone among the Democratic presidential aspirants, Bob Graham intended to oppose all the war resolutions.[34]

Graham's colleague John Edwards was also resolute, though in the opposite direction. The North Carolinian did not need any convincing that Saddam should be overthrown by military force. "I think Iraq is the most serious and imminent threat to our country," Edwards had declared back in February 2002—a position more strident than even Cheney had taken at that early juncture.[35] Edwards had also bought Bush's "axis of evil" premise, stating in a floor speech that there was "every possibility that he could turn his weapons over to these terrorists."[36]

Edwards had a different concern besides Saddam Hussein: Hillary Clinton, a likely rival for the presidency. He could see that the New York freshman senator was equivocating on her vote, trying to have it both ways. To contrast himself with Clinton, Edwards intended "to be the first out of the gate calling for action," according to one of his aides.[37]

Clinton was indeed immersed in painstaking deliberations. The former Vietnam War protester had achieved a hawkish makeover on the Hill, with admirers who included John McCain. The New York senator also felt a debt of gratitude to President Bush for the $20 billion in federal aid that was funneled to the city after 9/11.

She was still a Democrat, however, and not a signatory to the Bush doctrine of preemptive war. The peace groups that came to her office and the religious leaders who joined her in prayer carried some sway. Still, most of the advisers with whom she spoke were not anti-war. Clinton conferred often with her husband's former national security adviser Sandy Berger, who was convinced that Saddam retained a weapons stockpile.[38] She talked frequently as well with her husband's former ambassador to the UN, Richard Holbrooke, who regarded Saddam as "the most dangerous leader in the world today."[39] She also received at least three briefings with former Clinton NSC aide and CIA analyst Kenneth Pollack, who had published a book earlier that year entitled *The Threatening Storm: The Case for Invading Iraq.* While her anti-war visitors were appealing to Clinton on moral grounds, Pollack and the others had issued a stark warning: Saddam was simply too dangerous to ignore.[40]

But Clinton's calculations included other factors as well. As a former first lady, she was inclined to give deference to the president. And as a Democrat, she feared that the timing of the vote before the November midterms was forcing their hand. During a Senate Armed Services Committee hearing on the subject, she slid a note over to Chairman Levin. It read, "Carl, can we delay the vote on Iraq?"

They could not. On October 10, 2002, Senator Clinton took to the Senate floor—with the misfortune of following the lengthy, impassioned anti-war pleas of West Virginia Democrat Robert Byrd. "This is probably the hardest decision I have ever had to make," she said. But, she added, "I cast it with conviction."[41]

Her conviction was bolstered by the knowledge that the Senate's top Democrat, Tom Daschle, had already said that he, too, would vote for the Lieberman-Gephardt resolution. Daschle had his own political calculations at work. His fellow South Dakota senator, Tim Johnson, was facing a tough battle for reelection and was voting for the resolution. For Daschle to vote the other way would only serve to complicate Johnson's explanation.

Still, the majority leader did not claim, as Clinton had, to be casting his vote "with conviction." Instead, Daschle warned in his floor speech that the president had been wrong when he said, three days earlier in his Cincinnati address, that the situation with Saddam could hardly get worse than it was now. "Yes, it can," he said. "If the administration attempts to use the authority in this resolution without doing the work that is required before and after military action in Iraq, the situation there and elsewhere can indeed get worse. We could see more turmoil in the Persian Gulf, not less. We could see more bloodshed in the Middle East, not less. Americans could find themselves more vulnerable to terrorist attacks, not less."

After Daschle concluded, Byrd rose to compliment the majority leader. Taking a swipe at Gephardt, the eighty-four-year-old dean of the Senate intoned bitterly, "He is the one leader on this Hill in my party who didn't rush to judgment on this blank check we are giving the president of the United States."[42]

In all, seventy-seven senators voted for the authorization to use military force, with twenty-three opposed. Bush called Daschle after the vote to thank him. "I know it was a tough call for you," the president said. "But I think we'll prove to you that we did the right thing."[43]

Daschle continued to harbor doubts. Clinton maintained her posture of conviction all the way up until the morning of March 6, 2003, when several dozen representatives from the women's group Code Pink showed up to her Senate office and refused to leave until granted some face time. After nearly an hour of waiting, the women got their wish, and Clinton met them in her conference room. For fifteen minutes, she answered their questions in measured, solemn tones. But the dialogue took an ugly turn at the very end, when Code Pink cofounder Jodie Evans predicted that Clinton's vote for war would lead to the deaths of innocents.

"I am the senator from New York!" Clinton declared angrily. "I will never put my people's security at risk!"

"You are! You are!" they chanted as she stormed out of the conference room.[44] What the videotape of the encounter did not capture was the remark Hillary Clinton made to one of her aides after the women were out of earshot.

Muttered the senator, "I can't believe I signed up for this fucking war."[45]

CHAPTER FOURTEEN

===

A PASSING PHASE

W e don't do windows!"

When Steve Hadley learned from a CENTCOM staffer during the summer of 2002 that the war plans being briefed to President Bush concluded with a slide pertaining to postwar planning followed by that declaration—"We don't do windows!"—he thought: *Hmmm. Better look into this.*[1]

The sentiment had originated from a Bush campaign defense policy adviser named John Hillen, who in 1997 had written an article entitled "Superpowers Don't Do Windows."[2] Candidate Bush's campaign denunciations of nation-building—of Clinton recasting warriors as social workers in Kosovo and Bosnia—carried over into his presidency. When Lawrence J. Korb, a Reagan-era assistant secretary of defense, met with members of the Bush team early in the administration, he was surprised to hear the macho vow "We don't do windows" actually uttered.[3]

But to several service officers and civilians inside the Defense Department, an unsettling discrepancy had emerged by early 2002. While Secretary Rumsfeld had immersed himself in an epic and laborious reimagining of an invasion force into Iraq, very little thought had been devoted to what would happen after Saddam's army was defeated.

This disproportionality did not constitute an oversight on Rumsfeld's part. To the contrary, it reflected his predisposition. "Taking our hand off the bicycle seat so Iraqis know they have to pull up their socks, step up and take responsibility for their own country"[4] was in keeping with the secretary's low-budget, light-footprint, do-it-yourself-and-don't-call-us-we'll-call-you theology. Rumsfeld did not view rebuilding broken countries as part of his job description. He did not do windows. The post-conflict stabilization period termed Phase 4 by military planners would have to be someone else's business. As a result, remembered General John Batiste, who served as Wolfowitz's senior military aide, "I can recall the secretary issuing edicts that there would be no planning for post-fall Saddam. No post-reconstruction. No Phase 4. Forbidden within the Department of Defense."[5]

Still, the dearth of postwar planning was explained only partly by Rumsfeld's nonchalance. It originated principally from a series of rather bold assumptions, promulgated chiefly by Rumsfeld's deputy, Paul Wolfowitz. These assumptions posited that such planning was mostly unnecessary. Iraqis would rejoice at the sight of their Western liberators. Their newly shared sense of national purpose would overcome any sectarian allegiances. Their native cleverness would make up for their inexperience with self-government. They would welcome the stewardship of Iraqi expatriates who had not set foot in Baghdad in decades. And their oil would pay for everything.

These assumptions were not entirely products of the imagination. They were variously supported by fondly repeated anecdotes, by the experiences of altogether different countries in altogether different eras, by the brainpower of conservative scholars like Fouad Ajami who predicted that "the tormented people of Iraq would be sure to erupt in joy"[6] and by President Bush's unshakable conviction that all humans longed for freedom and would therefore sacrifice all else to preserve it once it was theirs.

What did not back up these dazzlingly optimistic propositions was intelligence of any sort. By comparison, the evidence of Iraqi WMD was ironclad and mountainous. The intelligence community's obsession with Iraq's weapons

and its military was matched by a near-total incuriosity about Iraqi culture
and psychology under Saddam—what U.S. Army War College professor
Jeanne Godfroy would term "the human terrain."[7]

And, as with the bleak assessments of Saddam's arsenal, the buoyant
projections of post-Saddam Iraq went mostly unchallenged within the Bush
White House. The administration's counterparts in the UK were discomfited
by such credulousness. After frequent conversations with his opposite number,
Doug Feith, on their classified line, Tony Blair's policy director in the Ministry of Defence, Simon Webb, wrote in a worried memo, "U.S. thinking has
not identified either a successor or a constitutional restructuring to provide
a more representative regime. . . . The idea that <u>anyone</u> would be better than
Saddam is unconvincing."[8]

It was not like Steve Hadley to step outside of his bureaucratic lane. The
deputy national security adviser saw no need in troubling the president with
accounts of the operatic dysfunction witnessed in the Deputies Lunches.
Hadley did not share with Doug Feith his private belief that the Feith group's
"Assessing the Relationship Between Iraq and al Qaida" briefing—which
Hadley had received together with Scooter Libby shortly after the CIA did,
in late August—struck him as thoroughly unconvincing. He certainly was
not going to tell the secretary of defense how to do his job. Still, the "We
don't do windows" briefing slide worried Hadley, all the more so because it
was not the only disquieting report to come his way.

Hadley conveyed the information to his direct superior, Condoleezza
Rice. She had been mostly in the dark about the war planning, as Rumsfeld
had zealously kept the national security adviser out of the loop. "Colin, have
you talked to your buddies in the Pentagon about this?" she asked Powell.
But the secretary of state was, for whatever reason, reluctant to interpose
himself.[9]

As Rice already knew, all sorts of people *were* thinking about "the day
after" an invasion of Iraq, even if Rumsfeld wasn't. Just one month after 9/11,
after observing the intense interest in deposing Saddam shared by Wolfowitz
and Cheney, Powell authorized the State Department to initiate the Future
of Iraq Project. Tom Warrick, the special adviser to Assistant Secretary Bill

Burns, led the project, whose first meetings with Iraqi expatriates took place in July 2002. The project's mission, said David Phillips, director of the project's Democratic Principles Working Group, "was based on the principle that you can't go to war in Iraq without talking to Iraqis. You couldn't sit on the sixth floor of the State Department and figure that all out."[10]

Over the course of nine months, the Future of Iraq Project held thirty-three meetings with Iraqi exiles, on topics ranging from agriculture to education to governance. Its expectation was not to provide an exhaustive blueprint for a post-Saddam landscape. Rather, said one State official who was deeply involved in the project, "the idea was to get Iraqis to network with each other. There was a fair amount of expertise out there in law, banking, the military, and other areas, but they weren't talking to each other. So let's get them discussing."[11]

The exiles were educated, highly opinionated, and at times cacophonous—all of which were encouraging harbingers for a representative democracy. At the same time, few of them had been to Iraq in recent years, though "everybody purported to have internal networks, because it made them feel important," said one participant.[12]

But what hamstrung the Future of Iraq Project was not so much the capabilities of the participants. Instead, it was the glaring absence of the only participant who mattered to the Iraq war hard-liners: Ahmad Chalabi. "Yeah, we didn't get involved in any of that," Chalabi's lieutenant Zaab Sethna recalled dismissively. "Future of Iraq was like a high school science project."[13] The specific reason for Chalabi's lack of involvement, said the State Department official, was that "Ahmad wanted to control it. And Allawi"—Ayad Allawi, a disaffected Baathist and head of the Iraqi National Accord—"wouldn't do it if Ahmad was in charge."[14]

The INC leader's nephew Sam Chalabi did attend some meetings, as did Chalabi's ally Kanan Makiya. Cheney's deputy national security adviser, Samantha Ravich, was an active participant. So was Feith's Iraq point man, Bill Luti, though his Office of Special Plans was intended to be doing the same activities as the Future of Iraq Project, thus leaving some to wonder whether Luti was more of a spy than an actual teammate. But it eventually became clear to the Iraqi participants that the project's original and unforgivable sin was that it was being run by State, the apostate agency.

"We had all these months of Future of Iraq meetings," recalled Makiya. "But DOD utterly despised the State Department. These interactions with the U.S. government, I'd leave feeling overwhelmed by this incredible hatred and jealousy and backbiting. Epithets a polite person wouldn't use—this was their language. It was complete chaos."[15]

BY MOST ACCOUNTS, GENERAL TOMMY FRANKS SHARED SECRETARY RUMS-feld's aversion to doing windows. "He had very little interest in it," recalled JCS chairman Richard Myers.[16] In September 2002, Franks briefed CENT-COM's final war plan, known as 1003-Victor, to Myers and the rest of the Joint Chiefs staff in the tank. After Franks had finished, Myers looked around the room and asked if there were any questions.

JCS director of operations General Gregory Newbold raised his hand. Somewhat perplexed, Newbold said to Franks, "I didn't hear anything be-yond a halt just before Baghdad. I didn't hear the plan for the rest of the country or what we're going to do after Saddam."

"Well," replied Franks, leaning back in his chair, "I like to preserve my flexibility. I'll handle the situation when it comes up."[17]

In reality, the swaggering Texan was attempting to bluff his way to vic-tory with the meager hand he had been dealt by Rumsfeld. Since June 2002, a team of five men stationed in Kuwait had been tasked by CENTCOM specifically with drawing up a post-conflict plan. Upon arrival at the base that month, the team's new leader, Colonel Kevin Benson, asked the lead planner of the Coalition Forces Land Component Command why they had not yet begun Phase 4 planning. When the weary planner handed Benson the terse communiqué from Wolfowitz—"We have a brigade on the ground. Why can't we go in now?"—the colonel laughed, thinking it had to be a prank: *This guy's busting my ass.*

Benson and his team were soon read into Franks's war planning. But while the CENTCOM planning team in Tampa remained overwhelmed by

Rumsfeld's endless tinkering with the invasion scheme, the post-conflict base planners toiled, in obscurity and under-resourced, for fully eight months. The plan Benson sent over in February 2003 lacked the benefit of knowing what kind of post-Saddam government it would be handing power over to. It simply assumed that there would be some governing body, and that other countries, along with the UN, would be there on the ground to assist with the reconstruction efforts.[18]

That the JCS lacked visibility into CENTCOM's Phase 4 planning only intensified the generals' concerns that post-Saddam preparations were a low priority. By the early summer of 2002, General George Casey, the JCS's director of strategy, had grown tired of waiting on Franks to furnish something. On July 10, Casey established the Iraq Political-Military Cell (IPMC) and put a Navy admiral named Bud Jewett in charge of it. In addition to numerous JCS staffers, the cell included members of the State Department and the CIA, as well as Bill Luti and Abram Shulsky, from Feith's office.

Over the next several weeks, the IPMC produced a flurry of papers and taskings on security, economic, and humanitarian issues. "We had pieces of the puzzle," one of the participants recalled, "but they weren't all integrated into a collective whole." As with State's Future of Iraq Project, Luti's presence did not seem altogether forthright. "I would say Bill Luti and OSD [the Office of the Secretary of Defense] got a lot more out of us than we did out of them," the participant added. "I don't think they were fully transparent, except in their opinion that Chalabi should be the anointed one."[19]

THE PROBLEM, THEN, WAS NOT THAT NO ONE IN THE BUSH ADMINISTRATION was talking about post-Saddam planning. The problem was that the right people were not listening.

Condi Rice sought to remedy this. She instructed Hadley to contact the NSC's director of defense policy, Frank Miller. In mid-August, Hadley called Miller's deputy, who reached his boss on vacation in New Hampshire, to congratulate him: Miller was now in charge of something called the Executive Steering Group.

Hadley did not need to do very much explaining. In recent weeks, Miller had been the notetaker at the contentious Deputies Lunches. The writing was on the walls, ceiling, and floors: military action against Iraq was very likely. Rice and Hadley wanted Miller to oversee a process that pushed all the bickering to the side. If war was imminent, the NSC and all relevant agencies needed to be ready.

The Executive Steering Group, or ESG, would supersede the Iraq Political-Military Cell and, at least in theory, Feith's Office of Special Plans as well. Miller's experience in the national security bureaucracy's apparatus dated back to the Reagan era. He had a wealth of back-channel contacts, had a healthy estimation of his own abilities, and was not easily cowed. Still, Miller had back-benched meetings where Rumsfeld, Wolfowitz, and Feith steamrollered the process. OSD was accustomed to having its way. Recognizing the jittery politics at hand, Miller announced that ESG meetings would be held not in the White House Situation Room but in the Pentagon. As Miller confided to his deputy, Tom Greenwood, "We're not going to get any cooperation out of these guys if we don't do that. It's a small compromise."[20]

Despite that concession, the principal reason for Rice and Hadley's having formed the ESG—to ensure that the war planning was adequate—was once again thwarted by the Defense Department. "Secretary Rumsfeld was very controlling," recalled Lincoln Bloomfield, Powell's assistant secretary for political and military affairs, who served as one of State's ESG designees. "His subordinates didn't have the authority to say yes to anything, but they had many creative ways of saying no, which was the only answer they were authorized to give. They would stop the conversation and say, 'Wait—if we're talking about oil now, that's not for this group. We're handling that.' Or, 'If it's about the Revolutionary Guard, let's take that off-line.' To be honest, the OSD circle removed from the process some very key issues that were in retrospect consequential."[21]

Similarly, Rumsfeld's generals were less than helpful at the ESG meetings. "That's under advisement and study," the CENTCOM rep would carefully reply to a question. Or, "We can't give this to you before the SecDef receives it, and he's supposed to get that update three weeks from now."

Apoplectic at Bill Luti's refusal to provide any information, a CIA participant demanded at the end of one meeting, "Then what are our next steps?" Luti did not reply; the CIA rep was not invited to future meetings. The DOD attendees, recalled one of the participants, "were not there to cooperate and help us advance the mission. They were there to collect information and then go back."[22]

In the end, subservience to DOD's wishes was the only way for the ESG to function. Miller asked for and received from Franks a list of more than a hundred things the group could assist CENTCOM with, from basing rights to a plan for retraining a conquered Iraqi army. Establishment of refugee camp sites, protection of oil fields, and preservation of cultural sites were hashed over at length. Not until December 2002, however, did Steve Hadley approach his harried ESG director and ask Miller the question that had prompted the NSC's intervention four months earlier.

Asked Hadley, "The president wants to know, how are we going to be running postwar Iraq?"

DURING THE SUMMER OF 2002, JIM THOMAS, THE SPECIAL ASSISTANT TO Wolfowitz, reacquainted himself with Gregory Schulte, whom he had known from the midnineties while doing NATO work in Brussels. Schulte had been the director of NATO's Bosnia Task Force and later helped oversee the postwar missions in Kosovo. Thomas asked him to come to the Pentagon to talk about postwar planning. As he listened to Schulte describe his experiences in the Balkans, two things occurred to Wolfowitz's special assistant: first, that the post-conflict challenges were profoundly complex, and second, that Greg Schulte understood how to meet those challenges better than almost any living American.

But even as Thomas later brought up to Wolfowitz the idea of bringing into the Pentagon the ultimate "day-after" expert to assist with Phase 4 Iraq planning, he could see from his boss's slack expression what Greg Schulte's name truly meant to Rumsfeld: *Clinton holdover.*

"It's not going to happen," Wolfowitz said—quietly, but with finality.[23]

Schulte, who would become Rice's executive secretary at the NSC the following year, could hardly have been surprised to learn that his experiences in the Balkans counted as a disqualifier to the Rumsfeld team. After all, that same summer he had given a talk at National Defense University about the need for postwar planning in Iraq. A few of Tommy Franks's war planners had attended.

Their response to his lecture, Schulte would recall, was "We don't escort kids to school. That's Clinton stuff. We fight wars."[24]

CHAPTER FIFTEEN

INSPECTORS

T hroughout the first six months of 2002, Cheney and Libby received a series of briefings on biological warfare from a CIA weapons analyst whose mustachioed good looks reminded Libby of Errol Flynn. The analyst, Jerry Watson, found the vice president to be polite and attentive—especially upon learning that Watson had spent part of the nineties accompanying the UNSCOM weapons inspectors through sites in Iraq.

"How well did you know them?" the vice president inquired.

When Watson responded that he knew the UNSCOM inspectors on a first-name basis, Cheney turned to Libby. "I've got to go do this videoconference with the president," he said. "But I want you two to keep talking about the inspections process." Cheney suggested that Libby continue his discussion with Watson in the Oval Office, since the president was out of town.

The two men resumed their conversation in Bush's office. Cheney's chief of staff pelted the CIA analyst with questions. Yes, Watson said, he'd had some concerns about UNSCOM. There was a French inspector on the team whom some suspected of leaking information to Saddam's regime, with the result that the sites would be suspiciously empty by the time UNSCOM arrived. By and large, however, Watson thought the inspectors had done excellent work.

Libby brushed past this. "What about the new team?" he wanted to know. "Will they be about as effective as the old one?"

Libby was referring to the United Nations Monitoring, Verification and Inspection Commission, or UNMOVIC, which had been established immediately after UNSCOM was disbanded in 1999. "Not at first," replied Watson. "They're new at it, so it's going to take them a while to learn all the deception patterns. They've got a long learning curve ahead of them."

Watson left the briefing figuring that he had simply stated the obvious. But then he watched Cheney's Nashville VFW speech on August 26, in which the vice president asserted that "a person would be right to question any suggestion that we should just get inspectors back into Iraq, and then our worries will be over." About two weeks after the speech, Watson and a second analyst gave a briefing to NSC staffers. To Condi Rice, who had recently returned from Crawford, Watson sheepishly confessed that he might have inadvertently supplied ammunition for Cheney's speech.

Rice was furious. Did Watson have any idea how much effort she, Powell, Blair, and others had expended trying to persuade the president to go to the UN and agree to a new inspections process?

"I got used," Watson acknowledged glumly.[1]

THE DIRECTOR OF UNMOVIC, DR. HANS BLIX, HAD RECEIVED A FORESHADowing of the skepticism he would face from the Bush administration when he visited Washington on January 10, 2002. Bush had yet to deliver his "axis of evil" speech. But Blix could see that attitudes toward Saddam had hardened since the UN inspector's previous visit to the White House, several months before 9/11. Back then, Rice had assured Blix that the new administration was supportive of the UN and that its policy toward Iraq remained one of containment. By January 2002, however, Rice had a darker view. Bush's national security adviser told Blix that she could envision Saddam giving his weapons to terrorists, or even using them himself. Rice offered no new intelligence to support this belief.

That same day, Blix went over to the Pentagon and met with Doug Feith. The defense undersecretary told the chief inspector that he was concerned about the team Blix was recruiting. What if they were secretly Saddam sympathizers? What if their real interest was not to master inspection techniques but to learn how best to thwart them?[2]

Blix did not meet Paul Wolfowitz during that trip to the Pentagon. Three months later, however, *The Washington Post* reported that around the time of Blix's visit, the deputy secretary had tasked the CIA with producing a study on the inspector's previous tenure as a nuclear inspector for the IAEA.[3]

Blix, a phlegmatic seventy-three-year-old Swedish diplomat, was unruffled by that disclosure. What he found more revealing was the story's suggestion that Wolfowitz and others feared "that new inspections—or protracted investigations over them—could torpedo their plans for military action to remove Hussein from power."[4]

Hans Blix was unaware that the topic of the UN and its inspectors had consumed the Bush administration throughout the spring and summer of 2002. The contours and sides in this debate were familiar. Powell and Armitage argued that an international coalition could be amassed only after first letting UN inspectors back into Iraq to determine whether Saddam had abandoned or reconstituted his weapons program. Rumsfeld, Wolfowitz, Feith, Cheney, and Libby maintained that Saddam was far too skilled a deceiver for UNMOVIC to ever discover the truth and that the fruitless inspections effort would surely drag on forever. Rumsfeld shared with Cheney a dim view of UN inspectors. Whatever they had found in Iraq during the nineties, the secretary inaccurately said to a group of reporters in April, was "a result of a defector giving them a heads-up."[5]

Rice and Hadley were once again caught in the middle. Bush had been persuaded by Powell that there was no point going to the UN without asking for a resolution that, through an inspections process, gave Saddam a final chance to comply. But Rice and her deputy could also see that the president's patience was wearing thin. It was additionally important for them not to alienate Vice President Cheney and the other Iraq militants. When Rice met with Hans Blix on June 18, she used a rhetorical formulation that had been coined by Libby: the United States' goal was to disarm Iraq, not merely inspect it.[6]

On the day of Bush's speech to the UN, September 12, the NSC released a twenty-one-page paper entitled "A Decade of Deception and Defiance: Saddam Hussein's Defiance of the United Nations."[7] The document was the Bush White House's way of warning the UN that the Iraqi dictator should not be awarded the benefit of the doubt. Five days later, on the 17th, Iraqi foreign minister Naji Sabri read aloud a letter from Saddam at the UN, welcoming inspectors "without conditions" to "remove any doubts Iraq still possesses weapons of mass destruction."[8] Fleischer's office fired off a press statement that same day, declaring such promises all too familiar and thus not to be taken at face value.[9]

At another NSC meeting in early September, Rice suggested an idea that she hoped would unite the war council. She and Hadley had met with a retired Air Force general named Charles Boyd, who proposed that the UN send armed inspectors into Iraq. Rice argued that the very act of Saddam's agreeing to let inspectors back into Iraq might prove so humiliating that the military would overthrow him.

Bush was momentarily intrigued by the idea. Then Powell scoffed, "What—if they can't get into a site, they'll shoot their way in? Get into a gunfight with the Iraqi army?" In a rare if unintended moment of unity, Cheney and Rumsfeld chimed in with disdainful comments of their own. "It got laughed out of the room," recalled one of the participants.[10]

Meanwhile, Libby had offered up a proposal during one of the Deputies Lunches in September. What if the deputies were to fashion an inspection regimen that was too impermeable for Saddam to puncture, and then insert it into a resolution for the UN to vote on? Libby and Wolfowitz had a few ideas along these lines. No site would be off-limits. No advance notice would need to be given for any inspection. Any Iraqi scientist the inspectors wished to interview could be flown out of the country, along with their families, to avoid being tortured or killed by Saddam's thugs.

Libby and Eric Edelman were sitting in the chief of staff's small office, adjacent to Cheney's in the West Wing, one day in September when his phone rang. It was Marc Grossman, Powell's undersecretary for political affairs. "We're not going to participate in this," Grossman told Libby. "An inspection regimen like that stands no chance of passing the UN. It's just setting up diplomacy for failure."

Libby and Edelman were stunned. State wasn't even willing to *discuss* this? To them it was another case, along with snubbing Chalabi, of Powell's department acting as a dissident faction rather than as part of the Bush team.

Grossman viewed things differently. He knew that working with the UN was not Cheney's preference—that the vice president had lost this argument to Powell and Blair—and that all of the hard-liners distrusted the inspectors. This new gambit did not strike Grossman as a willingness on OVP's part to view Hans Blix's team more confidently. More likely the tough-regimen idea was a poison pill guaranteed to get a "no" vote from the UN, allowing Bush to then say to Blair and the rest of the world, "Well, we tried."[11]

Grossman's skepticism was well founded. On the evening of September 22, Bill Luti sent Hadley (with copies to Cheney, Libby, and Edelman) a briefing presentation entitled "UNMOVIC: Building in a Disarmament and WMD Elimination Authority." After establishing the inspectors' failures during the nineties, Luti in his next slide listed several reasons why "UNMOVIC is weaker than UNSCOM" (among them Jerry Watson's observation that they lacked on-the-ground experience). "But," Luti's document observed, "even the most intrusive inspection regimen can only hinder Iraqi/WMD/missile development, not eliminate it." His proposed solution, then, was to add an American-led "Disarmament and Elimination authority" that could establish new no-fly zones, impound equipment, have unfettered access to Iraqi military bases, and obtain armed backup from CENTCOM. The modest proposal would in effect give Saddam a ludicrously untenable choice: allow Iraq to become a U.S.-led occupation zone or face war.[12]

Blix was surprised when he learned that some of the "coercive inspection" ideas expressed in Bill Luti's brief had now become American negotiating points for a UN resolution.[13] The U.S. ambassador to the UN, John Negroponte, seemed to Blix embarrassed by their draconian nature.[14]

Negroponte himself was being squeezed. To appease Wolfowitz, who distrusted any State official with the task of negotiating the resolution—though that was in fact a UN ambassador's job—Hadley had assigned the NSC's sharpest-elbowed conservative, Elliott Abrams, to assist. Upon his arrival in New York, Abrams met with the UN ambassador in his office and bluntly informed him, "You understand that my job here is to spy on you."[15] But then Abrams's wife became ill, and in his place Hadley sent Rice's general counsel, John Bellinger, to litigate every clause.

Wolfowitz, Libby, and Luti had already won one important battle: in Bush's Cincinnati speech on October 7, the president had demanded that inspectors be allowed to fly Iraqi scientists and their families out of the country to be interviewed. If the president said it, then it was going in the resolution. But the true must-have item that Negroponte and Bellinger were instructed to fight for was a magic clause: *Iraq has been and remains in material breach of its obligations.* "Has been and remains in material breach" meant that even if Blix's team found nothing, Saddam's *past* UN violations were sufficient to justify war.[16]

On November 8, the United Nations Security Council unanimously passed Resolution 1441. The UN was granting Saddam a final chance to declare his arsenal and comply with inspections—though, as a legalistic sword of Damocles, the resolution already found him "in material breach." The president called his UN ambassador right after the vote. "Hey, good going, Ponty!" Bush exclaimed, using the nickname Negroponte had been given at Yale, which the president's uncle Bucky Bush had attended at the same time.

Weeks would pass before John Negroponte finally learned just how much military planning and troop deployment had already been under way—all suggesting, the ambassador would later reflect, that "the resolution was just a bump in the road for those who wanted to invade."[17]

―――

HANS BLIX AND THE IRAQ HAWKS DID HAVE ONE VERY IMPORTANT THING IN common. Blix believed that Saddam had something to hide. So did the rest of his team.[18] Like soldiers and policemen, weapons inspectors are wired to expect that bad behavior is there to be uncovered.

But Blix hailed from a country that had no dog in this fight. He had Americans on his team, but far fewer than did UNSCOM. Unlike its predecessor, which participating nations funded, UNMOVIC was financed through Iraq's Oil-for-Food Program and was, as he would put it, "not in anyone's pockets." Blix wished to avoid the presence of embedded CIA agents, which had tainted UNSCOM.[19] His employer was the UN, and his job was to determine whether Saddam Hussein was in violation of its international standards, not to reinforce the Bush administration's case for war.

It was his job description more than his employer that would prove to be Hans Blix's greatest liability. "The findings were plausible," he later wrote of the National Intelligence Estimate, "but we needed evidence."[20] By contrast, the president was already on record as saying that he did not intend to wait for evidence while dangers gathered—that he refused to stand by until the smoking gun finally materialized in the form of a mushroom cloud. Where Blix's sole investment rested in discovering whatever the truth may be, Bush was haunted by the "plausible," and even the "possible," the dots yet unconnected.

The president was additionally haunted by the conundrum of coercive diplomacy. What if it succeeded? What would success even look like? If inspectors, after having free run of Iraq, found no weapons—then what? Or if they found an immense trove of WMD—then what? If Saddam proactively handed over his entire arsenal—then what? Under which of those eventualities would the United States invade? And under which would Saddam's fate be left to the judgment of his fellow Iraqis? Would the Americans be content to see another bushy-mustached Baathist step in and lead Iraq? Or an Islamic fundamentalist? Or Ahmad Chalabi? Or nobody?

Most if not all of these scenarios had been considered in NSC, principals, or deputies meetings. But no firm plans existed to confront any of them. The only plan on the books was a war plan.

On November 25, 2002, Blix and his team of inspectors would land in Baghdad. Over the next four months, and for the first time in nearly four years, UNMOVIC would slowly accumulate what the intelligence community and the U.S. government had lacked all this time. They would come closer than any non-Iraqi had to achieving ground truth.

How the Bush White House would respond to the truth was another open question.

"MR. BLIX, YOU DO KNOW THAT THESE IRAQIS HAVE WEAPONS OF MASS DE-struction?" Wolfowitz asked sharply.

It was October 3, 2002. Blix, chief nuclear inspector Mohamed ElBara-dei, and several members of their teams sat in a State Department conference room. Powell, Rice, and JCS vice chairman Peter Pace were also there. Blix, in fact, did believe that Saddam had retained a prohibited weapons program. His hope was that the dictator would use this final opportunity to claim that some Iraqi general had been hiding all these weapons without official per-mission and thereupon hand them over to UNMOVIC.

But Blix didn't disclose any of this, since he viewed his opinions on the matter to be irrelevant. Instead he pointed out to Wolfowitz that the re-ports he had seen thus far from the U.S. and UK intelligence sources were tantalizing—but, so far at least, lacking in evidence.

The deputy secretary leaned against the conference table, elaborately annoyed with Blix's seeming insistence that intelligence officials, rather than Saddam, shouldered the burden of proof. "It was 'Why are we wasting time with this old fool, let's get on with it?'" according to one participant.[21]

Wolfowitz felt that his condescension toward Blix was warranted. The deputy secretary had heard a rumor that when Blix worked for the IAEA in 1991, he was just about to pronounce the Iraqi regime purged of nuclear capa-bility when a different inspection team discovered alarming evidence to the contrary.[22] The Swede's passivity was rankling. It was Wolfowitz who had pushed for the clause in the UN resolution that would allow inspectors to fly Iraqi scientists and their families out of the country to be interviewed in a secure environment. Wolfowitz would later urge Blix to make use of this power. It would be like issuing the regime a subpoena, he told the inspector. The government would have to permit this or face dire consequences.[23]

Blix made clear that he thought Wolfowitz's idea was foolish. Would you extract not only a scientist's wife and children but also his cousins in Basra and his aunt in Mosul? What if the scientists and their families didn't want to leave Iraq? Would you remove them by force? (In the end, Blix never made use of this power.)[24]

At the meeting in the State Department, Rice was also talking tough— at least in front of Wolfowitz. She told Blix and ElBaradei that the inspection team's intelligence unit should be led by an American. "We trust our people," Rice said crisply.[25]

Blix did not back down on this matter. His intelligence unit was headed by Jim Corcoran, the former deputy director of the Canadian Security Intelligence Agency. Blix was confident that UNMOVIC would not leak under Corcoran. Furthermore, the Americans seemed to have the mistaken notion that Blix had picked a team that would be unlikely to offend the Iraqi regime. That supposition was preposterous. Saddam had not issued any demands, nor would Blix have heeded them if he had. Blix's team also included two highly qualified Russian inspectors, whose independence had not pleased the Russian government. In other words, Blix was his own man. He did not intend to be a "façade" for a U.S. operation or for anyone else.[26]

Rice did not back down, either. "As you are aware," she said, "the security of the United States is threatened, and it is therefore free to take whatever measures are necessary to protect its security."[27]

Still, Rice was pleasantly surprised by Blix's intestinal fortitude. The old diplomat was honest and he was tough, she concluded. She was less sure about ElBaradei, who had conveyed to her his belief that Saddam had not reconstituted his nuclear program. The IAEA had been wrong about this in 1991, she thought.[28]

Four weeks later, Blix and ElBaradei were summoned to the White

House to meet the president for the first time. First, however, they were led to the vice president's office. Cheney and his staff had a message to send, which was that the inspectors were on the clock. As one of Cheney's senior staffers would recall thinking, "Were they going to do what we needed them to do in the time we needed to give them to do it? And were they going to say the things that they would need to say to make it clear that material breaches had continued and that the jig was up?"[29]

Cheney received his guests from behind his desk and dispensed with pleasantries. "The U.S. is ready to work with the United Nations inspectors," he said. "But we are also ready to discredit the inspections in order to disarm Iraq."

The message could not have been more clear to Blix and ElBaradei. If they failed to find Saddam's weapons, the Bush administration would push UNMOVIC and IAEA aside and recover the weapons themselves.[30]

They were then ushered into the Oval Office. Bush played the good cop. The president was as warm and self-effacing as the vice president had been cold-blooded and tart. It was an honor to meet the chief inspectors, Bush assured them. Swiveling away from his desk and pantomiming a gunslinger, he said, "I'm not a trigger-happy Texas cowboy, with six-guns." His first choice, he assured them, was peace.

But, the president added, he did not intend to drag out this process, to watch as the UN replicated the impotence of the League of Nations. The United States and a "coalition of the willing" would take matters into their own hands. Like Cheney, Bush did not ask Blix and ElBaradei any questions about what they thought or what they expected to encounter in Iraq the following month. Both chief inspectors came away with the distinct impression that the Bush White House had stopped listening.[31]

In fact, Bush was torn between his gut instincts and the dutifulness inculcated by his father, himself a former ambassador to the UN. He did in fact want a coalition behind the United States; he did in fact want that coalition to be willing, not arm-twisted. At the same time, the French and the Germans were driving him crazy. When Bush spoke about UN inspections to his closest foreign ally, Tony Blair, on their secure line in November, the president did not bother to conceal his impatience. Blix's inspections needed to be quick and unpredictable, Bush said. He was frustrated by the Swede's intimation that the outcome of UNMOVIC's findings would dictate whether war was necessary.

"That is *our* judgment," the president told Blair. "He is *not* going to get between us and freedom. Once we strike, we go for it. We don't wait for the world to sing Kumbaya, to hold hands and wait for Saddam to develop a better karma."[32]

Bush vented freely to the prime minister, confident that Blair understood and would keep their discussions inside No. 10 Downing Street. (Which Blair did, except that his communications director, Alistair Campbell, was taking notes and would eventually publish his diary.) Blair also understood the singular burden of going to war. Hans Blix was not going to tell Bush what to do. Neither was Cheney or Powell or the Iraq weather charts, or even Tony Blair. Bush was making his own mind up—not altogether heedless to others, but also not asking new questions or demanding more information.

Still, he maintained that he had not yet decided.[33] The answer was coalescing inside him while he impatiently stalked the sidelines, waiting for Saddam's next play.

ON SATURDAY, DECEMBER 7, A YOUNG UNMOVIC STAFF MEMBER, ACCOMPA-nied by a UN security official, arrived in Baghdad. They were given hand luggage containing twelve thousand pages. About three thousand of those pages constituted Iraq's formal declaration of its weapons program, and the rest were support materials, mainly in Arabic. The two men flew with their cargo from Baghdad to Cyprus to Frankfurt to New York. From UN headquarters, the documents were transported by FBI helicopter to the CIA's office in Langley, where copies were made that Sunday evening for each of the five permanent members of the UN Security Council.[34]

At eight the following morning, several CIA analytical teams—focusing on biological weapons, chemical weapons, nuclear weapons, ballistic missiles, and imports—assembled in a conference room and began to pore over the documents. Rumsfeld had asked the analysts beforehand, *How will we know if Saddam's declaration amounts to compliance?* The agency's answer: *We'll know he has come clean by the way he responds to the assessments made in the NIE and the British intelligence dossier.*

Within a week's time, the CIA analyst entrusted with summarizing the day's findings in a Presidential Daily Briefing memo, Bill McLaughlin, realized that he was reporting the same thing over and over. Eventually McLaughlin briefed Tenet on Iraq's weapons declaration. "There was nothing new," he would recall, "and they certainly didn't address any of our concerns."[35]

"When Cheney's people saw this pile of rehashed old reports," recalled a senior administration official, "they wanted to go to war. They said, 'This is a continuation of the material breach.'"[36]

Still, by this time Blix's team had already been combing through sites in Iraq for the past few weeks, with no major discovery. The outlook did not look promising to Bush. As his communications director, Dan Bartlett, would recall, "Look, all the shenanigans with the inspectors was not confidence-inspiring. And this is what you do in a pre-9/11 world: inspectors running around, they're milking the clock, this is part of the playbook."[37]

On the ground in Iraq, Blix was interpreting the situation differently. The twenty sites they inspected during the first week on the job had yielded nothing of interest. Blix still suspected that there were weapons to discover. Was the U.S. intelligence community not telling him everything about where to look? He called a sympathetic ear, Colin Powell, and complained, "You're like a librarian sitting on all these books that you don't want to lend."[38]

Blix's concerns were shared by Senator Carl Levin. During a closed hearing of the Senate Armed Services Committee, Levin accused Tenet of withholding information from UNMOVIC about potential WMD sites. Tenet assured the senator that this was not the case.[39]

Another senior CIA official, WINPAC deputy director Andrew Liepman, was there at the hearing as well. Just a few days earlier, Liepman had been summoned to brief Vice President Cheney on how the CIA would support UNMOVIC's efforts. In front of Cheney's staff, Rice, Wolfowitz, and others, the vice president also asked about what information the CIA was giving Blix's inspectors. But he phrased the question differently than Levin had.

"We're not going to give them the really good intel, are we?" Cheney asked.[40]

The vice president's concerns were shared by Wolfowitz and others in the administration. As one intelligence official who sat in on this briefing would explain, "The fear was if we briefed this stuff to UNMOVIC, it would get leaked and the weapons would disappear. Better to save it as a cruise missile target when the war broke out."[41]

Liepman assured Cheney that "the really good intel" was not making its way to Blix. His answer was not substantively different from the one he and Tenet gave Levin a few days later. As Liepman reasoned to himself, there *was* no "really good intel," either to give or to withhold.[42]

But it was also the case that Blix's and Levin's suspicions were correct. As one senior administration official would carefully put it, "We shared with them what we could."[43] UNMOVIC was being set up for failure.

≡≡≡

CHAPTER SIXTEEN

THE MAGICIAN
AND THE WARRIOR

Sometime in May of 2002, President Bush received a CIA briefing that included perhaps the most alarming intelligence about Iraq he had yet heard. NSA intercepts had picked up communications between an Iraqi general and an Iraqi procurement agent who was based in Australia. The general had directed the procurement agent to buy equipment for Iraq's unmanned aerial vehicles (UAV) program. In the spring of 2002, the agent had given an Australian equipment distributor his shopping list. Among the items was Garmin GPS software that included maps of major cities in the United States. Alarmed, the distributor contacted the authorities.[1]

This PDB presented Bush with the first intelligence appearing to confirm his nightmare scenario: Saddam intended to attack the U.S. homeland. Why else would his military want mapping software of American cities? Of course, simply owning U.S. maps would not make Saddam dangerous. But the existence of Saddam's UAV program was well known; in fact, the same procurement agent in Australia had been part of that program. The regime's intention before the Gulf War to develop unmanned aircraft that could spray biological weapons onto a population had been divulged by Saddam's son-in-law Hussein

Kamel in 1995.[2] CIA analysts deduced that Saddam still harbored such ambitions. The mapping software strongly suggested that those ambitions now extended to attacking the United States.

And how would Saddam manage to do so? How would his BW-loaded aerial vehicle make its way from Baghdad to the United States? The PDB did not speculate. But where the intelligence left off, the imagination of the Bush administration stepped up to connect the dots. As Paul Wolfowitz and other Iraq hawks conceived it, the UAV could easily be shipped in a cargo container across the Atlantic, where a terrorist cell would then launch it from a boat and, by remote control, use it like a crop duster to poison the city of New York.[3]

This, along with the earlier intelligence extracted from Ibn al-Shaykh al-Libi in which Iraq was said to be training Al Qaeda terrorists to construct illicit weapons, marked a turning point for Bush, according to one of his senior advisers: "We get this report about they've bought this software that's supposed to be mapping the United States. He's hearing this intel, and the diplomacy is going nowhere. And so I think that's when he really starts thinking, *I've got to get something done in Iraq.* . . . It gets everybody's attention that this mapping software is out there. It did have a huge impact. It had an impact on everybody."[4]

The mapping software intelligence was only the darkest hue of a greater shadow enveloping the Oval Office. By the fall of 2002, Bush was no longer sunnily invoking the word "opportunity," as he had in the first months after 9/11. The menace of Saddam now loomed ever greater. In his Cincinnati speech on October 7, Bush had likened the dictator to Hitler—an indicator that the president could not foresee a diplomatic outcome.

Direness was Bush's daily bread. The PDBs, retooled to rivet the First Customer in the manner of a Tom Clancy novel, were replete with portent. These daily reports, the Commission on the Intelligence Capabilities of the United States Regarding Weapons of Mass Destruction (more commonly known as the WMD Commission) would later find, were, "if anything, more alarmist and less nuanced than the NIE"—and, "with their attention-grabbing headlines and drumbeat of repetition, left an impression of many corroborating reports when there were in fact few sources."[5]

Saddam was in fact *not* engaged in any new and diabolical activity that fall. But it certainly seemed that way, given that the intense demand for WMD information had produced a torrent of grim disclosures. Policymakers who had been consuming intel for decades had seen nothing like this before. As Marc Grossman, of the State Department, would recall, "Why was the intelligence on Iraq WMD the best intelligence I'd ever seen in my whole career? So acute, and so specific. And I don't think I ever said to myself, '*This looks too good to be true.*"[6]

It was not a coincidence that Bush's mornings had become a daily horror show of WMD scenarios. Now that it seemed evident to CIA director George Tenet that America was headed for war, he saw no profit in holding anything back. As a CIA senior manager would say, "George definitely wanted the president to see everything—that was definitely driven by George."[7]

But it was not just that Bush was getting so much more WMD intelligence of a particularly vivid nature. His presenters were also more theatrical than before. Even in normal times, the job of PDB briefer was understood to be a fast-track assignment, reserved for the agency's most politically attuned officials.[8] "You're not going to get picked for one of those positions by being an outlier," said one intelligence officer. "You're going to be a conformist, watch the body language, not tell him anything he doesn't want to hear. It makes careers."[9]

Now, however, Tenet had begun to supplement the daily briefers with his deputy director of operations, Jim Pavitt, and with case officers—"the ops guys," said another CIA senior manager, "who are fantastic salesmen."[10] If in the middle of a briefing Tenet sensed that the president was losing interest, the first senior manager recalled, the director would turn the floor over to his operations officer: "That's their job, to be gung-ho and proactive."[11]

"It was, I have to admit, very heady," recalled one of the agents who began briefing Bush in the fall of 2002. "As a case officer, you put out your intel, you don't see anything after that. And here you are watching this stuff that's having an impact. You have the president of the United States asking your opinion."[12] But the intoxicating exposure to the president affected that particular case officer's judgment, recalled one of the agency's senior officials: "I'd have to temper him. I'd say, 'We can't go into the Oval and say, '*Let's invade tomorrow!*'"[13]

But even the amped-up PDBs and their supercharged presenters did not fully account for the grimness surrounding George W. Bush that fall. It pervaded his White House. The shared language of a more innocent yesteryear—"soft bigotry of low expectations," "personal responsibility," "tax relief"—was now supplanted by a bleak vocabulary of mushroom clouds, deception and denial, imminent threats and securing the homeland. As the case officer who briefed Bush put it, "He's being fed stuff from OVP, OSD, their stuff is getting darker, their point of view is things are getting worse, and he's being fed all that."[14]

AS IT HAPPENED, THERE WAS A LESS DARK EXPLANATION FOR THE UAV MAP-ping software. Two CIA analysts and an Australian intelligence officer began following the Iraqi procurement agent and reading his emails in late August 2002. Eventually they brought him in for questioning and confronted him about the American maps. The Iraqi was stunned. He said that it was the Garmin hardware he had been interested in. The only reason he purchased the mapping software, he said, was because he thought the hardware wouldn't work without it. The presentation on the vendor's web page seemed to confirm this account.

By now it was late September and the NIE was nearly complete. It contained an alarming passage about Iraq's UAV program, saying that intelligence "strongly suggests that Iraq is investigating the use of these UAVs for missions targeting the United States."[15] The two CIA analysts flew home and implored John Landry, the national intelligence officer in charge of that section in the NIE, to soften the language by deleting the word "strongly."

"You're doing this *now*?" Landry asked incredulously. He refused to make the change.

On October 1, just as George Tenet was walking into the National

Foreign Intelligence Board meeting to formally approve the contents of the NIE, one of the CIA analysts approached the director. She urged Tenet to downgrade the UAV assessment from "strongly suggests" to "suggests." Annoyed, Tenet waved her off and stepped into the NFIB conference room.

The passage stayed as it was in the NIE. Meanwhile, the other CIA analyst—who happened to be Jerry Watson, Scooter Libby's Errol Flynn lookalike who had inadvertently stoked Cheney's criticisms about the UN weapons inspectors—was reviewing the text of Bush's upcoming Cincinnati speech. He came to a passage about Iraq's unmanned aerial vehicles: "We're concerned that Iraq is exploring ways of using these UAVs for missions targeting the United States."[16] Watson crossed out that sentence.

Two days later, Bush gave his speech. The passage about Iraq using UAVs to target the United States had been restored.

On October 9, eight days after the NIE had been published, Tenet requested a PDB memorandum explaining what the analysts had learned in Australia about the mapping software purchase. Watson wrote the PDB memo. The deputy director for intelligence, Jami Miscik, who personally approved everything that went into the PDB, argued to Tenet that it should be sent to the president. Tenet overruled her.

When Watson learned that his memo had been shelved, he appealed to Deputy Director John McLaughlin.

McLaughlin denied his request, saying, "Jerry, it looks like we're flip-flopping."[17]

It was shaping up to be a contentious year for McLaughlin, a beloved figure among the agency's analysts. Tenet's preoccupation with counterterrorism meant that supervising the WMD intelligence fell largely to his deputy. This entailed numerous hours being grilled by Senator Carl Levin while keeping tabs on the key passages in the NIE. He carried an aluminum tube as a prop to briefings on the Hill. As measured and even-tempered as Tenet was mercurial, the deputy wore natty suspenders but was otherwise a by-the-book professional who pored over classified documents with a ruler, sliding it slowly downward line by line. His one indulgence was performing sleight-of-hand coin tricks, which earned him the code name Merlin from the Secret Service. In 2009, he would bestow a copy of the book *Houdini's Texas Tours* to the outgoing president, whose nickname for him was Johnny Mac.[18]

Unlike Tenet, McLaughlin held out hopes that Bush's mind was not yet made up. Still, the magician in him had always been fascinated by an American psychologist's discovery, in 1899, that a sketch of an animal could seem to some viewers to be a rabbit and to others a duck. People saw what they wished to see. McLaughlin had spent much of the spring and summer embroiled in the debate between the CIA's analysts and Scooter Libby over Saddam's purported relationship with Al Qaeda. To the deputy director, Libby and his cohort were determined to see a connection that was not there. It did not occur to McLaughlin that the intelligence community might similarly be transfixed by the optical illusion of a weapons program in Iraq.[19]

Where Bush and Tenet could be coarse, McLaughlin was unfailingly analytical, a trait that his briefings reflected. Some viewed this as a shortcoming. Nicholas Calio, Bush's director of legislative affairs, had told Tenet that his deputy's briefings on the Hill were underwhelming. "We need someone like you, with a little bit of passion, who can sell it," Calio implored the director.[20] For that same reason, Rumsfeld's office often requested that it be Tenet who delivered his usual forceful briefing to senators who were on the fence. Not wishing CIA briefings on Iraq's WMD to be reduced to macabre entertainment, one of Tenet's staffers would claim that the director was already booked that day: "I wanted them to get the John McLaughlin version."[21]

In early December, word reached Langley headquarters that the White House wanted the CIA to prepare an oral presentation on Iraq's WMD program that would feature an "Adlai Stevenson moment"[22]—referring to the famous tableau in 1962 of the U.S. ambassador to the UN presenting open-and-shut photographic evidence of Soviet ballistic missile installations in Cuba. It wasn't yet clear who would make this presentation, or where or when. And indeed, the timing of the request seemed odd, given that Hans Blix's team was already in Iraq and would presumably be furnishing on-the-ground visual proof of Saddam's arsenal any day now. The fact that such a presentation was being ordered up was tantamount to a White House vote of no confidence in Blix.

The presentation was referred to internally as the Case. That Tenet and McLaughlin had not resisted partaking in what amounted to an advocacy brief for the Bush administration was telling evidence that the agency had crossed a red line. "The first thing they teach you in CIA 101 is you don't help them make the case," said an agency official who was involved in the project. "But we were all infected in the case for war, and it was bad judgment on John and George's part to lead that charge."[23]

McLaughlin met with Bob Walpole's analytical team. "The White House has asked for our best story on Iraq," the deputy director told the WINPAC analysts. The analysts sent up what visuals they had. McLaughlin reviewed them with astonishment. "This is all there is?" he asked.[24]

He also asked the analysts in the room, "Do we have any slam-dunk evidence of WMD?"

Larry Fox, WINPAC's senior chemical weapons analyst, did not watch basketball. He asked McLaughlin what "slam dunk" meant.

"Like a smoking gun," the deputy director explained. "Undeniable. Caught red-handed."

"Ah," said Fox. "Well, no. We don't have any."

For the next two weeks, several analysts fine-tuned the presentation. "It had to be short and succinct, and it also had to be graphic and visual, much different than a written document," recalled one who worked on the Case. "There's no 'We judge' or 'This is what we think they're doing.' More conversational style, and it had to have impact."[25]

On Friday afternoon, December 20, the Case was briefed at the Pentagon. The ideal presenter would have been Walpole, who had overseen both it and the NIE. But Walpole had fallen out of favor with the Iraq hawks after he expressed doubt about the Iraq threat at the deputies meeting where Libby muttered to Feith, "Who is this guy?"[26] Nor was Tenet ideally suited, as his familiarity with the WMD intelligence was limited.

The task as briefer therefore fell to McLaughlin. He stood in Rumsfeld's conference room before a group that included Wolfowitz, Feith, Franks, and

DOD undersecretary for intelligence Stephen Cambone. The deputy director went through a series of charts. He held up his aluminum tube. Notably absent from his presentation was any mention of the UAV mapping software. Even if McLaughlin didn't want to be seen as "flip-flopping" on the matter, Jerry Watson's PDB had raised enough doubt that the deputy director thought it better to leave the subject unaddressed.

Wolfowitz, of course, noticed the omission and was displeased by it.[27] Rumsfeld and his team were polite but visibly unimpressed. They asked few questions. The only visuals that seemed to catch their attention were photographs of a vehicle believed to be a mobile biological weapons lab, described by the former Iraqi chemical engineer code-named Curveball.

The Case had failed to animate the most zealous Iraq case-makers in the Bush administration, thought one of the meeting's participants, Bill McLaughlin, the weapons analyst who had briefed Tenet on Saddam's weapons declaration (and who was not related to the deputy director). He was somewhat unnerved, then, to be told upon returning to headquarters, "Yeah, well, you've got another meeting tomorrow morning."

That meeting would take place in the Oval Office.[28]

ON SATURDAY, DECEMBER 21, AT SEVEN IN THE MORNING, GEORGE TENET, John and Bill McLaughlin, the deputy director's executive assistant, Leah Florence, and PDB briefer Andy Makridis stepped into the West Wing. While Tenet, his deputy, and Makridis gave the president his morning briefing, Florence and Bill McLaughlin waited in the anteroom. They drank coffee from Styrofoam cups bearing the White House emblem while three young staffers busily divided Christmas gifts intended for one of three destinations: the White House, Camp David, and the ranch at Crawford. A small black dog entered and began to bark ferociously at Bill McLaughlin.

"That's just Barney," said an amused voice that belonged to the president.

Bush wore his cowboy boots bearing the presidential seal and was holding a plastic bottle of Deer Park water. Cheney, Rice, Card, Hadley, Libby, and the NSC's weapons director, Robert Joseph, were assembled in the Oval

Office. Bill McLaughlin positioned the flip chart in front of them, then sat and proceeded to take notes.

"This is a rough draft—it's still in development," John McLaughlin began. For the next twenty or so minutes, he spoke almost entirely uninterrupted. He began by citing the tons of biological and chemical agents that Saddam had not provided an accounting of after the Gulf War. His charts depicted images of prohibited ballistic missiles, of an alleged chemical facility, of UAVs. He recounted Curveball's depiction of a mobile BW trailer. Lastly, he played radio intercepts purporting to be discussions among Iraqi officials about nerve agents and concealing a suspected weapons facility.[29]

It was a smoother performance than McLaughlin's briefing the day before at the Pentagon. Bush and the others had listened intently. But a thick silence settled in after he had finished.

"Again, this is a first draft," Tenet assured the president.[30]

"Nice try," said the president to McLaughlin.[31]

He did not mean it sarcastically. Bush expressed his concern clearly: "Look, in about five weeks I may have to ask the fathers and mothers of America to send their sons and daughters off to war. This has to be well developed. We have to be aware of the need to sell this to the average citizen. So it needs to be more convincing. Probably needs some better examples."

It was manifestly clear to everyone in the room that Bush did not need convincing about the nature of the Iraqi threat and the need to topple the regime. The only question to him was whether the CIA had what it took to persuade the public that the Iraqi threat justified war.

"Maybe have a lawyer look at how to lay out the structure of the argument," Bush continued. "Maybe someone with Madison Avenue experience should look at the presentation."

He added, "And it needs to tie all this into terrorism, for the domestic audience."

Bill McLaughlin suppressed a groan. The president remained convinced that Saddam would give his weapons to a terrorist group like Al Qaeda. Still, the mention of a "domestic audience" hinted at the presentation's ultimate purpose: someone, presumably Bush, would be speaking not only to Americans but to the world—probably at the United Nations, where the last "Adlai Stevenson moment" had occurred.

In sum, Bush said, the presentation left much room for improvement. Then he asked, "Can you do this, George?"

The director nodded confidently. "Slam dunk," he said.[32]

In Bob Woodward's 2004 book *Plan of Attack,* this moment would be framed as one where a president, suddenly beset by doubt, would ask, "George, how confident are you?" and then be reassured—not once but twice, with arms thrown in the air to indicate a touchdown rather than a basket—that the "case" was "a slam dunk." Interviewed by the famed *Washington Post* journalist one year after this briefing, in December 2003, with eight months' worth of scouring Iraq for weapons having yielded nothing of interest, Bush seemed intent on reminding Woodward's readers that it was his CIA director, after all, who had assured him that Saddam had weapons. "That was very important," the president told Woodward.[33]

But Tenet's words were "important" only because they helped remove any doubt as to whether the CIA could mount a solid case. As Condoleezza Rice would say, "I think the President believed that there were WMD. But I think having his intelligence chief say, *No, no, no, don't worry, it's really there* was important, because the presentation had been kind of tepid."[34]

Another White House attendee of the "slam dunk" meeting said, "The issue was not 'Do you have lockers and lockers of evidence?' The issue was 'This is a lousy job of presenting the lockers and lockers of evidence.' The president wasn't at all shaken by it."[35]

To John McLaughlin, Bush's message was clear. "This was the outcome of that meeting: 'Take another look and make sure there's nothing you've missed. Try again.'"[36]

"I HEARD THE BRIEFING DIDN'T GO TOO WELL," GEORGE HERBERT WALKER Bush said three days later to Jami Miscik.

It was the morning of Christmas Eve at Camp David. The deputy director for intelligence had offered to give the usual PDB briefer, Andy Makridis, the day off. Briefing 41 and 43 together during the Christmas season had become a tradition with Miscik, going back to when the son was president-elect. Whatever misgivings the father might have previously harbored about invading Iraq were now sublimated. The former president's posture was that of supporting the current one.

Miscik acknowledged that, yes, the Case was still a work in progress.

President Bush excused himself to make a Christmas call to the troops stationed in Afghanistan. *Well,* the father said, *surely there's a way to make the presentation stronger.*

"We've asked them to go back and scrub it," Miscik said.

But then she confessed something to the former president. "Sometimes there just *isn't* any more." What was baffling, Miscik told the elder Bush, was that the CIA had satellite images of trucks leaving facilities just as Hans Blix's inspectors were entering. But the agency wasn't hearing the kind of panic-stricken, *oh my God they're coming, move all the weapons out right away* chatter corresponding with these truck movements.

"It's just weird that we're not picking up more on the intercepts," Miscik said, more to herself than to the father.

Sometime early on Christmas morning, Jami Miscik woke up from her sleep with an unsettling thought about Saddam Hussein. She later shared it with her deputy, Michael Morell:

"What if he doesn't have any of this stuff?"[37]

JOHN MCLAUGHLIN TRIED AGAIN. HE INSTRUCTED BOB WALPOLE TO MAKE the Case more persuasive. "Give me everything you've got," Walpole in turn told his weapons analysts. "Never mind sourcing or other problems." He wanted the kitchen sink.

The chemical weapons expert Larry Fox replied to the WINPAC officer: *Look, we can say more about how Saddam is going to lengths to hide things. But we don't know what he's hiding.*[38]

On December 28, Walpole and John McLaughlin went to the White House to discuss the Case with Condi Rice. McLaughlin thought that folding the NIE's key judgments into the presentation might make it sound more definitive. As Walpole began to recite the NIE's key judgments, he was surprised to see that the national security adviser appeared to be learning about the classified document's specific conclusions for the first time.

Just a couple of minutes into his summary, Rice stopped him. "Bob?" she said, with evident concern. "If these are just *assertions*, we need to know this now."

"They're analytical assessments," Walpole replied. "The agencies have attached confidence levels to them."

Rice studied her copy, frowning. "What's 'high confidence'?" she asked. "About 90 percent?"

"About that," he said.

The national security adviser gaped at Walpole and McLaughlin. "Well," she finally said, "that's a heck of a lot lower than what the PDBs are saying!"

Well, Walpole allowed, the intelligence community was *extremely* confident that Iraq possessed ballistic missiles that flew beyond the UN-prescribed 150-kilometer restriction. "But you can't go to war over a few tenths of a kilometer," he acknowledged. The CW and BW cases were based on inference. The nuclear case, Walpole said, was "the weakest."

Rice turned to McLaughlin. "You have gotten the president way out on a limb on this," she said.

McLaughlin thought: *I'VE put Bush out on a limb?* Still, he and Walpole returned to Langley, endeavoring to keep improving the presentation.

Rice would later regret that she had not asked McLaughlin which was more accurate—the PDBs or these more cautious assessments in the Case and the NIE. She did not, in any event, report the discrepancy to the president.[39]

That same day, Walpole emailed his weapons analysts. He made clear that the White House was not interested in qualifiers. In all capital letters, Walpole wrote, "WE HAVE TO SAY IRAQ HAS WMD."[40]

Two days later, on December 30, McLaughlin sent his own memo to the weapons analysts:

Bob and company—this is a good start, and I thank everyone for the hustle in getting it to this point. There are some things we still need to work on. Here's my list:

It still needs much more display of evidence—much more texture on why we think what we think. . . . Look for every opportunity to say here are the three or four pieces of evidence that leave us little choice but to conclude what we have. I think we still have a lot to do on this score.

It has too much "intellispeak"—phrases like, "we assess," "we judge," "this suggests," "our analysts believe. . . ."

Don't be shy about saying what the source is. . . . I've told the Principals that they won't want to use this unless they are on the verge of conflict, because to do what they've asked will jeopardize sources. . . .

The nuclear section seems very thin, although the discussion of tubes is rich and a pretty good example of what I mean about sourcing and detail.[41]

By January 2, 2003, Walpole's team had gone through six drafts. On January 6, Rice and Hadley saw the latest version. Hadley commented that the nuclear case was weak. Walpole agreed. He had, in fact, been warning Hadley and Rice of this all along.[42]

What Walpole's team did not realize was that this entire exercise had been a pointless one for the agency. Immediately following the "slam dunk" meeting in the Oval Office on December 21, Vice President Cheney had said privately to Bush, "You know, Scooter's already been working on something we could use."[43]

On Monday, December 23, Libby called his deputy, Eric Edelman, and told him about McLaughlin's weak presentation two days before. "The president doesn't think it's nearly persuasive enough," Cheney's chief of staff said. "It's all over the map. It's an intelligence product. It's not a prosecutor's brief. And so they've given OVP the assignment of redoing that. I need you and John Hannah to get involved."

The next morning, Cheney's staff got to work on their alternative presentation. Libby and his staff secretary, Neil Patel, would handle the section relating to Saddam's connections to Al Qaeda. Hannah would write the section on Iraq's illicit weapons program. Edelman and Samantha Ravich would enumerate Saddam's human rights and environmental malfeasances. Bush had been told that the project would be supervised jointly by Libby and Hadley. The NSC's role turned out to be marginal. This was Scooter Libby's baby.

Still, for all of Libby's obsession with the Iraq–Al Qaeda relationship, Hannah's work on the WMD issue would prove to be the most important. His primary source would not be the NIE but instead the vast collection of cables and papers stashed away in OVP's vaults. Libby had instructed his Middle East specialist to put every damning bit of raw intelligence he could find into his brief. The burden would then be on the CIA analysts to argue why this or that bit of intel should be thrown out. Libby also wanted a livelier, more vivid presentation, with photographs and recordings. He did not want a reprise of McLaughlin's "nice try" dud.[44]

On Saturday, January 25, Libby gave a preview of the new presentation in the Situation Room. The audience included Rice, Hadley, Wolfowitz, and Armitage. More notably, the political side of the White House—Karl Rove, Dan Bartlett, chief speechwriter Michael Gerson, NSC communications director Anna Perez, and former counselor Karen Hughes—was now hearing the case against Saddam for the very first time.

At last unfettered by the CIA's judgments, Libby pulled out all the stops. Mohamed Atta meeting an Iraqi agent in Prague. An intercept of terrorists affiliated with Zarqawi laughing about killing a donkey with ricin. Trucks moving, objects apparently being dug up and buried.

Wolfowitz thought Cheney's chief of staff had done a great job. Rove found much to admire about it as well. The others had their doubts, however. To Bartlett, Libby's case seemed entirely inferential, a case of dot-connecting gone berserk. Hughes—who was no longer on the White House staff but remained influential and deeply protective of Bush—was especially forceful. "You can't just say it, Scooter," she argued. "The American people shouldn't and won't accept that. You have to prove it."[45]

Despite the concerns voiced about Libby's evidence, the consensus that arose from the Situation Room that Saturday had nothing to do with whether the case against Saddam was factually grounded. Instead, because many in the group were communications specialists, the focus became the messenger rather than the message. Said Rove, "I recall the general sense was 'Who would be the best person to make this case at the UN?' And the obvious answer was Colin Powell. Chief diplomat."[46]

"ARE YOU WITH ME ON THIS?" PRESIDENT BUSH ASKED POWELL. THE TWO were alone in the Oval Office on January 13, 2003. "I think I have to do this. I want you with me."[47]

Powell had cautioned Bush a few months earlier about the consequences of invading Iraq. But the secretary of state had never voiced opposition to the idea. Now the president of the United States—who in the past few days had already expressed his thinking to Rumsfeld, Rice, Blair, and Cheney that he would probably have to declare war on Iraq—was putting the onus on Powell. He was either on one side of the line or on the other.

The secretary had privately articulated his belief that invading Iraq was a foolish idea.[48] What if he had said no to the commander in chief? Powell would almost certainly have been obligated to resign. Many if not all of his top staffers involved in the Iraq issue—Armitage, Bill Burns, Ryan Crocker, David Pearce, Tom Krajeski, Steve Beecroft, and Yael Lempert—would also have quit, as several had already considered doing before writing the "Perfect Storm" memo instead.[49]

If State's top team had emptied out their desks, what would Powell's close friend Jack Straw, the British foreign minister, have done? Straw shared his friend's dim view of going to war with Saddam. "Powell kept saying to me, 'Removing Saddam is the easy part, but then you end up becoming the proud owner of twenty-five million Iraqis in eighteen fractious provinces,'" he recalled. "And he was absolutely right. And he kept saying that. The other thing—it was completely obvious, but never properly factored in—is that if we removed Saddam, Iran would be strengthened."

In the lead-up to war, Straw himself had considered resigning. "I thought about it a lot," he said. "I'm sort of not the resigning type. Nor is Powell, and that's the problem." But, Straw added, "If Powell had decided to resign in advance of the Iraq War, I would almost certainly have done so, too." Blair's support in the Labour Party would have cratered; conservative Tories would be second-guessing their backing of the opposition leader.[50]

Had Powell and his senior team at State resigned, had Straw joined the other cabinet members Robin Cook and Clare Short in quitting, and had Blair withdrawn his support for war under pressure from Parliament or simply failed to win an authorization vote, the narrative of collapsed momentum would have dominated the media coverage for weeks. The doubters in the JCS would have been empowered to speak out. The WMD intelligence would have been reexamined. Democrats now liberated from the onus of the midterm election cycle would have joined the chorus.

Against that tide, with its inevitable effect on public opinion, would Bush still have plowed ahead? Had the plans even been *temporarily* postponed, thereby giving Hans Blix's inspection team the time to learn what would instead become evident mere months after the invasion, could war have been avoided entirely?

This domino effect required a first move by Bush's secretary of state. "But I knew I didn't have any choice," Colin Powell would say years later. "What choice did I have? He's the president. They call me the reluctant warrior—but if you want to go to war, I know how to do it."[51]

Bush did not ask Colin Powell how to go to war, however. Instead, he asked him to sell it.

THOUGH POWELL WOULD NOT ADMIT IT, THE PRESIDENT'S REQUEST ON January 28 that he be the one to make the case against Saddam to the UN was enormously flattering.[52] Yet again, as he had when angling for unanimous support for the UN resolution, Bush was turning to his secretary of state to bail him out. And the president was doing so with Cheney's explicit acknowledgment that Colin Powell was the right man for the job. As the secretary told one of his top aides, "The vice president said to me, 'You're the most popular man in America. Do something with that popularity.'"

But, Powell added to his aide, he wasn't sure he could say no to Bush anyway. "There's only so many times I can go toe to toe with the VP," he said. "The more I think about it, the more I realize it's important to keep my job."[53]

Once the decision was made that Powell would deliver the UN speech, Rice handed him the large text that Libby's team had prepared. The cover sheet included an image of a mushroom cloud.[54] Powell viewed the document suspiciously. It wasn't his habit to recite somebody else's speech, he told the national security adviser.

Rice and Karen Hughes also proposed to Powell that he deliver a three-part speech, spread over as many days—one part on WMD, one on the terrorism angle, and the last one on Saddam's human rights abuses. This idea struck Powell as laughable. Clearly, Rice and Hughes had never sat among a UN audience. He would be lucky if he managed to hold their attention for ninety minutes. Furthermore, Powell told them, he wanted to focus on the one threat that mattered to the entire world: Saddam's weapons of mass destruction.[55]

Powell's stipulation on the speech's content was both reasonable and profoundly consequential. As a senior member of Cheney's staff later remarked, "He's the one who decided to make it all about WMD. He's the author of his own embarrassment, honestly."[56]

Among the first things Powell noticed about Libby's text were the lurid intimations about Saddam's supposed ties with bin Laden's organization. "You guys really believe all this shit?" he scoffed to one of Cheney's deputies, thus making clear where the secretary stood on the subject.[57] Powell scrapped all the work that Libby and Patel had done.

Powell knew only the CIA's baseline judgments about Saddam's WMD program, not the specifics. Just as Cheney and Rumsfeld tended to cast aspersions on the viewpoints tendered by State, Powell was of the view that if Cheney and Rumsfeld's teams believed something, it should be eyed with heightened skepticism. Their reflexive embrace of the WMD worst-case scenarios was a case in point, and it was borne out by his own experiences as the JCS chairman. One afternoon in the fall of 2002, the secretary was killing time in the White House press office before an NSC meeting. After making small talk with Ari Fleischer, Powell observed, "You know, anytime an Iraqi wants to build a swimming pool, they would go to their backyard, put up some aluminum, and our intelligence would show that there is some type of radar facility in their backyard. And we'd drop bombs to take it out, and now they had the hole for their swimming pool."[58]

Powell knew, then, not to take John Hannah's WMD opus at face value. "Carl," he said to Carl Ford, the director of State's in-house intelligence bureau, INR, "have your people go over this and tell me what they don't like."

Ford's staff worked overnight.[59] Their memo of objections to Hannah's WMD section on January 31 came to six single-spaced pages and cited thirty-eight items that were deemed either "weak" or "unsubstantiated." The INR analysts warned that Iraq's alleged chemical weapon decontamination trucks could simply be water-conveying vehicles. As they had in their NIE dissent, the State analysts continued to think that the confiscated aluminum tubes were for rocket launchers, not nuclear centrifuges. The critique's three most common phrases were "plausibility open to question," "highly questionable," and "draft states it as fact."[60]

Meanwhile, Powell's chief of staff, Colonel Lawrence Wilkerson, was also hashing out the WMD text with John Hannah. The sources in the text weren't footnoted, and Wilkerson grimaced as he watched Hannah fumble through his binders. After one query, Hannah produced a *New York Times* article as his source. Between INR's factual objections and Hannah's halting command of the material, Powell was fast losing faith in the speech. He instructed Wilkerson to start from scratch. The secretary contacted Rice to see if he could have more time for the speech.

No, replied Rice. The president had already announced that Powell would be delivering a major speech to the UN on February 5. He had six days to prepare the most important address of his life.

Indeed, that same day, Bush offered a preview of Powell's speech to a roomful of reporters. "Secretary Powell will make a strong case about the danger of an armed Saddam Hussein," the president said as Tony Blair stood beside him. Unaware that Powell had already tossed out Libby's section,

Bush went on to say, "He will also talk about Al Qaeda links, links that really do portend a danger for America and for Great Britain, for anybody who loves freedom."[61]

It was George Tenet who came to the rescue. Tenet suggested that Powell base the new speech on the NIE. It was, after all, the consensus product of the U.S. intelligence community. What could go wrong?[62]

For the next three days, Powell sat in Tenet's conference room on the seventh floor in CIA headquarters with his speechwriting team. Line by line, data point by data point, the secretary read out the text and then asked, "Does that sound right? What's the source on this? Opposition? Kurdish? Asylum seeker? Can we trust him?" If the answer did not suit him, Powell's reply would be "I'm not comfortable with that. Throw it on the floor." He threw out the U.S. mapping software after it became clear that the intelligence community no longer stood firmly behind it. A chart purporting to show the current whereabouts of Saddam's original nuclear team struck Powell as an incoherent plate of spaghetti; he threw that out as well.[63]

The secretary wore a flannel shirt and jeans. His command of the conference room appeared to be absolute. To the outside observer, the process seemed methodical and professional. Dan Bartlett dropped by Langley over the weekend. There were no whirring faxes or multiple-edited drafts flying around, in the manner of a presidential address. Nor did the content have the outer-space quality of Libby's presentation in the Situation Room. "Everybody's in the room," Bartlett recalled. "He's got their undivided attention. This is going to be done right. I left thinking, *Okay, I feel good about this.*"[64]

Powell had reason to feel sanguine about the process as well. For Tenet was there, along with John McLaughlin and his aluminum tube prop, which at one point he rolled seductively across the conference room table.[65] The national intelligence officers were in the room. Whenever Powell seemed concerned about a particular claim, Tenet would usher in what seemed to be the proper analyst to affirm the source's validity. As one visitor during the marathon vetting process at Langley would recall, "Powell and his team are pounding away trying to get this as right as they can. Tenet is intimately involved. And analysts that he thinks he needs there are intimately involved."[66]

What Colin Powell could not have known was that George Tenet had assembled his own yea-sayers. In his agency, there were analysts who seriously doubted that Saddam had reconstituted his nuclear program. There were analysts who had come to doubt that the Iraqi regime was using trucks for CW decontamination. And there were analysts who had questions about whether Iraq had mobile BW laboratories.

Those analysts were not in the conference room. Tenet did not want any confusion, any show of uncertainty or discord. He was there to accommodate the First Customer's designated orator—and, just as much, to ease the concerns of the Bush White House that the CIA might not be capable of mounting an Adlai Stevenson–style case.

This was particularly evident when the subject turned to the primary source—the only source, really—of the mobile biological weapons facility tale. "The really strong stuff was Curveball," remembered CIA weapons analyst Bill McLaughlin, who was in the conference room on Saturday, February 3. "It carried a lot of weight. I think everybody was pretty wowed by the graphics. Rice and Hadley were there. I don't think they had seen this stuff before. They were pretty positive about it. It was the kind of specificity we needed to show. It was the centerpiece of the discussion."[67]

"The BW stuff," agreed one of Powell's speechwriters, Barry Lowenkron, "was the strongest of the strong."[68]

AS CIA DEPUTY DIRECTOR JOHN MCLAUGHLIN SUPERVISED THE WINPAC team's ill-fated "slam dunk" presentation of Iraqi WMD in December, it was becoming increasingly clear that the Case relied heavily on the claims of a German source to whom the U.S. intelligence community did not have any access. "We don't have a case officer in touch with this guy," Tenet muttered to one of his top officials.[69]

That fact was worrisome enough. (Though not enough to prevent the October 2002 NIE authors from upgrading earlier NIE assessments that Iraq "could" have biological weapons to the conclusion that it "has" such weapons and that the program had expanded.)[70] But Curveball's claims to have been part of a mobile BW program had also polarized the agency. More often than not, it was the case officers in the field—from the Directorate of Operations (DO)—who were gung-ho about the intelligence they had collected, while the analysts in the Directorate of Intelligence (DI), back at Langley headquarters, who studied the intel tended to be the skeptics.

In Curveball's case, it was the opposite. WINPAC's BW specialists—among them, the senior analyst Beth and Libby's "Errol Flynn," Jerry Watson—were convinced that the Iraqi engineer's description explained everything. The ops officers, who dealt firsthand with informants on a daily basis, believed they knew a liar when they saw one. In Curveball they saw a liar.

McLaughlin was aware that this rift between the DO and the DI on Curveball existed. But his hands were more than full assembling the Case. He asked his executive assistant, Steve Slick, to (as Slick would put it) "get to the bottom of a disagreement within the building about the veracity of one human source."[71]

On December 19, Slick met with the senior BW analyst Beth and Margaret Henoch, the DO's chief of the group of European countries that included Germany. Because the Curveball intelligence had been deemed sensitive, it had not been routed through Henoch's office. Only in September, when Tyler Drumheller, head of the DO's European division, informed her that the BW intelligence would figure heavily into the NIE, did she hear the code name for the first time.

"Look into Curveball," Drumheller instructed Henoch. Referring to the DO's deputy director, Jim Pavitt, he added, "Pavitt wants him to be vetted, because apparently we're going to use him to justify going into Iraq."

Henoch farmed the job out to two assistants. They dug up more than a hundred intelligence reports that had been circumnavigated past her office and over to Langley. But their discussions with the German intelligence agents had led them to conclude that Curveball was not on the level.

On December 19, Henoch argued this point to Slick. Turning to the BW analyst Beth, she said, "This is about asset validation, which I've been trained in. You guys are trained to write papers. You write to prove a thesis, rather than evaluating the information. And I think that's what you've done here."

Beth's rebuttal was equally forceful. Henoch, she argued, lacked the scientific training to comprehend Curveball's reports, which were technically exquisite. Another source had corroborated Curveball.

Henoch countered that the other source had corroborated only where Curveball worked, not what he did or saw. She added that Curveball's accuracy could be explained by his possibly reading UNSCOM reports off the internet.

A day later on December 20, Slick issued his opinion in a memo to WINPAC. "After an exhaustive review," he wrote, "the U.S. Intelligence Community [as well as several liaison services] . . . judged him credible." Slick himself would later admit that his own "exhaustive review" consisted of this single meeting.[72] Beth, he later explained to the WMD Commission, was "the master of the [Curveball] case."

But Slick acknowledged something else to the commission: there was "not much more" to the BW case than Curveball. At that moment, the day before Slick's boss was to present the Case to President Bush, the CIA was looking to deliver more, not less.

Slick was far from the only CIA official clearing the path for Curveball's mobile BW intelligence. When one analyst expressed concern about the source to WINPAC's WMD task force deputy, the latter's email response began, "Let's keep in mind the fact that this war's going to happen regardless of what Curveball said or didn't say, and that the Powers That Be probably aren't terribly interested in whether Curveball knows what he's talking about." The deputy then added, "However, in the interest of Truth, we owe somebody a sentence or two of warning, if you honestly have reservations."[73]

For that matter, Deputy Director Pavitt had distanced himself from the argument his subordinate Margaret Henoch was having with the analysts. He would later take strong issue with Steve Slick's adjudication of the matter, saying, "Margaret's views and the views of the Germans were known to the analysts. It's the analysts' tradecraft that broke down. And Slick had the responsibility to serve the deputy director as his executive assistant. His job was not to make analytic judgments on behalf of the DI."[74]

But on the day that Slick decided that Beth was "the master of the case," Pavitt essentially concurred, telling Henoch that she was not qualified to judge Curveball's claims. Pavitt also conveyed to a colleague, much as WINPAC's WMD deputy had, that war was inevitable, and those against it could "tap dance nude on Pennsylvania Avenue and it would make no difference."[75]

John McLaughlin would later insist that he was unaware that Margaret Henoch—or anyone else, for that matter—had expressed doubts about Curveball's veracity. Still, before Powell was to deliver his UN speech, the deputy director found time twice to dab his toe into the murky BW waters. First, McLaughlin spoke personally with Beth to receive the senior BW analyst's assurances that Curveball's intelligence was sound. And second, he directed his executive assistant, Steve Slick, to check on Curveball's "current status/whereabouts."

Slick's memo to European division chief Tyler Drumheller on February 3 said, "A great deal of effort is being expended to vet the intelligence that underlies SecState's upcoming UN presentation. Similarly, we want to take every precaution against unwelcome surprises that might emerge concerning the intel case; clearly, public statements by this émigré, press accounts of his reporting or credibility, or even direct press access to him would cause a number of potential concerns."

But Slick's memo made no mention of a cable that had been sent to him a week before this by the CIA's chief of station in Berlin, Joe Wippl. BND, the German intelligence agency handling Curveball, "has not been able to verify his reporting," Wippl warned. He added, "The source himself is problematical. Defer to headquarters but to use information from another liaison service's source whose information cannot be verified on such an important, key topic should take the most serious consideration."

Colin Powell knew nothing about these serious concerns. Joe Wippl was not in the room during the secretary's UN speech preparation. Margaret Henoch was not in the room. Beth was, along with George Tenet and John McLaughlin. And Curveball's intelligence was the room's star attraction.

"George was on the team, and that itself is an issue," Wippl would later reflect. "It was *Hey, guys we're going to war—and we'll find this stuff anyway once we're there*. It's something that, in retrospect, kind of makes you sick."[76]

ON THE EVENING OF FEBRUARY 4 AT UN HEADQUARTERS, POWELL WENT OVER his speech a final time. Poring over the text with the dutifulness of a GS-12 public servant, stripping out garbled language, the secretary also drew accent marks over particular syllables so that the intonations would be right. Those who had watched him during the entire preparation process marveled at Powell's professionalism and attention to detail. He seemed in every way to live up to the hype of the Colin Powell brand.[77]

Powell asked George Tenet if he felt comfortable with the facts marshaled in the speech. The CIA director said that he did. "Good," said Powell. "Because I want you sitting right behind me when I give it tomorrow morning."

Tenet resisted the secretary's request, saying that he had a trip planned. The director was aware that his sitting behind the secretary would give the appearance that the agency was bestowing the seal of approval to administration policy.

Tenet ultimately capitulated. He was way past the point of protesting. His agency had spent the entire month of December preparing the Case as a template for this presentation. Powell's speech had been assembled at CIA headquarters, which had made Deputy Directory for Intelligence Jami Miscik so uncomfortable that she had refused to participate in the process (though she did not prevent her analysts from being drawn into it).[78]

That same evening, Scooter Libby made one last run at including more information about links between Saddam and Al Qaeda. Earlier, Tenet had agreed to a compromise, directing one of his senior analysts, Philip Mudd, to write a passage describing Zarqawi's activities in northern Iraq. During the intel-vetting at Langley, Tenet had burst in at one point to proclaim, "We've just got some bombshell information." It was in fact year-old news, but again cleared by Tenet's analysts: the disclosure by al-Libi, under interrogation by Egyptian intelligence officials, that Iraqis had trained Al Qaeda operatives in how to make and use WMD. Powell didn't know the circumstances under which al-Libi had confessed. He directed that Wilkerson include that point as well.[79]

Now Libby pressed for more. On the phone with Powell speechwriter Barry Lowenkron, Cheney's chief of staff said, "Don't you find it interesting," and then began listing a series of aircraft bombings perpetrated by Islamic terrorists in the mid-eighties.

"This has nothing to do with Iraq," Lowenkron said before hanging up on Libby.[80]

At 10:30 the following morning, Secretary Powell stood before the international body. For the next seventy-six minutes, with UN ambassador John Negroponte sitting just behind him and to his left and a puffy-eyed Tenet to his right, he laid out the U.S. government's case against Saddam. "My colleagues, every statement I make today is backed up by sources, solid sources," Powell said in his calm but resolute and sonorous baritone. "These are not assertions. What we're giving you are facts and conclusions based on solid intelligence."

The story Powell told—in conversational language that marked a departure from the Bush administration's tape-loop evocations of madness, evil, and mushroom clouds—was an investigator's meticulous brief of institutionalized deception and murderous intent. Powell spoke of a key source, "an eyewitness, an Iraqi chemical engineer," who happened to be watching the speech at home with his wife in Erlangen, Germany.[81] He spoke of one of Curveball's confirming sources, "an Iraqi major"—surprising a DIA agent who was watching the speech while waiting for a ride to take him to the Atlanta airport, and who months earlier had interviewed the major and determined him to be a fabricator.[82] He spoke of decontamination trucks at chemical weapons factories, to the consternation of CW analyst Larry Fox, who had repeatedly objected to that questionable "signature" being used in Powell's speech and had been repeatedly overruled by his superiors.[83] And he spoke of aluminum tubes that "most experts think" were to be used for uranium enrichment—ignoring his department's own experts, including the

INR's director, Carl Ford, who became instantly heartsick when he heard that passage on TV and informed Powell three months later that he was resigning.[84]

The CIA's Red Cell had warned that Powell's speech lacked the requisite "Adlai Stevenson moment" and thus might not live up to its billing. Jami Miscik decided not to publish the team's paper. She was vindicated: few, if any, objected to the performance itself. The only scolds were those who had quarrels with the speech's substance. One of them was Hans Blix, who murmured as he watched the speech, "This is just shit."[85] Another was former UNSCOM chief inspector Rolf Ekéus, who said on *PBS NewsHour* after the speech, regarding Curveball's claims about mobile BW labs, "That sounds still a little difficult to believe"—a single note of skepticism among the coverage that caused PBS considerable heartburn at the time.[86] On the opposite side of the analytical spectrum, Vice President Cheney groused to his staff that Powell had left out too much damning intelligence.[87]

A young UNMOVIC inspector named Dawson Cagle happened to be recalled from Baghdad in time for him to attend the UN speech. Sitting next to Cagle was one of Blix's senior munitions experts who had also just returned from Baghdad. The expert's mouth opened when Powell displayed photographs of trucks moving into a suspected WMD bunker hours before an inspection team was due to visit, followed by a photo of the inspectors filing through a now empty bunker.

"I'm in that photo," the munitions expert whispered to Cagle. "I went into that bunker that those trucks pulled up to. There was a three-inch layer of pigeon dung covering everything. And a layer of dust on top of that. There's no way someone came in and cleaned that place out. No way they could've faked that."

Wow, thought Cagle. *So this is all just theater.*[88]

Another UNMOVIC inspector, Roman Mezencev, was watching Powell's UN speech in Baghdad with other members of his team. He found himself laughing out loud when the secretary displayed an image of Iraq's supposed mobile biological lab. Just a few days earlier, Mezencev had been training other inspectors at a huge outdoor storage facility of heavy equipment in New Jersey.

One of the pieces of equipment the new inspectors were training with was a soil remediation vehicle for treating crude oil spillages. To Mezencev, that vehicle in New Jersey looked identical to the one Powell was now saying could only be the ominous centerpiece of Saddam's biological weapons program.[89]

But back at the White House, Bush watched Powell's speech in his small dining room connected to the Oval Office. The president was on the edge of his seat. He was visibly pleased.[90]

On the Hill, at a Democratic Senate caucus meeting following the UN speech, Majority Leader Tom Daschle told his colleagues that he was now "really convinced" that Saddam had weapons of mass destruction. To the caucus he said, "You may not trust Dick Cheney. But do you not trust Colin Powell?"[91]

"Powell was catalytic in the war gaining credibility," Daschle would later say.[92] Nowhere was that more evident than on the op-ed page of *The Washington Post* the day after Powell's speech. The lead column, written by Pulitzer-winning writer and avowed anti-war liberal Mary McGrory, bore the headline "I'm Persuaded." Singling out Powell's passage about the mobile BW program—"I was struck by their ingenuity"—McGrory compared the Curveball intelligence to Nixon counsel John Dean's game-changing disclosures during the Senate Watergate hearings.

"I'm not ready for war yet," her column concluded. "But Colin Powell has convinced me that it may be the only way to stop a fiend, and that if we do go, there is reason."[93]

═══

CHAPTER SEVENTEEN

TRUTH AND THE TELLERS

P atrick Tyler, the chief correspondent for *The New York Times*, was among the dozens of reporters who covered Colin Powell's speech at the United Nations in New York on February 5, 2003. Shortly after Powell had finished, Tyler called the Washington bureau of the *Times* to survey the opinions of his colleagues on the Pentagon beat.

"I thought it was Powell's finest moment," one of them said.

Tyler was astonished to hear this. In his view, Powell's case seemed strained, a far cry from the "Adlai Stevenson moment" it was billed to be. After he hung up, Tyler turned to his editor and relayed what the Pentagon reporter had said. Nodding, the editor replied, "I thought it was his finest moment, too."[1]

Warren Strobel, of the Knight Ridder newspaper chain, was also covering Powell's speech inside UN headquarters. The speech had unnerved him as well, but for a different reason than it had Tyler. Where the *Times*—including Tyler, who co-wrote the first story claiming that Mohamed Atta had met in Prague with an Iraqi intelligence agent—had often been credulous in its Iraq reporting, Strobel and his colleagues at Knight Ridder had filed numerous stories that cast doubt on the Bush administration's assertions about Saddam Hussein. *But,* he thought, *this is Colin freaking Powell.* Strobel came away from the UN speech convinced that Iraq possessed at least a limited WMD arsenal. He wondered, momentarily, if there were other things his team had gotten wrong.[2]

Strobel and Tyler were both veteran reporters who had covered the Middle East and spent considerable time in Iraq. Two important factors separated them, however. Strobel had spent time in Baghdad for *U.S. News & World Report* in 1998 and 2000, when Saddam had thoroughly consolidated his power in Iraq and was content to rattle his saber at the West. In Baghdad, Strobel found little more than a Potemkin village run by a dictator luxuriating in his status quo—one whose "craving for the limelight is second only to his survival instinct," as he wrote in 2000.[3]

Tyler, on the other hand, had been to Halabja for *The Washington Post* in March 1988. His front-page story began, "More than 100 bodies of women, children and elderly men still lay in the streets, alleys and courtyards of this now-empty city, victims of what Iran claims is the worst chemical warfare attack on civilians in its 7 ½-year-old war with Iraq."[4] Three years later, for the *Times,* Tyler again visited Halabja after the Gulf War to cover the return of exiled Kurds to their homeland.[5] As Tyler would later acknowledge, "The part of my brain that might have been more skeptical about Saddam possessing WMD was psychologically burdened by my own experiences in Iraq, reporting on the human cost of those weapons."[6]

The other major difference between the two reporters was where they worked. Because Strobel and his colleagues Jonathan Landay, John Walcott, and Joe Galloway were employed by a chain of newspapers not situated in the Beltway and not driving Washington's daily narrative, the Bush White House essentially ignored Knight Ridder's reporting. To some degree, Strobel and his team were liberated by their relative anonymity, while the reporters at the *Times* were ever conscious of their status in the top echelon of what Tyler would call "the media-industrial complex." Careers could be made by wars. It was equally true that wars could be made by careerists, including those in newsrooms.

Strobel's lightbulb moment about Iraq occurred about three weeks after the 9/11 attacks. He received a tip from a diplomat that Paul Wolfowitz had arranged for a government plane to fly former CIA director and fellow Iraq hawk James Woolsey to London to speak with British intelligence officials about possible connections between Saddam and the World Trade Center terrorists. (Woolsey's efforts proved unsuccessful.) Strobel broke the story exactly one month after 9/11.[7]

Concurrently, Strobel's editor at Knight Ridder, John Walcott, had received two phone calls from former CIA operative Dewey Clarridge, a legendary freelancer in overseas adventurism. In the first call, Clarridge offered Walcott the scoop that Iraq had been training foreign terrorists how to hijack planes at a base in Salman Pak. Walcott looked into it. His intelligence sources told him that there were no foreigners at the Salman Pak base and that the Iraq operation there was intended to *thwart* Islamic hijackers, not to train them. In the second call, Clarridge was selling a different shiny gem: in the 1990s, a former Iraqi intelligence officer had traveled to Kandahar to meet with bin Laden and offer him safe haven in Iraq. Making calls afterward, Walcott learned that such a meeting *had* taken place. But Clarridge had failed to add the tale's coda: bin Laden turned down the offer, because he knew that it would have put him under Saddam's control.

Taken together, what became clear to Walcott and Strobel was that, in the days immediately following 9/11, some highly influential figures were desperately trying to tie Saddam to the 9/11 perpetrators. The Knight Ridder team thereafter investigated the Bush administration's case for war against Iraq with a pronounced degree of skepticism.[8]

But Dewey Clarridge's labors were hardly in vain. Chris Hedges, of the *Times,* bit on the hijacker story. Supplied with two key sources by Ahmad Chalabi's INC, his piece ran on November 8, 2001.[9] Eleven days earlier, the story about the Iraqi intelligence agent offering safe haven to bin Laden had landed in the *Times,* though without the critical detail that bin Laden had resisted being under Saddam's control. One of the two authors of that piece was Patrick Tyler. One of Tyler's sources was former CIA director James Woolsey, Wolfowitz's emissary to London.[10]

———

AS WITH THE BUSH WHITE HOUSE AND CONGRESS, THE EVENTS OF 9/11
threw the Washington media into a state of apprehensiveness and dismay.
Most of them "had never been in any kind of danger their entire lives," said
the veteran *Washington Post* reporter Walter Pincus, who had served in Vietnam. "When 9/11 happened, reporters at the *Post* were taping their windows
and getting gas masks."[11]

Few if any of them had seen such attacks coming. In the nine months
before the morning of September 11, not a single question by the White
House press corps to Ari Fleischer pertained to Al Qaeda.[12] Accompanying
their bewilderment were the jarring spectacles of smoke rising from iconic
buildings and evacuated White House staffers standing shoeless at the edge
of Lafayette Park, sobbing. The reaction to the attacks was even more visceral
and prolonged in New York. As one *Times* reporter would reflect, "There was
a very strong bias to believing that the worst could happen again. And we
really became engaged in an effort to protect a lot more people from getting
killed, even as we're literally still dragging more bodies out of the rubble of
New York."[13]

Drawn, by their failure to predict 9/11, into a catastrophist mind frame,
reporters in the ensuing months strode warily into the unknown. Were there
other terrorist sleeper cells in America? Were they carrying nuclear suit-
case bombs and targeting dams and subways? Were our own children, like
the Washington, D.C., native John Walker Lindh, slipping into Afghan
training camps to learn how to destroy us?

But, as with members of the Bush administration, reporters also reverted
to the familiar. The malevolence of Saddam Hussein was well known to
many of them—none so much as *The Washington Post*'s Jim Hoagland, twice
a Pulitzer Prize winner. Hoagland had interviewed the dictator in May 1975,
when Saddam was still the Baath Party's vice chairman and already according brutal treatment to the Kurds.[14] Hoagland was dismayed when the first
Bush administration failed to topple the dictator, and even more so when
President Bush encouraged the Shia uprising against Saddam and then did

nothing to protect them. After Hoagland went on TV and criticized the administration for not shooting down Saddam's helicopters, he received a call of support from an unexpected ally: Secretary of Defense Cheney's undersecretary, Paul Wolfowitz.[15]

Hoagland had also come to know Ahmad Chalabi during the seventies. Their hatred of Saddam formed the basis of a mutually beneficial relationship. When Chalabi's relationship with the CIA dissolved in 1997, he handed the scoop to Hoagland.[16] When Chalabi began his charm offensive on Capitol Hill in 1998, his friend the *Washington Post* columnist was there to memorialize Chalabi's newfound popularity.[17] When, that same year, Chalabi wanted to leak UN inspector Scott Ritter's evidence that Iraq had apparently used VX nerve gas in its missile warheads, he knew whom to call.[18] And, one month after 9/11, when the *Times* had published the INC-furnished scoop about the Salman Pak hijacker camps despite efforts by the CIA to discredit it, Jim Hoagland obligingly scolded the agency in print for its "dismissive" attitude toward Chalabi—and, in the same story, quoted Jim Woolsey lecturing his former employer as well.[19]

On September 12, 2001, Hoagland became the first major columnist to suggest in print that the previous day's attacks likely were masterminded by a state sponsor. (That column recycled Laurie Mylroie's theory, embraced as well by Wolfowitz, that Saddam was responsible for the 1993 World Trade Center bombing.)[20] By October 2001, the *Post* columnist was explicitly calling for Bush to move swiftly in Afghanistan "so that you can pivot quickly from it to end the threat Saddam Hussein's regime poses."[21] As the drumbeats for war grew louder, Hoagland publicly derided those who might slow the march. For failing to acknowledge Saddam's ties to Al Qaeda, Hoagland wrote that the CIA was "wrong close to 100 percent of the time on such an important subject as Iraq" (though he accepted 100 percent of the agency's WMD intelligence).[22] And, as Hans Blix's inspectors began their work in Iraq in November 2002, Hoagland dismissed Blix as "a studious, by-the-book Swedish treaty lawyer who failed to detect Saddam Hussein's nuclear program the first time around."[23]

But Hoagland was not *The Washington Post*'s only early protagonist for military action in Iraq. Columnist David Ignatius, who as a foreign editor for the *Post* during the Gulf War had come to know several Iraqi opposition figures, also endorsed the war, having—as he would later say—"seen the events through Iraqi victims whose stories I'd internalized."[24] Like Hoagland, Lally Weymouth, whose family owned the *Post*, had interviewed Saddam decades before and would write that "the only language he understands is force."[25] Most significantly, the paper's editorial board threw its support behind military action ten days after Powell's UN speech.[26]

Meanwhile, a number of *Post* reporters—among them Walter Pincus, Tom Ricks, and Joby Warrick—were filing stories that called into question the quality of the Iraq intelligence and the efficacy of the war plans. Many of these stories were relegated to the back pages, however. The enduring appetite among editors for conflict had been supplanted by a post-9/11 bias in favor of certitude. When, in October 2002, Ricks offered a piece entitled "Doubts," reflecting the concerns of retired military officials about the headlong rush to war, an editor killed the story.[27]

The *Post*'s most celebrated reporter, Bob Woodward, was now spending more time inside the Bush White house for his books than at the paper. From within, he had developed granular understanding of the dysfunction pervading the interagency process—and, in particular, of the squabbling between Powell's State and Rumsfeld's Pentagon. But among Bush's war council, not even Powell was seriously questioning whether Saddam had weapons of mass destruction. Woodward had little to no exposure to these midlevel conflicts— unlike Walter Pincus, who was not a fixture at the White House but had excellent contacts within the CIA. Those contacts revealed deep division in the agency about whether the evidence was anywhere near sufficient to justify war.

Again, however, these were portraits of uncertainty, not of action, and thus unlikely to receive marquee placement.[28] And in the meantime, recalled Ignatius, "when we should've been trying to surface the skepticism that existed, we instead were convinced Bush was going to war. And so we were scrambling to get training on how to operate in these combat environments, to get assigned to the right embed—spent more time on these things than on the fundamentals of what made sense."[29]

FIVE DAYS AFTER THE ATTACKS, THE VENERATED *MEET THE PRESS* HOST TIM Russert spoke with Cheney on his show. After reading Saddam's spiteful observation that "the American cowboy is reaping the fruits of crime against humanity," Russert asked the vice president, "If we determine that Saddam Hussein is also harboring terrorists, and there's a track record there, would we have any reluctance of going after Saddam Hussein?"

Obligingly, Cheney replied, "No." But, he also acknowledged, there was no hard evidence linking Saddam to the attacks.[30]

Six months later, Cheney returned to *Meet the Press,* where Russert reminded the vice president of his remark that there were no clearly established ties between Saddam and bin Laden. Then the host said, "There's an article in *The New Yorker* magazine by Jeffrey Goldberg which connects Iraq and Saddam Hussein with Al Qaeda. What can you tell me about it?"

"I've read the article," Cheney replied. "It's a devastating article, I thought." Again, however, the vice president issued a caveat: "We've not been able yet from our perspective to nail down a close tie between the Al Qaeda organization and Saddam Hussein. We'll continue to look for it."[31]

Goldberg's March 2002 story amounted to a coup for the Bush administration: an assiduously reported piece by a prominent and universally respected journalist for a decidedly left-of-center publication that would therefore instantly achieve accepted-wisdom status inside the Beltway. Furthermore, Cheney and others in the White House could honestly maintain that they had nothing to do with how the story came to be reported.

Goldberg, an award-winning Jewish American writer who had once served in the Israeli Defense Forces, subscribed to, as he would put it, "a fundamental belief that, in the post-Holocaust universe, the civilized world should not permit genocidal dictators to stay in power." Saddam's gassing of the Kurdish villages during the Iran-Iraq War in 1988 qualified him as a genocidalist, in Goldberg's view. A month after 9/11, Goldberg began pursuing a story about Iraq's link to terrorists. He was awarded an interview with German intelligence director August Hanning. On the record, Hanning stated, "It is our estimate that Iraq will have an atomic bomb in three years." The BND chief did not say how Saddam would achieve this, or on what assumptions his estimate was based, or whether other intelligence agencies concurred.

Goldberg then traveled to Kurdistan. In Halabja, he interviewed numerous survivors of the chemical weapons massacre in 1988. In the city of Sulaimaniya, Goldberg discovered something else. The Kurdish intelligence service had detained several members of Ansar al-Islam, the terrorists who had informal affiliations with Al Qaeda and, eventually, Zarqawi. The Kurdish intelligence chief encouraged Goldberg to interview the detainees—saying, Goldberg would write, "he hoped I would carry this information to American intelligence officials."

The detainees, who insisted to Goldberg that they had not been abused by their jailers—"There is nothing like torture here," one said as a guard stood nearby—disclosed remarkable things. They described direct links between Ansar al-Islam, Al Qaeda, and Saddam. One of them claimed to be a bodyguard for bin Laden's deputy, Ayman al-Zawahiri, and to have escorted him to Saddam's palace. Another, a twenty-nine-year-old Iranian Arab named Muhammad Mansour Shahab, elaborately recounted meeting bin Laden in a tent and smuggling chemical weapons from Iraq into Al Qaeda's hands.

"If these charges are true," Goldberg wrote, "it would mean that the relationship between Saddam's regime and Al Qaeda is far closer than previously thought." As to whether they *were* true, Goldberg hedged somewhat: "The stories, which I later checked with experts on the region, seemed at least worth the attention of America and other countries in the West."

The story's "experts" were a less-than-perfect fit with the subject at hand. Goldberg quoted Kanan Makiya, the chronicler of Saddam's human rights malfeasances, about Iraq's weapons program, though Makiya did not possess any more expertise on that subject than the average newspaper reader. He quoted a British scholar of the Halabja attacks who postulated, without any evidence, that "the Kurds were a test population" for later attacks Saddam might inflict on the West. He quoted Kurdish studies scholar Carole O'Leary speculating that Saddam's intelligence service "could" destabilize the Kurds by linking up with Islamic extremists, though she was not referring to Al Qaeda. And Goldberg quoted Ahmad Chalabi declaring of Saddam with typical fact-free flair, "He thinks he can kill one hundred thousand Israelis in a day with biological weapons."[32]

A few months after Goldberg's story "The Great Terror" was published, British journalist Jason Burke, of *The Observer*, visited the Sulaimaniya prison as well. Burke had lived in Pakistan for the past two years. Both there and in Afghanistan, he had spoken with numerous associates of bin Laden's. None of them were Iraqis, and their disdain for the Baathist regime was palpable. Burke had also reported more than once from inside Iraq. "I just couldn't see how you could reconcile what was going on there with bin Laden's clear antipathy towards apostate regimes that he would rail against in practically every speech," he said.

At the prison, Burke interviewed Muhammad Mansour Shahab, who had told Goldberg that he had met bin Laden in a tent and later ferried weapons from Iraq to Al Qaeda. "The story struck me as bullshit from the moment he started telling it," Burke later recalled. In this latest recounting to the British journalist, Shahab had met bin Laden in a cave, not a tent. He badly mischaracterized cities and travel times. The arsenal of mortars and RPGs Shahab described loading and unloading with five other men would have weighed about twenty tons—a feat that would have taken several days to accomplish, but Shahab claimed they had pulled it off in five or six hours. At the end of the interview, Burke accused Shahab of lying. The detainee laughed and said, "You are a clever man."[33]

Where Burke's approach to Shahab had been one of skepticism, Goldberg's point of departure was an aggressive willingness to believe. As Goldberg would later say, "Well before 9/11, Saddam struck me as uniquely evil. The pivot for me was when Hanning said, *This guy can get nukes*. Then it's off to the races. We know the man was capable of using chemical weapons on humans. We knew his cruelty was unimaginable."[34]

This formulation—Saddam had WMD and had used them in the past, and what he might do next was a dark feast for the imagination—became the shortest and straightest line to war for many Beltway intellectuals. Among them was Leon Wieseltier, literary critic of *The New Republic*, whose editorial voices were overwhelmingly pro-invasion. For Wieseltier, Saddam's attack on the Kurds at Halabja "showed at that time he had chemical weapons," he recalled. "And I was working on the assumption that he still did." His written support for the Gulf War was rewarded in 1991 by an invitation to a reception at the White House, where the liberal scribe mingled with Jim Woolsey and Doug Feith and was given a personal tour of the residence by President Bush (who, directing Wieseltier's attention to a portrait of Dolley Madison, noted admiringly, "Look at the rack on that woman!").

One afternoon, on a street corner in Northwest D.C., Wieseltier bumped into Zbigniew Brzezinski. The former national security adviser under Jimmy Carter opposed invading Iraq and had warned Rumsfeld that doing so would jeopardize the war on terror. By way of greeting, Brzezinski said to Wieseltier, of his latest column, "You know, you're wrong about Iraq."

Brzezinski argued that, the atrocity of Halabja notwithstanding, Saddam had been deterred from the use of chemical weapons ever since 1988. There was no reason to go to war with a dictator to seize weapons he had no intention of using.

"I appreciate the force of your argument," Wieseltier replied. "I, too, would like to tenaciously cling to my belief in the rationality of the actors here. But the idea that I'm going to bet on the decency and rationality of the man who already used chemical weapons on his own citizens . . . ?"

The two men agreed to disagree. Brzezinski was a Cold War realist who saw in an Iraq excursion a constellation of ugly geopolitical eventualities. Wieseltier was an idealist who nonetheless embraced the belief that a dictator who had killed some of his country's most defenseless inhabitants fifteen years earlier would next set his sights on the most powerful country on the planet.[35]

In the capital city, liberals like Leon Wieseltier and Andrew Sullivan found additional fodder for war at the residence of Christopher Hitchens and

Carol Blue, on Columbia and Wyoming NW. The *Vanity Fair* provocateur supported the removal of Saddam on humanitarian grounds, irrespective of whatever weapons the dictator did or did not possess. He considered Chalabi a patriot, Wolfowitz a visionary—"almost a quarter-century of being essentially right" when it came to Saddam—and hosted both of them frequently at dinner parties. The rotating cast also included Kanan Makiya, the Kurdish leader Jalal Talabani, and Senator John Edwards.

Hitchens was a pugnacious and original thinker who enjoyed reminding people that he had come by his anti-Saddam views "long before George Bush did." Still, after 9/11, Hitchens's considerable imagination took wing. Before an audience in Los Angeles during the run-up to war, Hitchens spoke of how, during the nineties, he had easily tracked down and interviewed the Palestinian secular terrorist Abu Nidal at a villa in Baghdad. Then, after asserting that Saddam "has sheltered Al Qaeda members, numbers of them, on its territory, since September 11," Hitchens concluded, "Yes, Iraq has always been an arsenal and backer of international gangsterism and remains so. To doubt this is foolish."[36]

Still, Hitchens, Wieseltier, Sullivan, *Terror and Liberalism* author Paul Berman, and other influential liberal writers exerted, above all, a moral justification for invading Iraq. The fall of the Berlin Wall and the subsequent liberation of Eastern Europe stirred the conscience of liberals who had spilled more ink decrying Reagan than Soviet totalitarianism. The swiftness of Operation Desert Storm had demonstrated to them that all wars need not be Vietnam. At the same time, that war's unhappy aftermath, with the elder Bush consigning the Marsh Arabs to massacre, along with Clinton's paralysis during the slaughter of the Tutsis in Rwanda three years later, horrified intellectuals of the left for whom "Never again" was civilization's blood oath.

Given the latter apostasies, Clinton's belated but effective efforts in the Balkans vindicated the arguments for neoliberal aggression. Sullivan would write that he "had seen the moral power of Western intervention in Bosnia and Kosovo."[37] But it was not simply that America had been moved to intervene that inspired Sullivan and others. It was that American intervention had, for a change, made things better rather than worse. As the neoliberal senator and Vietnam veteran Bob Kerrey would say, "It demonstrated our *capacity* to do something good with the use of force."[38]

Of course, overthrowing Saddam meant, for liberal journalists, the unsettling prospect of aligning themselves with Bush and Cheney. But they could console themselves in the company of "Iraq's Solzhenitsyn," Makiya, and by standing in solidarity with the courageous Kurdish warrior Masoud Barzani (and his more urbane, wine-and-cigar-toting fellow Kurd Talabani). If anything, the moral authority conferred on regime change gave them license to chide Bush for his overreliance on the WMD argument. As Berman thundered in a February 2003 column for *Slate*, "Bush has failed to present the current war and its impending new Iraqi front in terms of a democratic struggle against totalitarianism. He has failed to discuss in any serious way the moral aspect of the war, has failed to present the war as an act of solidarity with horribly oppressed Iraqis and other victims of Muslim fascism, has failed to show the humanitarian aspect of the war, has failed to present the war in the light of the long history of anti-totalitarianism."[39]

Such indignation did not welcome thoughtful and patriotic dissent. A leading pro-war columnist would later reconsider the scorn heaped on Brzezinski, Brent Scowcroft, and concerned generals like Gregory Newbold and Eric Shinseki: "It was such a consequential decision, with immensely respectable people along the way saying, 'Don't do this.' And what took place with some columnists was not just the usual Washington groupthink, but a strict enforcement of that groupthink—an attempt to shame others who would disagree."[40]

The more bellicose pro-war voices had more than just the Bush administration's support. They drew upon the sentiment of an injured, fearful, and outraged American public that had little appetite for nuance or self-inspection. Bill Maher learned this the hard way. Less than a week after the attacks, the *Politically Incorrect* TV show host took issue with Bush's characterization of the 9/11 hijackers as cowards, saying, "We have been the cowards, lobbing cruise missiles from two thousand miles away. That's cowardly. Staying in the airplane when it hits the building, say what you want about it—not cowardly." A few months later, ABC took Maher's show off the air.[41]

Beneath America's swelling ocean of moral righteousness, an undertow sought to drown the voices of dissent—at the Pentagon, at the CIA, at the NSC, and in newsrooms. At Knight Ridder, the publication of a story by Warren Strobel and John Walcott on February 13, 2002, entitled "Bush Has Decided to Overthrow Hussein," resulted in an avalanche of hate mail. Few took issue with the facts of the story, which had this lead: "President Bush has decided to oust Iraqi leader Saddam Hussein from power and ordered the CIA, the Pentagon and other agencies to devise a combination of military, diplomatic and covert steps to achieve that goal, senior U.S. officials said Tuesday."[42] What the readers objected to was a story that might compromise such plans—in the process putting at risk not so much American troops as an opportunity for retribution.

The discordant stories from Knight Ridder's D.C. bureau cost the chain significant advertising revenue. Cowed by the backlash, many of its papers stopped publishing reports by Strobel, Landay, Walcott, and Galloway. One editor at the Knight Ridder–owned *Philadelphia Inquirer* went so far as to assign two of his reporters the job of investigating and debunking the D.C. bureau's work.

In early September 2002, at a meeting of Knight Ridder editors in San Jose, California, discussion turned to the Bush administration's intensifying rhetoric about Saddam's weapons program. John Walcott, the D.C. bureau chief, spoke up. His sources in the intelligence community had expressed doubts that Iraq was anywhere near having nuclear capability.

Another editor said that Walcott's sources were wrong. As evidence, the editor held up a story that had just come over the wires.

"It's *The New York Times!*" the editor exclaimed. "It's Judith Miller. We have to go with that."[43]

FOUR MONTHS AFTER WINNING A PULITZER FOR A SERIES OF STORIES SHE had coauthored about Al Qaeda, Judy Miller was approached by one of her editors at the *Times*. Cheney had just given his VFW speech on August 26, citing with certainty Saddam Hussein's possession of deadly weapons. The editor said that the paper's executive editor, Howell Raines, wanted Miller and military correspondent Michael Gordon to investigate the Bush administration's claims. They had two weeks.

On Thursday, September 5, 2002, three days before their story was set to run, Gordon received a tip from an intelligence official about the seizure of aluminum tubes thought to be used for a nuclear centrifuge. Miller contacted the NSC's resident Iraq hawk, Robert Joseph, seeking confirmation. After checking with his boss, Condoleezza Rice, Joseph and his deputy, Susan Koch, met with Miller and Gordon on the morning of Friday the 6th. On background, Joseph and Koch confirmed the tip about the tubes and furnished more details. Deputy National Security Adviser Hadley also served as a confirming source for the story.

All the quotes relating to aluminum tubes used by Miller and Gordon in their front-page Sunday story, "U.S. Says Hussein Intensifies Quest for A-Bomb Parts," were attributed to "a senior administration official," meaning Joseph, Koch, or Hadley.[44] That same Sunday morning, three even more senior administration officials took to the airwaves. On *Fox News Sunday*, Secretary of State Colin Powell referred to "reporting just this morning" about Saddam's attempts to acquire aluminum tubes.[45] On *Meet the Press*, Vice President Dick Cheney observed, "There's a story in the *New York Times*" describing Saddam's efforts to acquire "the kinds of tubes that are necessary to build a centrifuge."[46] And on CNN's *Late Edition with Wolf Blitzer*, National Security Adviser Condoleezza Rice cited the tubes and then refrained a line that had appeared in Miller and Gordon's story: "But we don't want the smoking gun to be a mushroom cloud."[47]

Ironically, on the evening of Friday the 6th, while Miller and Gordon were writing their story, another *Times* front-page story was being finalized as well. That piece, by Elisabeth Bumiller, divulged a "meticulously planned strategy" by the White House to sell the public, Congress, and U.S. allies on the need to disarm Saddam. With the infamous quote by Chief of Staff Andy Card that, "from a marketing point of view, you don't introduce new products in August," Bumiller's story was destined to make news.[48] But Howell Raines decided to publish her piece on Saturday the 7th and award the marquee Sunday space to Miller and Gordon.

It was an ill-considered decision. The aluminum tubes story had been rushed; its authors were completely unaware at the time of the heated debate within the intelligence community about whether the tubes were intended for centrifuges or rocket launchers. But the *Times*'s determination to find ammunition to support Bush and Cheney's WMD assertions caused the editors to overlook the strong possibility that the administration was using threadbare evidence to build a case for war in major media outlets. That the White House would resort to such a tactic was, of course, the premise of Elisabeth Bumiller's story. As a result, the Sunday-show echo chamber of that morning's front-page *Times* story fulfilled the prophecy of the previous morning's lead article.

A great deal of negative commentary about Judy Miller's reporting would ensue in the year to follow. Despite her unquestioned reporting skills, "all of us at the *Times* saw her as somewhat captive to a group of sources and the stories they were spinning," said one fellow *Times* reporter.[49] Those sources included Chalabi and Scooter Libby, the latter of whom also frequently communicated with others in the D.C. bureau, including bureau chief Jill Abramson.[50]

But Miller was responsible only for the stories she wrote. She was certainly not responsible for the ones written by her colleagues that the *Times* editors decided not to publish. One of these, by Patrick Tyler on August 22, examined the records of Rumsfeld and Cheney pertaining to Saddam's weapons program. The 1,500-word story reminded readers that in 1983, special envoy Rumsfeld had met with the dictator to solidify relations with the United States and elected not to bring up the fact that the Iraqi regime had just used chemical weapons on the Iranians. Similarly, Tyler pointed out that when Cheney sat on the House Intelligence Committee in 1988, he took no action as a bipartisan bill to sanction Iraq for the gassing of the Kurds in Halabja died in committee after Reagan threatened to veto it.

Tyler's editors sat on the story for several days. On the morning of August 26, Tyler emailed Cheney's communications staff, requesting "input from the VP." He did not hear back. Later that day, Cheney delivered his VFW speech. Raines reacted by assigning to Judy Miller and Michael Gordon the story about Saddam's new WMD arsenal, which they furnished with the aluminum tubes scoop. Tyler's story on Cheney's tolerance of Saddam's previous use of WMD never ran.[51]

During the fall of 2002, the *Times* reporter assigned to the intelligence community, James Risen, received a tip from the CIA. His source called into question the story published a year earlier—by Tyler and John Tagliabue, of the *Times*, as well as several other news outlets—that the hijacker Mohamed Atta had met with an Iraqi intelligence officer in Prague. "I met with a bunch of top government and intelligence officials in Prague," Risen recalled, "and they were all laughing that the U.S. had taken this seriously." Risen's editor deliberately snuck his story into a Monday edition in the hopes that Raines would not notice. The executive editor of the *Times* was displeased when he saw the story (though Raines does not remember that being the case).[52]

Risen was also hearing reports from CIA sources that the WMD intelligence was shaky. These intimations were frustratingly elliptical. But that itself indicated a fear that speaking out, at a time when the Bush White House's charge toward war appeared to be at a full gallop, would lead to reprisals.

Risen wrote a series of stories during the period from November 2002 to March 2003 that reflected serious doubts about the prewar intelligence. Later he would recall that the stories "sat in the *Times* computer system for days, then weeks, untouched by editors." One story finally ran in truncated form, in the back pages, unnoticed.[53]

To a large extent, what had transpired at the CIA after 9/11 was also taking place at the *Times* and other news organizations. Assuming the worst, leaning into the powers of the imagination and away from evidence-based reason, counted perversely as the most welcome news of the day. Doubt was not banned. It was simply back-paged. "It's like any corporate culture," James Risen said, "where you know what management wants, and no one has to tell you."[54]

CHAPTER EIGHTEEN

≡≡

THINGS FALL APART

In December 2002, Saddam Hussein convened a meeting with his generals. Though war with the United States seemed inevitable, the dictator had been assuring his military commanders that they had nothing to fear, that he had—as his deputy prime minister and minister of military industrialization, Abd al-Tawab Mullah al-Huwaysh, would later put it—"something in his hand." His war council took that to mean WMD.

At this meeting, however, Saddam had news for his generals: Iraq's illicit weapons program had been discontinued. There were no WMD. His generals would be fighting the Americans with conventional arms.[1]

The generals were astonished. As Colin Powell's speech to the UN would disclose two months later with recorded intercepts, Iraqi Republican Guard Corps commanders had been busily discussing "nerve agents" and searching "Al-Madinah battalion for any chemical agents." These conversations were not about concealing an existing weapons program, however. They were instructions by Saddam to remove any residual evidence of the *former* program, in advance of Hans Blix's inspections.[2]

Later, Saddam advised his generals that there were other ways to slay the American invaders. He stood before several devices arrayed on a table-top. They included a crossbow, a blowgun, several Molotov cocktails, and a slingshot.

"Let's use all the methods we can," said the dictator to his commanders. But these "methods" would be asymmetrical. Saddam was foreshadowing a war not of apocalyptic weaponry but of insurgency.[3]

THE FIRST INSPECTIONS REPORT RELEASED BY BLIX, ON JANUARY 27, 2003, took the form of a not-so-friendly warning. "Iraq appears not to have come to a genuine acceptance—not even today—of the disarmament which was demanded of it and which it needs to carry out to win the confidence of the world and to live in peace," he told the UN Security Council.

The UNMOVIC chief acknowledged that the Iraqis were "cooperating rather well." But Iraq had yet to provide a satisfactory explanation for its unaccounted-for anthrax and VX nerve gas. Implicitly, Blix was declaring Saddam to be in material breach. Though he stopped short of deploying that phrase, which would be used by the Bush administration to justify war, he believed the message he had delivered was a severe one.[4] Indeed, many of Blix's inspectors on the ground thought his report was far too harsh: the Iraqis had never once obstructed their work.[5]

The next evening in Washington, President Bush delivered his State of the Union address. After praising the Bush tax cuts, inveighing against medical lawsuits, introducing a faith-based initiative, urging a ban on human cloning, and describing a landmark effort to curb AIDS in Africa, the president turned his attention to national security. Bush assured the audience, "We've got the terrorists on the run." More pointedly, the president made clear that he sought no one else's permission to protect the nation. "Whatever action is required, whenever action is necessary, I will defend the freedom and security of the American people," he pledged.

Bush reserved the climax of his address for Saddam. He reiterated Blix's concerns about Iraq's invisible BW and CW programs. He also referenced Saddam's mobile BW labs program—the Curveball intelligence—as Powell would again the next week at the UN. But Bush added his own darkly fantastical post-9/11 flourish, an echo of his October speech in Cincinnati: "Imagine those 19 hijackers with other weapons and other plans, this time armed by Saddam Hussein. It would take one vial, one canister, one crate slipped into this country to bring a day of horror like none we have ever known."

The State of the Union address also happened to include something that had been deleted at the last minute from his Cincinnati speech, and which Powell would also omit from the UN speech: "The British government has learned that Saddam Hussein recently sought significant quantities of uranium from Africa."[6]

Without explicitly saying so, Bush was referring to Saddam's supposed attempts to purchase yellowcake uranium from Niger. George Tenet had previously persuaded Steve Hadley to remove the yellowcake line from the October speech, largely on the grounds that (as a memo from a CIA analyst to the White House would put it) "the evidence is weak."[7] But by the time of the State of the Union address, the administration was determined to press the case that Saddam constituted a nuclear threat. The White House knew that the U.S. intelligence community had doubts about the Niger connection. But the British intelligence services found it credible. At the urging of Hadley and Cheney, NSC nonproliferation staffer Robert Joseph reached out to the CIA's WINPAC director, Alan Foley. Was there any classification reason why the president could not say that "the British government" had produced this intelligence? Foley could not think of one.[8]

A week after Bush's speech, one of the IAEA nuclear inspectors, Jacques Baute, studied the purported letters of agreement in 2000 between Iraq and Niger. Seeing the name of Niger's foreign minister, Allele Habibou, Baute performed a Google search. Habibou had left office more than a decade before the letter of agreement was written. It was a forgery.[9]

The IAEA's director general, Mohamed ElBaradei, sought to break the news gently to the Bush administration. Hadley offered to resign. The president declined his offer. Though annoyed by ElBaradei's public disclosure in early March that the Niger document was a forgery, Bush was no more deterred by the IAEA's finding than he was the day before the State of the

Union address when ElBaradei told the UN that his inspectors on the ground had assessed that Iraq's aluminum tubes "would not be suitable for manufacturing centrifuges."[10]

ElBaradei and Blix had expected that their inspectors on the ground would encounter resistance from the Iraqis. But it was the Americans who were throwing up roadblocks. The CIA was holding back information on some of the suspected weapons sites—and, when asked by Senator Carl Levin in February why this was happening, Tenet's answers were elliptical.[11] In the case of the suspected chemical weapons facility in the northern Iraq city of Khurmal, Feith and his deputy, Bill Luti, prepared a top secret briefing to argue the pros and cons of either giving the site details to Blix or saving them for a cruise missile attack during an all-out invasion of Iraq.[12]

Blix had been boxed into a catch-22 predicament. On the one hand, the Bush administration was withholding information on which sites might be worthy of inspection. On the other, Wolfowitz and other administration officials were grousing about UNMOVIC's failure to find WMD[13]—and speculating that this failure served as proof that Blix's team was incompetent, or worse. As the inspectors descended on one suspected chemical weapons facility, John Bolton—Powell's undersecretary for arms control and international security and State's most ardent Iraq hawk—became convinced that the Iraqis were already evacuating the site's contents. (These were the suspected "decontamination trucks" that could also have been water-spraying vehicles conducting their usual rounds.) In a secret memo, Bolton's assistant, David Wurmser (who had moved there from Cheney's office, and before that from Feith's) wrote, "John Bolton strongly advises that public disclosure of the compromise be made prior to the completion of the inspection of the site." Publicly charging that the inspections were hopelessly tainted before invading Iraq would, Wurmser argued, "lay an important moral mark to justify such a decision."[14]

Blix, like the Bush administration, had not felt terribly sanguine during the early stages of the inspections. He, too, believed some if not all of the WMD intelligence. But even after his harsh report to the UN Security Council on January 27, Blix kept thinking about the conversation he'd had ten days prior with Jacques Chirac. The French president believed that Saddam had discontinued his weapons program. Blix reminded him that his own intelligence officials thought otherwise.

Chirac was dismissive. Intelligence agencies tended to "intoxicate each other" with worst-case scenarios, he said.[15]

Blix returned to Baghdad on February 8 to find an even greater level of cooperation from the Iraqi regime. U-2 overflights were now permitted. Documents were more promptly produced. When Blix's team expressed concern about the unaccounted-for anthrax, the Iraqi scientists suggested that UNMOVIC extract a soil sample from where the Iraqis claimed the anthrax had been dumped in 1991. The test came back positive. The Iraqis proceeded to generate a full list of the individuals who had been involved in the destruction of the anthrax.

Meanwhile, the sites provided by the CIA continued to yield only "very, very meager" results, Blix would say: empty artillery shells in the desert containing traces of mustard gas that apparently had been produced during the Iran-Iraq War; a few jumbles of documents in this or that scientist's house; forty-foot metal tubes at a chicken farm that turned out to be chicken feeders. Blix's team also inspected mobile food-testing labs and refrigerated trucks. None of them turned out to be a biological weapons lab on wheels.[16]

Following Powell's UN speech on February 5, the CIA suddenly began to flood UNMOVIC with so-called special inspections: closely held, last-minute orders for searches of hot targets, often provided by Iraqi informants. One was highly specific: according to a source, inspectors should visit a particular university building, where, in the men's restroom located in the basement, a loose tile could be flipped back, revealing buttons that, after punching in a secret code, would in turn reveal a secret biological weapons laboratory behind a wall. But the building in question did not have a basement.

Another such inspection was ordered when overhead imagery picked up the outlines of what appeared to be a Scud missile buried in the athletic field of a primary school. An angry mob loudly protested as Iraqi soldiers despoiled the schoolyard. The large metal object turned out to be an unconnected sewer pipe.[17]

A third "special inspection" was specified for a site that, according to the Iraqis, had previously been used to manufacture spray tanks for agricultural purposes. U.S. intelligence sources insisted that an active BW-spraying-device program was housed there. Roman Mezencev led a BW team to the supposed hot target. They encountered a rusted junkyard of farm equipment.[18]

Twice the UNMOVIC inspectors descended on the facility at Djerf al-Nadaf where Curveball had said the mobile BW labs were kept. Climbing over a wall and into the building, inspector Rocco Casagrande encountered what he would recall as "a shed filled with four feet of dusty-ass corn, obviously not put there recently." The chief biological inspector, Kay Mareish, insisted that they visit a second time and take samples. All tests came back negative.[19]

On February 14, Blix went before the UN and gave a speech that was a jarring contrast to Powell's address nine days before. The four hundred inspections accomplished thus far had been leakproof and unimpeded, the chief inspector said. Of Powell's litany of WMD, Blix said, "So far, UN-MOVIC has not found any such weapons."[20]

Tony Blair was livid. Blix's speech was "a total disgrace," he told Alastair Campbell.[21] A few days later, the prime minister let his feelings be known to Blix in a phone conversation—though, in typical Blair fashion, he said that it was the Americans who were disappointed in his speech, rather than him.[22]

The inspector did not back down. He reiterated what he had told Condi Rice a few days earlier—namely, that the intelligence was looking quite weak. Then, as he would later recall, "I added that it would prove paradoxical and absurd if 250,000 troops were to invade Iraq and find very little."

Blair responded that he had faith in the intelligence.[23] And in any event, Rice would also argue to Blix, Saddam was on trial here, not the intelligence. The dictator was guilty until proven innocent. From the standpoint of the Bush administration, Blix's endeavor should not be a scavenger hunt. Iraq could end this twelve-year charade once and for all. The regime should volunteer where the weapons sites were and then lead UNMOVIC to them. That the Iraqis had yet to do so simply confirmed the White House's view that, to answer the elder President Bush's rhetorical question, this leopard would never change his spots.

But the progress made by the inspectors in Iraq was beginning to make others feel queasy. At *The Washington Post*, reporter Walter Pincus called Blix, whom he had known since 1960, when the two met in Ghana as delegates of the World Assembly of Youth. Hanging up after their conversation, Pincus realized that Bob Woodward and others at the *Post* were being taken for a ride on the WMD narrative.[24]

In the Pentagon, Wolfowitz's special assistant, Jim Thomas, said to Rumsfeld's undersecretary for intelligence, Steve Cambone, "God, what if they go into Iraq and they don't find anything?"

Laughing, Cambone replied, "How can you possibly be that naive? If anything, we're going to find a program that's bigger than anyone thought!"[25]

(Cambone's boss, of course, preferred to hedge his bets. On February 9 at the Munich Security Conference, German foreign minister Joschka Fischer stared directly at Rumsfeld and exclaimed in English, in a quavering voice, "You have to make the case! And in a democracy, you must convince by yourself! Excuse me, I'm not convinced!" A few days later, Rumsfeld sent a snowflake to his communications director, Torie Clarke: "I am concerned that we are not using all the arguments and leverage we have. The WMD issue is front and center."[26])

At CIA headquarters in Langley, WINPAC director Alan Foley plopped down in a chair next to his senior chemical weapons analyst, Larry Fox. "Larry, am I going to have a job in two months?" he asked.

"What do you mean?" asked Fox.

"Are they going to find the WMD?"

"Well," Fox said, "there's a 60 to 70 percent chance they will." Just four months earlier, Fox had rated the likelihood at 90 percent.[27]

Up on the seventh floor at Langley, Deputy Director John McLaughlin said to Tenet's chief of staff, John Moseman, that Blix's team was doing impressive work.

Then he closed his eyes and quietly sighed, "God, I hope we're not going to do this."[28]

Down in Tampa, CENTCOM commander Tommy Franks interrupted an intelligence briefing on suspected Iraqi WMD locations with a fusillade of curses. "Where the fuck is it?" he demanded. "Show me! Is it here? There? Nowhere? Do we not fucking know?"[29]

To another colleague, Franks growled, "You know, there's plenty of bad things you can say about Saddam. You don't have to make shit up."[30]

And in Cairo, two old friends, David Welch and John Sawers—respectively, the U.S. and UK ambassadors to Egypt—were sitting together over drinks one evening in February 2003 when Welch mournfully observed, "John, we've been looking for WMD for the last twelve years. We've searched everywhere, exhausted all the intelligence, and still found nothing. The most likely conclusion, John . . . *is that it's just not there.*"

Said the American ambassador, "The beginning of any regime's downfall is hubris, when it overreaches in its use of power."[31]

ON MARCH 1, AMERICAN AND PAKISTANI INTELLIGENCE OFFICERS DESCENDED on a suburban house near Islamabad and captured Khalid Shaikh Mohammed, the mastermind of the 9/11 attacks. He was secreted away to a succession of interrogation sites. Eventually, after being subjected to repeated waterboarding and other harsh interrogation techniques, Mohammed would confess to having planned the 9/11 hijackings, the 1993 World Trade Center bombing attempt, the murder of *Wall Street Journal* reporter Daniel Pearl, and numerous other acts of terror. On any involvement between Iraq and Al Qaeda, however, bin Laden's top lieutenant had nothing whatsoever to offer.

But a few days after Mohammed's arrest, Jim Risen and David Johnston of the *Times* divulged an association between the terrorist and a different country: Qatar, a purportedly staunch American ally. According to the account, in 1996 top government officials in Qatar had tipped off Mohammed that the FBI was preparing to arrest him, thereby facilitating the terrorist's safe passage out of the country.

There was little the Bush administration could say to the Qataris by way of rebuke. After all, the dramatic next act in the war on terror was about to be commandeered by Tommy Franks from Camp As Sayliyah, with a nearby newly built $1 billion military airstrip. Qatar's sins of the past would remain unaddressed throughout Bush's presidency.[32]

Even as the case that Saddam had weapons of mass destruction was beginning to come undone, the Bush administration was struggling to convince other countries to join the war effort. Rumsfeld's the-mission-determines-the-coalition outlook was not shared by Bush, Rice, and Powell. In their view, as one of CENTCOM's military planners would put it, "every flag was a good flag."[33] A sizable "coalition of the willing" would serve to demonstrate that America's cause was just and that Bush did not intend to go it alone.

The task of forming a coalition had begun with Cheney's trip to the Middle East in March 2002. By the fall, numerous U.S. ambassadors, Frank Miller's NSC Executive Steering Group, and CENTCOM's planners had become intensely involved in the effort. On January 30, 2003, Feith reported to Rumsfeld, "Overall, 33 countries may be said to be currently in the 'Coalition.'" That figure seemed impressive on paper, given that the Gulf War's famous coalition consisted of thirty-four countries (though it fell well short of the Operation Enduring Freedom coalition in Afghanistan, which involved sixty countries). Every one of those nations in 1991 contributed military personnel, however. Of the countries referred to in Feith's memo, only three—the UK, Australia, and Poland—offered military forces, while twenty-five were passively supporting the United States via "access, basing and overflight."[34]

Even those agreements were piecemeal and hard-won. "We should be graded like Olympic divers, with the degree of difficulty factored in," one of the participants would later say.[35] Many countries were willing to grant overflight rights for humanitarian-related aircraft only. After initially granting overflights, Austria—where 85 percent of the public opposed any involvement in a military invasion—reversed itself in February. Quietly, however, Debra Cagan, the State Department's lead coalition builder, managed to convince the Austrian government to supply chemical-and-biological-weapon vaccinations from its large pharmaceutical firms.[36]

One Eastern European country could offer only a dental unit, prompting the CENTCOM planners to mutter among themselves, "Uh, probably not gonna take a hill with a dental chair."[37] The king of Tonga, on the other hand, signed on early and enthusiastically to the coalition, promising a small contingent to provide security for the Marines as gratitude for America's defense of Tonga during World War II.[38]

More often than not, however, such overtures came at a price. Hungary offered a transportation battalion but expected uniforms, weapons, and money in return. Did the Hungarian soldiers intend to show up naked? It delighted the Bush administration when the Poles eagerly agreed to contribute military personnel to the invasion force. But first the Polish government inquired as to whether it might receive preferential treatment in access to Iraqi oil contracts after the war. After the Bush administration advised that such an arrangement would not be possible, the Polish government agreed to supply about two hundred troops, largely to secure the oil fields and provide anti-CW backup.[39]

The request for oil profits by the Poles was not unreasonable. After all, in January 2003 only 21 percent of the Polish public supported participation in the Iraq war coalition, while 72 percent found it unjustified.[40] Risking the lives of Polish soldiers for so profoundly unpopular a cause should be worth some stake in the future of Iraq, went the thinking. And there were other calculations made by would-be allies with which the coalition builders had to contend. "It was a constant process of *Who's got an election coming up? Is this participation going to do damage to the government?*" recalled one of them. "And then just the practical problems: 'The Lithuanians are willing to do night patrols in Sadr City in Baghdad, that's huge and brave, all they want is night vision goggles, but they're still classified as a Warsaw Pact country and so DOD claims they can't give them night vision goggles, and OMB is insistent that we cannot expend money this way—who can we talk to on the Hill who can do a drug deal that essentially says, '*Yes, we're going to violate the law, won't you please help us?*' That kind of stuff was the daily aggravation."[41]

A scramble was under way to find U.S. personnel in the reserves who worked in law enforcement and would be willing to help train the police in Baghdad after the invasion. In this and other civilian recruiting efforts, the coalition builders heard a continuing refrain: *How secure will it be there?* The answer, of course, was: *Not very secure, if we can't get sheriffs and cops to come help us train the Iraqi police!*

Then there was the matter of the Free Iraqi Forces, the brainchild of Paul Wolfowitz and Ahmad Chalabi. Though the deputy secretary of defense had hoped for upwards of ten thousand Iraqis to sign up for combat, by January 2003 the more realistic hope was five hundred. Because most of the recruits were likely to come from Europe, it fell to Debra Cagan to find a place to house and train them. (It also proved necessary to find a home for the hundred or so Iraqi Americans who had begun their training at Fort Bliss, in El Paso, Texas, only to have it determined that this was against U.S. Army rules.)[42] The U.S. Air Force base in Ramstein, Germany, adamantly refused. Where would they find beds for hundreds of Iraqis? Cagan finally located a willing partner in Hungary, whose government had embarked on a charm offensive to improve its relations with NATO. In January, the United States and Hungary announced that "up to 3,000" Iraqis would soon be arriving at Taszár Air Base for a mission that had yet to be specified.[43]

By February 2003, the Bush administration's NATO allies were showing up weekly to the Pentagon to be briefed on the robust coalition that the president had pledged to assemble. Frank Miller's aide Tom Greenwood had created a PowerPoint chart of the supporting countries. Under each country's flag was a listing of the support offered. One morning, Miller and Greenwood appraised the graphic, with its feeble entries: one dog platoon from this country, two chemical decontamination spray units from that country.

"Damn," muttered Miller. "This is not going to make the president happy."

"Well," sighed Greenwood, "guess I'll make the flags bigger."[44]

FOR ALL THE INTENSE EFFORT THAT WENT INTO THE MONTHS OF DRAWING up the invasion plans, those who were finally privy to them during the first two months of 2003 were astounded by their immaturity. There was no provision for WMD seizure and disposal, no troops allotted to guard ammunition depots or to seal the country's borders.[45] In mapping out air strikes for Baghdad, CENTCOM sought to avoid hitting embassy buildings but did not know where many of them were.[46]

By contrast, Wolfowitz and Feith spent considerable effort on the Free Iraqi Forces. They were also deeply preoccupied with how the invasion plan might affect Israel. "There was clearly a concern on the part of Wolfowitz and certainly Feith that this was about protecting our friends in Israel, and that Saddam wouldn't do something that would affect them," one of the CENTCOM planners recalled. "It was very clearly a part of the discussion and part of our planning effort. Were there certain trip wires that might bring the Israelis into the fight early? They asked a lot of questions about how we were going to ensure that this does not occur. Having Israel making some decision to enter this would polarize the Arab world and was high-risk."[47]

At one deputies meeting, Feith introduced the idea of "catastrophic success." What if the war was over more quickly than the planners had anticipated? The question was worth asking. But the undersecretary did not propose any remedy, or even a recommendation that the matter be given further study.[48] It was difficult to tell whether Feith was truly concerned with such a scenario or if—in the manner of the "Rumsfeld Mini-Me" that State officials believed he had become—the undersecretary simply wished to demonstrate his mastery of the right questions without the burden of having to answer them.

Rumsfeld had a final riddle of his own to unsheathe. In March, the secretary asked a gathering that included Wolfowitz, JCS chairman Myers, and JCS vice chairman Pace, "How long does everyone think combat is going to last in Iraq?"

Myers demurred. "That's an unknown," the chairman said, hoping that his deployment of Rumsfeld's parlance would let him off the hook. Rumsfeld was insistent, however. Gamely, each man supplied an answer, ranging from days to weeks.

When Rumsfeld's turn came, the secretary awarded them a cockeyed grin. "You think I'm stupid enough to guess?" he said.[49]

Studying the final war plans one day in January 2003, Condi Rice thought, *This doesn't look like an invasion force to me.* It did not seem at all clear how the troops would be sufficient to hold the territory they had just conquered. The Pentagon's answer—that the Brits or the Aussies or some other entity would "backfill" the invading force—struck the national security adviser as dubious. (That was especially true when the frugal Rumsfeld became aware of the UN pay scale for peacekeeping forces and announced his disinclination to delegate this mission to other countries.)[50]

In February, Rice finally managed to get the matter of "rear-area security" on the agenda for a briefing with the president. Bush opened the discussion by saying to the JCS generals, "This is something that Condi has wanted to talk about." Perhaps unintentionally, the president had sent a signal to the generals that the topic did not merit his concern and therefore need not merit theirs. They offered only their usual "backfilling" notions, and the matter was dropped.

Even the placid Hadley was stupefied by Bush's condescension. "I would have resigned after that comment by the president," he told Rice after the meeting.

Rice felt humiliated. "What were you *doing*?" she demanded to Bush later. "You just knocked the legs out from under me."

The president began to bristle, but Rice was not finished. "And by the way," she added, "you don't have a plan for what happens after this, after you defeat Saddam's forces. They haven't told you what they're going to do."

Rice brought up the matter of inadequate rear-area security again the following morning in the Oval Office. This time, however, Cheney was present. "You know," said the former defense secretary, "you really shouldn't be questioning the Pentagon."

The national security adviser was well aware that she was playing out of her lane. Still, she repeated to Bush, "Mr. President, they don't have a plan for you for what happens after they've defeated Saddam's forces."[51]

To Rice, the fault lay with Rumsfeld and the generals. She was there in the Cabinet Room in March 2003 when Bush asked the Joint Chiefs, "Do you support this plan?" That was their opportunity to voice to the commander in chief the complaints so many of them would publicly disclose months and years after this moment in the Cabinet Room. And instead, whether out of can-do military spirit or fear of Rumsfeld, to a man they replied, "Yes, sir." Only Jim Jones, the commandant of the Marines, would offer a slight caveat: "Well, I had some concerns, but they've now been addressed."[52]

But it was also true that Bush—he of the gut intuition, who could effortlessly eviscerate a flabby speech draft and pick apart an equivocating CIA briefer—did not press the generals. He did not ask the what-if, the how-do-you-know, that so often stumped his White House staffers. Bush let the generals off easily. They were telling him what he wished to hear.

ON JANUARY 20, PRESIDENT BUSH SIGNED NATIONAL SECURITY PRESIDEN-tial Directive No. 24, establishing that the Iraq postwar planning tasks be overseen by the Department of Defense. The directive had been drafted thirteen days earlier, by Bill Luti in Feith's office.[53]

State Department officials objected vigorously to Luti's draft. Its open-ended timetable fed "perceptions that our real objective is not to disarm Iraq but rather to exploit Iraq's oil sector," argued Assistant Secretary of State for South and Central Asian Affairs Robert Blake. The draft also made no mention of rapidly establishing a diplomatic presence in Iraq.[54] In the end, State's concerns went largely unaddressed. The final version changed one of DOD's postwar tasks from "protecting energy supplies" to "protecting natural resources." It made mention of a chargé d'affaires in Baghdad but did not say when it would be established or what power it would be given.

Later that week, at the gated Georgetown home of Ahmad Chalabi, a gathering that included Richard Perle, David Wurmser, Laurie Mylroie, and Chalabi's lobbyist, Francis Brooke, celebrated the news. One of Chalabi's aides kneeled before the INC leader, as one attendee would recall, "to celebrate the fall of Colin Powell." Brooke later turned to the same party guest and proclaimed, "If you're nice to me, you can come visit me when I'm Iraq's foreign minister."[55]

A few days after NSPD-24 had been signed by the president, the *New York Times* columnist Thomas Friedman dropped by the Pentagon to meet with Donald Rumsfeld. Friedman had not interviewed the secretary until now. Though he had generally written in favor of overthrowing Saddam as a post-9/11 means of transforming the Middle East, the Pulitzer Prize–winning columnist worried that the Bush administration had not thought through the postwar challenges. He intended, then, to build his next column around the man who would now be in charge of this very matter.

Rumsfeld offered Friedman a tuna sandwich. The *Times* columnist then asked the secretary to explain his plan for "the morning after."

Friedman sat quietly through Rumsfeld's long-winded, tangent-riddled, quasi-Socratic, and ultimately nonresponsive reply. "His disquisition made absolutely no sense to me," he would recall. Friedman did not manage to fashion a column out of his encounter with Rumsfeld, though the material was there in front of him: with war imminent, the Bush administration had little clue about what would follow the collapse of Saddam's regime.[56]

The fault began with the president. Bush had ordered that a postwar planning office be delayed, for fear that a leak about its existence would undercut diplomatic efforts.[57] It was a laudable sentiment, but one without logic. The State Department's Future of Iraq Project had been conducting meetings with Iraqi exiles for months now. Tens of thousands of U.S. troops were massed in Kuwait. Administration officials had fanned out across Europe and Asia, requesting overflight and basing access.

Each of these activities had leaked to the press, as had the broad outlines of the Pentagon's invasion plans. And though most American allies opposed an invasion of Iraq, among their reasons for doing so was that the Bush administration was rushing to war without adequate forethought for "the morning after." A sign to the contrary might have reassured rather than alienated them.

Now, as of January 20, Feith's shop had supervision over postwar planning. Henceforth, Rice's NSC would have even less visibility into the most significant national security decision of George W. Bush's presidency. Rice pressed Frank Miller and his deputy, Tom Greenwood, to shake down their Pentagon sources. Were Feith and Wolfowitz still obsessing over their Free Iraqi Forces, a concept so half-baked and ineffectual that Rice had not even bothered briefing the president on it? (Yes.) Were they seeing to it that U.S. military personnel on the ground would have sufficient interpreters? (No.)[58]

Hadley convened a deputies meeting in the Situation Room with Feith, Luti, Miller, NSC official Elliott Abrams, and a few others. The president wanted a postwar plan, Hadley told them, adding, "You're not leaving the room until it's finished."

Feith promptly got up to leave. "He's my ride back," said Luti, by way of also saying goodbye to the other deputies.[59]

For months, Abrams and another NSC official, Robin Cleveland, had been developing plans to provide humanitarian relief for the Iraqi people following the invasion. It came as a surprise, then, when in January, Feith approached Abrams and said, in effect, *You and Robin stand down. We're taking command of this.* Feith's shop made no further use of Abrams's and Cleveland's expertise after that.[60]

In London, Minister of Defence Geoffrey Hoon announced at a meeting of Blair administration officials that his American counterpart, Rumsfeld, had been put in charge of post-conflict humanitarian issues. The news, Alastair Campbell would recall, "was met with laughter mixed with shock all around the table."[61]

ON JANUARY 10 AT 2:15 IN THE AFTERNOON, BUSH, CHENEY, RICE, CARD, Fleischer, and NSC official Zalmay Khalilzad met in the Oval Office with three Iraqi exiles: Kanan Makiya, Rend al-Rahim Francke, and Hatem Mukhlis. Khalilzad, whom Bush had appointed the president's "envoy to the Free Iraqis" just a month before, had hand-selected the trio. The well-known Makiya, as well as Francke, the executive director of the Iraq Foundation, had been avid voices for regime change for more than a decade. Both were proxies for Chalabi. Mukhlis, a New York–based surgeon, was a Sunni from Tikrit, Saddam's birthplace—"and it was a huge fight to get Mukhlis in there," recalled a State official. "He was also an oppositionist, but he could speak with a little more sobriety."[62]

Bush began by telling his three guests, "I believe in freedom and peace.

I believe Saddam Hussein is a threat to America and to the neighborhood. He should disarm. But he won't. Therefore, we will remove him from power. We can't change his heart. His heart is of stone."

Francke said that she agreed. Then she assured the president, "The Iraqi people can practice democracy if they're given the opportunity. It's a large and rich country."

Bush wanted to hear their personal stories. The three exiles had not been to Iraq in decades and lived comfortable lives. But Mukhlis told Bush that his father had been killed a few years earlier by Saddam's thugs after a failed coup attempt. "All the Iraqis are ready to get rid of Saddam," he said. "The fear is what comes after."

"Does the average citizen in Iraq hate Israel?" Bush asked.

"No," Mukhlis assured him. "They're self-absorbed. Inward-looking."

Makiya then spoke sweepingly of the Iraqi people's suffering under the regime. "You're going to break the mold," the *Republic of Fear* author told the president. "You will change the image of the United States in the region. Democracy is truly doable in Iraq."

"We're planning for the worst," Bush said.

As if to suggest that this would not be necessary, Makiya replied, "People will greet the troops with flowers and sweets."

"How do you know?" Bush asked.

"This comes from people on the inside," Makiya said.

Bush took this in. "My most important job," he said, "is to convince the American people that this is the right thing to do."

Makiya did not disagree. But he emphasized something that Wolfowitz and Chalabi had long been arguing: "You need Iraqis to go in with you."

Bush was noncommittal on this point. There were, in effect, two armies, the president told them. "The first will be to topple Saddam and his regime. The second will be to rebuild Iraq. And plans are already well under way for that."

Mukhlis said that he was glad to hear this. But the window to achieve this was perhaps two months. If the Americans failed to deliver on its reconstruction promises, he warned, "you could see Mogadishu in Baghdad."

Bush was emphatic: they would deliver. He looked over to Rice for confirmation. She nodded and recited a litany of doctors, engineers, and technicians who would constitute the postwar "army."

Bush was curious about what U.S. troops would face on the ground. Would they find starving Iraqis? (No, came Francke's answer, but likely malnourished people who would need immediate medical attention.) Would they encounter sectarian tensions? (No, Makiya said: "The Sunni/Shia conflict is top-down-driven," meaning it was a rivalry created by Saddam, and by implication would likely disappear with the dictator's removal.) Would the Iraqi diaspora return to their homeland? (Absolutely, said Makiya.) Did Iraqis send emails? (Judiciously, as the internet was state-owned.) How long would the U.S. military have to stay? (Two to three years, Francke estimated.)

Cheney interjected for the first and only time: "We need to have a light hand in the postwar phase," he said.

True, Makiya agreed. "But you need to find the right people now."

Then Bush asked, "How do we deal with the impression that the U.S. is bringing in a leader who will impose our will?" It was a question Bush had wrestled with for some time. Though he was glad to hear from his three guests that the Iraqi diaspora would return home to help put into practice their own experiences of living in a democracy, the president had frequently voiced to his aides the concern that the exiles had avoided the hardships of their countrymen and thus had not earned a stake in the country's future.

"That's an outside issue, not internal," replied Makiya—implying that the Iraqi people would be fine with whoever replaced Saddam.

Wrapping things up, Bush told the three exiles, "We haven't reached any conclusions. I view you and the Iraqi diaspora as our partners. Your job is to gather the people who want to help, and rally their hearts and souls. My job is to rally the world and win the war. I'm not sure it's my job to pick [the next Iraqi leader]."

Standing, Bush said, "I truly believe that out of this will come peace with Israel and the Palestinians. Maybe one year from now, we'll be toasting to victory and talking about the transition to freedom."[63]

Makiya left the Oval Office mostly pleased with what he had heard from the president. Still, he could not shake the feeling that Rice's subdued body language suggested a lack of confidence in the postwar effort. Two weeks later, Makiya was asked to meet a retired general named Jay Garner at the Pentagon. Garner had just been hired by Rumsfeld to lead the postwar planning effort known as the Office of Reconstruction and Humanitarian Assistance (ORHA). Makiya found him in a small office, sitting alone.

Garner had heard a lot about Makiya. "Come help me do this thing," the new ORHA director said.

Taken aback, Makiya said, "I'm sorry, but I'm not really an administrator. I'm more identified with the opposition."

He asked Garner, carefully, "Who do you have working with you so far?"

Just a secretary, Garner replied.

Makiya then remembered Bush's pledge of a "second army" and Rice's unenthusiastic posture. It was late January. He knew, of course, that his months of participation in the Future of Iraq Project now constituted a waste of time, since, as he would later say, "DOD utterly despised the State Department." Makiya left wondering why Rumsfeld had insisted on taking on a responsibility for which he had little to no enthusiasm.[64]

The fault did not lie with Garner, whom Rumsfeld already knew from a space commission they had served on together two years earlier. The Army general had supervised the humanitarian assistance to 400,000 Kurds in northern Iraq following the Gulf War and was a beloved figure there.[65] But the ORHA director was given no plan, "just a bunch of papers, most of them from Feith's policy shop," he would say.[66] Garner had no time, no resources, and no autonomy.

That latter fact became obvious to Garner a month after Rumsfeld hired him. In late February, Garner received from Secretary Powell a long list of potential ORHA hires. One of them, Meghan O'Sullivan, worked under Bill Burns in the Bureau of Near Eastern Affairs at State. Another adviser to Burns, Tom Warrick, had been the director of the Future of Iraq Project and had thought about post-conflict issues more than anyone Garner had yet encountered. He wanted them both on his team.

But Rumsfeld nixed them both. When Garner protested that they were two of his most knowledgeable recruits, the secretary said firmly, "It's well above me. You have to get rid of them."[67]

Though Garner was unaware of it, the matter was not "well above" Rumsfeld at all. O'Sullivan had been one of the architects of Powell's "smart sanctions" policy, which was anathema to Rumsfeld and Cheney. (Libby enjoyed saying that smart sanctions were neither.)[68] Warrick had gotten on Wolfowitz's bad side. The deputy secretary had told his boss that Garner was considering Warrick. Rumsfeld then did the honors of short-circuiting the appointment while claiming to Garner that it was "well above me."[69]

At the end of February, Garner proposed having twenty-three "senior ministry advisors" who would each preside over an important postwar area such as trade, justice, education, oil, or agriculture. Rumsfeld liked the idea. Then he saw the nominees. Eight of them were from State. Rumsfeld crossed out their names. He wanted people from his building.[70]

Powell was enraged. It was one power grab too many. He sent Marc Grossman to a Deputies Committee meeting to set things right. As Feith began to explain Rumsfeld's thinking—many of these proposed hires were retired diplomats; Garner could surely find better alternatives—Grossman stood up and said, "I'm not going to listen to this," and walked out.

Feith later called Grossman at Hadley's behest. "I can't explain it," the undersecretary stammered. Powell's undersecretary for political affairs was not mollified. Garner, in the meantime, would fly off to the Middle East with those eight positions unfilled, since Rumsfeld had no DOD recruits in mind—only objections to the State recruits.[71]

Underlying Rumsfeld's inattentiveness—and adding to Garner's stress— was the secretary's abiding belief that this whole postwar planning exercise was not America's responsibility anyway, that Iraqis had better learn how to ride the bicycle themselves. And they would do so gladly, Wolfowitz and others argued. General Tim Cross, who became Garner's British counterpart in postwar planning, would come to realize that "the plan is that we do not need a plan. The plan is that once we have moved into Iraq, then the Iraqi people, generally speaking, will welcome us"—which meant that, after tidying up a few of the inevitable war-related humanitarian complications, Iraq would soon be left to bask in joyous self-determination.[72]

But this begged perhaps the most important question of all, the one whose answer would remain unsettled as President Bush plunged into war: *How* would Iraq be governed after Saddam? Here was where the administration departed from its Afghanistan model. That country's leader, Hamid Karzai, had been selected at the Bonn Conference and escorted into Kabul. Rice would later observe that the West had little choice but to install Karzai, as "everybody had been run out of Afghanistan by the Taliban."[73]

By contrast, Bush had been convinced that Iraq was teeming with able leaders-in-waiting. Perhaps, he suggested to his aides, such individuals were buried somewhere in Baghdad's technocracy, or running the nation's oil sector. Perhaps they were in jail. But the stories of Iraqi suffering told by Makiya—who, like Chalabi, strongly advocated a transitional government led by exiles—had produced the opposite of the intended effect. Bush concluded that it was Saddam's victims who deserved the opportunity to rule, not those who had escaped the suffering.[74]

Such a leader would not emerge overnight, however. And despite the rosy promises of Makiya, Chalabi, and others that democracy in Iraq was "truly doable," this—like the idea of Saddam spraying New York City with anthrax from his fleet of unmanned aerial vehicles, or handing his nuclear program over to bin Laden—required an Olympian leap of the imagination. As Paul Pillar, of the CIA, warned in a January 2003 paper entitled "Principal Challenges in Post-Saddam Iraq," "Iraqi political culture does not foster liberalism or democracy. Iraq lacks the experience of a loyal opposition and effective institutions for mass political participation. Saddam's brutal methods have made a generation of Iraqis distrustful of surrendering or sharing power."[75] ("This is something you guys ought to read," John McLaughlin said as he dumped a stack of copies of Pillar's just-published paper on the conference table of the Situation Room at the beginning of a Deputies Committee meeting. Feith and others gamely accepted a copy, but McLaughlin did not hear a word about the paper after that and would come to regret not having pushed them to heed its warnings.)[76]

The self-starting Iraq that Makiya and Chalabi conjured up in their dreamy monologues had taken great strides backward in the past two decades, Pillar wrote. Per capita income had plunged. Its literacy rate was now a meager 50 to 60 percent. Less than half the population had electricity and clean water. Democracy was not uppermost in the minds of Iraqis.

Wolfowitz and Feith continued to insist otherwise, and to maintain that an exile-led transitional authority would be the most expeditious pathway to that goal. Each went a step further: at successive NSC meetings in January 2003, first Wolfowitz and later Feith said, "When Chalabi's in charge . . ."

In both cases, Bush cut them off. "We're *not* putting Chalabi in charge," the president said sharply. "The Iraqi people are going to decide that."[77]

On the other side, Powell, Armitage, and others at State argued that Chalabi would have no legitimacy inside Iraq—that he barely had any *outside* of it—and that a multiyear U.S. occupation was the only realistic option.

Indecision on this one crucial matter paralyzed the entire postwar apparatus. As Bill Burns wrote Powell in a memo, "The fundamental question of the structure of the post-conflict government—whether Iraq is governed by a U.S. military administration or, alternatively, by an international civilian transitional authority—has limited our ability to plan effectively and reach out to potential partners."[78]

Even State had predicated its Future of Iraq Project on the belief that the Iraqi exiles had a role in post-Saddam Iraq. How much of a role, and when, were the outstanding issues. After a year's worth of bickering on the subject, the task now fell to Zal Khalilzad. Having worked for Cheney and Libby in the first Bush administration, Bush's new "special presidential envoy and ambassador at large for the free Iraqis" was indebted to them for his job at the NSC, particularly after having failed to impress Rumsfeld in his interview for the undersecretary job that ultimately went to Feith. Because Khalilzad had OVP's imprimatur, Hadley afforded him a long leash.[79] Before 9/11, part of his roving portfolio included interfacing with Iraqi opposition members like Chalabi, whom Khalilzad had known for a decade.[80] As a native Afghan, he suddenly became indispensable after 9/11 and the fall of the Taliban as the administration's chief intermediary with tribal leaders.[81]

In December 2002, as Bush was assigning Khalilzad his new Iraq post, Feith's deputy, Bill Luti, and David Pearce, of the State Department, visited Chalabi at his home in London just before a White House–sponsored conference of Iraqi exiles was about to begin. They presented Chalabi with a letter signed by Wolfowitz, Armitage, and Libby—an unambiguous affirmation of White House policy. The letter made clear Bush's opposition to any kind of interim government being formed until Saddam was overthrown. "It was a tough moment," recalled Pearce. "Not so much 'It's never going to happen.' More 'It's not going to happen when you want it to.'"[82]

Chalabi was angry but undeterred. The following month, he and Makiya traveled to Iran and entered Kurdistan on foot. They and other opposition figures insisted on another conference to discuss a provisional government of exiles. Khalilzad met with them in the mountain village of Salahuddin on February 12.[83]

Insisting that the exiles be a governing force in post-Saddam Iraq, Chalabi warned Khalilzad, "We are your friends, but not your agents." He reminded Bush's envoy, "We fought Saddam Hussein before you knew of him."[84]

But the facts had not changed. Khalilzad informed Chalabi that the U.S. government would not be anointing a successor to Saddam.

Until now, Chalabi had assumed that his foes were the CIA and Powell's State Department. Khalilzad's message was a sobering revelation. The president himself opposed an interim government. His national security adviser felt the same way. It had not escaped Condoleezza Rice's notice that the Iraqi exiles seemed incapable of reaching consensus. In this manner, as she told one confidant, they reminded her of the Polish opposition exiles during World War II.[85]

Still, Chalabi's long war was far from over. He continued to have backing from the offices of Rumsfeld and Cheney. In early February, one of Chalabi's key supporters approached Jay Garner. "You know," said Doug Feith, "you could make things a lot easier on yourself if you just appointed Ahmad president when you got there."

"Doug, I'm not going to do that," Garner replied. "We're going to let the people choose their leaders. That's my policy, and that's the same policy as your boss." Garner was referring to Rumsfeld, who was cordial with Chalabi but also careful to maintain a healthy distance from the controversial INC leader.

Shortly before Garner left for Kuwait at the end of February, Rumsfeld brought him to an NSC meeting. As the new ORHA chief began his briefing on the plans his team was developing, Bush spoke up.

"Why do you talk like that?" the president asked, referring to the general's southern accent.

"I was born and raised on a ranch in South Florida," Garner replied.

Bush put up a thumb. "You're in," he said.

Once Garner had finished his briefing and the meeting drew to a close, the president had one last thing to say to Garner. "Hey, Jay," he said. "Kick ass. And if you have any problem with that governor down in Florida, let me know. I've got some control over him."

Garner smiled, thinking, *He didn't ask me a single question.*[86]

CHAPTER NINETEEN

LIBERATOR

I s Iraq capable of democracy?"

"Yes! Yes! Yes!"

Paul Wolfowitz stood in his blue dress shirt and red tie before some three hundred Iraqi Americans inside the Fairlane Club, in Dearborn, Michigan, and basked in the chanting. It was a snowy Sunday afternoon, February 23, 2003, and the deputy secretary of defense had just flown in on a C-9 at the invitation of the Iraqi Forum for Democracy. Many of the attendees wore native dress. Some spoke in Arabic. At one point, several of them rose from their folding chairs and began to sing and dance on the parquet floor. Wolfowitz himself greeted the audience in Arabic and quoted from the Koran.

Though Wolfowitz was visiting the Detroit suburb for the first time, the encounter seemed redolent of the past—bringing him full circle back to his romantic tour of service, fifteen years earlier, as ambassador to Indonesia, where he first became a believer in tolerant Muslim societies. As in Jakarta, many in the Dearborn audience had learned a bit about this man and how he had supported their cause back when few other Americans did. Though Wolfowitz had never been much of an orator, the crowd listened raptly, knowing that he spoke for the president and that their hour of deliverance was soon coming.

President Bush had not yet decided whether to go to war, he reminded them. But, Wolfowitz added, "it is not too early for the rest of us to be thinking about how to build a just and peaceful and democratic Iraq after Saddam Hussein is gone." He laid out the administration's objectives, beginning with "the overarching principle: The United States seeks to liberate Iraq, not to occupy Iraq." After the applause died down, the deputy secretary listed the other goals: ridding Iraq of its WMD, destroying its terrorist infrastructure, maintaining its territorial integrity, and rebuilding the country.

Eventually, Wolfowitz arrived at the real purpose of his visit. The Bush administration needed their help. They needed Iraqi Americans who were willing to return to their birthplace—as civilian contractors, as interpreters, and of course as members of the Free Iraqi Forces, for whom "training has already begun at a military base in Hungary." Less than a month before combat operations, Paul Wolfowitz was scrambling to fill a yawning void in how peace would be kept in Iraq.

The moderator, an oncologist named Maha Hussain who had attended medical school in Baghdad, took the microphone after Wolfowitz had concluded his remarks. Listing the U.S. government's support for dictators, its neglect of the Iraqi people, and its disengagement from the Middle East peace process, Dr. Hussain then pointedly asked, "Why should we be here, with all due respect, why should the people outside in Iraq trust or believe what you just said or what the United States government says?"

Wolfowitz smiled and spoke ruefully of having to field so incisive a question. But no one in the Bush administration was better prepared for it than the deputy secretary. He began by acknowledging that he could understand her sentiment and might even agree with a few specific grievances. Then he said:

> Remember, it was the United States and United States blood and courage that liberated the people of Kuwait. It was the United States military that saved the people of Somalia from starvation. It was the

United States military that ended ethnic conflict in Bosnia. It was the United States military and a coalition that ended ethnic cleansing in Kosovo. It is the United States military that led to the liberation of Northern Iraq and has protected it since. And it was the United States military and other countries and our president and a lot of other people, but above all the courage of American soldiers, sailors, airmen and marines that liberated Afghanistan. And that's by my count, six times that we've come to the aid of Muslim populations. The Iraqis will be the seventh.

But let me say one other thing because I know there's a lot of history and some of it is personal and bitter. This is a time not to look to the past but to look to the future. This is a time not to talk about our differences but to pull together.

We have a president of enormous courage who says what he means and means what he says and his word you can count on. We have one of the most powerful military forces ever assembled ready if the president decides they're needed to do what has to be done. And if we commit those forces we're not going to commit them for anything less than a free and democratic Iraq.

Applause engulfed Wolfowitz. At the end of the event, after the reporters were led out, about a hundred participants stepped forward and presented their contact information to CENTCOM's deputy commander, Michael DeLong— saying, as DeLong would later write, "if there was a war, they wanted to be part of it." (When war came, CENTCOM contacted these individuals "to be interpreters or translators," DeLong wrote. "Most said no; they wanted only positions of power or leadership in the new Iraq.")

Wolfowitz also shook the hand of a thirteen-year-old boy named Ahsan Alwatan, whose family home had been invaded by Saddam's troops in 1991, during the Shia uprising. The Alwatans were accused of taking part in the insurrection. In front of his mother, one-year-old Ahsan was kicked repeatedly in the head. The boy was partially brain-damaged but survived. He and his family had made it to America three months before 9/11.

Now he would live to see his new countrymen topple the regime of his old one. Ahsan Alwatan would nonetheless elect to stay in America—where, at age twenty-six, he was fatally shot in the head after an altercation at a gas station in Detroit.[1]

TWO DAYS AFTER WOLFOWITZ RETURNED FROM DEARBORN, ARMY CHIEF OF staff General Eric K. Shinseki was summoned to a Senate Armed Services Committee hearing on Capitol Hill. During an otherwise uneventful proceeding, Senator Carl Levin took the opportunity to ask Shinseki a question that he felt the Bush administration had been evading for some time:

"General, could you give us some idea as to the magnitude of the Army's force requirements for an occupation of Iraq, following a successful completion of the war?"

When Shinseki replied that it would be hard to offer a specific number, Levin pressed, "How about a range?"

"I would say that what's been mobilized to this point, something on the order of several hundred thousand soldiers are probably a, you know, figure that would be required" was Shinseki's answer.[2]

Wolfowitz was furious when he received word of Shinseki's testimony later that day. The two had a history, going back to the Army chief's decision in early 2001 to allow all members of the Army to wear black berets. In a June 2001 commencement speech at West Point, the deputy secretary had cited Shinseki's courage in battle while suffering "horrendous wounds" during the Vietnam War. Even then, however, Wolfowitz viewed him as an antagonist— an alleged reformer who was principally interested in protecting the status of the Army and bloated projects like the Crusader missile program. In April 2002, barely halfway into his four-year term as chief of staff, Pentagon officials leaked to *The Washington Post* that Rumsfeld had lost patience with the "lack of fresh thinking in the Army" and intended to replace Shinseki.[3]

Wolfowitz's quarrel with Shinseki's assertion of "several hundred thousand soldiers" had less to do with the substance of that prediction than with its potential to disrupt the momentum toward war. Rumsfeld, on the other hand, was offended on theological grounds. An Army general, having the gall to say that a light footprint in Iraq would not suffice! The secretary directed Wolfowitz, according to a senior Pentagon official, "to go up there and refute Shinseki."[4]

On February 27, two days after Shinseki's remarks, Wolfowitz appeared before the House Budget Committee. Ostensibly, the deputy secretary was there to discuss the DOD's budget request for fiscal year 2004. But midway through his prepared testimony, Wolfowitz begged the chair's indulgence to digress. "I am reluctant to try to predict anything about what the cost of a possible conflict in Iraq would be—what the possible cost of reconstructing and stabilizing that country afterwards might be. But some of the higher-end predictions that we have been hearing recently, such as the notion that it will take several hundred thousand U.S. troops to provide stability in post-Saddam Iraq, are wildly off the mark."

But of course, Wolfowitz had himself made many such predictions about Iraq in the past. Now he proceeded to do so again. He predicted that "even countries like France will have a strong interest in assisting Iraq's reconstruction." He predicted that "the Iraqis themselves can provide a good deal of whatever manpower is necessary." Wolfowitz predicted, "I am reasonably certain that they will greet us as liberators, and that will help us to keep requirements down." He predicted that the "$15 to 20 billion a year in oil exports" and the "billions that are closeted away by Saddam Hussein and his henchmen" would pay for the bulk of postwar expenditures.

He reserved his most audacious prediction for the end of his testimony. "But I will tell you," Wolfowitz told the House committee, "in the aftermath, I think if you want a glimpse of what it is going to be like, I would urge you to do what I did a week ago Sunday and go to Dearborn, Michigan, where the largest Iraqi American community in this country lives, some 400,000, I was told." The deputy secretary said that in addition to the terrifying stories he had been told, he had also heard words of hope:

"One of them even told of getting a call from a friend of his who is a son of a minister in the Iraqi government. They are just unanimous in their hope that we will help to liberate Iraq. These are Arabs, 23 million of the most

educated people in the Arab world, who are going to welcome us as liberators. When that message gets out to the whole Arab world, it is going to be
a powerful counter to Osama bin Laden."[5]

WOLFOWITZ'S TAKEDOWN OF SHINSEKI—WHO WOULD RETIRE FROM THE
Army less than four months later—reverberated throughout the Pentagon.
"It sent a signal, absolutely, like Rumsfeld calling out Newbold for saying
'eviscerated,'" recalled General Mark Hertling. "Those two were leaders. It
sent a message that you're better off being a follower."[6]

The price of admission for Wolfowitz that day on the Hill was having to
answer questions from Congress about the costs of invading Iraq. In particular, several House Democrats were unamused to hear about the financial in-
ducements Wolfowitz and other administration officials had been dangling
to Turkey in exchange for assisting the invasion. "You know, in the very week
that we negotiated with Turkey, the administration also told the governors
there wasn't any more money for education and health care," observed Illinois congressman Rahm Emanuel. He added with a smirk, "So I would
recommend to the governors that they may want to hire the person that has
been negotiating for Turkey on their behalf, because he has done a very
good job."[7]

Since July 2002, Wolfowitz had spearheaded the United States' efforts
to court Turkey as a northern front for the invasion. The Turks shared a one-
hundred-mile border with Iraq. It was already understood that the Saudi
government would not permit American troops to use Saudi Arabia as a
southern front, as they had in 1991. That left Kuwait as the only other entry
point for a ground invasion. Franks and his planners feared that 150,000
American and British troops moving through the narrow southern corridor
would be vulnerable to a chemical weapons attack. A second front from the
north would not only mitigate that eventuality but also divide Iraq's Republican Guard while removing a Baath leadership escape route to Saddam's
birthplace of Tikrit. British general Anthony Pigott had argued forcefully

for the "Northern Option." By October, it had become an essential feature of CENTCOM's final war plan. All of this presupposed Turkey's willingness to be a staging ground for an American-led invasion of its neighbor.[8]

Wolfowitz felt confident that he could convince the Turks to join the war effort. In Turkey's secularity, the deputy secretary saw glimmers of his beloved second home. "One of the striking facts about Indonesia," he observed in a speech at Washington's Willard Hotel in June, "is that it's only one of two countries, Turkey being the other, with a Muslim majority in which Islam is not the state religion." Like Indonesia, Turkey had made a "historic commitment to modernity."[9] A month later in Istanbul, he again highlighted this commonality: "Turkey's courage to embrace both tradition and modernity offers great promise for all Muslims today, especially as we consider the war on terrorism."[10]

But Turkey had reason to "consider the war on terrorism" through a different lens. Its war, for the past fifteen years, had been against the Kurdistan Workers' Party, or PKK, a separatist group with ties to Ansar al-Islam in northern Iraq whose suicide bombings and other terrorist acts had resulted in fatalities greater than ten times what the United States had experienced on September 11.[11] Several of the Kurdish leaders who were among the Iraqi exiles were already pushing for an autonomous Kurdistan, which Turkish leaders felt would gravely destabilize the region. When Wolfowitz met with Prime Minister Bülent Ecevit, the frail seventy-seven-year-old poet declared that the situation with the Kurds was already spinning out of control.[12]

Wolfowitz assured Ecevit that the United States opposed an independent Kurdish state. He argued, "If we can liberate the Iraqi people, Turkey's real reward will be having a democratic, prosperous neighbor."[13] But the Turks viewed Saddam through a different lens as well. The $1 billion in bilateral trade between the two countries was crucial to Turkey's recession-plagued economy.[14] The Baathist regime had been a bulwark against Kurdish empowerment. As State's Marc Grossman would say, "The Turks worked with Saddam a lot to keep the Kurds in between a hammer and an anvil."[15] Saddam was the devil they knew.

Meanwhile, only 30 percent of the Turkish public identified themselves as pro-American, according to a Pew Research poll conducted in November 2002. Fully 58 percent of Turks opposed America's war on terrorism. Only 13 percent supported letting U.S. troops use Turkish bases for an invasion of Iraq.[16]

Nonetheless, Wolfowitz departed Ankara believing that they had the makings of a deal. But, just as the Bush administration was advising that America did not require Turkey's assistance while very much desiring it, the Turks were also playing a double game: trying to convince Bush to "abandon the idea" of war, as Ecevit said in October, while seeking to maximize Turkey's benefit if war proved unavoidable.[17] By the time Wolfowitz returned to Ankara at the beginning of December, Ecevit's party had lost power, Abdullah Gul was the new prime minister, the newly reigning Justice and Development Party (AKP) had distanced itself from strict Islamic governance, and the political climate suddenly seemed to favor the Americans.

Wolfowitz and Grossman met with Gul on December 3. The deputy secretary made his offer. Turkey would receive $2 billion annually for the next two years, plus another $1 billion in oil donations and $500 million in local defense procurements. In return, the United States wanted access to several Turkish air bases and seaports and permission to deploy upwards of eighty thousand U.S. and British troops in southeastern Turkey. Wolfowitz said that he wanted an answer by December 6.

"By the end of the week?" Gul exclaimed. The government was brand-new and had barely been briefed on Bush's war plans. "We have followed this issue, but of course, it's different when you are in government," the new prime minister said. "To give a political decision, we need some time, frankly speaking."

Then Wolfowitz's Turkish counterpart, Undersecretary of Foreign Affairs Ugur Ziyal, spoke up. The United States' offer was too low for what they were demanding in return, he said. Furthermore, on December 12 the European Union would vote on whether to establish an accession date for Turkey to enter the EU. Ziyal, clearly interested in leveraging the United States' influence, told Wolfowitz that any decision would have to wait until after the EU vote.

Turkey's admission into the EU, Wolfowitz replied, would amount to "an incredible strategic opportunity for the EU and I hope it doesn't blow it." The deputy secretary then defended the Bush administration's offer to Turkey. "The numbers may not be big to you," he said, "but they are big to our government. They represent a major presidential commitment."

Wolfowitz continued his hard sell later that day. To prove their resolve to Saddam, he told a roundtable of new government officials, the United States needed to begin surveying sites and proposed sending six thousand engineers and logisticians to Turkey immediately. Ideally, U.S. and British troops would begin arriving in a month. When asked about the composition of the coalition, the deputy secretary correctly replied that most of the other twenty-four members and aspiring members of NATO were with the United States—though he chose not to add that only three of them were offering military support. Daring to dream, Wolfowitz also predicted that the French and Russians would come on board.[18]

As he had in July, Wolfowitz expressed confidence after the December negotiations, telling reporters, "Turkish support is assured."[19] Hardly for the first time, however, the Bush administration had failed to appreciate that not everyone saw the post-9/11 world as the president did. The Turks did not share Bush's urgency about Saddam. Wolfowitz's insistence on a quick decision, combined with a perceived lowball offer, struck them as insulting. So did subsequent intimations in the press that the negotiations had become a rug-merchant-like "bazaar," with Turkey focused only on cashing in, rather than on avoiding war, with its potentially devastating human and economic consequences. The rose-colored lenses through which Wolfowitz viewed "moderate Islamic" nations somehow blinded him to how an act of American aggression in the Middle East would be received in the region.

On February 27, while testifying before the House Budget Committee about Shinseki and the costs of war, Wolfowitz measured his words carefully, fully aware that imprudence could upend months of effort. "It is a fact that Turkey has great reason to be concerned," he said, "that if there is a conflict in Iraq, they are going to sustain some significant short-term economic costs and burdens." But, he maintained, "the long-term benefits to

Turkey's economy are enormous. And if Turkey helps us, they are not only helping us, they are helping themselves."[20]

Two days later, on March 1, the Turkish parliament voted on a bill to authorize the deployment of 62,000 U.S. troops in Turkey. For all of Wolfowitz's stated fidelity to democracy, he had based much of his confidence on the influence of Turkish military leaders, who had seemed highly receptive to a partnership throughout all the talks.

In the end, however, it was the Turkish public and its 95 percent opposition to war that spoke the loudest. More than fifty thousand anti-war demonstrators massed outside parliament as the roll call began. The measure failed by four votes.[21]

THE NORTHERN OPTION HAD DISINTEGRATED. CENTCOM'S WAR PLANS WERE now scrambled. Thirty 4th Infantry Division ships would hover for more than two months in the Mediterranean before sailing through the Suez Canal, across the Red Sea, and finally to the Persian Gulf.[22]

But by March, Wolfowitz's concerns had shifted away from where they had been the previous summer, when he'd told Bill Keller of the *Times*, "I think the getting in is the dangerous part."[23] The fears he had expressed to Keller—of CW attacks on the troops, of protracted urban warfare—had hardly been allayed by Hans Blix's inspection activities, which Wolfowitz continued to ridicule as "a cruel joke,"[24] or by the meagerness of the "coalition of the willing." And his confidence in Iraq's desire to become "the first Arab democracy" remained unflagging.

He was not a fool, however. President Bush had yet to endorse a governing concept for Iraq. General Jay Garner had left for Kuwait to run a reconstruction project that was woefully understaffed and clueless about what resources would assist them in Baghdad. The Free Iraqi Forces had successfully recruited less than 1 percent of what he had hoped for. And perhaps Eric Shinseki's estimate of "several hundred thousand soldiers" was, as Wolfowitz insisted, "wildly off the mark." But that was only because Rumsfeld had imposed his will on the war plans, with the result being an invasion force that was well short of overwhelming.

The deputy secretary was heading down the elevator to the Pentagon parking lot one evening in March. Within a week's time, the president would be giving the order. His military aide, Colonel Steve Ganyard, accompanied him, carrying the usual armload of classified documents for his boss to read that evening.

"Are you nervous about the fight?" Ganyard asked.

Wolfowitz paused for several seconds. "No," he finally replied. "I'm worried about what comes after."[25]

=≡=

CHAPTER TWENTY

A MAN IN THE WORLD

T he decision was George W. Bush's. By January 2003, he had decided. He knew where his war council stood. Dick Cheney believed that, after a long string of inaction—following the USS *Cole* bombing off the coast of Yemen in 2000, the African embassy attacks in 1998, the Khobar Towers explosion in Saudi Arabia in 1996, and, for that matter, Saddam's massacre of the Shiites in 1991—the United States had sent a message of timidity to the Middle East. After 9/11, in the vice president's view, America could not afford another failure of nerve.[1]

Condoleezza Rice, Bush's national security adviser, did not agree with Cheney on much. But by January she, too, believed that America's credibility was on the line. Saddam was toying with Hans Blix's inspectors and, by extension, with international law. It was time, Rice believed, for the games to end with military action.[2]

Donald Rumsfeld—well, it was not like the secretary of defense to speak definitively. Nor, when it came to the subject of removing Saddam by force, had Bush ever asked him to.[3] But, in Rumsfeld's riddling manner, he had observed that, absent unambiguous capitulation on Saddam's part, there were risks in *not* going forward with military action. Conversely, Rumsfeld had not offered any thoughts to Bush on what the risks of war might be.[4] (He had in fact ticked off twenty negative eventualities in his October 15, 2002, "parade of horribles" snowflake. But, for reasons of his own, Rumsfeld elected to disseminate this list only to his staff. "He was writing for history," one senior White House official would wryly reflect.)[5]

CIA director George Tenet had told Bush repeatedly, in person and in writing, that Iraq had WMD, was actively seeking nuclear capability, had sought to obtain maps of U.S. cities, and had associated frequently with Al Qaeda throughout the years. In the meantime, Tenet had not volunteered to the president any concerns about going to war. His volubility on the deadliness of Saddam's arsenal counted for Bush as an endorsement of military action.[6]

Only Secretary of State Colin Powell had hinted at reservations. But when Bush had expressly asked him, "Are you with me?" on January 13, the reluctant warrior said that he was.

What Bush did not know was that Tenet, Powell, several of the generals, and even Rice had long suspected that war was a fait accompli. They had suspected this even when the self-proclaimed "decider" repeatedly insisted, both publicly and privately, that he had *not* decided. Though the decision was finally his and only his to make, it will never be known what George W. Bush's course of action would have been if, during the spring, summer, and fall months of 2002, even one member of his administration had tested his professed receptiveness to an argument against war.

In truth, Bush had stacked his own deck. Prizing loyalty above all else, he had surrounded himself with subordinates who believed that their job was to support the president's value judgments rather than to question them. To walk into the valley of the shadow of Bush's peevishness and tell him something he did not want to hear was not so brutal an experience, in the end. The president appreciated candor, did not shy away from admitting error, and almost never held grudges (except against members of the media).

But to the extent that his White House staff challenged Bush, those qualms invariably related to messaging and process. Almost never did they question what his father once referred to clumsily as "the vision thing." The younger Bush had espoused a single vision since his days as governor: every individual deserved freedom, and in return for that freedom, every individual was obligated to take personal responsibility for his or her actions. As commander in chief after 9/11, he regarded it as his sacred duty to protect free Americans from evil. But his "vision thing" had dilated over time: the entire world, he now believed, yearned to be free from evil's tyranny.

Details mattered, but only up to a point. They could also distort the vision—specks of nuance and equivocation conspiring to blot out all clarity. They provided an excellent excuse for doing nothing. At best, details were tactical, thus falling beneath Bush's job description, or so he believed, as did many presidents before him and since. All presidents learn on the job, and Bush would be well into his—suddenly faced with an unholy trinity of endless war and natural disaster and a collapsing economy—before he came to understand that the devil was not in the details but rather in inattention to them.

"This guy tried to kill my father," he had said after an Iraq intelligence briefing in early 2003—apropos of nothing, leading the CIA briefer to think, *Wow. This is personal.*[7] And it was, but not in a dispositive manner. His animus toward the dictator had never once overtaken him. Even now, Bush maintained that his hand was forced. The choice was not his, but rather Saddam's: *Disarm or be disarmed.* "He's the person who gets to decide war and peace," Bush told a White House press pool on February 7, two days after Powell's UN speech.[8]

Instead, the dictator sat back in his palace while Hans Blix's eighty-four inspectors stumbled through a country the size of California. Bush had come to view Blix as weak and no match for Saddam's trickery.[9] On March 6, the day before Blix reported to the UN that Iraq had been cooperating with UNMOVIC in earnest and that there appeared to be no evidence of a nuclear program, a White House press release categorically stated, "The inspections are not working."[10]

And how did the president know this? "They could have shown up at a parking lot and he could have brought his weapons and destroyed them," Bush pointed out at a news conference on March 6. "That's not what he chose to do."[11]

Bush saw his own choice as a bleak one. With Saddam's refusal to disarm, the president could scarcely envision withdrawing the troops from Kuwait and in effect confirming to the world that UN resolutions meant absolutely nothing and that gathering dangers would in fact go unheeded.[12] This had been the way of the world before 9/11—back when, as Bush audaciously told a Republican audience on February 9, "it was very difficult to link a terrorist network and Saddam Hussein to the American soil."[13] In the president's mind, this link was now inarguable.

Still, he prayed for a way out of war. In February, a single alternative had presented itself. The chief of Egypt's intelligence office, Omar Suleiman, had received word from an Iraqi intermediary that Saddam could be financially induced to leave the country. Egypt's president, Hosni Mubarak, passed this information on to Bush. Italian prime minister Silvio Berlusconi conveyed a similar message, which he had received from Libya's autocrat Muammar Qaddafi: Saddam was open to an exit strategy.

The price was steep: more than $1 billion. Saddam also wanted more than a hundred friends and family members taken with him to another destination in the Middle East. "Well, that would be an interesting appropriation request," Rice commented when she heard about the proposal.

The thought of Saddam Hussein—who knew only one country, and whose entire life had been devoted to ruling that country—fleeing to a foreign destination completely stripped of his power seemed like a ludicrous fantasy. But for the sake of avoiding war, Bush was receptive to it.

By March, however, the scenario had dissipated. To the Bush White House, it was easy to understand why. After all, the French, the Germans, and the Russians had made evident their intentions to oppose the war. Without their support, Saddam had likely calculated, America would do what it had always done: nothing.[14]

"GIVE MY REGARDS TO YOUR FATHER," JACQUES CHIRAC WOULD FREQUENTLY say at the end of his conversations with Bush.[15] Perhaps the French president meant this fondly. But Chirac also brought up the elder Bush in the middle of their dialogues—usually as a means of drawing a not-so-subtle comparison with the less genteel, more visceral son. Such references also served to underscore Chirac's seniority and, by extension, diminish Bush.[16]

"Jacques Chirac and I didn't agree on much," Bush would later write, with terse understatement.[17] The disagreements had begun two months into the latter's administration, when the Frenchman chided the United States in a speech not only for withdrawing from the Kyoto Protocol on climate change but also for continuing to allow the death penalty.[18] Face to face, the professorial Chirac seemed to enjoy bringing up subjects about which Bush knew little, such as the political dynamics in Lebanon. Meanwhile, Bush's body language—slumping in his chair, legs splayed out, eyelids drooping—signaled how unimpressed he was with the Frenchman's windy discourses.[19]

But Iraq had driven an even deeper wedge between the two leaders. Chirac and his minister of foreign affairs, Dominique de Villepin, were actively lobbying other UN Security Council members to join France in opposition to war. Bush was convinced that Chirac's position was driven by economic interests. "We are both moral men," he had told Bush two days after Powell's UN speech. "But in this case, we see morality differently." Bush wondered how someone could invoke morality and in the same breath argue that Saddam should be left in power.[20]

Privately, Chirac predicted that the dictator would not remain in power much longer anyway.[21] He believed that Saddam had no WMD and that Blix would soon confirm this.[22]

The French president was also convinced that Bush would come to regret declaring war on a country in the Middle East. "Don't invade—this will end very badly," Chirac's ambassador to the United States, Jean-David Levitte, warned NSC official Daniel Fried.[23] But it was also true that France had a compelling interest in the primacy of the UN, that Chirac sought relevance on the global stage, and that an overwhelming majority of the French public opposed U.S. intervention in Iraq.[24]

At the same time, being at odds with France was hardly tarnishing Bush's domestic standing—particularly among Republicans, whose displeasure with Chirac reached its apogee in early March when two GOP congressmen succeeded in renaming French toast and French fries "freedom toast" and "freedom fries" in the House cafeterias.[25] Germany was a somewhat different matter. It was Bush who had embarrassed Gerhard Schröder in March 2001 when, on the day of the German chancellor's visit to the White House, the president pulled out of the Kyoto accord. Schröder remained unflappable, and Bush quickly grew fond of him. But Bush felt betrayed after the chancellor, who in January 2002 had pledged to support overthrowing Saddam, campaigned for reelection as a staunch opponent of war. When Schröder's minister of justice compared the Bush White House's war propaganda to that of Hitler, the president was livid, and Rice declared the two countries' relationship to be "poisoned."[26]

On February 11, Chirac, Schröder, and Vladimir Putin, of Russia, announced their alliance in opposition to war.[27] Rice would react with a glib bit of advice for Bush: "Punish France, forgive Russia, and ignore Germany."[28] The president also felt inclined to show Putin greater leniency. The sanctions against Saddam's regime had blocked sales of Russian farm equipment that the UN had deemed to be of dual-use capability. Though it had startled Bush when the Russian leader told him on the phone that he feared that an invasion would cause oil prices to plummet, at least Putin had been up front about his motivations.[29]

In fact, the three European leaders shared more than economic ties to Baghdad. All of them had expressed deep sympathy after 9/11 but were at pains to grasp the national trauma that lingered in the United States. In turn, Bush did not seem to understand the perspective of three great nations watching helplessly as the lone remaining superpower sought to remake the Middle East, unchecked and oblivious to global outcry. Iraq, in the meantime, was seen as useful by the Europeans precisely because it was one Arab country that the United States did not control. And though Putin saw mainly downside to war, he was also intrigued by the possibility of the United States squandering its status and its resources in a protracted conflict, much as the former Soviet Union had done in Afghanistan.[30]

Bush's one unshakable European ally remained Tony Blair. It was because of the British prime minister that the president reluctantly agreed to pursue a second UN resolution citing Iraq's continued refusal to hand over its weapons, thereby justifying military force. As both a legal and political matter, Blair maintained that he could not receive permission from Parliament to send troops into battle without the additional nod from the UN Security Council. Bush continued to maintain that the first UN resolution, 1441, had given him all the authority he needed.[31]

But he could see his British counterpart braving headwinds that Bush himself did not have to face. Blair was interacting with Chirac, Schröder, and Putin more often than he was. British opposition to war was heavy; fully 81 percent regarded a second UN resolution as an "essential" prerequisite for joining the United States in war.[32] For Blair's sake, Bush gamely threw himself into the Security Council vote-lobbying effort.

One member Bush did not have to worry about was Spain. Its prime minister, José María Aznar, was, at fifty, close to Bush's age and more similar in his conservative outlook than other European leaders. Despite the fact that 91 percent of the Spanish public opposed the war, with violent protests soon to erupt in the nation's cities, Aznar displayed unflinching support for overthrowing Saddam.[33] But even Aznar advised Bush on February 22, while visiting the president's ranch in Crawford, "It is very important to have a resolution."

Bush replied that he understood. He and Blair would in fact be offering a new resolution in two days. To the president, the entire matter was pro forma. Its wording was immaterial to him. Aznar should feel free to tinker with the language. Bush just wanted it done—it and the whole inspections process. "This is like water torture," he said. "We must put an end to it."

"I agree," said the prime minister, "but it would be good to have the maximum possible number of people. Have a little patience."

"My patience is exhausted," said Bush. "I don't intend to wait longer than the middle of March."

Reiterating the sentiment he had expressed to King Abdullah of Jordan in the Oval Office the previous August, Bush said to his guest, "When history judges us years from now, I do not want people to ask themselves why Bush or Aznar or Blair did not face up to their responsibilities. In the end, what people long for is freedom."

After a time, Aznar said to the president, "The only thing that worries me about you is your optimism."

"I'm optimistic," Bush replied, "because I believe that I'm in the right. I'm at peace with myself."[34]

Like Aznar, Bush faced demonstrations wherever he went. He was unmoved by them. There had been protests in Austin when then-Governor Bush refused to stay the execution of murderer turned Christian Karla Faye Tucker. Both then and now, he sought wisdom and strength through prayer and proudly ignored polls. On the walls of the Oval Office, great leaders haloed him. He was not alone.

BUSH NEEDED NINE VOTES FROM THE UN SECURITY COUNCIL'S FOURTEEN other members—a supermajority—to get a resolution passed for Blair and Aznar's sake. As it now appeared, France, Germany, Russia, China, and Syria would vote against it. That meant the United States, Spain, and the UK needed votes from every one of the seven remaining countries on the Security Council: Pakistan, Bulgaria, Mexico, Chile, Angola, Cameroon, and Guinea. Among them, only Bulgaria was a sure "yes."

The day before Bush met with Aznar in Texas, Assistant Secretary of State for African Affairs Walter Kansteiner and his British counterpart, Valerie Amos, landed in Angola. They found President Jose Eduardo dos Santos in a transactional frame of mind. The United States had been providing military training to the country's ranger battalion. Dos Santos requested that this training be extended. Kansteiner quickly determined that this would not be a problem.

Next, the two diplomats contacted Cameroon's president, Paul Biya, who expressed his regrets that he could not host them the next day, as he would be in Paris for the Franco-African summit. Kansteiner and Amos flew to Paris and met Biya in his hotel suite. The Cameroonian leader let it slip that he had never been in the Oval Office before. Less than a month later, Paul Biya's wish would come true.[35]

Kansteiner then traveled alone to Guinea. He met President Lansana

Conte in his palace. The president alternated between smoking cigarettes and breathing heavily into an oxygen mask. Guinea relied on U.S. military assistance, which Conte wanted continued. Even so, he remained noncommittal. On the way to the airport, Kansteiner asked Guinea's foreign minister, François Fall, where he thought Conte stood.

"The president will travel to his village for the weekend," Fall said. "His shaman will throw the bones. Then we will know."

Kansteiner called Powell and Armitage with the update. "We need all three African members," said Powell, who then alluded to France's foreign minister, who was also making the rounds in Africa. "De Villepin's right on your heels."

A few days later, Fall called the assistant secretary. "Walter, I'm sorry," Guinea's foreign minister said. "The shaman threw the bones, and the bones read that President Conte is closer to his end than to his beginning. The shaman says that you should always vote for peace as you come to the end of your time. So the president is going to vote against you, and for peace."

"Oh, François, this is really not good," Kansteiner groaned. Then a thought occurred to him: "Is this always the same shaman he uses?"

"Oh, no," replied Fall. "He uses multiple shamans."

At Kansteiner's urging, Fall persuaded Conte to receive a second opinion. A second shaman threw a second set of bones.

"We're with you," the Guinea foreign minister informed him. Walter Kansteiner had gone three for three in Africa.[36]

But it would not be enough.

BUSH VIEWED AZNAR, BLAIR, AND POLISH PRESIDENT ALEKSANDER KWAS-niewski as the core of a twenty-first-century European coalition that reflexively aligned itself with America's interests.[37] He had anticipated a similarly reliable alliance with Latin America's leaders, beginning with Texas's former neighbor to the south, Vicente Fox of Mexico.

Much had happened since Bush and his cowboy boots had visited Fox's hacienda during the fourth week of his presidency. Anti-war sentiment among Mexicans now ran as high as 83 percent, and Fox's party faced challenging midterm elections in May.[38] When Bush called him in early March to lobby for his vote on the second resolution, Fox pretended not to understand what resolution the president was talking about.

"If I can give you some advice," said Bush, "you should not be seen teaming up with the French."

Fox responded that he would mull it over and get right back to him. Instead, he checked into a hospital for back surgery.[39]

Ricardo Lagos, the president of Chile, was another equivocator on the Security Council. Blair had asked Bush to work over Lagos, but lightly. "Don't worry—I'll be more subtle than you fear," Bush teased his British friend. "I'm not going to say to Lagos, 'Hey, you mutha, I'm gonna crush you like a Chilean grape!'"[40]

But when Bush called Lagos on March 11, just after his call to Fox, he was not much more subtle than he had been with Mexico's president. "Ricardo, what's your vote?" he said.

Lagos believed that the inspectors were making progress. He suggested that Saddam be given a few more weeks.

More time would make absolutely no difference, Bush said. Saddam had been given years to comply. Things could not be dragged out any longer.

Chile's president informed Bush that his vote would be "no."

"I just don't understand these guys," Bush told Blair later.[41]

What Bush did understand was that the UN resolution was sure to fail, which in turn imperiled Blair's standing back home. He told the prime minister that he would rather lose him as a war ally if it ensured that Blair would keep his office. The offer was sincere, and Bush was sincerely unsurprised when Blair refused it.[42] The prime minister had *cojones*, regardless of his allegiance to process, a discipline that Bush had come to admire anyway. Where Cheney and Rumsfeld would have prodded him to go it alone, Tony Blair had kept Bush tethered to the outside world.

But the connection was tenuous and became even more so seemingly every time Bush opened his mouth. Whether lecturing the UN about its creeping irrelevancy or hectoring individual Security Council members to pony up with their votes, the president's imperfections on the world stage only made Blair's job harder.[43] The moral case was not catching on. Nelson Mandela, the president of South Africa, to whom Bush had awarded the Presidential Medal of Freedom in June 2002 for his decades of fighting apartheid, and who had been effusive in his support for Operation Enduring Freedom, condemned his rush to war: "All that [Bush] wants is Iraqi oil."[44]

The estimated fifty thousand protesters who gathered outside the White House on March 16 provided a message of their own.[45] But Bush was not there to hear it. He was on Air Force One to meet Blair and Aznar—not in the UK or in Spain, where his presence would have drawn a crush of demonstrators, but instead in the tranquil Portuguese islands known as the Azores.

The Azores summit was a show for Blair's benefit, a supposed last-ditch effort among the three pro-invasion allies to weigh their diplomatic options.[46] No such options existed, other than the "Chinese water torture" of letting the inspections continue. And though Bush had vowed on March 6 that he would demand a vote from the Security Council even in defeat—"It's time for people to show their cards, to let the world know where they stand when it comes to Saddam"—cooler heads had since prevailed.[47] In two days, Blair would receive a vote from the House of Commons on whether to authorize war. If the authorization failed, Blair intended to resign. As Alastair Campbell warned his U.S. counterpart, Dan Bartlett, a few untoward words by the president could push a few votes in the wrong direction.[48]

At a press conference following the pro forma meeting, Bush declared that the diplomatic road had come to an end, leaving "a moment of truth for the world." Unless by some miracle France dropped its veto threat and the Security Council sided with him the following day, the president would instruct UN Ambassador John Negroponte that same day to take down the resolution. That would leave two scenarios. "Saddam Hussein can leave the country, if he's interested in peace," Bush said. Otherwise, there would be war.[49]

Just after the discussions among the leaders had concluded, Bartlett and NSC aide Daniel Fried stood outside and gazed out somberly at the verdant archipelago spilling out into the Atlantic. Murmured Bush's communications director, "Pretty nice place. If the war doesn't go well, we'll all be seeking asylum here."[50]

"WE'RE PLANNING FOR THE WORST," THE PRESIDENT HAD SAID IN THE OVAL Office to his three Iraqi American visitors on January 10. And indeed, as March proceeded and the possibilities of any diplomatic outcome slipped away, Bush at last turned his attention to the minutiae of wartime. On the morning of March 10, he and his National Security Council discussed the capturing and prosecution of Iraqi war criminals; the possibility of establishing a "truth and reconciliation commission"; the need to dismantle and replace the regime's intelligence network; and the desirability of retaining an Iraqi police force. (The importance of the latter was underscored to Bush in person by the Kurdish leader Barham Salih, who told him in the Oval Office, "If you have a domestic dispute between an Iraqi husband and wife, you're not intending to settle it with a soldier from Arkansas, are you?")[51]

On March 11, he participated in an NSC meeting in which he and the principals agreed that an Iraqi Interim Government composed of both resident Iraqis and expatriates would team with Jay Garner's Office of Reconstruction and Humanitarian Assistance to take the first steps in rebuilding post-Saddam Iraq and establishing a new government. At the same meeting, Bush and his war council decided to request the UN's help in post-conflict issues. He also agreed that U.S. dollars would be used in Iraq and stashes of Saddam dinars be confiscated until a new Iraqi currency could be established.[52]

On March 12, Bush's NSC discussed the need to reshape the Iraqi military. The president accepted the recommendation by Garner (who was not there but who composed the original briefing slides) and Feith (who had Luti rewrite them and who subsequently gave the briefing at this meeting) to retain and reform the existing army rather than assemble a new one from scratch.[53]

Mindful that the Arab world was already speaking edgily about Western crusaders invading a Muslim population, by March the president was taking every opportunity to guarantee that the Iraqi people would immediately encounter food and medical care—that their days of suffering were soon to end. As he said in the Azores, "Iraq's liberation would be the beginning, not the end, of our commitment to its people."[54] The humanitarian effort, like the protection of Iraq's oil fields, received the lion's share of post-conflict planning attention—a well-intended fixation on scenarios that never came to pass.[55]

By early March, the president's morning Presidential Daily Briefing was being followed by a separate briefing conducted by Iraq Operations Group chief Luis Rueda, whose information—some of it retrieved just two hours earlier—represented the most current on Iraq that the U.S. intelligence community had to offer. They discussed the Iraqi military's positioning and the covert activities of the sixty or so Baghdad-based informants known within the agency as ROCKSTARS. During one briefing where Rice, Card, and Tenet were also present, Bush asked Rueda, "So what do you think about what we should do with the Baathists?"

"Well, it's kind of like the Communist Party," the IOG chief replied. "In Iraq, if you want to be a schoolteacher or a cop, you've got to join the Baath Party. It doesn't mean they're Saddam die-hards."

Then he added, "Now, there are probably two to five thousand hardcore Baathists we'll have to round up and kill . . ."

"Uh, the president doesn't need to be hearing about this," Rice interrupted. The subject was dropped.[56]

Even as he was steeling himself in anticipation of the worst, Bush sought out comforting reminders that the cause was just and its aftermath auspicious. On the afternoon of February 27, the Nobel Peace Prize recipient and author Elie Wiesel visited Rice in the White House. Hearing that the legendary Holocaust survivor was in the building, Bush dropped by Rice's office fifteen minutes into their conversation. Wiesel argued that had America and European nations taken action against Hitler in 1938, World War II could have been averted. "In the name of morality, how can we not intervene?" he said. "Iraq is a terrorist state."

"That's very wise of you," Bush said. Referring to Saddam, he added, "A killer hears the protests of respectable people and thinks they're for him."

Bush mentioned that he had read the historian Michael Beschloss's best-selling book *The Conquerors: Roosevelt, Truman and the Destruction of Hitler's Germany, 1941–1945*. In it, Wiesel was quoted as saying that the Auschwitz concentration camp should have been bombed by the Allies, even though Wiesel himself was inside it. Then the president said, "If we don't disarm Saddam, he will put a WMD on Israel. And they'll do what they have to do in Israel. We have to avoid that."

"I'm against neutrality," said Wiesel, "because it doesn't help the victim. It only helps the aggressor."[57]

As Bush would later write, "The force of his conviction affected me deeply. Here was a man who had devoted his life to peace urging me to intervene in Iraq."[58]

On March 14, the fifteenth anniversary of the massacre at Halabja, three Iraqi Americans who survived the chemical attack were brought into the Oval Office. As they discussed the dictator's deadly use of WMD, one of the survivors, a geologist named Katrin Michael, intoned, "Saddam's blood is a chemical weapon to Iraq."[59]

As Bush took in the stories of such atrocities, his determination to liberate a tormented people was redoubled. He had thoroughly internalized the exhortations of the Iraqis who had visited him on January 10 and March 14. "As our troops advance, we'll be behind the lines, improving everything," Bush pledged one day to a staffer in the Oval Office. "And they're going to embrace freedom. And they'll also demand that their lives be made better. And we're ready. We're not just going to end the terror. We're going to reconstruct Iraq."

Said the staffer years later, "He really believed this."[60]

ON THE EARLY AFTERNOON OF MARCH 17, AFTER INSTRUCTING AMBASSADOR Negroponte to take down the UN resolution, the White House announced that the president would be addressing the nation that evening. At eight o'clock Eastern time, George W. Bush stepped behind a podium set up in the broad corridor on the first floor of the White House residence known as the Cross Hall. The long walkway extended back to a flag of the Stars and Stripes, symbolizing the journey he had taken, this man in America, to solicit the world's alliance, if not its permission, in his quest to end a tyrant's regime. Now back home, his words were for America. "My fellow citizens," he began quietly, as if in grief, "events in Iraq have now reached the final days of decision."

Bush referred to Hans Blix's inspection efforts as a failure. The intelligence, he said, "leaves no doubt that the Iraq regime continues to possess and conceal some of the most lethal weapons ever devised." Asserting that Iraq "has aided, trained and harbored terrorists, including operatives of al Qaeda," Bush once again evoked the specter of Saddam confederating with terrorists to kill "hundreds of thousands of innocent people in our country." Taking a shot at France, he said that certain "governments share our assessment of the danger, but not our resolve to meet it."

America would meet it. "Saddam and his son," he said, "must leave Iraq within 48 hours. Their refusal to do so will result in military conflict, commenced at a time of our choosing."

Yet again, Bush addressed the Iraqis to assure them of his sincere intentions. "We will tear down the apparatus of terror," he vowed, "and we will help you to build a new Iraq that is prosperous and free." He warned the Iraqi military to lay down their arms, to leave the oil fields intact. He also assured terrorists that an attempt to strike America would be met with "fearful consequences." Finally, he reminded America that this fateful next step was a necessary one against a highly weaponized Iraq: "With these capabilities, Saddam Hussein and his terrorist allies could choose the moment of deadly conflict when they are strongest. We choose to meet that threat now, where it arises, before it can suddenly appear in our skies and cities."[61]

The next day, Tuesday, March 18, Bush followed the vote in British

Parliament as if it were his own election. Though three senior members of the Blair administration resigned in protest over going to war, the prime minister prevailed in the House of Commons by a comfortable margin. "Landslide," Bush said in his congratulatory phone call to Blair. "You showed *cojones*. You never blinked. A leader who leads will win, and you are a real leader." Bush predicted to Blair that his countrymen would ultimately view him as a hero for toppling Saddam.[62]

That morning in Baghdad, a convoy of vehicles shuttled UNMOVIC's inspectors to Saddam Hussein International Airport. In the airport lounge, a member of the Republican Guard served the inspectors tea. Then a chartered L-100 flew Hans Blix's team to UNMOVIC's logistics base on Cyprus.[63]

Later that day, Bush and his NSC team held a videoconference with General Tommy Franks and several other generals. With no word indicating Saddam's departure from Iraq and with war a near certainty, the president now had the safety of his troops on his mind. Were they adequately prepared for chemical warfare? he wanted to know. Several of the generals on the videoconference had children who would be sent into combat. It felt oddly reassuring to these military men that, even on the eve of war, the commander in chief palpably wished to avoid bloodshed.[64]

Meanwhile, a British intelligence official had conveyed to CIA deputy director John McLaughlin a startling development. According to an informant who worked in the Republican Guard, Saddam's military was moving the regime's WMD across the border into Syria. Satellite imagery had captured the movement of the trucks.

McLaughlin and Tenet presented the photographs to Bush. The president was clearly alarmed. McLaughlin called his British friend again. "Are you sure?" the deputy director asked. "Because the president is paying attention to this."

Yes, the British intelligence official said. The sourcing was solid.

The source was later determined to be a fabricator. The trucks contained money and furniture belonging to senior Baath Party members now fleeing the country.[65]

———

EARLY ON THE MORNING OF WEDNESDAY, MARCH 19, LUIS RUEDA SPOKE ON
the phone with the operations officer who was supervising most of the Iraqi
ROCKSTARS from his base in northern Iraq. One of the officer's informants was a member of the Republican Guard who functioned as a sort of
advance man for Saddam, traveling to the dictator's next destination and
setting up communication lines. It had thus come to this guard's attention
that Saddam would be arriving very late that evening at Dora Farms, a
residence on the Tigris River frequently used by Saddam's wife. A second
ROCKSTAR happened to be in charge of security at Dora Farms. He confirmed that there would be a family gathering there that evening. Satellite
imagery detected an unusually large number of vehicles parked beneath the
palm trees.

Rueda and Tenet informed Bush that this was as good as intelligence got.
Saddam was expected to arrive at Dora Farms sometime between one and
four in the morning. The president polled Cheney, Rice, Powell, and Rumsfeld. All of them agreed: an opportunity to decapitate the regime, without
any troop casualties, was well worth the risk of the intelligence proving
faulty.

At 7:12 p.m., Bush gave the order. Two F-117 stealth fighter aircraft took
off from Qatar bearing bunker-buster bombs. Three hours later, the president
addressed the nation for the second time in three days. U.S. forces, Bush
stated, had begun to conduct the "opening stages of what will be a broad and
concerted campaign."

He concluded by promising, "We will bring freedom to others and we
will prevail. May God bless our country and all who defend her."[66]

THE BOMBS FROM THE F-117 HAD KILLED ONE OF THE ROCKSTARS WHO HAD
furnished the tip to the CIA.[67] The intelligence had been inaccurate. Saddam
and his family were not at Dora Farms at the time of the bombing. Saddam

would later tell his American interrogators that he had not been at the farm that day at all.[68]

G-Day nonetheless commenced on March 20, with a convoy of U.S. and British ground forces rolling out of Kuwait toward the oil fields of southern Iraq. Meeting only light resistance, the 3rd Infantry Division continued to push west and then northward, into the heartland of the Shia, whose American liberators had forsaken them back in 1991. By the 22nd, the 3rd Infantry Division had penetrated 150 miles into Iraq. The troops wore protective gear, but no chemical weapons had yet been detonated. The Iraqi regular army was neither aggressing nor surrendering; it seemed to have disintegrated altogether.

On Sunday the 23rd at An Nasiriyah, the guerrilla fighters known as the Fedayeen Saddam ambushed the eighteen-vehicle convoy of the 507th Maintenance Company, killing eleven of the thirty-three U.S. soldiers. Another seven were captured, including one who would die in an Iraqi hospital and another who was seriously wounded: nineteen-year-old Private First Class Jessica Lynch, from West Virginia.

On the 24th, the 1st Marine Expeditionary Force descended on An Nasiriyah to clear the city and was promptly swallowed up by a massive sandstorm. Another sandstorm on the 25th thwarted the 3rd Infantry Division's strike on the Republican Guard at Karbala. The division ultimately crossed the Karbala Gap, a great victory but an even greater puzzle, as this had been the last of four red lines at which U.S. forces had expected to encounter a CW attack.

As the U.S. troops now sped unimpeded toward Baghdad, the British 7th Armoured Brigade rolled northward on the old Highway of Death and fought its way into the Shiite stronghold of Basra, Iraq's second-largest city. Two British soldiers were captured by the Fedayeen on the outskirts of the city and later killed, while two others were killed by friendly fire. While under siege, Basra was plunged into darkness, its rickety electrical grid now in tatters.

President Bush stood in the Oval Office reception room one day in early April and watched on television as peace at last returned to Basra. Standing next to him was Secretary of State Colin Powell, Bush's reluctant warrior. They watched in silence as the cameras panned across a city occupied by British tanks and helicopters. Smoke rose from the intelligence service headquarters. The gates of the city prison were thrown open. Looters fleeced the state buildings of their desks and chairs and water tanks. The residents of Basra, newly liberated, stared at the cameras. Bush the liberator stared back at them, his expression intense as he attempted to reconcile what he had imagined in his heart for so many months with what his eyes were now seeing for the first time.

Then he asked, "Why aren't they cheering?"[69]

CHAPTER TWENTY-ONE

===

THE DAY AFTER

On the afternoon of April 4, 2003, as the U.S. 3rd Infantry Division prevailed in a tank battle and secured control of Baghdad International Airport, Bush taped a radio address to the nation that would air the following day. His remarks, sixteen days into war, were somber rather than triumphalist. "With each new village they liberate, our forces are learning more about the atrocities of the regime and the deep fear the dictator has instilled in the Iraqi people," the president said.[1]

It was Bush's subtle way of acknowledging to Americans that the invading U.S. troops were not encountering flowers, sweets, and chants of joy. No longer operative was the idea that a traumatized country could be instantly healed with precision air strikes and a few truckloads of emergency rations.

An hour after the taping, Bush welcomed a dozen Iraqi Americans into the Roosevelt Room of the White House. Yet again, the president asked to hear their stories of oppression and torture. He basked in their gratitude, pledging, "We will take this tyrant out. And then we'll build a modern Iraq that will serve as a model for other countries in the Middle East."

"Mr. President, we're excited to see these changes," said one of the visitors. His name was Jacob Bacall, a real estate developer in the Detroit area whose family had left Iraq in 1975. Bacall was Chaldean, a Catholic from a village near Mosul called Tel Kaif that had been a Christian enclave for centuries. Though that religion had been marginalized in the greater Arab world, many Chaldeans had prospered under Saddam, who perceived his principal adversaries to be Islamic clerics. The dictator's longtime foreign minister, Tariq Aziz, was himself a Christian from Tel Kaif.

Bacall nonetheless regarded Saddam as a butcher whose demise he welcomed. He rejoiced at the prospect of his native country becoming a democratic model for others in the region. That Iraq had momentarily descended into looting sprees was an unsettling spectacle for him, especially given that many of the victims were Chaldean shop owners. But it was impossible for him to imagine that this might continue for long—or, worse still, that Christians might later be targeted for ransoms and massacres, that they might ultimately flee in droves across the border into Syria and then Lebanon, abandoning Tel Kaif for good.

The president has a plan, Bacall assured himself. It was the Detroit developer's dream to bring his children and grandchildren to his birthplace one day, to be a builder of the new Iraq.

And as to when this all might be possible? Bush seemed to be reading Jacob Bacall's mind when, after excusing himself from the gathering, he paused in the doorway of the Roosevelt Room and said a single word to the émigrés: "Soon."[2]

ELEVEN DAYS LATER, ON APRIL 15, AHMAD CHALABI RETURNED TO BAGHDAD for the first time in forty-five years. Accompanying him was an armed militia of six hundred Iraqi expatriates whom the Iraqi National Congress leader had culled from the United States and Europe, plus Shiites in the south, Kurds in the north, and refugees from camps in Iran.

Fittingly, Chalabi's presence in Iraq was both authorized and not. In early April, after taking stock of the 3rd Infantry Division's struggles in the south, General John Abizaid at CENTCOM had heard of reports that Chalabi was training a fighting force at a makeshift camp in Kurdistan. He reached out, thinking that an Iraqi face on the invasion might expedite victory.

Abizaid balked when Chalabi insisted on traveling with them. "This is a military campaign—we don't want politicians," the general said.

But Chalabi held all the cards. He called Paul Wolfowitz on his satellite phone.

On the early morning of Sunday, April 6, two U.S. Air Force C-17s ferried Chalabi and his men south to Tallil Air Base, after which the military abandoned them without food or water and they were forced to encamp in a few abandoned warehouses outside Nasiriyah. A few days later, the INC leader's nephew, Sam Chalabi, drove up from Kuwait in a convoy of rented vehicles. They proceeded northward, taking care to steer clear of Fedayeen and coalition tanks.

The Baghdad Chalabi beheld on April 15 was nothing like what he remembered or could have predicted. It seemed more reminiscent, he would later say, of "an impoverished capital on the African coast."

Just three days earlier, Secretary of Defense Donald Rumsfeld had put a jaunty face on the widespread looting. "Freedom's untidy, and free people are free to make mistakes and commit crimes and do bad things," he memorably quipped, in effect putting the country on notice that America's hand was off the bicycle seat and whatever happened thereafter was up to the free Iraq. But now Chalabi could see for himself what he and the other well-heeled exiles had not known: the UN sanctions had left the country in tatters. The free-for-all pillaging of the capital city augured Darwinian travails for years to come.

Upon his arrival in Baghdad, Chalabi knew exactly where to go. In the once affluent suburban neighborhood of Mansour, the owners of the Hunting Club—a country club founded by the Baathists, with tennis courts and a swimming pool—wanted protection from looters and offered up their facilities to the INC leader and his militia. Within days, Chalabi, at his new outpost, was receiving hordes of suitors from the former regime, pledging fealty and requesting work.

One of them happened to mention that the headquarters of the Iraqi

Intelligence Service was among the many government offices that was both deserted and unguarded. The INC leader dispatched his men. In the basement of the IIS, they scooped up the repository of Saddam's intelligence files and delivered them to Ahmad Chalabi.[3]

Survivor and creature of improvisation that he was, Chalabi was already several steps ahead of the Bush administration's designated man in Iraq, General Jay Garner. For almost a month since the air strike on Dora Farms, Garner and his Office of Reconstruction and Humanitarian Assistance team were stranded in Kuwait. The reason for ORHA's state of limbo was the same reason for why U.S. troops had whizzed past hundreds of abandoned ammunition depots en route to Baghdad: thanks to Rumsfeld's insistence on a lean invasion force, Tommy Franks had no extra troops to spare for security.[4]

With all major cities—Basra, then Baghdad, then Mosul and Kirkuk, and at last Tikrit on April 14—now in the hands of the coalition, Franks was eager to put a bow on Operation Iraqi Freedom and take his victory lap in Washington. From Baghdad, he called Wolfowitz on a secure phone. "Mr. Deputy Secretary," said the CENTCOM commander, "things are going great here. I've got a favor to ask. I'd like to come back home for the White House Correspondents Dinner"—referring to the annual black-tie Beltway self-celebration that would be taking place on April 26. (Franks did in fact jet home for the gala, taking his place with Colin Powell, Hans Blix, and Bush himself. Within days of the Correspondents Dinner, Franks informed Rumsfeld that he intended to retire.)[5]

Eager as Franks was to hand over post-conflict duties to Garner, the ORHA director could not take over without security resources from CENTCOM. Even when they arrived in Baghdad on April 21, six days after Chalabi, Garner's team could not move about freely. When they were at last able to do so, the ORHA team discovered that all the ministry buildings had been stripped bare by looters. The notable exception was the Ministry of Oil, which the Pentagon had singled out as meriting heavy security. It was nonetheless evident to Garner that Iraqi oil would not come close to paying for the rehabilitation of a shattered country. Who *would* foot the bill? He glumly recalled what Rumsfeld had said to him a month before the invasion, when

Garner predicted that a reconstruction effort could run into the billions of dollars.

"My friend," the secretary breezily informed him, "if you think we're going to spend a billion dollars of our money over there, you are sadly mistaken."[6]

Thanks to Rumsfeld's vetoing of several State Department recruits, Garner had arrived in Iraq with only eleven of the twenty-four ministry director positions filled.[7] Woefully understaffed, moving through the city only when a military convoy was available, the ORHA team eventually succeeded in locating many of Baghdad's leading technocrats and slowly reassembling the ministries.

Garner's alliance with Chalabi was a wary one. Both had been leery of the other's motives initially. Garner also did not share Chalabi's belief that a new Iraqi government should be almost completely purged of Baath Party members. When they met for dinner one evening in Baghdad, Garner warned Chalabi, "I'm not going to help you take over. If the people want to elect you, that's another thing."

Acknowledging this position, Chalabi then asked if Garner would assist in helping Chalabi's daughter, Tamara—who was seated next to him—to become the minister of education. Garner was noncommittal.[8] Still, both men shared an overarching goal: the sooner Iraqis were able to select their own leaders, the better.[9]

That had been Bush's goal as well. But the protracted battles with the Fedayeen, the disturbing images of looting on CNN, and the harried reports to Condoleezza Rice from Margaret Tutwiler—James Baker's longtime communications director, now on loan to ORHA in Baghdad—together evoked an atmosphere of chaos that seemed beyond Jay Garner's ability to surmount it. Within a matter of days, the Bush White House began reassessing its long-held belief that Iraq would easily transition into a state of self-governance.[10]

On the evening of April 24, Garner spoke to Rumsfeld by phone and updated him on ORHA's progress. The secretary complimented him on his work. Then he mentioned that the president would soon be announcing Garner's replacement, former ambassador to the Netherlands and Kissinger protégé L. Paul "Jerry" Bremer III.[11]

As startling as this bit of news was to Garner, who had arrived in Baghdad only three days earlier, it would have surprised Bush, too, as the president had yet to meet Jerry Bremer. But, as was so often the case in the Iraq saga, the cake had been baked before the president had an opportunity to order it.

Scooter Libby had first reached out to Bremer in late March, just after Operation Iraqi Freedom had begun and well before Garner was in theater. Though Bremer had no work experience in the Middle East, he had served in a couple of counterterrorism posts in previous administrations and was known for his take-charge personality. Libby inquired if Bremer would be interested in an unspecified job in post-conflict Iraq. After Bremer indicated that he would be, Wolfowitz summoned him to the Pentagon. The deputy secretary asked Bremer if he believed in democracy in the Middle East. Bremer gave the correct reply: "Yes, absolutely. I don't believe there are any people in the world that aren't capable of self-government."[12]

Wolfowitz himself had been interested in the high-profile job of U.S. envoy to Iraq. But his reputation as a disorganized administrator disqualified him from overseeing the rebuilding of a shattered nation. Rumsfeld also would not have liked to see his deputy under so prominent a spotlight. The secretary let it be known that he might be interested in the job as well. Bush did not take this scenario seriously, however.[13] Karl Rove also dangled the position to former Democratic senator Bob Kerrey, who indicated that he might be interested but then never heard back.[14] For, after April 24, the job was Jerry Bremer's to lose.

On that morning, Bremer met with Rumsfeld. The secretary apparently saw something of himself in the alpha-male diplomat. It happened that, in early 2001, Reagan-era secretary of state George Shultz had recommended Bremer to Rumsfeld as a candidate for some future envoy post, much as Shultz had tabbed Rumsfeld for such an assignment in the early eighties.[15] Sounding very much like Rumsfeld, Bremer pointed out that if he were to take this job, not only would Garner have to be sidelined but so would Zalmay Khalilzad, who was currently in Baghdad serving as Bush's political liaison to the Iraqis. Nor did Bremer wish to have a U.S. ambassador in

Baghdad during his stay. There would be one American viceroy in Iraq, and that would be Jerry Bremer.

"I have had a good talk with him," Rumsfeld effused in a memo to Andy Card later that afternoon. "I like him. I think he is the man." Rumsfeld added that he had already run Bremer's name by Tenet and Powell and neither had raised objections. The secretary requested that Card schedule an introductory meeting with the president for the next day, the 25th.[16] Then the secretary called Garner and advised him that Bremer would be his replacement.

Bush met with Bremer at ten the following morning. Three days later, at a rally in Dearborn, Michigan, the president declared, "I have directed Jay Garner and his team to help Iraq achieve specific long-term goals. And they're doing a superb job."[17] Already, however, Bush had decided that Garner's days in Iraq were numbered.

ON MAY 1, PRESIDENT BUSH STOOD ON THE DECK OF THE USS *ABRAHAM Lincoln* and declared to the world, "Major combat operations in Iraq have ended. In the battle of Iraq, the United States and our allies have prevailed. . . . The battle of Iraq is one victory in a war on terror that began on September 11, 2001, and still goes on. . . . The liberation of Iraq is a crucial advance in the campaign against terror. We have removed an ally of Al Qaeda and cut off a source of terrorist funding."[18]

Unforgettably—and thus unfortunately—Bush had arrived aboard the USS *Lincoln* dressed in combat fatigues and helmet, swaggering his way to a podium underneath a banner that proclaimed MISSION ACCOMPLISHED. The slogan accurately reflected the Bush administration's wishful thinking and grandiose sense that history had already been made. When the longtime British Ministry of Defence official Kevin Tebbit came to visit the White House just after the fall of Baghdad, he was surprised to receive an embrace from his old friend Condoleezza Rice.

"We've done it, Kevin!" Rice exclaimed. "It's just like the fall of the Soviet Union!"[19]

A gathering disquiet accompanied the self-congratulation, however. Five days after Bush's "mission accomplished" speech, he publicly announced that Garner would be replaced with Bremer. Three days later, at an NSC meeting on May 9, Bush essentially discarded the concept of an Iraq Interim Authority, instead telling his team that the United States would not be in any hurry to set up an Iraqi-led administration.[20]

Rumsfeld, to whom Bremer answered, also furnished the new Coalition Provisional Authority CEO with a memo entitled "Principles for Iraq—Policy Guidelines," which he also handed out to his peers at a Principals Committee meeting. The memo reflected an astonishing reappraisal of the ground truth in Iraq. In it, the authority of Bremer's CPA was codified: "There will be clarity that the Coalition is in charge, with no conflicting signals to the Iraqi people, Coalition partners or neighbors." The memo concluded by acknowledging that democracy in Iraq would "likely evolve over years"— adding, "Rushing elections could lead to tyranny of the majority."[21] The following day at an NSC meeting, Bush reiterated the thrust of Rumsfeld's memo when he said, "We're going to take the time needed to get this right."[22]

Bremer arrived in Qatar on May 11. Garner met his replacement there. He advised Bremer that a gathering of key Iraqi opposition leaders had been scheduled to meet with the new CPA chief in a week. "I don't think that's going to happen," Bremer briskly replied.[23]

The new U.S. envoy arrived in Baghdad the next day, carrying with him a document that Doug Feith had handed Bremer the day before his departure, saying, "This has been fully cleared in the interagency."[24] CPA Order No. 1, as it came to be known, purged the upper three layers of Baath Party membership from all government jobs. Garner and his deputies protested that this was lunacy. To be a schoolteacher or an engineer, an Iraqi had to join the Baath Party. De-Baathification would wipe out the already hobbled country's technocracy.

"I have my orders, and I'm going to implement them," Bremer replied.[25]

He was not done yet. Quietly, without the knowledge of President Bush or the NSC, Feith had been working with Walter Slocombe, the CPA's incoming senior adviser for security and defense, on what to do about the Iraqi army. Together they had produced a document blandly entitled "Dissolution of Entities." It called for the disbandment of the entire army—in one fell swoop putting 350,000 armed Iraqi men out of work.[26]

The CIA's new chief of station in Baghdad, Charlie Seidel, was stunned to learn of Bremer's plans. Slocombe had informed Bremer that, since the Iraqi army had effectively demobilized, it made sense to simply build a new army from scratch. Seidel knew this was untrue. He and General David McKiernan had regularly been meeting with a dozen or so Iraqi generals. The generals supplied them with hard drives listing all of their troops. The integrity of their units had been maintained.[27]

"We can easily reconstitute their army," Seidel argued to Bush's envoy. "What's more, if you do this, these guys don't have second careers. So what do you think they'll do next? They'll go back to their village, commiserate with other guys who don't have jobs, gather all the weapons from the places we haven't been able to control—I mean, they're going to be disenfranchised! What do you think is going to happen?"[28]

Bremer was unmoved. He informed the NSC in a videoconference on May 22 that he intended to reverse Bush administration policy and disband the army. Powell, Rice, and Frank Miller exchanged looks of stupefaction.

By way of granting permission, President Bush replied, "You're our man on the ground."[29]

Just after the meeting, Miller pleaded with Steve Hadley to have the principals revisit the issue. Hadley refused. By executive authority, postwar matters were exclusively in DOD's hands. Rumsfeld had insisted on autonomy, as he always did. Hadley had gone so far as to shut down both the Executive Steering Group and the Deputies Lunches to afford the Pentagon a wide berth. It made no sense, the deputy national security adviser reasoned, to jerk Bremer's chain barely a week into his tour of service.

Hadley thought of himself as a "process person." For Miller, what was striking was how diminished a role process had played in the president's decision-making. Here was a major reversal of policy being undertaken without the prior knowledge of the national security adviser, the secretary of state, or the CIA director. As with Bush's decision to invade Iraq, and then his decision as to how post-Saddam Iraq would be governed, there had been no "process" of any kind.[30]

Jay Garner departed Baghdad on June 1. As part of the rebooting of their postwar Iraq policy, Bush administration officials extolled Jerry Bremer's blue-ribbon résumé while intimating to reporters that Garner had been out of his depth. The general returned home to Florida, humiliated and depressed.

Ten days later, Garner was summoned to the White House. Bush was alone and staring out the window onto the Rose Garden when Garner and Rumsfeld stepped into the Oval Office. "Mr. President," Garner began cautiously, "you've got the weight of the nation on your shoulders. So let me just shake your hand and let you get back to work."

"No," Bush protested. "You're going to sit down and talk to me."

Garner and Rumsfeld sat across from the president. Cheney and Rice filed in as well and took their seats. "Okay, let me give you a report," the general began.

Bush cut him off. "No, I don't need that," he said. "Just tell me some stories."

For the next forty-five minutes, Garner regaled the president, Rumsfeld, Cheney, and Rice with slices of life in liberated Iraq. He told them about the Shia cleric whose affection for America was so great that he had requested to Garner that Iraq be made the fifty-first state—"and if you do that," vowed the imam, "I'll worship Jesus Christ." Garner mentioned how he had confessed his distrust of a certain Kurdish leader to Jalal Talabani, prompting the latter to pat Garner on the knee and wisely reply, "It is better to have him inside the tent than outside it."

The president nodded and grinned. *It was nice to deliver good news to such a burdened man,* Garner thought. He did not think to tell Bush and the others what he had conveyed to Rumsfeld just a few moments earlier—that in his view, Jerry Bremer had erred dreadfully in disbanding the army, exiling Baath Party members from government jobs, and refusing to empower an Iraqi Interim Government.

The defense secretary had responded to Garner's words with a show of helplessness: "Jay, those are good points, but I think we're too far down the road to do anything about it." To press the points further to Bush might seem disrespectful, Garner figured. In any event, the president himself did not ask for Garner's advice based on his on-the-ground experiences. Neither did Cheney or Rice. In fact, it occurred to Garner later that *no one* in the White House had *ever* solicited his thoughts—not before he was sent off to Iraq, and not after. Only Rumsfeld had asked for his opinions; and when Garner had given them, the defense secretary had replied that it was too late, or simply ignored the advice.

Before leaving the Oval Office, Garner offered a few compliments about his successor Bremer. "You picked a good man," he said.

"Hell, I didn't pick him," Bush replied. "Rummy picked him. Just like he picked you."

Garner tried not to appear startled. The defense secretary had told him that it was Bush, not he, who had chosen Bremer. The general left Washington that day reflecting on the fact that Donald Rumsfeld, the closest thing to a friend that Garner had in the Bush administration, had worked in stealth to replace him.[31]

ON APRIL 12, DR. AMER AL-SAADI, THE BRAINS BEHIND SADDAM HUSSEIN'S weapons program, strolled out of his Baghdad villa with his German wife, Helga, and turned himself in to coalition authorities. A German TV network was there to document his surrender as the first high-value detainee in Iraq. Facing the camera, al-Saadi proclaimed, as he had repeatedly over the years, that Iraq no longer had a WMD stockpile. "I never told anything but the truth, and time will bear me out," he predicted.[32]

Bush administration officials characterized the Iraqi scientist now in custody as a potential gold mine of information. For intelligence analysts, however, al-Saadi's vow was unsettling—all the more so given that, after three weeks of combat, coalition troops had yet to encounter chemical weapons. With the collapse of the regime, inspectors could freely roam Iraq. The truth would be learned. Al-Saadi had to know this. And so what incentive did he have now to boast with such confidence that his claims of no WMD would be proven true?[33]

Shortly after the fall of Baghdad, the intelligence community opened its floodgates and the WMD hunters came pouring in. "We had over a thousand intelligence agents looking," recalled JCS chairman Dick Myers. "It was a White House priority. That was the focus. We weren't as focused or as smart about what was going on inside the country."[34]

Exactly one week after al-Saadi's surrender, a seemingly major discovery took place in northern Iraq. Near a checkpoint at Tel Kaif, a Kurdish militia apprehended a looter who had stolen a military truck with a rather curious gooseneck trailer attached. Inside the trailer was a tall stainless-steel tank and other metal equipment with color-coded valves affixed to the floor. The interior smelled of ammonia. The Kurds transported the trailer to a nearby air base. A team of military investigators studied it and pronounced the trailer capable of being a biological weapons laboratory. A second group judged that the trailer had the more innocuous purpose of producing hydrogen. A third team, composed of scientists, asserted that the mobile lab could produce both hydrogen *and* BW.[35]

Photographs of the trailer and its interior were ferried to Germany and presented by a BND analyst to Curveball. Was this the famed mobile BW lab that he had been talking about since early 2000? Studying the images, the defector carefully replied that he recognized some of its components.[36]

"We found the trailer," CIA executive assistant to the deputy director Steve Slick crowed to Directorate of Operations group chief Margaret Henoch on April 29. Curveball, he added, had been shown the photograph and confirmed it.

The skeptical Henoch replied, "Did you show him another trailer? You know, a control group?"[37]

On May 7, DOD undersecretary for intelligence Steve Cambone announced the discovery, saying that the trailer had been confirmed by "the defector" cited in Powell's UN speech. "The experts have been through it,"

Cambone said of the trailer. He added, incorrectly, "And they have not found another plausible use for it."[38]

Four days later, on May 11, a second suspected BW trailer was discovered, in the parking lot of a research-and-development facility in Mosul. Its interior tested negative for chemical and biological agents. The designer of the trailer insisted that it was for hydrogen generation.[39]

NBC broke the news of the second trailer. David Kay, a former IAEA inspector who was now one of the network's commentators, had gained access to the Mosul site. Speaking into the camera while gesturing at the trailer, Kay said, "Literally, there is nothing else you would do this way on a mobile facility. That is *it*."[40]

(Recalled CIA deputy director John McLaughlin, "David Kay on television saying, *This is the real deal*—what effect do you think *that* had on us?" One effect was that a month to the day after Kay's scoop, Tenet appointed the gung-ho former inspector to lead the U.S. hunt for Iraq's illicit weapons.)[41]

Judy Miller of *The New York Times* called former UNSCOM inspector Scott Ritter as soon as she saw Kay's breathless revelation. "I've seen those before," Ritter said of the trailers. "They produce helium for weather balloons. We inspected a facility in 1992 that had them. We know what they are."

Miller chose not to go with Ritter's assessment.[42] Her story, "Trailer Is a Mobile Lab Capable of Turning Out Bioweapons, a Team Says," ran on the *Times* website that same day. It contained no mention of Ritter's alternative theory, instead devoting all its space to the affirmative case for the trailer as a BW facility.[43]

On May 26, senior BW analyst Beth and Jerry Watson, two of the agency's foremost Curveball believers, churned out a paper on the two trailers. President Bush was delighted with the paper's findings. He wanted it declassified as a white paper and made public immediately. So did Powell, who had been under considerable strain with the failure thus far to uncover weapons that would confirm his claims before the UN three months earlier.

"You need to hold a press conference!" the secretary of state yelled at John McLaughlin, who was startled by Powell's vehemence. McLaughlin argued that the administration should wait until more facts were gathered, to no avail.[44]

Watson and Beth's white paper, "Iraqi Mobile Biological Warfare Agent Production Plants," was published on the CIA's website on May 28. The authors asserted that the trailer discovered by the Kurds was "strikingly similar to descriptions provided by a source," meaning Curveball. Then they proceeded to excuse away the various reasons why it might well *not* be Curveball's mobile BW lab. First, the trailer had been manufactured after Curveball had already defected—which meant that it must be "second- or possibly third-generation." The presence of a cooling unit and the mounting on a heavy transporter rather than on a flatbed trailer "probably reflect design improvements." The explanation that the trailers were used for hydrogen production "would be a plausible cover story," Beth and Watson wrote. Seemingly nothing would convince the two CIA analysts that the discoveries did not validate Curveball's information.[45]

"Well," chuckled a DIA case officer named Dan after reading the white paper, "they're not going to be happy with my report. Because it says the exact opposite." Dan had finished leading six detained Iraqi scientists to the trailers, which had been relocated to Camp Slayer, the military base at Baghdad International Airport. One of them was General al-Saadi, who gazed at the trailers and then scoffed, "Anyone who told you this is bio should be fired."[46]

The day after the CIA white paper was published, Bush was interviewed by a Polish TV station in advance of his trip to that country. When the interviewer commented that no WMD had been found, Bush shot back, "We found the weapons of mass destruction. We found the mobile laboratories."[47]

One of the intelligence agents at the State Department happened to hear the president declare that the United States now possessed two of Saddam's mobile BW labs. He raced over to INR chief Carl Ford. "We've been on a secure fax talking to the technicians looking at the trailer," the analyst said. "They're saying it's not for BW. Tell the secretary not to go too far out on a limb with this."

Ford conveyed this information in a note to Powell. The secretary, in turn, passed the note on to George Tenet. The CIA director promptly summoned the INR chief to Langley.

"How dare you write this note?" Tenet demanded, waving the offending object in the air.

"It's what my people are getting from the people who are actually looking at the trailers," Ford replied. "We thought it appropriate to warn the secretary that it's possibly not what you think it is."

"You don't know everything," Tenet cryptically insisted.

"I don't?" Ford shot back. "Why? Are you holding something back from me?"[48]

Tenet did not elaborate. But during a meeting at Langley headquarters a few days later, an analyst informed Tenet that there was growing evidence of insurgent groups clustering throughout Iraq. "We probably need to be researching this," the analyst advised.

The CIA director glared at the analyst. "My ass is hanging out twenty-six miles on WMD," Tenet said. "I don't care about anything else."[49]

Tenet now had reason to regret his acquiescence to President Bush's desire for a public airing of the "mobile BW labs" intelligence. A veteran biological weapons inspector named Hamish Killip flew into Baghdad from London and was driven directly to the trailers at Camp Slayer. "It took two or three minutes to conclude that they weren't BW labs," Killip would say later.[50]

On June 3, Jerry Watson arrived in Baghdad. By now the CIA's BW analyst had read the DIA's counter-analysis and begun to wonder if he and Beth had been premature in their white paper's judgments. At Camp Slayer, Jim Burans, a highly regarded DOD microbiologist Watson knew, was already examining the trailer.

"Hey, Jerry! What are you doing here?" Burans asked.

"Checking out the trailer," Watson replied.

"Thank God you're here," said the microbiologist. "Some idiot wrote a white-paper saying this was for BW."

"I'm one of the idiots," Watson confessed.

Burans gave the CIA analyst a tour of the trailer, ticking off the reasons why it could only be a facility for producing hydrogen and not biological weapons. Somewhat dazed, Watson retreated to the agency's Baghdad station, which was little more than a trailer. He sent a cable back to Langley, urging the agency to recall the white paper.

No, came the reply. The so-called experts were wrong. The evidence was conclusive.

What the hell is going on? Watson thought.

"WELL, IT'S A GOOD THING WE STILL HAVE CURVEBALL," CHEMICAL WEAPONS analyst Larry Fox said in June to a CIA case officer, referring to the failure thus far to find any WMD.

"Oh, we have our doubts about him, too," the case officer replied.

Fox flew to Baghdad in July. He spent a month conducting interviews with Saddam's detained scientists. One of them was Dr. Mahmud Farraj Bilal, who had overseen the weaponization of Iraq's biological and chemical agents. Bilal insisted to Fox that all CWs had been unilaterally destroyed by the regime in 1991.

Why then? Fox wanted to know.

It was just after the IAEA had discovered Saddam's illicit nuclear program in the wake of the Gulf War, Bilal replied. The dictator feared that if the UN discovered the full extent of Iraq's WMD program, the United States–led coalition would return and remove Saddam by military force. "I got a call in the middle of the night," the scientist said. "I was told, 'Get rid of everything in forty-eight hours.'"

But, persisted Fox, if the Iraqis had destroyed all their weapons, then why did they continue to be evasive to the UNSCOM inspectors?

Because, Bilal replied, he and other Iraqis hated the inspectors. UNSCOM was full of spies who had ulterior motives for searching through government buildings.

But then what would explain the numerical discrepancies in your weapons declarations? Fox asked.

The answer: when Iraq destroyed its weapons, it destroyed most of the records as well. The declarations were simply guesses. The UN had better records of Iraq's destroyed weaponry than Iraq did.

What felt like a gigantic pillar collapsed inside of Fox. The analyst proceeded to write a series of papers arguing that his own assessments about Saddam's CW program that had been published in the October 2002 National Intelligence Estimate were wrong and warranted correction. The agency refused to publish them.

Jerry Watson had also begun to interview the detainees. Since he had been one of the investigators of the UAV mapping software that Saddam had supposedly wanted for the purpose of targeting American cities, he sought out the engineers and military officers who were part of Iraq's UAV program. The detainees patiently explained to the CIA analyst that the UAVs were used only for electronic surveillance and reconnaissance. Watson then obtained documentary evidence that backed up their assertions. He sent a report back to Langley discrediting the CIA's stance on Iraq's UAV program. It met the same fate as Fox's report.

Bill McLaughlin, the analyst who had taken careful notes during the fateful "slam dunk" briefing to Bush the previous December, also had been talking to Iraq's scientists. In April, his supervisor, Jane Green, dispatched McLaughlin to the Emirates, where one of the deans of Iraq's weapons programs had been located. For the remainder of the week, the analyst interviewed the scientist in a hotel suite. The Iraqi was polite, rational, and at the same time insistent that the regime had destroyed all its weapons. On the sixth day, the scientist agreed to a polygraph test. He passed it.

Bill McLaughlin flew back to Washington and attended the 4 p.m. daily Iraq meeting on the seventh floor. Tenet and all the other relevant supervisors were in attendance. The Iraq branch chief of the agency's Counter Proliferation Division led the briefing. He described McLaughlin's view that the polygraph results had validated the scientist's claims that Iraq had long since disposed of its illicit weapons.

Then the branch chief said of the scientist, to McLaughlin's astonishment, "He's lying through his teeth."

By the end of July, Larry Fox was wrapping up his interviewing in Baghdad. The CW analyst thought that David Kay, the director of the Iraq Survey Group, should know about what the analysts were hearing from the detained scientists. Each time Fox attempted to get on Kay's calendar, he was informed that the chief inspector was too busy.

On Fox's last night in Baghdad, he visited a bar in the secure Green Zone. There was Kay. The CW analyst introduced himself to the ISG director. The words began to tumble out. Fox's biases had blinded him. The Iraqi scientists had completely plausible alternative explanations for everything. To speak to them was to see their world as they did, rather than through the tainted lens of a suspicious intelligence community. But, Fox added, his superiors back at CIA headquarters seemed to have little interest in the uncomfortable truth. Fighting back tears, he implored Kay to help him get his papers published so that the agency would face up to the facts.

Kay said nothing. But his expression conveyed more than just sympathy. Months later, after resigning from the Iraq Survey Group, the chief inspector would tell Jim Risen of the *Times* that analysts had come to him "almost in tears. . . . I have had analysts apologizing for reaching the conclusions that they did."

"Larry," a colleague warned him after the story was published, "you need to watch out. The seventh floor is angry with you."

"What? Why?" Fox sputtered.

"Something about you crying to David Kay," the colleague said.[51]

"RUMSFELD'S BACK," PAUL WOLFOWITZ PROCLAIMED TO THE *NEW YORK Times* columnist Tom Friedman during the summer of 2003. "He's engaged."

Friedman swallowed the obvious rejoinder: *Wait. You mean the secretary of defense was not engaged during wartime until now?*[52]

No one could level such an accusation against the deputy secretary, however. The liberation of Iraq had been Wolfowitz's animating cause for more than a decade. Now that it had at long last occurred, he tended to the preoccupation he had voiced to his military aide, Steve Ganyard, just before the invasion: *I'm worried about what comes after.*

He was in fact worried about many things. His Free Iraqi Forces, once imagined to be a mighty squadron in the tens of thousands, had mustered only seventy-six graduates by the time the program was suspended on March 31.[53] Wolfowitz had been in constant communication with the CENTCOM planners now in Qatar via secure video teleconference—"dealing with every-thing from ethnically designed menus that we would cater during combat operations to coordinating transport to vetting the list of who could and who couldn't come to meetings," one of the planners would recall.[54]

He was worried about how Operation Iraqi Freedom was being com-municated to the region. During another SVTC with the CENTCOM team in Qatar, the deputy secretary argued that the coalition should be character-izing Operation Iraqi Freedom's goal as establishing Iraq "as a cornerstone of democracy in the Middle East."

A member of the CENTCOM team gently suggested "representative government" as an alternative phrase—adding, "To be honest, 'democracy' isn't a word that resonates favorably in the Arab world."

Wolfowitz became angry. "Why is everyone fighting this?" he de-manded. "Making Iraq the cornerstone of democracy *is exactly what we're doing here!*"[55]

(That summer, the deputy secretary tasked the CIA with producing a paper entitled "Can Iraq Become a Democracy?" The conclusion, said the analyst who wrote the paper, "was that the best we can hope for is that Iraq will look something like the Kurds after 1990: tough going, probably a civil war, and if they do things right it'll be a quasi-representative government that's at least somewhat more respectful of human rights than Saddam Hus-sein's regime—which is of course a very low bar.")[56]

He was also worried about American public opinion. The Bush admin-istration had made the case for war on the basis of dangerous weapons that the inspectors had thus far failed to find. "We were going through all the intelligence reports while the ISG guys were hitting dry hole after dry hole," recalled one of Wolfowitz's aides. "He just didn't believe it. 'They moved it to Syria. It's out there. You just have to keep looking.'"[57]

"He'd seen all the intel, and he'd latch on to what he thought were the facts," affirmed another aide. "Chasing down everyone—*I've got a friend who's got a brother who heard something*—we did that all the time, these wild goose chases."[58]

Most of all, however, Paul Wolfowitz was worried about how Iraq was faring in its transition from tyrannized nation to "cornerstone of democracy in the Middle East." On July 17, he visited for the first time, taking with him six journalists who had supported the invasion, including Christopher Hitchens of *Vanity Fair* and Stephen Hayes of *The Weekly Standard*. The deputy secretary and his entourage toured the notorious Abu Ghraib prison, where, they were told, Saddam had executed more than 100,000 Iraqis. A specter such as Abu Ghraib, Wolfowitz commented, "can help you understand why the fear of Saddam Hussein hasn't left this country, especially because people are convinced that he's still alive."[59] (Which in fact he still was.)

While in Baghdad, the deputy secretary and Hitchens sought out a tree where, according to a well-circulated story, two Iraqi women had been tied up and raped. An elderly resident helpfully guided the two men to a withered and half-dead specimen. As the deputy secretary stood, solemn-faced, before the pathetic tree, a member of the entourage watched skeptically, thinking, *Ehhhh . . . where's the evidence?* But to Wolfowitz, belief stepped in where proof was absent.[60]

Two days after returning to Washington, Wolfowitz held a briefing and volunteered to the reporters that the Bush administration's postwar planning had gotten a few things wrong. They had assumed there would be a refugee crisis, an outbreak of malnutrition, and destruction of oil fields and dams. None of these things had occurred, he acknowledged. They had also assumed that the Iraqi army would be standing by compliantly "so that we could use them as Iraqi forces with us today." They had operated on the peculiar assumption that the Iraqi police force would be efficient and corruption-free.

Most regrettably, said Wolfowitz, the coalition had not expected guerrilla warfare. He did not say "insurgency"—the dreaded I-word that

Rumsfeld was doing everything possible to expunge from the Pentagon's vocabulary. Instead he attributed the continued violence to "the criminal gang of sadists and gangsters who have run Iraq for 35 years."[61]

By the time of Wolfowitz's July visit, practically every commanding officer in the field was accumulating powerful anecdotal evidence that Bremer and the Pentagon's orders to de-Baathify the government and disband the Iraqi army had fostered resentments that were fueling the insurgency.[62] But to Wolfowitz, according to one of his aides, "It was always the Baathists, and the years of oppression by the Sunnis. Never our fault."[63]

Wolfowitz's conviction that the insurgency was purely a Baathist phenomenon had been buttressed by an op-ed in *The Washington Post* by a former Marine Corps officer named Gary Anderson. In the column, Anderson advised building a "people's army" in Iraq—essentially what Bremer, Feith, and Slocombe had in mind—and confidently predicted that the Baathist guerrilla war could be "put out of its misery."[64] Wolfowitz subscribed to Anderson's argument, though not to his boss Rumsfeld's dismissive sentiment that the Iraqi resistance amounted to "pockets of dead-enders."[65] To the deputy secretary, the insurgency, whatever its composition, constituted a serious threat to the country's future. As an aide put it, "Wolfowitz got it in a way that Rumsfeld never did."[66]

In September, Wolfowitz gamely accepted an invitation to the New Yorker Festival to be interviewed onstage by writer Jeffrey Goldberg. "I think I'm glad to be here," he said abashedly after his introduction met with a mixture of applause and boos.

It was Goldberg's March 2002 *New Yorker* piece about the Kurds that had first mainstreamed the notion that Saddam and Al Qaeda had confederated. As such, the moderator did not challenge Wolfowitz's assertion that "the lesson of 9/11 is that there are interlocking groups with the potential to do great harm." What gave Goldberg pause was Wolfowitz's reply when the moderator asked the deputy secretary if it concerned him that a future democratic election in Iraq might produce an Islamic extremist as its leader.

"Look," the deputy secretary replied, "50 percent of the Arab world are women. Most of those women don't want to live in a theocratic state. The other 50 percent are men. I know a lot of them. I don't think they want to live in a theocratic state."

"*Shit*, I thought," Goldberg later wrote, by way of explaining how he came to be disillusioned with the Iraq War.[67]

WOLFOWITZ RETURNED TO A DIFFERENT IRAQ IN OCTOBER. THE PENTAGON'S plan to draw down the troop level to thirty thousand had been quietly shelved. That many U.S. troops now occupied Baghdad alone.[68] On August 7, a car bomb exploded outside the Jordan embassy in Baghdad, leaving eleven dead and sixty-five wounded.[69] The next day, CPA chief Jerry Bremer complained to Tenet that the CIA's preoccupation with the hunt for WMD was coming at the expense of counterterrorism and counterinsurgency expertise. Help did not arrive until the end of the year.[70]

On August 19, a bomb detonated at Baghdad's Canal Hotel, the headquarters for the UN. Among the twenty-two dead was Sergio Vieira de Mello, the UN's envoy to Iraq.[71] As horrific as the attack was, a far more portentous event took place ten days later when a car bomb outside the Shrine of Imam Ali, in Najaf, killed at least 125, including a prominent Shiite cleric.[72] The mosque bombing left little doubt that guerrilla warfare against the Western occupiers might be the least of the coalition's worries. Against all the assurances by leading exiles to President Bush and other administration figures that Iraqis of all stripes would joyously coalesce around freedom, a bloody Sunni-Shia sectarian struggle was now under way.

The Pentagon had again rounded up several reporters to accompany Wolfowitz on his October trip. The American press had been obsessed with negativity, the reporters were told; a far bigger story of progress was there to be written.[73] But the deputy secretary was equally concerned about the message being conveyed to the Arab world. Yes, Iraq badly needed stabilizing, but, as Jamil Mroue, publisher of the Beirut-based *Daily Star*, had warned Wolfowitz over dinner recently, the American presence in Iraq had to be about more than security. Justice needed to be emphasized as well.[74]

On October 24, Wolfowitz visited a newly erected women's rights center in the ancient Babylonian city of Hilla. "There are people in the world who say that Arabs can't build a democracy," he told the women. "I think that's nonsense."

Then he added, almost beseechingly, "So please do it."[75]

Wolfowitz spent much of the next day in Tikrit, Saddam's birthplace. Meeting with new recruits for the Iraqi army—some of whom had previously fought for the dictator—the deputy secretary pronounced this development "an amazing success story."[76] Just after he and his entourage departed for Baghdad that afternoon, however, insurgents fired rocket-propelled grenades at a Black Hawk helicopter, injuring five U.S. troops.[77]

Late that afternoon, the Americans reposed at al-Rashid Hotel, in Baghdad. Wolfowitz sat for drinks with two companions: *Washington Post* columnist David Ignatius and Ahmad Chalabi. Ignatius did not trust Chalabi. Wolfowitz had begun to reappraise his own high regard for the INC founder. His aides had been warning him that Chalabi had his own agenda and was not above deception in the furtherance of it.[78]

Ignatius could not resist commenting that President Bush had come to take a dim view of Chalabi. The previous month at Camp David, he said, King Abdullah of Jordan had brought up the INC leader. Bush's immediate response was "Piss on him."

Chalabi affected nonchalance. Then he gazed around the hotel, seen by many Iraqis after the invasion as an oasis of Western decadence, filled with CPA workers and assorted profiteers.

"I think," he said to Wolfowitz, "this is a dangerous place for you."[79]

Later that evening in the bar, Chalabi said to a reporter, "The Baathists are coming back. I can feel it."[80]

Wolfowitz was awake and in the shower at six the next morning when a great *whoosh* swept through the air outside. What appeared to be a large generator parked across the street spat out a fusillade of seventeen rockets that flew over a concrete barrier and crashed into the hotel, killing one U.S. soldier and wounding fifteen others.

With Bill Luti, Wolfowitz scrambled down twelve floors to the lobby. The deputy secretary promptly announced that he intended to continue with his schedule. "There's a small number of bitter-enders who think they can take this country back by destabilizing it and scaring us away," he declared to the assembled press, who had also been staying at al-Rashid.

Pledged Wolfowitz, "They are not going to scare us away."[81]

Within a few weeks' time, thirty of the individuals thought to be behind the attacks were arrested after a series of targeted raids conducted by coalition forces. In interrogating the suspects, a notable fact emerged about the men characterized by Wolfowitz as "bitter-enders." They were, for the most part, former members of the Iraqi army who had been thrown out of work by the CPA's disbandment order. "That was the bread and butter of who we rounded up, absolutely," recalled Colonel Rob Baker, commander of the 2nd Brigade Combat Team of the 1st Armored Division that carried out the raids. "The more military training and leadership they had, the more effective they were."[82]

Before Wolfowitz left Baghdad, he visited 28th Combat Support hospital. A fifty-four-year-old Army colonel named Elias Nimmer had been badly wounded during the attack on the hotel and had just been wheeled out of surgery. A large piece of shrapnel was removed from Nimmer's spinal column, saving his life. But shrapnel remained in his body from head to toe. Acid burns from unspent fuel covered his face.

"Where are you from?" the deputy secretary asked him.

Groggy from anesthesia, Nimmer replied that he was from Arlington, Virginia. Before that, he added, from Lebanon.

Then Wolfowitz asked, "How do you feel about building a new Middle East?"

Nimmer managed to raise a thumb. Then he took off his oxygen mask and posed for a photograph with the deputy secretary.[83]

It was a memory that would stay with Wolfowitz.[84] Nimmer's more searing recollections in Iraq preceded the attack. How, for example, when the trained health-care technician first arrived in Baghdad, full of admiration for the brilliance of the military invasion, he reported for duty to the Coalition Provisional Authority and asked the civilian commanders, "So can I read the plan? Or is it classified?" And he was told, "You *are* the plan."

And how, when speaking in his fluent Arabic with former members of the Iraqi army, Colonel Nimmer heard their blunt assessment of the Pentagon's disbandment order: "When an officer is sent home without a salary and can no longer feed his family, his wife will tell him to get out of the house. What do you think he will do then? How do you think he will feel?"[85]

ON THE AFTERNOON OF OCTOBER 6, THE NSC STAFF GATHERED A COLLECtion of government officials who had recently returned from Iraq. It was almost exactly six months since the fall of Saddam, and the White House was mounting an aggressive public relations campaign to quell rising concern over the disarray in Iraq. In the coming days, Bush, Cheney, and Rice would hit the road, telling audiences not to be swayed by the media's negativity. Today this gathering of U.S. officials would inaugurate the effort with testimony on the White House lawn about their own affecting experiences.

Bush, whose day was largely preoccupied with a state visit by Kenya's president, Mwai Kibaki, met with the group briefly in the Roosevelt Room. He offered each of them a handshake, then wanted to know what they thought his next steps should be in Iraq. Given that there were about ten of them and only as many minutes with the president, the scenario did not lend itself to trenchant observations. "Don't give up, Mr. President—stay the course," said Deputy Assistant Secretary of State Ryan Crocker, who had come to believe that the only idea worse than invading Iraq was abandoning it now.

Crocker and his State colleague Yael Lempert were the only officials in the gathering who did not work for Bremer's CPA. Lempert had spent May, June, and July in Iraq. In that span of time, she had watched the heartbreaking spectacle of the American-led occupation stoking all the discontents that she, Crocker, and others had foreseen in State's "Perfect Storm" memo. It astonished her that no one in the room was conveying to the president the chaos that each of them had plainly witnessed.

When it came Lempert's turn to speak, she began on a positive note. The State official described the excitement in Baghdad on the evening of July 22 when the skies in Iraq erupted in celebratory gunfire after two hundred

U.S. troops dragged the bullet-riddled bodies of Uday and Qusay Hussein from a villa in Mosul.

Just then, Chief of Staff Andy Card stepped into the room. It was time for the president to rejoin his Africa-related meetings. Lempert never received another opportunity to share her concerns about Iraq with the president.[86]

Three days later, Bush defiantly told a crowd of Republican donors in Kentucky, "We're making great progress. I don't care what you read about. Just ask anybody who's been there."[87]

Bush knew better, however. While in Bangkok on October 18 for the Asia-Pacific Economic Cooperation forum, he and Colin Powell were visiting in the president's hotel suite at the Grand Hyatt Erawan when his briefer entered to give a casualty report. Four American soldiers had lost their lives in the previous two days: three while negotiating with a group of armed Iraqis after curfew and another when his vehicle ran over an improvised explosive device. The death toll among U.S. troops had now reached 353. October had been the deadliest month since Bush declared the end of major combat operations, on May 1.

Bush fell silent after the briefing. He and Powell rode the elevator together. The president said nothing as they descended. Walking through the kitchen and outside to where his limousine awaited him, Bush at last spoke.

"Colin," he said quietly, "you warned me."[88]

TWO MONTHS LATER, GOOD NEWS ARRIVED IN IRAQ. ON DECEMBER 12, A close associate of Saddam Hussein's was captured and interrogated by the U.S. Army. In exchange for obtaining the freedom of forty family members, the associate described the former dictator's whereabouts: a remote farm compound a few miles south of Tikrit that the military had previously searched. Inside the kitchen, a Delta Force operator kicked away a loose slab of flooring. From the exposed hole in the ground, two raised hands materialized, followed by a wild head of hair and two wide eyes beneath.

"I am Saddam Hussein," he said. "I am the president of Iraq, and I am willing to negotiate."

The former president was extracted from his hiding place—along with a Glock, an AK-47, and $750,000 in U.S. hundred-dollar notes—and ferried by helicopter to Baghdad.[89] Though it was a military operation, it was CPA administrator Jerry Bremer who made the announcement: "Ladies and gentlemen, we got him." Images were soon released of Iraq's former leader lying, bedraggled, in the dirt—and, later, being examined by a military physician for head lice and gum infections while his captors gleefully recounted Saddam's having been "caught like a rat" in a "spider hole."

The televised humiliation of an Arab leader did not lead to ill effects on the ground at first. Following a post-combat peak of eighty-four U.S. casualties in November 2003, the numbers proceeded to tick downward: forty-nine in December, forty-three in January 2004, and thirty-one in February. Bush had reason to hope that Saddam's capture had kicked the legs out from under the insurgency.

"The once all-powerful ruler of Iraq was found in a hole and now sits in a prison cell," the president declared to thunderous applause from Congress on the evening of January 20, during his State of the Union address. Later in his speech, he gestured up to the balcony and said, "And tonight we are honored to welcome one of Iraq's most respected leaders: the current president of the Iraqi Governing Council, Adnan Pachachi."[90]

The cameras panned upward to capture Pachachi standing and applauding, with Laura Bush standing next to him. Directly behind the first lady, another council member also stood and clapped, the discerning smile unmistakably that of Ahmad Chalabi.

Bush had in fact met with Chalabi, Pachachi, and a third council member, Abdul-Aziz al-Hakim, in the Oval Office that morning. Following his address, Bush shook Chalabi's hand and the two men spoke briefly.

But the president was not happy to see the INC leader there. "What was Chalabi doing sitting behind Laura last night at the State of the Union?" he demanded to a roomful of White House staffers the next morning.[91]

Bush's profane assessment of Chalabi to King Abdullah four months previously—"Piss on him"—reflected an accumulation of misgivings. That same month, in September, while the White House was seeking an $18 billion reconstruction budget from Congress, Chalabi was on the Hill insisting to members that Iraqis had sufficient wealth to pay for the rebuilding themselves. "I'm really pissed at Chalabi," the president told Bremer. He added that he had seen Chalabi the previous day at a UN diplomatic reception and would have lit into him but for the fact that Chalabi's daughter was standing next to him.[92]

Saddam's weapons arsenal had yet to be found, and Bush now believed that Chalabi's INC had been passing phony intelligence to the U.S. government. (Those suspicions would be borne out as information supposedly taken from the Iraqi Intelligence Service files now in the possession of the INC was transmitted to U.S. authorities and fed into the Harmony database. One brazenly forged document purported to be a letter of alliance signed by both Saddam and Osama bin Laden.)[93]

Bush also blamed Chalabi for promoting de-Baathification and the disbandment of the Iraqi army.[94] As the president would later write, "In retrospect, I should have insisted on more debate on Jerry's orders, especially on what message disbanding the army would send and how many Sunnis the de-Baathification would affect. Overseen by longtime exile Ahmed [*sic*] Chalabi, the de-Baathification program turned out to cut much deeper than we expected, including mid-level party members like teachers."[95] (In November 2003, as Chalabi was presiding over the de-Baathification process, Scooter Libby called Bremer in Baghdad. "Well," Cheney's chief of staff said, "Chalabi has about run out of support here.")[96]

More recently, at the end of 2003, Chalabi had argued that the Mahdi Army, the militia formed by Shia cleric Moqtada al-Sadr, could help provide security in Iraq. Bremer condemned the idea. In early April 2004, the CPA chief termed al-Sadr an "outlaw" and referred to Sadrists killed by coalition forces as "the enemy."

"These are not the enemy!" Chalabi exclaimed during an Iraqi Governing Council meeting, and pounded the table as he glared at Bremer. "These are Iraqis you're killing!" Chalabi stormed out and never spoke to Bremer again.[97]

In April 2004, Bush learned of yet another transgression committed by

Chalabi. Jim Risen of the *Times* had approached Rice for confirmation of a bombshell scoop: the exile had tipped off leaders of Iran's spy service that the U.S. intelligence community had been reading their intelligence cables. Learning of Risen's investigation, NSA director Michael Hayden contacted *Times* editor Philip Taubman and convinced him to hold the story.[98]

The disclosure nonetheless percolated up to Bush, who was irate. "Does this guy Chalabi still work for us?" he snapped during an NSC meeting in April.

"Sir," said Rob Richer, the CIA's chief of Middle East clandestine operations, "I believe he is working for DOD."

Wolfowitz confirmed this. "Chalabi has a relationship with DIA and is providing information that is saving American lives," the deputy secretary said.

The president looked skeptical. "I want an assessment of that," he said to Rice. "But in the meantime, I want him fired."

A few weeks later, Rice, Richer, and Undersecretary for Intelligence Steve Cambone reconvened in the Oval Office to discuss Chalabi's relationship with the U.S. government. Rice confirmed that the DIA had been paying the INC $350,000 a month. She said that there was no conclusive evidence to support Wolfowitz's claim that the INC's intelligence was "saving American lives."

"We fired him, though," said Bush. "Right?"

"Well," hedged Cambone, "we're still maintaining contact with him."[99]

The DIA terminated its contract with Chalabi's INC on May 14.[100] Six days later, Iraqi police and U.S. military personnel raided the Hunting Club and Chalabi's residence, seizing computers and files.[101]

The American media widely chronicled Ahmad Chalabi's fall from grace with the U.S. government. Chalabi himself knew better. "I've been blackballed more times than I can possibly count," he told an associate.[102] Blame, he knew, would be widely distributed as the Iraq saga continued. The INC's WMD intelligence would prove to be no worse than that of the vaunted CIA. Yes, his limited relationship with President Bush—whom Chalabi would later describe as "a man with very little skill and knowledge"—had now come to an end.[103]

But for all his flaws, Chalabi himself had never been accused of lacking cleverness and substance—or, for that matter, survival skills. He would outlast this latest blackballing. In November 2005, Ahmad Chalabi, the new deputy prime minister of Iraq, would return to Washington, even while still under FBI investigation, for secret meetings with Dick Cheney, Donald Rumsfeld, and Condoleezza Rice.[104]

SADDAM HUSSEIN HAD BEEN A PRISONER OF THE U.S.-LED COALITION FOR A week when CIA analyst John Nixon began the interrogations on December 20, 2003. The former dictator was not in a good mood. Before his captivity, he had written approximately seven hundred pages of a novel, set in Arabia in the seventeenth century, and he wanted his manuscript returned to him.

The megalomaniacal madman of the Bush administration's collective imagination had, according to interviews conducted with his subordinates, largely checked out of running Iraq's affairs. Since 2001, Saddam had increasingly delegated authority to his deputy prime minister, Tariq Aziz; his vice president, Taha Yassin Ramadan al-Jizrawi; and the deputy secretary of the Baath Party, Izzat Ibrahim al-Duri. He was spending his days writing fiction and poetry. After 9/11, he imagined that Iraq and the United States would ally against Muslim extremists. He did not expect war. He thought Chirac and Putin would talk Bush out of it. After finding out differently on March 20, 2003, the day U.S. troops crossed Kuwait into Iraq, Saddam loaded up on American currency at the Central Bank of Iraq, gave a speech standing on top of his car, waved, and drove through three checkpoints north to Tikrit, his birthplace. Not for a second had he ever considered leaving Iraq.

Bill McLaughlin took over the interrogations in mid-January. Like Nixon, McLaughlin could see that Saddam was at peace with the knowledge that his execution was imminent. A malignant narcissist who was frequently manipulative and at times menacing, Saddam also could be self-deprecating and even charming, freely dispensing advice on matters of love and getting ahead in life. He maintained that Iraq had no weapons program, that the weapons declaration his regime had submitted to Hans Blix in December

2002 was accurate, that the inspectors would find nothing because there was nothing to find. It mystified Saddam that the Americans had imagined him as a closet Islamist. He told McLaughlin that he had left Iraqis free to practice their religion, so long as it stayed in places of worship. "If they engaged in politics based on their religion," he said simply, "we took action."

At one point, Saddam offered a peculiar insight into American history. "The reason the South lost the Civil War," the former dictator told John Nixon, "was that it was always fighting uphill."

Nixon suppressed a smile. It was Saddam's misunderstanding of America's psychology, rather than of its geography, that had proved fatal for him. But the ignorance worked both ways, Nixon thought. Fully four years would pass before Saddam Hussein's interrogators would be invited to the White House to shed light on the man who had driven George W. Bush to war.[105]

"AND DESPITE SOME PUBLIC STATEMENTS, WE ARE NOWHERE NEAR 85 PERcent finished," George Tenet declared at Georgetown University on February 5, 2004.[106]

The CIA director was referring to the recent comment by former Iraq Survey Group chief David Kay that "I think we have found probably 85 percent of what we're going to find."[107] Kay had also testified to the Senate that "it turns out that we were all wrong."[108] With his Georgetown speech, Tenet's point-by-point rebuttal of the agency's critics on the prewar intelligence, profoundly defensive in tone if heavily caveated with "provisional" conclusions, reflected a dawning awareness that he was the likeliest candidate for Bush administration fall guy in the misbegotten run-up to war.

One week later, Tenet was in Baghdad. At ISG headquarters, the director hollered to the inspectors, *"Are we 85 percent done?"*

"No," a few of them mumbled.

"Are we 85 percent done? I want to hear you!"

"No!" came the more fervent reply.

"Maybe it was an American thing," recalled the British biological weapons inspector Hamish Killip. "Like: *'Who let the dogs out—who, who, who who*

who!' But it was wholly inappropriate at the 'time. What mattered was that we actually got to the truth."[109]

At the ISG meeting, Tenet also introduced the inspectors to Kay's replacement, former UNSCOM inspector Charles Duelfer. "This man is as weird as shit," the director said as he squeezed his arm around the embarrassed ISG chief. "But he knows a hell of a lot about Iraq."[110]

Duelfer did know a lot about the country. And what he knew, judging from the reports he had gleaned from the field, was that Tenet was wrong and Kay was right. The inspection work *was* nearly complete. The intelligence community *was* wrong. Saddam had no illicit weapons, nor any weapons program. The only thing left to learn was where and when the WMD had been disposed of.[111]

This was not just the opinion of inspectors like Duelfer. During a video-conference of CIA senior weapons analysts in December 2003, each of them acknowledged that they had reassessed their previous dire judgments.[112] Among them, only Beth, the Curveball advocate, remained a holdout. But to anyone not still under the spell of prewar biases, the mobile BW lab case had collapsed as well. In March 2004, Tenet finally persuaded the Germans to permit one of his analysts to interview Curveball. On May 26, a CIA memo concluded that the Iraqi defector had "lied about his access to a mobile BW production project."[113]

The supposed Al Qaeda connection had crumbled as well. In January 2004, Ibn al-Shaykh al-Libi—the terrorist who had told Egyptian interrogators that Iraq had been training Al Qaeda members in how to produce and deploy WMD—recanted to CIA debriefers his previous disclosures. Al-Libi explained that the Egyptians had placed him in a small box for seventeen hours, then beaten him for fifteen minutes. After this, he had told his interrogators a made-up account of three Al Qaeda members acquiring information about nuclear weapons from Iraq. Al-Libi was then returned to his cell and given food. He told the CIA that the Egyptians also beat him for not providing information about Iraq's having provided anthrax to Al Qaeda. He said that he had not been able to invent a story on the spot because he did not understand the term "biological." CIA cables describing al-Libi's recantation were sent to Langley headquarters on the day before and the day of Tenet's speech at Georgetown.[114]

The other crucial peg in the Saddam–Al Qaeda argument had also been dislodged. At the request of Dick Cheney, in early 2004 the agency undertook an appraisal of Abu Musab al-Zarqawi's relationship with the former Iraqi regime. The paper concluded that the relationship did not exist and that Saddam had not abetted Zarqawi's terrorist activities in northern Iraq. To the contrary: the Iraqi Intelligence Service was hunting for Zarqawi, just like the Americans were.

"You're moving the goalposts," Cheney growled when John McLaughlin briefed the national security team on the paper's findings.

"It's our obligation to tell you when we have new information that changes our assessment," the deputy director pushed back. (Cheney elected not to be swayed by the reassessment. In his vice presidential debate against John Edwards that fall, Cheney cited the CIA paper, saying, "The report also points out that at one point some of Zarqawi's people were arrested; Saddam personally intervened to have them released, supposedly at the request of Zarqawi." The vice president's statement "was the exact opposite of what the paper said," recalled one of the analysts who had helped produce the assessment.)[115]

That obligation stated by McLaughlin did not extend to the general public. By the fall of 2003, chemical weapons expert Larry Fox and biological weapons analyst Jerry Watson were pressing their superiors to publish papers acknowledging that the CIA had erred in its judgments about CW stockpiles and mobile BW labs. The agency's managers refused to do so. Watson and Fox continued to complain. Both were ultimately moved out of headquarters to other offices.[116]

Tenet knew that the intelligence case for war had fallen apart. On February 11, the day the CIA director flew to Baghdad to rally his inspectors, his deputy for intelligence, Jami Miscik, gathered the agency's employees for an "all-hands meeting" in the CIA auditorium. "While some of the criticisms will be unmerited," Miscik told them, "we have to recognize that many will be justified." Among the deserved criticisms, she cited single-sourcing, failing to electronically post fabrication notices, inheriting rather than reexamining past assumptions, and neglecting to let superiors know when a judgment might be intuitive rather than fact-based.

Miscik then instructed all office managers to conduct follow-up sessions with their subordinates, beginning that afternoon.[117] The ensuing re-education would focus on matters such as "analytic word creep"—or, as Iraq group chief Jane Green would put it, "When do we use 'probably,' and is 'probably' equivalent to 'is likely to'? But that was irrelevant to the problem. The problem was the seventh floor pushing us *not* to use probabilistic language, but to be as clear and definitive as possible. Jami read all the source information we used and reviewed virtually everything that went to senior policymakers, and she wasn't shy about making changes. She knew what George wanted. George wanted to please the First Customer. And the First Customer wasn't pleased by the use of caveats."[118]

But by the time he had selected Charles Duelfer to lead the Iraq Survey Group, Tenet was aware that his own legacy hung in the balance. Duelfer was a popular choice to succeed Kay. "They saw me as sort of a kindred spirit, somebody who's not against them, who was of the view that Iraq would be better off without Saddam," he recalled.[119]

Duelfer was also astute enough to recognize the political sensitivity of his task. He had not even begun his work in early February of 2004 when Rumsfeld's undersecretary for intelligence, Steve Cambone, asked the new chief inspector, "Can't this wait until after the election?"

It would have made little sense for the new ISG chief to begin his work by parroting what his predecessor Kay had been saying about there being no WMD, even if the facts dictated that he do so. The ISG staff had already concluded that Iraq never had a mobile BW lab program and that the aluminum tubes it had purchased were intended for rocket bodies rather than nuclear centrifuges.

Duelfer did not include those findings in his interim report to Congress on March 30, 2004. Instead, his report was packed with red meat for the administration. The most important work was yet to be done, he implied, given that "we have yet to identify the most critical people in any programmatic effort." (The reason for this was that no WMD program existed for any people to be a part of.) The ISG had found "equipment suitable for the production of biological agents." (But no evidence existed that such equipment was being used for this purpose.) Iraq had recently built new facilities "for the production of chemicals." (But the chemical in question, dicyclohexylcarbodiimide, was a commonly used dehydrating agent in the pharmaceutical industry.) As for Saddam's nuclear program, Duelfer refused to rule out a dark purpose for the aluminum tubes, saying that there were "still a number of discrepancies to examine with regard to these tubes."[120]

Duelfer's approach bought him goodwill with the Bush administration. But his omissions came at a cost: three of the ISG's top inspectors quit in protest.[121]

Still, Duelfer was only buying time in the face of the inevitable. Throughout the spring and early summer of 2004, his inspectors continued to hit dry holes. It seemed evident that the ISG would be bearing bad tidings once again. In August, Duelfer informed Steve Hadley that "I'm at like a nine confidence level" that no weapons existed.[122]

Duelfer issued his final report on September 30, five weeks before the presidential election. Intended or not, Duelfer's conclusions amounted to a gift to Bush and Tenet. Though no weapons had been found, the ISG chief wrote, Saddam's "strategic intent" was to reconstitute his program once sanctions were lifted.

In fact, none of the regime's scientists or military officials had said this explicitly to their American interrogators. No physical evidence of such intentions had been found. To his inquisitors, Saddam repeatedly denied that he intended to resume a weapons program. Both John Nixon and Bill McLaughlin, of the CIA, concluded that the dictator had lost his appetite for the attenuated cat-and-mouse game that had cost his country so dearly. Only when his third and final interrogator, FBI agent George Piro, leadingly raised the specter of Iran attacking Iraq did Saddam acknowledge that he "would have done what was necessary" to protect his country—though the ex-dictator also volunteered his hope that, under such a scenario, the United

States might see fit to protect his country against the Iranian aggressors. On this thin reed, Bush, Cheney, and Tenet could now confidently assert that the Butcher of Baghdad would have remained a threat to the world.[123]

Even so, Bush and Cheney's claim that Saddam was an imminent threat to the United States required an element that Charles Duelfer could not provide and in fact did not believe. Had a shred of evidence emerged that the dictator intended America harm?

"No," Duelfer would later say. "Nothing. It was like when Wolfowitz asked the agency, before the war, to go through all of Saddam's speeches and count up the times he threatened the United States. And they did. And they came up with zero.

"And after 9/11, Saddam felt, 'Okay, now you have to deal with me.' But as an ally! It never occurred to him that he would be conflated with the Islamicists—who he hated!"[124]

But Duelfer did not include this insight in the ISG final report. The confection of Saddam Hussein's encompassing menace was allowed to stand. Still, the acknowledgment that no illicit weapons had been found—which had been the intelligence community's consensus view going back to the previous December—was at last made public. In that ten-month span, 632 American soldiers had lost their lives in a war to eliminate a threat that had not existed.[125]

There was, to be fair, a standby argument for the Bush administration. In the course of conducting combat patrols throughout Iraq, U.S. troops occasionally came in contact with residual mustard gas and sarin found on munitions from the Iran-Iraq War, half-buried in the desert and long forgotten. That was particularly the case in the village of al-Aziziyah, bordering Iran, where vicious battles had been fought and the fields were littered with expended chemical weapons.[126] When the CIA briefed the NSC on these discoveries, observing that the missile shells had been produced before the 1991 Gulf War, the president seemed annoyed by the hairsplitting.

Muttering under his breath, Bush told an aide seated nearby, "I don't remember saying pre-'91 or post-'91. I said the son of a bitch had WMD!"[127]

AS IRAQ SPIRALED INTO CHAOS, DONALD RUMSFELD WAS FOCUSED ON THE things that really mattered.

It bothered him greatly when, on May 6, 2003, Bush had neglected to invite the secretary of defense to his hiring of Jerry Bremer. "POTUS had lunch with him alone—shouldn't have done so," he noted to himself that day. Such actions, Rumsfeld believed, "contributed to a confused chain of command."[128]

A month later, in June, as the first clear signals of a brewing insurgency began to emerge, Doug Feith showed up to a Deputies Committee meeting with a proposal from his boss. It was time to rethink the "coalition of the willing," according to Rumsfeld's undersecretary. The countries that were not providing troops should be kicked out of the coalition. As always, Hadley cautiously affirmed that the secretary's idea was "an interesting subject for study." He assigned the matter to an NSC aide, who quietly studied the matter into an early grave.[129]

In November 2003, as a means of upholding the DOD's personnel policy, Rumsfeld and his undersecretary for personnel, David Chu, announced that a force rotation would soon take effect, such that all 150,000 forces in theater would be replaced. CENTCOM planners argued that this was foolhardy. As one of them would recall, "Chu and Rumsfeld had that compact with the servicemen of '365 days of boots on the ground.' I understand the compact. But it's like this: Take out the whole police department from Houston or Brooklyn and put in a whole new group, and see what happens. That's what happened in Iraq. You pull that many people out of the provinces and you put new people in there—it gave the insurgency room to breathe. But the bottom line was, Chu and Rumsfeld's personnel policy took primacy over everything else.

"It was probably the worst thing I was a part of in my military career. It was one of the stupidest things I ever saw."[130]

The following year would bring new matters of bureaucratic fixation for

Rumsfeld. In May 2004, when Chalabi's Baghdad properties were raided, the secretary indicated his displeasure in a snowflake to General John Abizaid, the commander of CENTCOM. What bothered Rumsfeld was not the treatment of Chalabi, but rather that Bremer had authorized the raid through Rice and not him. Issues of such sensitivity "should be elevated up to [General Ricardo] Sanchez"—the three-star general now leading coalition troops in Iraq after Tommy Franks's departure—"[and then] he should elevate them up to you, and you should elevate them up to me," he insisted.[131]

Throughout it all, Rumsfeld continued to maintain that no insurgency was occurring and that the CIA and the media did not know what he knew.[132] But in late April 2004, the press—specifically, CBS's *60 Minutes* and Seymour Hersh of *The New Yorker*—had an unwelcome surprise to spring on Rumsfeld. In the U.S.-occupied Baghdad prison known as Abu Ghraib, photos had been taken of Iraqi inmates with dog collars around their necks, with women's underwear over their faces, and naked in piles.

Bush was understandably upset that the Pentagon and the media had seen the Abu Ghraib photos before he had. Rumsfeld was summoned to the Oval Office after the scandal broke. Communications Director Dan Bartlett stepped into Bush's office after Rumsfeld had left.

Holding up a letter from the defense secretary, Bush said, "Guess who just offered to resign."

The president was ruefully impressed. "That's the smart old infighter. He knows I'm not in a position to fire him."[133]

But the prisoner abuse scandal was more than just a regrettable news day. The months of positive momentum in Iraq following Saddam's arrest had evaporated. So, incidentally, had the president's popularity among Arab American voters. By the summer, the voting bloc that White House political director Ken Mehlman said "got us here" in the previous election cycle was now supporting the Democratic nominee, John Kerry, by a two-to-one ratio.[134]

Bush enjoyed telling audiences and journalists how indifferent he was to polls. By 2004, he did not need to consult public opinion data to know that domestic support for the war was eroding badly. "We need an Iraqi leader to say to the U.S., 'Thanks for your sacrifice,'" he snapped during an NSC meeting in May. "I don't expect a toady. But he should be grateful for what we've done. We want the American people to support our mission."[135]

The president faced conflict in both countries. The publication in April of Bob Woodward's explosive book *Plan of Attack* revealed the bitter infighting between State and DOD, the machinations of Bush's vice president, and his own seeming indifference to the failure to find WMD in Iraq.

Perhaps most of all, Woodward's book appeared to scapegoat George Tenet, who would retire from the CIA in June. Though Bush would award the former director the Presidential Medal of Freedom at the end of 2004, recriminations between the White House and the agency persisted. Bush later told a CIA official that he was convinced the agency was leaking embarrassing material to the press in hopes that he would lose the election.[136] Bush was getting fed up with the negativity in his morning Presidential Daily Briefing sessions. The briefers in turn began conducting an "open feud" with the agency's analysts, one CIA senior manager said, "because we had a duty to tell him the bad shit, and there was a lot of bad shit. There was a lot of pressure from the PDB briefers to stay in the game and be one of Bush's fraternity brothers in this process."[137]

As global opinion began to swerve hard against the war, the agency's alternative Red Cell unit produced a paper for Bush on European attitudes. The president's jaw stiffened when he came upon the word "schadenfreude."

Tossing the paper back at his briefer, he said, "Tell those sons of bitches never to use a foreign word in one of these again."[138]

BUSH WENT ON TO PREVAIL IN THE GENERAL ELECTION, DEFEATING JOHN Kerry with 51 percent of the popular vote, even with Rumsfeld's baggage and without the support of Arab Americans. In an exit poll, 52 percent of Americans believed that the Iraq War had not made the country safer.[139] And yet the Bush campaign, directed by Rove and Mehlman, gambled that a jittery electorate in a time of war would be reluctant to change presidents. The campaign therefore deliberately devoted nearly half of the issue contents of Bush's campaign speeches to terrorism and Iraq, often conflating the two.[140] The wager paid off. Among those voters who cited terrorism as their primary issue of concern, Bush won a staggering 86 percent.[141]

To the surprise of many, Bush elected to keep Rumsfeld for a second term. The bureaucratically peerless secretary had set up the situation beautifully a year earlier when the president complained to Rumsfeld about the ongoing war between State and DOD that was making its way into the press. "All the evidence suggests that it is State trashing us," Rumsfeld insisted. "If anyone has any information that my folks at DOD are leaking anything or trashing anyone, tell me."

Of course, Bush was unaware that Wolfowitz and Feith's fiefdoms included several prolific leakers. Rumsfeld may well not have known, either. (Though this would have qualified as a "known unknown.")

Still, the secretary proceeded to make a Stradivarius out of the president, telling him with concern, "What is happening is hurting you. If it gets to a point where the solution is for me to leave, I will do so in a second." He added, "It's certainly not my first choice, but we need you in the White House, and if my leaving would help, I'm ready."

Replied Bush, "I'm working hard on Powell and Armitage. I've seen the recent articles and I know what's going on."[142]

It was Powell who would be thrown overboard. Though the secretary of state had offered his continued services to the president, Bush instead elected to replace him with Condi Rice. Unlike the unctuous Rumsfeld, Powell continued to embarrass Bush in the press, as when the secretary theorized to the *Washington Post* editorial board in 2004 that the United States might not have gone to war had it been known that Saddam did not possess weapons of mass destruction. (Rice later called an editor at the *Post* and demanded a retraction.)[143]

Powell remained more popular than anyone else in the administration. Just after the election, Gallup ranked his approval rating at a stratospheric 87—thirty-six points higher than the president.[144] But his reputation had suffered greatly among the Washington elite who had put their trust in Powell's case for the war at the UN and now believed they had been lied to.

"I know that the first line of my obituary is going to include the phrase 'who made the false case for war,'" Powell told a group of reporters, and he repeated it later to a member of his staff.[145] Though stoic in his bearing, he had lost his temper more than once while receiving sheepish calls from the CIA as one data point after another from his UN speech was found not to hold water. When the call came in from Tenet about Curveball, the secretary uncharacteristically unleashed a torrent of profanities.

Hanging up, he turned to an aide in disbelief. "All he had to say for himself was 'Well, I guess I was wrong,'" he muttered.[146]

A former ambassador ran into Powell at a party in Washington after Bush's new personnel moves were announced at the end of 2004. The diplomat offered warm words, expecting that the loyal general would respond with niceties.

"He just unloaded," the former ambassador recalled. "They had lied to him. All the crap about the so-called biological vans. Cheney and the neocons pushing on the CIA. He was furious that he'd been made a patsy."[147]

RUMSFELD WOULD STAY. BUT HIS TOP TWO SUBORDINATES DEPARTED IN 2005.

Doug Feith did not particularly share the Bush administration's embarrassment over the failure to find illicit weapons in Iraq. In the undersecretary's view, Saddam's apparent bluffing about WMD to keep the Iranians and Kurds at bay was his problem, not America's. As for America's problem, Feith believed that the United States had historically projected to the outside world a feckless materialism, an unwillingness to die for a cause. At long last, America had proved the world wrong. Saddam had thought the United States was a paper tiger; now he sat in prison awaiting his execution.

As Feith would later say, "We went to war for a reason: to get rid of Saddam and his sons and the threats they posed. And we should take credit for that."

Feith himself had never served in combat. His two visits to Iraq after the invasion exposed him only minimally to the tragedies of war. For the undersecretary, sending sons and daughters off to fight six thousand miles away was justifiable even if Saddam Hussein did not possess WMD and even if he did not have a relationship with Al Qaeda. The dictator was, by his past deeds and by his recent rhetoric, a threat to the region and an offending object to the United States. His removal by force was a good thing. America deserved credit.

Feith would later protest, over and over, that it had never been his animating desire to install Ahmad Chalabi as Iraq's new leader. He simply did not wish to see "Saddamism without Saddam." Feith's objective was to remove the threat. What came after was important, but was not the motive or justification for the war. In this manner, the undersecretary belied the term "neoconservative." It had in fact rankled Feith that the theme of President Bush's May 24, 2004, speech on Iraq at the U.S. Army War College was "helping construct a stable democracy after decades of dictatorship."[148] As he argued in a memo to Rumsfeld, "democracy for Iraqis" was *not* "the strategic rationale for war." What if democracy in Iraq failed, just as the search for weapons had failed?[149]

For all the controversy that Doug Feith generated during his four years as undersecretary for policy, he left the Pentagon citing the most banal of Washington exit lines: to spend more time with his family.[150] In his retirement speech at the Pentagon on August 8, 2005, Feith quoted a little-known stanza from Francis Scott Key's "Star-Spangled Banner:" *Then conquer we must, when our cause it is just . . .*

"This is a striking line," Feith then told the audience. "It drives home that what makes America great is that Americans are not supposed to assume, uncritically, that everything we do as a country is wise and just."[151]

Thus consigning his work to the judgment of history, the undersecretary thanked his colleagues, exited stage right, and, with his family, spent his retirement shuttling between two houses, one in Bethesda and the other in Jerusalem.

ONE AFTERNOON IN AUGUST 2006, MARGARET HENOCH, OF THE CIA, WAS walking from the agency parking lot at Langley headquarters when a car pulled up and a familiar figure stepped out.

"What are you doing here?" George Tenet called out.

Henoch smiled at her retired boss. "The better question is: What are *you* doing here?" she asked.

"They let me keep an office here," Tenet said.

The former European group chief and the ex-director made small talk for a few minutes. After the crashing and burning of the Curveball episode, Henoch's warnings had been vindicated and she had received a promotion. Still, she had not forgotten the dismissiveness of her superiors and the senior BW analyst named Beth. None of them had been penalized for their errors. Not a single head rolled at the CIA in the wake of the sweeping intelligence failures. On the contrary, Tenet had received his Presidential Medal of Freedom, John McLaughlin had been elevated to acting director, and career paths for their subordinates continued to be dictated by bureaucratic vagaries, as before.

Henoch told Tenet that after twenty-three years in the agency, she was thinking about retiring soon. Perhaps she would take a job on Capitol Hill.

The former House Intelligence Committee staff director shook his head. "You'd hate the Hill," he said. "And they'd hate you." Henoch laughed, knowing that this was a salute to her bluntness, about which she had never made any apologies.

Then Tenet said, "Whatever you do, you have to stay true to yourself."

Somewhat taken aback by his seriousness, she replied, "I think I always do."

Said the former director wistfully, "I wish I had."[152]

IT IS A TRUISM THAT THERE IS LITTLE TO PREPARE ONE FOR THE UNIQUE experience of the presidency, thus requiring that the officeholder do most of

his or her learning on the job. By the end of 2006, George W. Bush had
learned quite a bit. He had at last fired Rumsfeld, one day after losing both
the House and the Senate in the November midterms. (Bush timed this decision to avoid the appearance of having political motivations, to the chagrin
of his fellow Republicans, who felt that the delay had cost them several Senate seats.) His reliance on the vice president had noticeably declined, as had
the insecurity that drew Bush to Cheney in the first place. (In his memoir,
Bush would divulge that he had momentarily considered Cheney's offer to
remove him from the ticket in 2004—in part because of the "myth that Dick
was actually running the White House. . . . Accepting Dick's offer would be
one way to demonstrate that I was in charge.")[153]

On January 10, 2007, Bush announced to the nation that the deteriorat-
ing situation in Iraq warranted a dramatic surge of twenty thousand U.S.
troops into the country. The change in strategy was not surprising. After all,
the prospect of withdrawing the American presence in Iraq, being an implicit admission of defeat, was anathema to who Bush was. But the deliber-
ateness by which he came to the decision, with attention to and ownership
of every particular detail, contrasted sharply with the detached means by
which he had decided to invade Iraq in the first place.[154]

A month before the surge announcement, Bush told this author, "I've got
Iraq on my mind. A *lot*. You know, every day I see the casualties, I get the
reports—I am *immersed* in this war."[155] Unspoken but implied was that this
immersion was a new development, tragically overdue.

Bush's belatedness in taking charge of the Iraq War fed into a narrative
that had begun to take hold in early 2005, after the newly reelected president—
perceiving himself to be loaded up with political capital that he could not
wait to spend—promptly bungled a major legislative initiative to partially
privatize Social Security. In August of that year, Hurricane Katrina breached
the levees of New Orleans and laid waste to the city, with the Bush administration's response lagging days behind the unfolding catastrophe.

Together, these events conveyed the image of an incompetent administration. Such a portrayal was understandably galling to the Harvard Business
School graduate who had sworn off alcohol and endured the grind of two

presidential campaigns, who insisted on rigorous punctuality and on proper White House decorum, who had seen a nation through trauma without once giving away his own rattled nerves. Bush was outraged by *The Washington Post*'s characterization of his tenure as "The Imperiled Presidency" and refused to sit for interviews with Peter Baker, the 2007 series's award-winning correspondent who subsequently wrote an acclaimed book about the Bush administration, *Days of Fire*.

But the architecture of his errors now loomed over Bush's presidency. It was he who had selected Donald Rumsfeld, who had been out of government for a quarter of a century. It was he who had been insufficiently attentive to the threat posed by Osama bin Laden. It was he who internalized the evidence-free claims by Paul Wolfowitz and others that Saddam likely had a hand in the 9/11 attacks. And then it was he, above all others, who promoted the spectacle of the Iraqi dictator handing over his imaginary weapons to a group of terrorists so as to fulfill the imaginary ambition of destroying America. It was the president's imagination that had run fatally wild.

It was Bush, the commander in chief, who saw no need for rigorous debate among his war council. Not on the advisability and necessity of invading Iraq. Not on the composition of the invasion force. Not on what would follow the invasion.

Bush, more than anyone else in the administration—more even than Wolfowitz—lived by the unassailable credo that all humans deserved to be free. Proceeding from that belief were several unfortunate leaps of logic. Iraqis yearned for freedom above all else. All sectarian grievances would give way to the desire to preserve a free Iraq. The Middle East would take note of this new blossoming; its deserts would erupt in a flowering of freedom. And along the way, to any tactical question, freedom served as the strategic answer.

This impulse would persist throughout his presidency. But by 2007, Bush had come to recognize that it would take more than the hunger for freedom to fix the quagmire in Iraq. That year, the president named Ryan Crocker the U.S. ambassador to Iraq. The longtime habitué of troubled countries had last been to Baghdad in 2004, when Iraq's condition was decidedly shaky. Three years later, he would recall, "it was for all the world as if I had landed in Beirut in 1983. The same guys were dishing it out to us—the Iranians and Syrians."

On Crocker's first NSC videoconference from Baghdad, the ambassador offered up his dour assessment. "I've now met with all the senior members of Iraq's national unity government," he began. "Here are my preliminary thoughts. It's by no means national. It's the antithesis of unified. And it doesn't pass any test of government."

Steve Hadley, now Bush's national security adviser, called Crocker the next day. "The president wants you to speak your mind," Hadley said. "But did it have to be so negative on the first call?"

At the next meeting by SVTC, Bush peered up at the monitor. "Okay, what have you got for me today, Sunshine?" he said to Crocker.[156]

But Bush's joke was not as pointed as it would have been four or even three years earlier. Ryan Crocker was encountering, in 2007, a president whose earlier preoccupation with sunshine had all but stricken him blind. Now, with Crocker as his chief diplomat and General David Petraeus as his surge commander, Bush could count on two flashlights to serve as reliable if belated beacons of truth.

Still, even the way out of the darkness did not open up onto the panorama of democracy in the Middle East that Bush had envisioned as the "fantastic opportunity" presented by the September 11 attacks. Democratic regimes would not spring up in the region during his presidency. (The only other country in the Middle East to introduce elections, Palestine, elevated the Islamic extremist group Hamas to power in 2006.) Elsewhere, democracies would fall rather than rise, in somber counterpoint to the "freedom agenda" that Bush hoped to inaugurate with his second term.

The war in Iraq would claim more than 4,400 American lives, wounding over 32,000. As many as 300,000 of the 1.5 million U.S. troops who served in Iraq would return home suffering from post-traumatic stress disorders. The effort that Wolfowitz imagined would be paid for with Iraqi oil, that Rumsfeld could not fathom costing a billion dollars, would ultimately exceed $2 trillion.[157]

The toll was heaviest for the liberated. An estimated 405,000 Iraqis would die as a result of the 2003 invasion.[158] Instead of Saddam, Iraq now had other forces of Sunni brutality. First there was Zarqawi, the leader of Al Qaeda in Iraq; and later would come the Islamic State, commonly known as ISIS. Though participatory democracy had more or less taken root, the dominant motif in Iraq was not freedom, as Bush had hoped, but rather violence, instability, and unending recrimination.

In 2008, the final year of his presidency, Bush at last invited Saddam Hussein's three interrogators to the Oval Office to hear what they had learned about his former adversary. John Nixon volunteered that he had seen the dictator the evening he was helicoptered into Baghdad from his spider hole.

"So what was he like?" the president asked. "Did he know he was going to be executed?"

Then Bush asked, "Why didn't he just take the deal we offered him?"

The question was put casually. But its poignancy was not lost on Nixon. By asking it, the president was in effect saying: *Saddam could have saved himself. Everything that's happened—Saddam could've saved us from all this.*[159]

DURING THE LAST WEEK OF GEORGE W. BUSH'S PRESIDENCY, A HILL STAFFER named Michael Briggs who served as the communications director for Vermont senator Bernie Sanders happened to be walking through the National Portrait Gallery. He stopped to gaze at the new oil-on-canvas depiction of the forty-third president of the United States. Though gray-haired and etched with wrinkles from eight years in office, Bush still looked vigorous and confident in his blue shirtsleeves.

What gave Briggs pause, however, was the accompanying plaque. It described Bush's presidency as one that took place during "the attacks on September 11, 2001, that led to wars in Afghanistan and Iraq."

That afternoon, Briggs drafted a letter for Senator Sanders to send to the National Portrait Gallery's director. "When President Bush and Vice President Cheney misled our country into war with Iraq," the letter said, "they certainly cited the attacks on September 11, along with the specious claim that Iraq possessed vast arsenals of weapons of mass destruction. The notion, however, that 9/11 and Iraq were linked, or that one 'led to' the other, has been widely and authoritatively debunked."

The gallery director immediately agreed to change the wording. To Sanders, the lesson was plain. "We have got to get our history right," he said.[160]

But the plaque had the history right the first time. In his mind, the president saw the link, a red line eighteen months and six thousand miles long. He would never unsee it.

IN THE DOWNTOWN OFFICE BUILDING OF A WASHINGTON THINK TANK called the Center for Strategic and International Studies, about eighty defense specialists took their seats one morning in May 2019 to listen to scholars and journalists discuss the Army War College's recently published postmortem of the Iraq War. The 1,500-page, two-volume anthology, drawing on interviews from virtually every key player in the Bush administration—including the president, but not including Secretary of Defense Donald Rumsfeld—amounted to a dispassionate but jarring indictment of how the war, particularly its post-conflict operations, had been prosecuted.

Paul Wolfowitz arrived ten minutes into the presentation. He was alone, a seventy-five-year-old man wearing a somewhat ill-fitting blue suit and a hearing aid in his right ear. Wolfowitz had arrived on foot from the American Enterprise Institute, a prominent conservative think tank where he was now a visiting scholar. AEI had awarded the post to him after his three decades of government service ended ignobly, in July 2007, when his tenure as director of the World Bank was cut short by the disclosure that he had assisted his female companion in obtaining a well-paying federal job.

Wolfowitz was still lionized in some conservative quarters, but hardly in all of them. He had publicly supported Hillary Clinton over Donald Trump in 2016. His aggressive foreign policy idealism had, for the moment at least, fallen out of favor. And to the larger public, Paul Wolfowitz was something of an obscure demigod, a comic book supervillain for the left, just as Saddam Hussein had once been to Wolfowitz—the architect of a fiasco, a neocon cabalist, a burlesque vampire memorably rendered in slow motion, wetting his comb with his own saliva, in the Michael Moore documentary *Fahrenheit 9/11*.

The sentimentalism that had blotted Wolfowitz's vision about a liberated Iraq remained with him after things went south. Quietly, with no entourage except a military aide, he often visited Section 60 of Arlington National Cemetery, where the fallen U.S. soldiers in Iraq and Afghanistan were buried. And after these visits, Wolfowitz would head north, to the Walter Reed National Military Medical Center, in Bethesda. The veterans who had lost their limbs were accustomed to seeing celebrity visitors take a perfunctory lap through Walter Reed. The blue-ribbon guests would speak a few clumsy words, then pose for photos with the amputees that would wind up on their personal websites. Wolfowitz visited at least three days a week and never brought a camera. He lingered by their bedsides and asked the recovering soldiers if they were getting all they needed. He invited them to come to his house for steak dinners as soon as they were released. As it turned out, Wolfowitz would make good on his offer.

On the afternoon of January 31, 2005, the soon-to-be-departed deputy secretary entered the room of a former Army helicopter pilot he often visited, Captain Tammy Duckworth. Two months earlier, Duckworth had been severely wounded when several RPGs fired by Iraqi insurgents hit her Black Hawk helicopter. She had lost both of her legs.

Wolfowitz had brought photographs. They were from the previous day's parliamentary election in Iraq, the first electoral contest since the fall of Saddam Hussein. Duckworth stared at the images of women in hijabs standing in line at polling places, of Iraqis proudly holding up their purple index fingers to indicate their new status as voters. Then her vision went blurry with tears as Wolfowitz said to the future U.S. senator, "You made this happen."[161]

Notably, Wolfowitz was the only member of the Bush administration in attendance at the Army War College presentation. As the speakers carried on, the former professor sat quietly in the back, scratching out notes on a white legal pad. Studiously, he scribbled as one of the scholars argued—twisting a memorable phrase of Rumsfeld's—that the Bush administration should have known that "you go to war with the enemy you have, not the enemy you want." The former deputy secretary of defense folded his arms around his chest but otherwise said nothing when a veteran journalist observed that "this idea of a short, winnable war was a fiction." When the same journalist recounted how "a senior officer in Al Anbar province saw a rising insurgency but said he couldn't say that, because civilian leadership in the Pentagon won't allow it," Wolfowitz seemed to jot down every word.

One of the speakers erroneously stated that the foolhardy disbandment of the Iraqi army had been the brainchild of "Paul Wolfowitz, the undersecretary for policy." Wolfowitz emphatically shook his head. (She meant Doug Feith.) More galling to him, however, was when an audience member asked whether Iraqi exiles like Ahmad Chalabi had ever been given an opportunity to lend assistance on the ground.

"Well, there was an initial effort," the speaker, Army War College professor Jeanne Godfroy, answered. "It was called the FIF—Free Iraqi Forces. They were given a chance, but it didn't work out so well."

After the event, Wolfowitz dutifully applauded with everyone else. On his way out the door, he saw a familiar face: an Iraqi American named Kadhim al-Waeli. The forty-six-year-old Shiite native of southern Iraq had fled the country after the Gulf War and wound up in the refugee camp in Saudi Arabia that then-Undersecretary Wolfowitz had helped establish. Al-Waeli ultimately made his way to East St. Louis. In late 2002, he volunteered for the FIF—where, he was told, the objective would be to liberate Iraq and install Ahmad Chalabi as the country's new leader.

"Kadhim," Wolfowitz called out. "Why don't you go tell her what the FIF did? How you saved a battle from breaking out at the Shrine of Imam Ali?"

Wolfowitz was referring to a confrontation, three weeks into the invasion, when U.S. troops approached the fabled thousand-year-old mosque in Najaf and were then surrounded by suspicious Shiite men who began to throw stones. Al-Waeli, of the FIF, happened to be embedded with the battalion as a cultural guide; he convinced them to drop to one knee and lower their weapons. In this way bloodshed had been averted.[162]

It was a small episode in an epic eight-year war, barely even qualifying as a blip. Four months later, a bomb outside the mosque in Najaf would claim the lives of more than 125 Iraqis. The UN headquarters explosion, the Abu Ghraib prison scandal, the grisly battle of Fallujah, the bombing of the Samarra mosque—these scarifying events would describe the sickly cascade until 2007, when the surge and the Sunni Awakening at last began to stanch four years of continual bloodshed.

Still: for that single moment at the Shrine of Imam Ali, things had proceeded in Iraq just as Paul Wolfowitz had always prescribed them. Staring at the muscle of America, the Iraqis had seen benevolence. And there had been peace. That, in his imagination, had always been the point of this war. Peace.

NOTE ON SOURCES AND ACKNOWLEDGMENTS

═══

In attempting to reconstruct any event that took place more than a decade ago, a journalist inevitably confronts frail memories—but also memories that have been rearranged, sometimes unintentionally, to conform to the public's judgment of that event. That phenomenon particularly holds true when the event in question is one as controversial as the decision to invade Iraq.

It's nonetheless a fact that this book could not have been written without the indispensable contributions of more than three hundred individuals who took part in the Iraq saga in one manner or another. I'm deeply gratified by the willingness of several key actors—Colin Powell, Richard Armitage, Condoleezza Rice, Steve Hadley, Paul Wolfowitz, Douglas Feith, Eric Edelman, George Tenet, John McLaughlin, General Richard Myers, General Gregory Newbold, General Jay Garner, Paul Bremer, Dan Bartlett, and Ari Fleischer, among others—to revisit their important roles in the Iraq narrative. No doubt doing so yet again was fatiguing. Their participation in this project was anything but rote, however. I'm especially grateful to Edelman for helping to demystify the activities of the Office of the Vice President, and to Fleischer for providing his detailed notes of a few important White House meetings.

While books may gain a certain prestige from the participation of blue-ribbon sources, it's axiomatic among journalists that the most reliable information often comes from those operating in the middle tiers—the actual doers who were in a position to know a great deal but who do not have legacies to protect. This book's greatest debt is therefore to the many dozens who worked in the Department of Defense, Department of State, National Security Council, Office of the Vice President, and the intelligence community during the run-up to war and elected to share their historical insights and recollections in these pages for the first time.

Among the latter, I want to express deepest thanks to the roughly seventy former analysts, case officers, station chiefs, and middle- and upper-management officials of the Central Intelligence Agency with whom I spoke. Five former CIA employees deserve special mention for their wisdom and endless patience: Jane Green, the Iraq group chief in the Directorate of Intelligence, Office of Near Eastern and South Asian Analysis; Bill McLaughlin, who worked in Green's division after serving as a UN weapons inspector; Luis Rueda, the chief of the Iraq Operations Group in the Directorate of Operations; Jerry Watson, a biological weapons analyst in the agency's Weapons Intelligence, Nonproliferation and Arms Control Center (WINPAC); and Bill Harlow, who served as the agency's director of communications. I also want to thank former Defense Intelligence Agency senior intelligence officer Gary Greco for his early and sustained support.

I undertook to convince as many sources as possible to be interviewed on the record—and was delighted to find a number who required no convincing at all. Inevitably, however, the sensitive nature of intelligence-gathering and presidential decision-making required that I honor the wishes of many that they be allowed to speak only "on background." I have also respected the wishes of a small handful who refused to be identified as sources in any manner and would speak only off the record. In those interviews, we proceeded with the understanding that I could use the material only if I independently confirmed it with a second source, without having divulged who my initial source was.

I should also acknowledge here this book's most prominent non-interviewee: President George W. Bush. Though apparently displeased with my 2007 biography *Dead Certain: The Presidency of George W. Bush*, for which he had cooperated extensively, he did not protest when other senior White House officials spoke to me for this project. I'm grateful for their help—which, in addition to my own knowledge of the president (owing to my previous years of proximity to him), has yielded a portrayal of George W. Bush in these pages that I hope will be thoroughly recognizable to those who knew him.

For this book, I made extensive use of government documents that have only recently been released to the public. Among the most useful of these are the fruit of numerous Freedom of Information Act requests by the heroic National Security Archive at George Washington University, as well as the staggering volume of declassified British government documents and testimony from the UK's Iraq Inquiry, also known as the Chilcot Report. The voluminous *Iraqi Perspectives Project*—a meticulously assembled collection of documents captured in Baghdad after the invasion—was released by the Institute for Defense Analyses in 2007 and was immensely helpful in my research. So, too, was the Army War College's remarkably candid two-volume anthology *The U.S. Army in the Iraq War*, published in January 2019. Among U.S. government investigative products, three publications stand out: the report of the 9/11 Commission, which principally concerns the attacks on the American homeland; the 2005 WMD Commission report co-chaired by Laurence H. Silberman and Charles S. Robb; and the succession of Iraq-related reports generated between 2004 and 2006 by the Senate Select Committee on Intelligence. These government-sponsored compilations are invaluable. It must be said, however, that much documentary information on Iraq continues to be withheld, for reasons that do not in any way appear to serve the public interest.

Though my ambition is for this book to serve as a fresh and important accounting of an immensely consequential foreign policy decision, I freely acknowledge a considerable debt to the many books on the Iraq War that precede mine. The most famous of these is Bob Woodward's one-of-a-kind

2004 opus *Plan of Attack: The Definitive Account of the Decision to Invade Iraq*, with its headline-grabbing contemporaneous interviews of the administration's principal characters, including Bush. Woodward's former colleague at *The Washington Post*, Thomas E. Ricks, produced in 2007 his own brilliant chronicle, *Fiasco: The American Military Adventure in Iraq*. Ricks's book was a narrative game-changer then and remains a classic today. George Packer's *The Assassins' Gate: America in Iraq* represents the best of that legendary journalist's work. *Cobra II: The Inside Story of the Invasion and Occupation of Iraq*, by Michael R. Gordon and Bernard E. Trainor, contains important reporting and is assiduously fair. Perhaps the most underrated feat of book-length journalism on the subject is David Corn and Michael Isikoff's 2007 epic *Hubris: The Inside Story of Spin, Scandal, and the Selling of the Iraq War*, which covered more territory and penetrated layers of intelligence more deeply than any other book published at the time. I'm genuinely grateful for the seminal work accomplished by all these gifted journalists.

I would also be remiss if I didn't express sincere gratitude for the essential newspaper and magazine reporting furnished in the lead-up to and aftermath of the war, by titans of the profession such as James Kitfield, Nicholas Lemann, Seymour Hersh, Dexter Filkins, James Risen, Thom Shanker, David Sanger, Elisabeth Bumiller, David Barstow, Bill Broad, Jeff Gerth, Peter Baker, Barton Gellman, Karen DeYoung, Joby Warrick, Dana Priest, Walter Pincus, and—please, let's not forget—the small but fearless Iraq team at Knight Ridder: Warren Strobel, Jonathan Landay, Joe Galloway, and John Walcott. And though memoirs are by design self-serving, there was much I found useful in the autobiographical works of George W. Bush, Donald Rumsfeld, Dick Cheney, Condoleezza Rice, Colin Powell, George Tenet, Michael Morell, Bill Burns, and (perhaps above all) Doug Feith.

The Iraq saga was a moving target during the time I was researching *Dead Certain* between late 2004 and early 2007—and, to be honest, I felt that my authorial efforts were best expended burrowing into Bush's West Wing rather than attempting to compete against the likes of Woodward, Ricks, Packer, Gordon, et al. Questions relating to Iraq gnawed at me in the decade to follow. When and how had Bush decided? Did the intelligence ultimately matter? Could anyone or anything have talked him out of the decision? In the late summer of 2017, it was Lawrence Wright, the esteemed *New Yorker* journalist, who suggested that I return to the topic of Iraq. After about five seconds of consideration, I decided that Larry's idea would be my next book project—and that I would do well to study the deep reporting and restrained elegance of his Pulitzer Prize–winning work *The Looming Tower: Al Qaeda and the Road to 9/11* as a model for my own approach.

It took my literary agent of more than two decades, Sloan Harris of International Creative Management, only slightly longer than it took me before agreeing that this was a worthy undertaking. Sloan's significance in my life is not fully measurable in contracts, dollars, or glasses of wine. I'm so lucky to have his friendship.

My relationship with Penguin Press is much newer but no less fortunate. Penguin Press's former executive editor Warren Bass showed such enthusiasm for my book idea, not to mention such expertise on the subject of Iraq (he was a former State Department aide and 9/11 Commission investigator), that I could not see myself saying no to Ann Godoff's legendary publishing outfit. When Warren decided to return to daily journalism midway into my research, my sorrow was instantly assuaged by the news that my new editor would be the great Scott Moyers. Scott and I had nearly collaborated on salvaging another writer's book back in 2011; later, I watched with envy as talented colleagues like Joshua Green and Mark Leibovich became Moyers's authors. Now I find my book benefiting from the thoughtful support of two editors. Talking through this book in full with Scott—title, structure, characters, narrative pacing—has been one of the great pleasures of my writing career. His guidance was augmented at Penguin Press by Scott's wonderfully efficient assistant editor, Mia Council. Will Palmer did an absolutely superb job copyediting the manuscript, as did Celeste Phillips with her discerning litigator's eyes. I'm additionally grateful to Penguin publicist Gail Brussel and marketing director Danielle Plafsky for their energetic efforts. Two good friends also merit shout-outs: Tom Rollins, for lending his critical eye to the first draft; and Matt Berninger, for cowriting the song by the National, "Start a War," that inspired my book's title.

I am seldom described as a cheery optimist, but every day I rejoice at having somehow fulfilled my childhood dream of writing for a living. It's an immense privilege, not to mention an enormous responsibility, and I try never to take any of it for granted. The love and support I've been shown from day one by my family—my almost mythically wonderful parents, Bob and Claire Draper; my brother and best friend John; my deceased older brother Eli—have sustained me all my life. A few months before this book was published, my father died at the age of eighty-nine. It is still too early for me to put into words how profoundly his fundamental decency has inspired me.

When I set out to become a writer, few else believed in me, with good reason, because frankly I sucked. Still, I found crucial support during my ignominious freelance years from literary pals like Bob Simmons, Ed Ward, Jan Reid, Joe Nick Patoski, Lee Smith, Hal Crowther, and Alan Cheuse. After a plucky agent named Madeleine Morel and a terrific editor at Doubleday, Paul Bresnick, took a chance and conspired to make a published author out of me, I was hired as a staff writer by Gregory Curtis, the editor in chief of *Texas Monthly*. I absorbed more from Greg and that magazine's uncanny roster of writing talent in my first six months on staff than I have ever learned about narrative writing before or since.

All that said, a writer needs friends. In addition to those I've already mentioned, this book benefits from the camaraderie and wisdom supplied by these ink-spattered eminences: Peter Baker, Julia Ioffe, Paul Kane, Mark Salter, Mark Leibovich, Susan Dominus, Mimi Swartz, Pam Colloff, Frances and Ed Mayes, Allan Gurganus, Jim Shahin, Mike Paterniti, Sara Corbett, Manuel Roig-Franzia, and Ann Hornaday. I've also been lucky to work for more than a decade now at two of the most esteemed magazines in America: *The New York Times Magazine*, under Jake Silverstein and Charles Homans; and *National Geographic*, under Susan Goldberg and John Hoeffel. I count Susan, John, Jake, and Charlie as not just talented editors but also friends whose encouragement and patience have meant the world to me.

The experience of writing this book over a furiously compressed six-month period was made strangely joyous because of where I accomplished it: in the Washington, D.C., home I share with my fiancée, Kirsten Powers, and our canine progeny. My long hours seven days a week on the top floor of our townhouse—half-engulfed in interview transcripts, with our sixteen-year-old Lhasa apso, Ellie, snoring at my feet—were serenely abided by Kirsten throughout. More than that: she was, and remains, an inspiration so encompassing that merely dedicating this book to her, as I've done, seems a woefully inadequate expression of my love and appreciation. She has made this book, and so many other things, possible.

NOTES

Chapter One: *Idée Fixe*

1. Paul Wolfowitz, interview with the author.
2. Donald Rumsfeld, *Known and Unknown: A Memoir* (New York: Sentinel, 2011), 334.
3. Donald Rumsfeld, "Remarks at Pentagon's Riverfront Entrance," September 10, 2004.
4. Rumsfeld, *Known and Unknown*, 338.
5. Peter Chiarelli, personal account, in *Then Came the Fire: Personal Accounts from the Pentagon, 11 September 2001*, ed. Stephen J. Lofgren (Washington, D.C.: Center of Military History, 2011), 100–103, https://apps.dtic.mil/dtic/tr/fulltext/u2/a562210.pdf.
6. Wolfowitz interview.
7. "Raven Rock Mountain Complex," White House Info, https://whitehouse.gov1.info/raven-rock/index.html.
8. Wolfowitz interview.
9. Fred Baumann (classmate of Wolfowitz), interview with author.
10. Wolfowitz interview.
11. Baumann interview.
12. Gerald M. Boyd, "Indonesia Bars Two Journalists in Reagan Party," *New York Times*, April 30, 1986.
13. Paul Wolfowitz, "A Conversation with Paul Wolfowitz," Miller Center, University of Virginia, October 26, 2009.
14. Wolfowitz interview.
15. Ibid.
16. Interview with former Defense Department official.
17. Wolfowitz interview.
18. Richard Cheney, "Richard B. Cheney Oral History, Secretary of Defense," Presidential Oral Histories, Miller Center, University of Virginia, March 16–17, 2000.
19. Cheney Oral History, Miller Center.

20. Wolfowitz interview.
21. Michael R. Gordon and General Bernard E. Trainor, *Cobra II: The Inside Story of the Invasion and Occupation of Iraq* (New York: Pantheon, 2006), 12.
22. George H. W. Bush, "Remarks to Raytheon Missile Systems Plant Employees in Andover, Massachusetts," February 15, 1991, https://bush41library.tamu.edu/archives/public-papers/2711.
23. George H. W. Bush, press conference, White House, March 1, 1991, https://www.c-span.org/video/?16868-1/status-events-persian-gulf&start=398.
24. Wolfowitz interview; interview with former Defense Department official.
25. Kanan Makiya, interview with the author.
26. School of Advanced International Studies, Johns Hopkins University, "President Bush Nominates SAIS Dean Paul Wolfowitz as Deputy Secretary of Defense," press release, February 4, 2001, https://sais.jhu.edu/content/president-bush-nominates-sais-dean-paul-wolfowitz-deputy-secretary-defense.
27. Laurie Mylroie, *Study of Revenge: The First World Trade Center Attack and Saddam Hussein's War Against America* (Washington, D.C.: AEI Press, 2000), xvii–xviii. Also mentioned in her acknowledgments are Francis Brooke, the lobbyist for Ahmad Chalabi's Iraqi National Congress; David Wurmser, who would work for both Doug Feith in the Defense Department and Scooter Libby in the Office of the Vice President; and John Bolton, whom Cheney arranged to have hired by Colin Powell's State Department.
28. Laurie Mylroie, "The World Trade Center Bomb: Who Is Ramzi Yousef? And Why It Matters," *National Interest,* Winter 1995/96.
29. Interviews with two FBI agents investigating the 1993 World Trade Center bombing.
30. Wolfowitz interview.
31. Discussion participant, interview with the author.
32. Paul Wolfowitz and Zalmay Khalilzad, "Overthrow Him," *Weekly Standard,* December 1, 1997, https://www.weeklystandard.com/zalmay-m-khalilzad-and-paul-wolfowitz/overthrow-him.
33. Paul Wolfowitz, statement at House National Security Committee Hearings on Iraq, September 16, 1998.
34. Paul Wolfowitz, remarks in the Senate, *Congressional Record,* March 2, 1998, S1180.
35. Joe Ralston, interview with the author.
36. Condoleezza Rice, interview with the author; Condoleezza Rice, *No Higher Honor: A Memoir of My Years in Washington* (New York: Crown, 2011), 3.
37. Wolfowitz interview.
38. Ibid.
39. Ari Fleischer, interview with the author; Wolfowitz interview; "Army Recalling China-Made Black Berets," *New York Times,* May 2, 2001.
40. Wolfowitz interview.
41. John Batiste, interview with the author; interview with Defense Intelligence Agency intelligence official.
42. Batiste interview; Richard Clarke, interview with the author; Paul Kurtz, interview with the author; Roger Cressey, interview with the author.
43. Austin Yamada, interview with the author.
44. Interview with Bush administration official.
45. Wolfowitz, Libby, Perle, and Khalilzad were all signatories to a petition calling for Saddam's removal by the Project for the New American Century. Feith, Wolfowitz, Khalilzad, Luti, and Wurmser were among those who signed a similar 1998 petition circulated by the Committee for Peace and Security in the Gulf.

46. Danielle Pletka, interview with the author.
47. George W. Bush, first Bush-Gore presidential debate, Boston, October 3, 2000.
48. Zaab Sethna (Iraqi National Congress senior staffer), interview with the author.
49. Interview with Bush administration official.
50. Gary Greco, interview with the author. The email was retrieved by another intelligence official and read to the author.
51. George Tenet with Bill Harlow, *At the Center of the Storm: My Years at the CIA* (New York: HarperCollins, 2007), 177.
52. Interview with meeting participant #1.
53. Interview with meeting participant #2; Gordon and Trainor, *Cobra II*, 18.
54. Interview with meeting participant #3; Peter Baker, *Days of Fire: Bush and Cheney in the White House* (New York: Doubleday, 2013), 144.
55. Interview with meeting participant #4.
56. Cofer Black, interview with the author. Wolfowitz did not recall the exchange with Black but acknowledged that it might have happened. Black said that after the meeting broke up, Wolfowitz sat next to him at lunch and engaged in light conversation, asking Black where he had gone to college.
57. Meeting participant #1 interview; Colin Powell, interview with the author. Black recalled that Bush said "it" rather than Iraq, though the president clearly was referring to Iraq.
58. Hugh Shelton, *Without Hesitation: The Odyssey of an American Warrior* (New York: St. Martin's Press, 2010), 444.
59. Richard Myers, interview with the author. Also Richard Myers with Malcolm McConnell, *Eyes on the Horizon: Serving on the Front Lines of National Security* (New York: Threshold Editions, 2009), 166.
60. Rice, *No Higher Honor*, 86.
61. Rice interview.
62. Bill Burns, interview with the author.
63. State Department official, interview with the author.
64. Black interview.
65. Rice, *No Higher Honor*, 87.
66. Wolfowitz interview; also confirmed by one of those present. See also Gordon and Trainor, *Cobra II*, 18–19, and Bill Keller, "The Sunshine Warrior," *New York Times Magazine*, September 22, 2002.
67. Thomas E. Ricks, *Fiasco: The American Military Adventure in Iraq* (New York: Penguin Press, 2006), 6–11.
68. Gregory Newbold, interview with the author.
69. Paul Wolfowitz to Donald Rumsfeld, "War or [sic] Terror—Coordination with Joint Staff," memo, September 17, 2001.
70. Condoleezza Rice, statement to the 9/11 Commission, April 8, 2004, cited in *Final Report of the National Commission on Terrorist Attacks upon the United States* ("The 9/11 Commission Report"), (Washington, D.C.: Government Printing Office, 2004), 335.

Chapter Two: A Man in America

1. Alastair Campbell, *The Burden of Power: Countdown to Iraq—The Alastair Campbell Diaries* (London: Hutchinson, 2012), 23; Alastair Campbell, interview with the author.
2. Campbell, *Burden of Power*, 14; Campbell interview.
3. Campbell, *Burden of Power*, 13; Campbell interview.

4. Campbell, *Burden of Power,* 24; Campbell interview.
5. George W. Bush, "Address to a Joint Session of Congress and the American People," U.S. Capitol, September 20, 2001.
6. Charles Krauthammer, "The Silent Imams," *Washington Post*, November 23, 2001.
7. Interviews with two White House officials.
8. George W. Bush, "Remarks by the President at Islamic Center of Washington, D.C.," September 17, 2001, https://www.c-span.org/video/?166111-1/presidential-visit-islamic-center.
9. Brian H. Levin, statement, *Increase in Religious Hate Crimes: Hearing Before the Senate Committee on the Judiciary*, May 2, 2017.
10. Douglas Wead, interview with the author.
11. Jack Straw, interview with the author.
12. Suhail Khan (White House aide), interview with the author. Two exit polls in Florida, both pseudo-scientific even by the standards of exit polls, suggested that Bush had captured anywhere from 88 to 91 percent of that state's Muslim electorate. Alexander Rose, "How Did Muslims Vote in 2000?," *Middle East Quarterly* 8, no. 3 (Summer 2001): 13–27, https://www.meforum.org/13/how-did-muslims-vote-in-2000.
13. Hamza Yusuf Hanson, interview with the author.
14. Interview with senior intelligence official.
15. Cofer Black, interview with the author.
16. Robert Draper, *Dead Certain: The Presidency of George W. Bush* (New York: Free Press, 2007), 149–50.
17. Ari Fleischer, interview with the author. The report about a truck bomb headed for the Washington Hospital Center turned out to be false.
18. Karen Hughes (counselor to the president), interview with Scott Pelley, CBS, August 22, 2002, internal White House transcript.
19. Interview with Camp David participant. See also Michael Morell, *The Great War of Our Time: The CIA's Fight Against Terrorism* (New York: Twelve, 2015), 63.
20. Draper, *Dead Certain*, 90.
21. Robert Draper, "Favorite Son," *GQ*, September 1998.
22. Karen Hughes, *Ten Minutes from Normal* (New York: Viking, 2004).
23. White House, "Press Conference by President Bush and Russian Federation President Putin," Brdo Castle, Slovenia, June 16, 2001, https://georgewbush-whitehouse.archives.gov/news/releases/2001/06/20010618.html.
24. Morell, *Great War*, 41.
25. Interview with CIA analyst.
26. "CIA Briefs Bush on National Security," *Washington Post*, September 3, 2000.
27. John McLaughlin, interview with the author.
28. Fleischer interview.
29. Third Gore-Bush presidential debate, St. Louis, October 17, 2000, transcript.
30. Interview with senior White House official.
31. Richard Clarke, interview with the author.
32. Interview with a former CIA analyst who was a part of the agency's daily "feedback" meetings to discuss what interested those being briefed.
33. Interview with Al Qaeda analyst.
34. Ibid.
35. Interviews with four analysts from the NSC, CIA, and DIA.
36. Richard A. Clarke, *Against All Enemies: Inside America's War on Terror* (New York: Free Press, 2004), 231–32. Wolfowitz has disputed that he said this. In an interview, Clarke

stood by his writing. One of Clarke's deputies, Roger Cressey, attended the meeting in question and confirmed in an interview that Clarke's depiction was correct. A second Clarke deputy was briefed on the meeting immediately after it took place and confirmed this depiction as well.

37. Morell, *Great War*, 41.
38. This intelligence briefing was declassified in 2004 (https://fas.org/irp/cia/product /pdb080601.pdf). It has frequently been alleged that the suspects' confessions were coerced, beginning with a March 1995 inquiry by Amnesty International (see Amnesty International, MDE 17/02/95, March 23, 1995, https://www.amnesty.org/download /Documents/172000/mde170021995en.pdf). Ultimately, many of the sentences were reduced or commuted, though the fate of al-Ghazali remains unknown.
39. Interview with senior CIA analyst.
40. Al Qaeda analyst interview.
41. Morell, *Great War*, 55.
42. Geoffrey Hoon, interview with the author.
43. Hayley Watson and Frank Furedi, "Review of Existing Surveys on Public Opinion of Security," unpublished working paper, University of Kent, 2010, table: National Threat Perceptions.
44. Frank Furedi, interview with the author.
45. The prototype for the box cutter appears to have been patented by Robert Lloyd Wright, of Salem, Ohio, on May 9, 1922, patent application #US559504A.
46. Roger Cressey, interview with the author.
47. Interview with NSC official.
48. Condoleezza Rice, interview with author.
49. Fleischer interview.
50. George W. Bush, news conference, October 11, 2001, transcript.
51. George W. Bush, address before Joint Session of Congress, September 20, 2001, transcript.
52. Daniel M. Filler, "Terrorism, Panic and Pedophilia," *Virginia Journal of Social Policy & the Law* 10, no. 3 (2002): 345–82.
53. Colin Powell, interview with the author.
54. Central Intelligence Agency, "The Attack That Failed: Iraq's Attempt to Assassinate Former President Bush in Kuwait, April 1993," declassified, https://www.cia.gov/library /readingroom/docs/DOC_0000756374.pdf.
55. David Von Drehle and R. Jeffrey Smith, "U.S. Strikes Iraq for Plot to Kill Bush," *Washington Post*, June 27, 1993.
56. George W. Bush, Republican presidential candidates debate, Manchester, N.H., December 3, 1999, transcript; Fleischer interview.
57. George W. Bush, interview with Jim Lehrer, *PBS NewsHour*, February 16, 2000.
58. Condoleezza Rice, "Campaign 2000: Promoting the National Interest," *Foreign Affairs* 79, no. 1 (January/February 2000).
59. Gregory Newbold, interview with the author; Jeremiah Gertler et al., *No-Fly Zones: Strategic, Operational, and Legal Considerations for Congress*, Congressional Research Service, May 3, 2013.
60. David Sanger, interview with the author; David Sanger and Frank Bruni, "From the Ranch, President-Elect Gazes Back and Looks to Future," *New York Times*, January 14, 2001.
61. Press conference, President George W. Bush and Mexican President Vincente Fox, February 16, 2001, https://www.c-span.org/video/?162643-1/us-mexico-relations.

62. Fleischer interview; Rice, *No Higher Honor*, 27.
63. Newbold interview; Frank Miller, interview with the author.
64. Rice, *No Higher Honor*, 28.
65. Powell interview; "US and Britain Roundly Condemned over Iraq Attack," *Irish Times*, February 17, 2001.
66. Richard Haass, interview with the author; Richard Haass, *War of Necessity, War of Choice: A Memoir of Two Iraq Wars* (New York: Simon & Schuster, 2009), 181.
67. Christopher Williams to Paul Wolfowitz, "A Strategy to Liberate Iraq," memo, April 23, 2001, declassified.
68. Donald Rumsfeld to Condoleezza Rice, "Iraq," memo, July 27, 2001, declassified.
69. Doug Feith, interview with the author.
70. Morell, *Great War*, 79; Morell interview.
71. Clarke, *Against All Enemies*, 32; Richard Clarke, interview with the author. Roger Cressey was present for Bush's order and confirmed this account, as did Paul Kurtz, who was tasked by Clarke with carrying out Bush's order. The Bush White House impugned Clarke's credibility when his book was published during the 2004 election season but never denied that this took place, and Rice confirmed to CNN that the Bush administration considered Saddam "a likely suspect" in the 9/11 attacks.
72. Clarke interview; Cressey interview; Kurtz interview.
73. Kurtz interview; Clarke interview.
74. Donald Rumsfeld, *Known and Unknown: A Memoir* (New York: Sentinel, 2011), 425. In his book, Rumsfeld recalled that Bush specified that he "wanted the options to be 'creative,' which I took to mean that he wanted something different from the massive land force assembled during the 1991 Gulf War." Given Rumsfeld's distaste for massive land forces, and given Wolfowitz's September 17, 2001, memo stating that the Joint Chiefs were unlikely to conceive of a "creative" option unless it reflected the president's thinking, it would seem likely that Rumsfeld encouraged Bush to advise such a path. Bush himself has never made reference to this meeting.
75. Rice interview.
76. Bush's September 2001 public events are archived at https://georgewbush-whitehouse.archives.gov/news/releases/2001/09.
77. Fleischer interview; Ari Fleischer, *Taking Heat: The President, the Press, and My Years in the White House* (New York: William Morrow, 2005), 189.
78. David Rose and Ed Vulliamy, "Iraq Behind U.S. Anthrax Outbreaks," *Guardian*, October 14, 2001. In the story, the reporters did not name Woolsey as the source. However, Rose subsequently did so in a story that *Vanity Fair* commissioned but never published, a copy of which he supplied to the author.
79. Campbell, *Burden of Power*, 56.
80. John McCain, interview with David Letterman, *The Late Show with David Letterman*, CBS, October 18, 2001, https://www.youtube.com/watch?v=jMiDXoYJbN4.
81. White House spokesman Ari Fleischer even warned ABC News not to go with a story from its reporter Brian Ross that the anthrax had come from Saddam. Ross did so anyway on October 29, 2001. Fleischer interview.
82. John King, "Bush Vows to Wage War, Even If Public Tires," CNN, October 17, 2001.
83. George W. Bush, presidential address to the nation, October 7, 2001.
84. David Friend, interview with the author. Friend was present for the entirety of the photo shoot.
85. Interview with White House official #1.

86. Interview with White House official #2.

87. "Saddam Hussein: In His Own Words," DOD internal document, October 22, 2002.

88. Simon Webb (policy director, UK Ministry of Defence), interview with the author.

89. Frank Carlucci to Bill Burns, letters, September 27, 2001, and October 8, 2001, declassified.

90. George W. Bush, remarks to troops and families stationed at Fort Campbell, Kentucky, November 21, 2001.

91. Rumsfeld, *Known and Unknown*, 427.

92. George W. Bush, interview with Asian editors, October 16, 2001, transcript.

93. Draper, *Dead Certain*, 134.

94. Jonathan Powell (Blair's chief of staff), testimony in Chilcot Inquiry, January 18, 2010.

95. George W. Bush, remarks to the Warsaw Conference on Combatting Terrorism, via satellite from White House, November 6, 2001, transcript.

96. Draper, *Dead Certain*, 168.

97. Baker, *Days of Fire*, 186.

98. Matthew Scully (White House speechwriter), interview with the author; John McConnell (White House speechwriter), interview with the author.

99. Tommy Franks with Malcolm McConnell, *American Soldier* (New York: Regan Books, 2004), 346–54; Bob Woodward, *Plan of Attack: The Definitive Account of the Decision to Invade Iraq* (New York: Simon & Schuster, 2004), 52–64; Gene Renuart, interview with the author.

100. Interview with CIA senior official.

101. Ibid.

102. Franks, *American Soldier*, 350–51.

103. Ibid., 355–56.

104. George W. Bush and Tommy Franks, press conference, December 28, 2001, transcript.

105. CIA senior official interview.

106. George W. Bush, State of the Union address, January 29, 2002, transcript.

107. Rice, *No Higher Honor*, 150.

108. Draper, *Dead Certain*, 169.

109. Campbell, *Burden of Power*, 203.

110. George W. Bush, *Decision Points* (New York: Crown, 2010), 233.

Chapter Three: The Supervillain

1. Jeff Simons (American wrestler), interview with the author; "Jeff Simons," Hall of Fame, Illinois Wrestling Coaches and Officials Association, https://iwcoa.net/hall-of-fame-2/jeff-simons.

2. Ryan Crocker, interview with the author.

3. Peter Hahn, "A Century of U.S. Relations with Iraq," *Origins* 5, no. 7 (April 2012).

4. "Oil Take-Over Pact Announced by Iraq," *New York Times*, March 1, 1973.

5. "Soviet and Iraq in 15-Year Pact," *New York Times*, April 10, 1972.

6. Allen Keiswetter (State Department official), interview with David Ruther, Foreign Affairs Oral History Project, Association for Diplomatic Studies and Training, 2011.

7. Allen Keiswetter, interview with the author.

8. Crocker interview; Keiswetter interview.

9. A. David Fritzlan (Baghdad counselor of embassy), interview, "Iraq Country Reader," Association for Diplomatic Studies and Training, 2011, 15.

10. House Select Committee on Intelligence, Report, January 19, 1976. The full report of the so-called Pike Commission, minus its recommendations, was leaked to the Village Voice, which published lengthy excerpts in its February 19, 1976 edition.

11. Bruce Riedel, "What Iran's Revolution Meant for Iraq," *Order from Chaos* (blog), Brookings Institution, January 24, 2019.

12. Edward L. Peck (minister-counselor in Iraq), "Iraq Country Reader," Association for Diplomatic Studies and Training, 2011.

13. Crocker interview; Keiswetter interview; Christopher Straub (Pentagon official), interview with the author; Charles Tripp, *A History of Iraq* (Cambridge, UK: Cambridge University Press, 2000), 217.

14. Tripp, *History of Iraq*, 214–22.

15. Jerrold M. Post, "Saddam Hussein of Iraq: His Personality and Political Behavior," unpublished paper, September 1990. Post is a former CIA analyst.

16. Alain Barluet, "Quand Paris Courtisait le Maitre de Baghdad," *Le Figaro*, October 15, 2007.

17. Crocker interview.

18. Interview with U.S. government official.

19. UK Joint Intelligence Committee, "Saddam Hussein, Psychological Profile, Updated," November 14, 2002, declassified.

20. Post, "Saddam Hussein of Iraq"; JIC, "Saddam Hussein."

21. Jim Hoagland, "Saddam, Iraq's Suave Strongman," *Washington Post*, May 11, 1975.

22. Adel Darwish, "Why Saddam Has Cast Himself as the Godfather of Baghdad," *Telegraph*, March 21, 2003.

23. Neil Armstrong, "Oliver Reed, Saddam Hussein and the True Story of the World's Most Bizarre Film," *Telegraph*, July 24, 2016.

24. JIC, "Saddam Hussein."

25. Ibid.

26. Interview with the CIA official in question.

27. Donald Rumsfeld to Jordan embassy, "Dispatch from Rumsfeld," State Department cable, December 23, 1983, declassified.

28. Central Intelligence Agency, *Intelligence Update: Chemical Warfare Agent Issues During the Persian Gulf War*, April 2002.

29. William Eagleton to George Shultz, "Iraq Reacts Angrily to U.S. Condemnation of CW Use," State Department cable, March 7, 1984, declassified.

30. Bernard Gwertzman, "U.S. Restores Full Ties with Iraq but Cites Neutrality in Gulf War," *New York Times*, November 27, 1984.

31. Central Intelligence Agency, *Intelligence Update: Chemical Warfare*.

32. "Poison Gas: Iraq's Crime," *New York Times*, March 26, 1988.

33. Maureen Dowd, "Bush Assails Use of Chemical Weapons," *New York Times*, October 22, 1988.

34. Rolf Ekéus (UNSCOM inspector), interview with the author; Rod Barton (UNSCOM inspector), interview with the author.

35. Fred Francis, *NBC Evening News*, April 11, 1990.

36. Alan Friedman, "US Officials Ignored Objections to Dual-Use Exports to Iraq," *Financial Times*, September 19, 1990; "Iraqgate," *US News & World Report*, May 18, 1992, 42–51.

37. Robert Pear, "Khomeini Accepts 'Poison' of Ending the War with Iraq," *New York Times*, July 21, 1988.

38. Human Rights Watch, *Genocide in Iraq: The Anfal Campaign Against the Kurds* (New York: Human Rights Watch, 1993), chapter 7.
39. Interview with attendee of the NSC meeting.
40. Saddam Hussein, statement at military ceremony, April 1, 1990.
41. Skip Gnehm, interview with the author; Don Oberdorfer, "Missed Signals in the Middle East," *Washington Post*, March 17, 1991.
42. Department of State, *The Implications of the Iran-Iraq Agreement*, May 1, 1975, declassified.
43. April Glaspie to Robert Dole, "Briefing Paper," cable, April 11, 1990; Robert Dole, press conference, Tel Aviv, April 12, 1990.
44. Saddam Hussein visiting U.S. Senators, April 16, 1990, transcript provided by Baghdad Domestic Service. The translation tracks with handwritten notes taken by Dole aide Alfred Lehn. These documents, along with the itinerary of the trip, were found in the Dole Archives at the University of Kansas. Also see Jack Anderson and Dale Van Atta, "Metzenbaum and Innocence Abroad," *Washington Post*, August 14, 1990; Nick B. Williams Jr. and Daniel Williams, "Iraq Threatens Israel with Use of Nerve Gas," *Los Angeles Times*, April 3, 1990.
45. Keiswetter interview.
46. April Glaspie to James Baker, "Iraq and Terrorism," cable, June 27, 1990, declassified.
47. Transcript, meeting between Saddam Hussein and the American ambassador to Baghdad, Baghdad, July 25, 1990.
48. A remarkable reconstruction of this momentous end to Operation Desert Storm was captured by Rick Atkinson in "'A Merciful Clemency': Scenes of Enemy Slaughtered in Retreat Persuaded Powell to Put Brakes on War," *Washington Post*, October 5, 1993. The statistics related to Desert Storm are from Tyler Rogoway, "Operation Desert Storm by the Numbers on Its 25th Anniversary," *FoxTrotAlpha* (blog), *Jalopnik*, January 16, 2016.
49. Charles Duelfer (Iraq Survey Group director) to CIA, transmittal message, September 23, 2004.
50. Except where otherwise noted, the passages pertaining to UNSCOM relied on interviews with six UNSCOM inspectors and two embedded CIA analysts. Also: Hans Blix, *Disarming Iraq* (New York: Pantheon, 2004), 23–40; Charles Duelfer, *Hide and Seek* (New York: PublicAffairs, 2009), 91–161; Rod Barton, *The Weapons Detective* (Melbourne: Black Inc. Agenda, 2006), 94–288; and Mohamed ElBaradei, *The Age of Deception: Nuclear Diplomacy in Treacherous Times* (London: Bloomsbury, 2011), 9–36.
51. Robert Gallucci, address at "Understanding the Lessons of Nuclear Inspections and Monitoring in Iraq: A Ten-Year Review," Institute for Science and International Security, June 14, 2001, transcript.
52. Central Intelligence Agency, *Intelligence Update: Chemical Warfare*, April 2002.
53. "Regime Strategic Intent, Key Findings," *Comprehensive Report of the Special Advisor to the Director of Central Intelligence on Iraq's Weapons of Mass Destruction*, September 30, 2004, https://www.cia.gov/library/reports/general-reports-1/iraq_wmd_2004/Comp_Report_Key_Findings.pdf.
54. Ekéus interview.
55. Barton, *Weapons Detective*, 250.
56. Duelfer interview.
57. Interview with 661 sanctions committee member.
58. Interview with UN weapons inspector.

59. Barbara Crossette, "Iraq Orders Freeze on Arms Inspections," *New York Times*, January 22, 1998.
60. Duelfer, *Hide and Seek*, 154.
61. Barton, *Weapons Detective*, 254.
62. Duelfer interview.
63. Interview with CIA official #1.
64. Interview with CIA official #2.
65. Interview with CIA official #3.
66. Douglas Jehl, "Assassination of Shiite Cleric Threatens Further Iraqi Unrest," *New York Times*, February 22, 1999.
67. Israel Defense Forces/Military Intelligence, *Iraqi Support for and Encouragement of Palestinian Terrorism*, September 30, 2002.
68. Interview with CIA military analyst.
69. William Clinton, address to the Joint Chiefs of Staff and Pentagon staff, February 17, 1998, transcript.
70. William Cohen, remarks at town hall meeting, Ohio State University, February 18, 1998, https://1997-2001.state.gov/www/statements/1998/980218.html.
71. Iraq Liberation Act of 1998, H.R. 4655, 105th Congress, October 5, 1998.
72. Ron Paul, remarks in the House, *Congressional Record*, October 5, 1998, H9489.
73. Edward Walker to Madeleine Albright, cable, August 21, 2000, declassified; Edward Walker, interview with the author.
74. Interview with CIA analyst.
75. Brian Whitaker, "Saddam Hussein, the Great Survivor," *Guardian*, January 2, 2001; "A Decade of Deception and Defiance," White House background paper on Iraq, September 12, 2002.
76. Blix, *Disarming Iraq*, 55.
77. Carl W. Ford to Colin Powell, "Iraq—Saddam Riding Higher Than Ever," State Department INR memo, September 7, 2001, declassified.
78. Skip Gnehm to Colin Powell, "Saddam's Regime Prosperous and Confident According to [Redacted]," cable, May 16, 2002, declassified; Bob Woodruff, "Saddam Images Omnipresent at Birthday Bash," *ABC News*, April 30, 2002.

Chapter Four: "Above All, Precision!"

1. Gregory Newbold, interview with the author.
2. Interview with CIA official.
3. Interview with White House official.
4. Gene Renuart, interview with the author.
5. Interview with Bush administration official.
6. Interview with Defense Department official.
7. Defense Department official interview.
8. Pentagon briefing, October 16, 2001, transcript.
9. Pentagon briefing, October 25, 2001, transcript.
10. Mark Hertling, interview with the author.
11. Dan Bartlett, interview with the author.
12. Donald Rumsfeld, interview with Marvin Kalb, *The Kalb Report*, April 10, 2002, transcript at http://media.leeds.ac.uk/papers/vp0133fe.html.
13. *Saturday Night Live*, NBC, November 17, 2001, https://www.nbc.com/saturday-night-live/video/donald-rumsfeld-cold-opening/n11521.

14. Rumsfeld to Larry DeRita, "War on Terrorism," memo, September 23, 2001, declassified.

15. Eric Schmitt and James Dao, "The 43rd President: Choosing a Cabinet; GOP Split Slows Bush's Selection for Defense Post," *New York Times*, December 22, 2000.

16. Donald Rumsfeld, *Known and Unknown: A Memoir* (New York: Sentinel, 2011), 279–82.

17. Rumsfeld, memo, December 28, 2000.

18. Interviews with three Bush administration officials.

19. Jane Perlez, "Bush Team's Counsel Is Divided on Foreign Policy," *New York Times*, March 27, 2001; Douglas Feith, *War and Decision: Inside the Pentagon at the Dawn of the War on Terrorism* (New York: Harper, 2008), 43; Zalmay Khalilzad, *The Envoy: From Kabul to the White House, My Journey Through a Turbulent World* (New York: St. Martin's Press, 2016), 95.

20. Rumsfeld, memo, May 31, 2001.

21. Defense Department official interview.

22. Snowflakes: Rumsfeld memos dated (respectively) April 9, 2001, April 10, 2001, and August 16, 2001.

23. Defense Department official interview.

24. Handwritten note from Rumsfeld aide, September 11, 2001, 2:40 p.m., documented in *Final Report of the National Commission on Terrorist Attacks upon the United States* ("The 9/11 Commission Report"), (Washington, D.C.: Government Printing Office, 2004).

25. Interview with Bush administration official.

26. Robert Andrews (deputy undersecretary of defense for counterintelligence and security), interview with the author; "little birds": Andrews interview; Douglas Feith, interview with the author.

27. Douglas Feith to Donald Rumsfeld, "Strategic Planning Guidance for the Joint Staff," memo, September 18, 2001, declassified.

28. Defense Department official interview.

29. Ibid.

30. Bob Grenier, interview with the author; Defense Department official interview.

31. Interview with CENTCOM planner.

32. Interview with Bush administration official.

33. Donald Rumsfeld, "Transforming the Military," *Foreign Affairs*, May/June 2002.

34. Interview with CENTCOM war planner.

35. Bob Woodward, *Plan of Attack: The Definitive Account of the Decision to Invade Iraq* (New York: Simon & Schuster, 2004), 25; Colin Powell, interview with the author.

36. Interview with White House official.

37. Interviews with three Defense Department officials.

38. Interview with NSC staffer.

39. Rumsfeld, *Known and Unknown*, 322.

40. White House official interview.

41. Interview with NSC official #1.

42. Interview with NSC official #2.

43. Stephen Hadley, interview with the author.

44. Interview with Rumsfeld aide.

45. Interviews with three NSC officials and two State Department officials.

46. Interview with NSC official.

47. Feith interview.

48. Interviews with three Defense Department officials and one CIA official; "paperhanger": Rumsfeld to Rice, "PC Meeting," memo, December 13, 2001.

49. Interview with three Defense Department officials.
50. DOD official, interview with the author.
51. Rumsfeld to unspecified, memo, September 21, 2001.
52. Feith interview.
53. Ibid.
54. Interview with Pentagon official. The dynamics of Rumsfeld and the deployment book were confirmed by four other Defense Department officials.
55. Defense Department official interview.
56. Paul Wolfowitz, interview with the author.
57. Feith, *War and Decision*, 17.
58. John Abizaid, "Preparing for War After 9/11," West Point Center for Oral History, April 9, 2012, transcript. Notably, Feith's seven-page description in his book of his conversation with Abizaid omits any speculation about Iraqi involvement. When asked in an interview whether he had concluded on the plane ride that Saddam needed to be deposed, Feith replied, "No, no, no. 'Depose Saddam' goes too far."
59. Newbold interview.
60. Interview with meeting participant.
61. Interview with PCTEG member.
62. Interview with Marc Grossman.
63. Michael R. Gordon and General Bernard E. Trainor, *Cobra II: The Inside Story of the Invasion and Occupation of Iraq* (New York: Pantheon, 2006), 38–39. The authors wrote that the meeting took place on January 12, 2002, but Macgregor's memo (referred to in the next footnote) indicates that it was held one week later.
64. Interviews with three CENTCOM planners; Macgregor to unspecified, "USCENT-COM Trip Report," memo, January 19, 2002, declassified.
65. Wolfowitz to Rumsfeld, "Special Military Planning," memo, January 24, 2002, declassified.
66. Interviews with two CENTCOM planners.
67. Bob Graham, interview with the author; interview with a CENTCOM planner who debriefed Franks after the meeting with Graham; Bob Graham, *Intelligence Matters: The CIA, the FBI, Saudi Arabia, and the Failure of America's War on Terror* (New York: Random House, 2004), 123–26.

Chapter Five: The Man Who Feared Too Much

1. *Meet the Press*, NBC, September 16, 2001, transcript.
2. Interviews with three OVP passengers.
3. Dick Cheney, *In My Time: A Personal and Political Memoir* (New York: Threshold Editions, 2011), 190–93.
4. Bob Woodward, *Plan of Attack: The Definitive Account of the Decision to Invade Iraq* (New York: Simon & Schuster, 2004), 111.
5. News releases for February 2002 on the Bush White House website, https://georgewbush-whitehouse.archives.gov.
6. George W. Bush, "President Discusses Ag Policy at Cattle Industry Convention," Denver, February 8, 2002, transcript.
7. George Tenet with Bill Harlow, *At the Center of the Storm: My Years at the CIA* (New York: HarperCollins, 2007), 259.
8. Interview with OVP official.

9. Bill Burns, interview with the author, and Richard Armitage, interview with the author.

10. Michael R. Gordon, "Middle East Turmoil: Diplomacy; Cheney, in Jordan, Meets Opposition to Military Move in Iraq," *New York Times*, March 13, 2002.

11. Interview with Egypt-based American and British diplomats.

12. Douglas Jehl, "Attack on Iraq: In the Gulf; U.S. Fighters in Saudi Arabia Grounded," *New York Times*, December 19, 1998.

13. Interview with CIA Saudi Arabia specialist.

14. Interviews with two State Department officials and two OVP participants.

15. Interview with CIA analyst who gave Cheney this briefing.

16. Interview with OVP participant.

17. Interview with attendee at the NSC meeting.

18. George W. Bush and Dick Cheney, briefing to press, March 21, 2002, transcript.

19. Kevin Tebbit, interview with the author.

20. Cheney, *In My Time*, 264.

21. "Minority Report," Understanding the Iran-Contra Affairs, project at Brown University, https://www.brown.edu/Research/Understanding_the_Iran_Contra_Affair/h -thereport.php.

22. Paul Wolfowitz to Dick Cheney, "Defense Planning Guidance—Major Comments Received," memo, May 5, 1992, declassified.

23. Interviews with OVP staff.

24. Powell interview.

25. Interviews with three White House officials.

26. Interview with senior NSC staffer.

27. Stephen Hadley, interview with the author.

28. Eric Edelman, interview with the author.

29. Hadley interview.

30. Ibid.

31. Dick Cheney, *Fox News Sunday*, July 30, 2000, transcript.

32. Interview with DIA officer; confirmed by a second DIA officer.

33. Edelman interview.

34. Interview with CIA analyst #1.

35. Interview with CIA analyst #2; confirmed in interviews with two others.

36. Interview with one of Cheney's CIA briefers.

37. Interview with Oval Office briefing attendee.

38. John McLaughlin, interview with the author.

39. Cheney, *In My Time*, 385; "Dark Winter," Center for Health Security, Johns Hopkins Bloomberg School of Public Health, http://www.centerforhealthsecurity.org/our-work /events-archive/2001_dark-winter/.

40. Interviews with CIA analysts who briefed Cheney and Libby on those topics.

41. Edelman interview.

42. Dick Cheney, speech at Conservative Political Action Conference, January 30, 2003, transcript.

43. Interview with OVP official.

44. Interviews with five CIA officials and analysts. Two retrieved documents did discuss the prospects of relocating some components of Al Qaeda to northern Iraq, an area not under Saddam's control. Interview with CIA military analyst; also Carl Ford to Colin Powell, "Pros and Cons of Iraq as a bin Laden Haven," State Department INR memo, January 22, 2002.

45. Interviews with two CIA officials and one DIA official; Douglas Jehl, "Qaeda-Iraq Link U.S. Cited Is Tied to Coercion Claim," *New York Times*, December 9, 2005; Michael Isikoff, "Terror Watch: Case Decidedly Not Closed," *Newsweek*, November 18, 2003.

Chapter Six: "History Has Called Us"

1. Christopher Meyer, testimony in Chilcot Inquiry, November 23, 2011.
2. Christopher Meyer, *DC Confidential: The Controversial Memoirs of Britain's Ambassador to the U.S. at the Time of 9/11 and the Iraq War* (London: Weidenfeld & Nicolson, 2005), 217–18, 245.
3. David Manning to Tony Blair, "Your Trip to the U.S.," memo, March 14, 2002, declassified.
4. Christopher Meyer to David Manning, "Iraq and Afghanistan: Conversation with Wolfowitz," memo, March 18, 2001, declassified.
5. Christopher Meyer to David Manning, Alastair Campbell, and Jonathan Powell, "PM's Visit to Texas: Bush and the War on Terrorism," cable, April 1, 2002, declassified.
6. Interviews with three Blair administration officials.
7. Alastair Campbell, *The Burden of Power: Countdown to Iraq—The Alastair Campbell Diaries* (London: Hutchinson, 2012), 12, 23.
8. Ibid., 64.
9. William J. Burns, *The Back Channel: A Memoir of American Diplomacy and the Case for Its Renewal* (New York: Random House, 2019), 167; Bill Burns, interview with the author.
10. Bob Woodward, "CIA Told to Do 'Whatever Necessary' to Kill bin Laden," *Washington Post*, October 21, 2001.
11. The phrase "pound sand" was in wide circulation in the Bush White House following the 9/11 attacks; see William Safire, "On Language: Pound Sand," *New York Times*, March 31, 2002.
12. Blair to Bush, October 11, 2001, declassified.
13. Manning to Rice, November 8, 2001, declassified.
14. Blair to Bush, memo, December 4, 2001, declassified.
15. "The Blair Doctrine," Global Policy Forum, April 22, 1999, transcript.
16. Farish to Powell, "Iraq Coalition-Building: UK Labor Party Not Yet Convinced," cable, April 2, 2002, declassified.
17. Hoon to Blair, memo, March 22, 2002, declassified.
18. Straw to Blair, memo, March 25, 2002, declassified.
19. Meyer, *DC Confidential*, 246–48.
20. David Manning, testimony in Chilcot Inquiry, November 30, 2009, transcript; George W. Bush, *Decision Points* (New York: Crown, 2010), 232; Tony Blair, *A Journey: My Political Life* (New York: Vintage, 2011), 398–401.
21. Manning, Chilcot testimony.
22. George W. Bush, "President Bush Calls for New Palestinian Leadership," White House, June 24, 2002, transcript.
23. Elliott Abrams, interview with the author.
24. Rice, *No Higher Honor*, 144.
25. Burns to Powell, "Rice Meeting with Israelis," email, June 13, 2002, cited in Burns, *Back Channel*, 185.
26. Rice, *No Higher Honor*, 145.
27. Bush speech, September 21, 2001, transcript.
28. Campbell, *Burden of Power*, 64; Campbell interview.

29. An excellent catalog of Bush's post-9/11 use of "opportunity" can be found at 911blogger.com: http://911blogger.com/news/2007-11-10/great-opportunity-president -bush-describes-911.

30. Bush speech, June 24, 2002, transcript.

31. Interviews with two of the meeting's attendees, one of whom shared notes from the meeting.

32. Skip Gnehm, interview with the author.

33. "King and Queen Return Home," King Abdullah II official website, August 4, 2002.

34. Interview with Blair administration official.

Chapter Seven: Secret Lunches

1. Condoleezza Rice, interview with the author.

2. Rice interview.

3. Interviews with three NSC senior staffers.

4. Condoleezza Rice, *No Higher Honor: A Memoir of My Years in Washington* (New York: Crown, 2011), 82.

5. Richard Clarke, interview with the author; one of Clarke's NSC deputies confirmed this.

6. Rice, *No Higher Honor*, 18.

7. Bill Burns, interview with the author.

8. Interview with NSC aide.

9. Campbell, *The Burden of Power: Countdown to Iraq—The Alastair Campbell Diaries* (London: Hutchinson, 2012), 249.

10. Elisabeth Bumiller, *Condoleezza Rica: An American Life* (New York: Random House, 2007), 35.

11. Interview with NSC official.

12. Kenneth Pollack, interview with the author.

13. Ben Rhodes, interview with the author.

14. NSC senior staffer interview.

15. Interview with Principals Committee attendee.

16. Donald Rumsfeld to Condoleezza Rice, "Interagency Process," memo, August 20, 2002.

17. NSC senior staffer interview.

18. Rice, *No Higher Honor*, 22.

19. Richard Armitage, interview with the author.

20. NSC aide interview.

21. Interview with senior White House official.

22. Armitage interview.

23. Kevin Tebbit, interview with the author.

24. Colin Powell with Joseph Persico, *My American Journey* (New York: Random House, 1995), 261.

25. Richard Armitage, interview, *Capital Sunday*, WJLA (Washington, D.C.), October 12, 2001.

26. Donald Rumsfeld to Colin Powell, "Coalitions," memo, October 18, 2001.

27. Interview with Deputies Committee participant.

28. Interview with top NSC aide.

29. Ari Fleischer, interview with the author.

30. Interview with State Department diplomat.

31. Donald Rumsfeld to Condoleezza Rice, "NSC," memo, October 16, 2002.

32. Douglas Feith, interview with the author.

33. Interview with NSC staffer.

34. Interview with Deputies Committee participant.

35. Interviews with five Deputies Committee participants.

36. Armitage interview.

37. Interview with CIA operative.

38. Interviews with two State Department officials.

39. Interview with State Department official.

40. Interview with one of the deputies.

41. Interviews with three Deputies Lunch attendees; Douglas Feith, *War and Decision: Inside the Pentagon at the Dawn of the War on Terrorism* (New York: Harper, 2008), 237–42.

42. Frank Miller, interview with the author.

43. John McLaughlin, interview with the author.

44. Interviews with four Deputies Lunch participants.

45. McLaughlin interview.

46. Armitage interview.

47. Interviews with four Deputies Lunch participants. In his book, Feith maintained that this meeting took place in January, though he did not attend lunches until March. The other attendees believed that the lunches did not begin until later, and one of them suspected that this topic was raised in February.

48. This account, except where otherwise noted, is based on interviews with two of Chalabi's closest INC aides, Entifah Qanbar and Zaab Sethna.

49. Ahmad Chalabi, interview by Ghassan Charbel, *Al-Hayat* (London), March 28, 2009.

50. Richard Bonin, *Arrows of the Night: Ahmad Chalabi and the Selling of the Iraq War* (New York: Anchor, 2012), 57.

51. Bob Kerrey, interview with the author.

52. Stephen Rademaker, interview with the author.

53. Ahmad Chalabi, testimony to Senate Committee on Foreign Relations, March 2, 1998, transcript.

54. Bonin, *Arrows of the Night*, 193.

55. Chalabi, *Al-Hayat* interview; Jim Hoagland, interview with the author; Scott Ritter, interview with the author; Jim Hoagland and Vernon Loeb, "Tests Show Nerve Gas in Iraqi Warheads: Finding Contradicts Claims by Baghdad," *Washington Post*, June 23, 1998.

56. Krajeski to Powell, "Grossman Tells Iraqi National Congress USG Supports You but Not Inside Iraq Yet," cable, November 16, 2001, declassified.

57. Clark Kent Ervin, interview with the author.

58. General Accounting Office, *State Department: Issues Affecting Funding of Iraqi National Congress Support Foundation*, GAO-04-559, April 2004.

59. Armitage interview.

60. "U.S. Halts Support for Iraqi Exile Group," *New York Times*, January 6, 2002.

61. Yael Lempert to Colin Powell, "Grossman Meeting with INC Leadership Council," cable, February 7, 2002, declassified.

62. Donald Rumsfeld to Paul Wolfowitz, "Iraqi Exile Support," memo, January 8, 2002.

63. Stephen Hadley, interview with the author.

64. Ryan Crocker, interview with the author.

Chapter Eight: The Murky Paper

1. Susan Hasler, interview with the author.

2. John McLaughlin, interview with the author.

3. *Final Report of the National Commission on Terrorist Attacks upon the United States* ("The 9/11 Commission Report"), (Washington, D.C.: Government Printing Office, 2004), 228.
4. CIA analyst #1, personal journal, August 23, 2002.
5. Interview with CIA analyst #1.
6. Interview with CIA analyst #2.
7. Ibid.
8. Interview with CIA official #1.
9. Interview with CIA official #2.
10. Interviews with two meeting attendees.
11. McLaughlin interview.
12. Here and below, unless otherwise noted, details relating to Tenet's biography and his interactions with Bush came from interviews with more than a dozen CIA senior officials, analysts, and case officers.
13. Interviews with four CIA officials.
14. Dan Bartlett, interview with the author.
15. Interviews with two CIA officials.
16. Interviews with three CIA officials.
17. Interviews with four CIA officials.
18. Interviews with two CIA officials.
19. Interview with CIA official #3.
20. Interview with CIA official #4.
21. Interview with CIA analyst #3.
22. Dick Cheney, interview with Tim Russert, *Meet the Press*, NBC, December 9, 2001, transcript.
23. Interview with CIA analyst #4.
24. Interview with CIA official #5.
25. Interview with OVP official.
26. Interview with Defense Department official. A second DOD official, in an interview, made the same observation verbatim.
27. Interview with CIA official #6.
28. Hal Rooks, interview with the author.
29. Frank Furedi, *Invitation to Terror: The Expanding Empire of the Unknown* (New York: Continuum, 2007), xxiv, 84.
30. George Tenet with Bill Harlow, *At the Center of the Storm: My Years at the CIA* (New York: HarperCollins, 2007), 185.
31. Here and below, unless otherwise noted, information pertaining to the Red Cell comes from interviews with Red Cell members.
32. Furedi, *Invitation to Terror*, 72.
33. Ibid. xxii.
34. Interview with intelligence official.
35. Intelligence official interview.
36. Jim Hoagland, "What About Iraq?," *Washington Post*, October 12, 2001.
37. Intelligence official interview.
38. Interview with CIA analyst #5.
39. Interview with CIA analyst #6.
40. Zaab Sethna, interview with the author; Entifah Qanbar, interview with the author.
41. Interview with CIA official #7.
42. Aram Roston, *The Man Who Pushed America to War: The Extraordinary Life, Adventures and Obsessions of Ahmad Chalabi* (New York: Nation Books, 2008), 213.

43. "Saddam's Ex-Mistress Recalls Ruthless Man," ABC News, September 12, 2002.

44. Interview with CIA official #8.

45. CIA official #7 interview.

46. Ibid.

47. CIA official #8 interview.

48. CIA official #7 interview.

49. Interview with CIA analyst #7.

50. Interview with CIA official #9.

51. CIA analyst #1 interview.

52. CIA analyst #7 interview.

53. Jeffrey Gettleman, "The Reach of War: A Profile in Terror; Zarqawi's Journey: From Dropout to Prisoner to an Insurgent Leader in Iraq," *New York Times*, July 13, 2004.

54. Carl Ford to Colin Powell, "Iraq/Terrorism—Al-Qaida Operatives Moving into Baghdad," Department of State INR memo, May 24, 2002, declassified.

55. Joel Rayburn and Frank K. Sobchak, *The U.S. Army in the Iraq War, Vol 1: Invasion, Insurgency, Civil War, 2003–2006* (Carlisle, Pa.: Strategic Studies Institute, 2019), 47.

56. Interview with CIA analyst #8.

57. Central Intelligence Agency, "Iraq and al-Qa'ida: Interpreting a Murky Relationship" (the "Murky Paper"), June 21, 2002, declassified and redacted.

58. Jane Green, interview with the author.

59. Interview with CIA official #7.

60. Interview with CIA official #8.

61. CIA, "Murky Paper," scope note.

62. George W. Bush, "Remarks by the President at the Republican Party of Florida Majority Dinner," Orlando, June 21, 2002, transcript.

63. Interview with "Murky Paper" coauthor.

64. Doug Feith to Paul Wolfowitz, "Creation of the Policy Counter Terrorism Evaluation Group (PCTEG)," memo, November 26, 2001, declassified.

65. Interviews with three Pentagon officials who read the document.

66. Paul Wolfowitz, interview with the author; interviews with six different CIA analysts who responded to taskings by Wolfowitz on significant Saddam–Al Qaeda connections by saying that there was none.

67. Kevin Tebbit, interview with the author.

68. Pentagon official interview.

69. Christina Shelton, interview with the author.

70. Senate Select Committee on Intelligence, "Senate Report on Prewar Intelligence on Iraq," July 9, 2004, 308.

71. Shelton interview.

72. Donald Rumsfeld, *Rumsfeld's Rules: Leadership Lessons in Business, Politics, War and Life* (New York: Broadside Books, 2013).

73. Department of Defense, "Assessing the Relationship Between Iraq and al Qaida," working paper, undated, declassified.

74. Paul Wolfowitz to Christina Shelton, Christopher Carney, Jim Thomas, Abe Shulsky, and Doug Feith, "Today's Briefing," email, August 8, 2002, declassified.

75. Interview with CIA official #9.

76. Doug Feith, interview with the author.

77. Interview with DOD meeting participant.

78. Interview with CIA meeting participant #1.

79. CIA participant #1 interview.

80. Interview with CIA meeting participant #2.

81. Interview with CIA meeting participant #3.

82. Interview with CIA meeting participant #4.

83. Interview with CIA meeting participant #5.

84. Interviews with ten of the meeting's participants. Tenet, in his memoir, wrote that he pulled DIA director Jacoby from the meeting and instructed him to "get this back in intelligence channels" (*Center of the Storm*, 348). No one else interviewed for this book recalled this directive.

85. Interviews with four participants in the follow-up meetings.

86. CIA analyst #7 interview.

87. Central Intelligence Agency, "CTC: Iraqi Support for Terrorism," January 29, 2003, declassified and redacted.

88. Interviews with three CIA senior officials.

89. Interview with individual familiar with the exchange.

90. Rooks interview; interviews with two analysts who confirmed his account as well as the content of his memos.

91. CIA official #2 interview.

92. Interviews with five participants in the meeting.

93. Interview with meeting participant #1.

94. Interview with meeting participant #2.

95. Interviews with two participants in the meeting.

96. George Tenet to Bob Graham, letter, October 7, 2002.

Chapter Nine: The Ugly Duckling

1. Marc Grossman, interview with the author.

2. Interview with State Department official #1.

3. Interview with State Department official #2.

4. Colin Powell with Joseph Persico, *My American Journey* (New York: Random House, 1995), 271.

5. Allen Keiswetter, interview with the author.

6. Interview with State Department official #3.

7. Interview with State Department official #4.

8. State Department official #2 interview.

9. Richard Cheney, "Richard B. Cheney Oral History, Secretary of Defense," Presidential Oral Histories, Miller Center, University of Virginia, March 16, 2000.

10. State Department official #1 interview. Powell, in his memoir, cited these two instances as earning disfavor from Cheney.

11. Interview with State Department official #5.

12. Interview with State Department official #6.

13. State Department official #3 interview.

14. Interview with State Department official #7.

15. Interview with senior White House official.

16. Ibid.

17. State Department official #5 interview.

18. Interview with State Department official #8.

19. State Department official #1 interview.

20. Senior White House official interview.

21. State Department official #5 interview.

22. State Department official #2 interview.
23. Ibid.
24. Ari Fleischer, interview with the author.
25. Colin Powell, interview with the author.
26. Interview with State Department official #9.
27. State Department official #6 interview.
28. Interview with State Department official #10.
29. Bill Burns, interview with the author.
30. Interview with State Department official #11.
31. State official #6 interview.
32. Interview with CIA senior official.
33. James Zogby, interview with the author.
34. Interview with State Department official #12.
35. Eric Edelman, interview with the author. In a separate interview with the author, Marc Grossman said that he did not recall this meeting but added that he had no reason to distrust Edelman's depiction of it.
36. State Department official #9 interview.
37. Ibid.
38. Interviews with three State Department officials.
39. Bill Burns to Colin Powell, "Iraq: The Perfect Storm," memo, July 2002, declassified.
40. Donald Rumsfeld, "Iraq: An Illustrative List of Potential Problems to Be Considered and Addressed," memo, October 15, 2002, declassified.
41. Burns to Powell, "Iraq: The Perfect Storm."
42. Ibid.
43. William J. Burns, *The Back Channel: A Memoir of American Diplomacy and the Case for Its Renewal* (New York: Random House, 2019), 169.
44. Bob Woodward, *Plan of Attack: The Definitive Account of the Decision to Invade Iraq* (New York: Simon & Schuster, 2004), 149, 153.
45. Colin Powell with Tony Koltz, *It Worked for Me: In Life and Leadership* (New York: Harper, 2012), 210.
46. Powell interview.
47. The reconstruction of the Hamptons meeting is based on interviews with the three participants: Colin Powell, Jack Straw, and Simon McDonald. Blair and Straw meeting: Simon McDonald, interview with the author.
48. Interview with State Department official #13.

Chapter Ten: The Decider, Deciding

1. "Blair Flies In with Ceasefire Agenda," BBC News, April 6, 2002.
2. White House, "President Bush Meets with Australian Prime Minister," news release transcript, June 13, 2002.
3. Interview with White House official.
4. George W. Bush, "A Distinctly American Internationalism," speech at Ronald Reagan Presidential Library, November 19, 1999, transcript.
5. George W. Bush, "Address Before a Joint Session of the Congress on the Response to the Terrorist Attacks of September 11," September 20, 2001, White House transcript.
6. Peter Baker, "Bad Blood: Saddam and Bushes," *New York Times*, December 31, 2006; the remarks were made on September 26, 2002.

7. White House, "Remarks by the President at South Dakota Welcome," news release transcript, October 31, 2002.
8. Interview with White House aide.
9. White House, "Remarks by the President at Thaddeus McCotter for Congress Dinner," news release transcript, October 14, 2002.
10. Interviews with three CIA officials.
11. John McLaughlin, interview with the author.
12. Dick Cheney, interview with Tim Russert, *Meet the Press*, NBC, September 8, 2002, transcript.
13. White House, "President Bush Meets with Prime Minister Blair," news release transcript, January 31, 2003.
14. Tom Daschle, interview with the author.
15. "Presidential Approval Ratings—George W. Bush," Gallup Historical Trends, https://www.gallup.com/poll/116500/presidential-approval-ratings-george-bush.aspx.
16. White House aide interview; Maia Jachimowicz, "DHS May Axe Special Registration of Foreign Visitors," Migration Policy Institute, December 1, 2003.
17. Interview with CIA official.
18. Robert Draper, *Dead Certain: The Presidency of George W. Bush* (New York: Free Press, 2007), xi.
19. White House, "President Discusses European Trip," news release transcript, July 16, 2001.
20. Bush unveiled these paintings at the George W. Bush Presidential Center in Dallas on June 26, 2018.
21. Draper, *Dead Certain*, 417. In a May 8, 2007, interview, Bush told this author that he identified with Churchill as portrayed by Olson, who had received a fan note from Rove.
22. Lynne Olson, "Yes, George Bush Does Recall a British Wartime Prime Minister: Chamberlain," *Guardian*, August 27, 2007.
23. Winston Churchill, *My Early Life*: A Roving Commission (London: Thornton Butterworth Ltd., 1930), 246.
24. Philip Zelikow, interview with the author.
25. Jack Reed, interview with the author.
26. Brent Scowcroft, *Face the Nation*, CBS, August 4, 2002, transcript.
27. Brent Scowcroft, "Don't Attack Saddam," *Wall Street Journal*, August 15, 2002.
28. Antony Blinken, interview with the author.
29. White House official interview.
30. Mark K. Updegrove, *The Last Republicans: Inside the Extraordinary Relationship Between George H. W. Bush and George W. Bush* (New York: Harper, 2017), 320.
31. Updegrove, *Last Republicans*, 324.
32. Ari Fleischer, interview with the author.
33. Interviews with four members of the White House Iraq Group.
34. White House Iraq Group member interview.
35. Richard Cheney, "Richard B. Cheney Oral History, Secretary of Defense," Presidential Oral Histories, Miller Center, University of Virginia, March 17, 2000.
36. Interviews with several OVP officials.
37. White House, "Vice President Speaks at VFW 103rd Convention," news release transcript, August 26, 2002; interview with OVP official.
38. Interview with senior CIA weapons analyst.
39. Colin Powell, interview with the author.

40. Fleischer interview.
41. White House, "Vice President Honors Veterans of Korean War," news release transcript, August 29, 2002.
42. Interview with OVP official.
43. Senior White House official interview.
44. Campbell, *The Burden of Power: Countdown to Iraq—The Alastair Campbell Diaries* (London: Hutchinson, 2012), 285.
45. David Manning, testimony in Chilcot Inquiry, November 30, 2009.
46. Senior White House official interview.
47. Tony Blair to George W. Bush, "Note on Iraq," letter, July 28, 2002, declassified.
48. Campbell, *Burden of Power*, 294.
49. Colin Powell, interview with Charlayne Hunter-Gault, *Inside Politics*, CNN, September 4, 2002.
50. Rice interview.
51. Interview with OVP official #1.
52. Interview with OVP official #2.
53. Fleischer interview.
54. Alaistair Campbell, interview with the author.
55. Condoleezza Rice, *No Higher Honor: A Memoir of My Years in Washington* (New York: Crown, 2011), 181.
56. Bob Woodward, *Plan of Attack: The Definitive Account of the Decision to Invade Iraq* (New York: Simon & Schuster, 2004), 178.
57. Campbell, *Burden of Power*, 296.
58. Powell interview.
59. Interview with senior Blair official.
60. Campbell, *Burden of Power*, 300.
61. George W. Bush, address to the UN General Assembly, September 12, 2002, transcript.
62. Simon McDonald, interview with the author.
63. Draper, *Dead Certain*, 181–82.
64. Fleischer interview.
65. Powell interview.
66. Interview with individual familiar with this communication.

Chapter Eleven: Drumbeats

1. Interview with CIA case officer.
2. Joel Rayburn and Frank K. Sobchak, *The U.S. Army in the Iraq War, Vol 1: Invasion, Insurgency, Civil War, 2003–2006* (Carlisle, Pa.: Strategic Studies Institute, 2019), 56.
3. Interview with CENTCOM planner #1.
4. Colonel Kevin Benson, interview with the author. Benson read the Wolfowitz note.
5. Jeffrey Goldberg, "The Great Terror," *New Yorker*, March 17, 2002.
6. George Tenet with Bill Harlow, *At the Center of the Storm: My Years at the CIA* (New York: HarperCollins, 2007), 350–51.
7. Tom Fingar to Ryan Crocker, "Iran's Reaction to U.S. Strike in Northern Iraq," INR memo, July 5, 2002, declassified.
8. Condoleezza Rice, *No Higher Honor: A Memoir of My Years in Washington* (New York: Crown, 2011), 178; Donald Rumsfeld, *Known and Unknown: A Memoir* (New York: Sentinel, 2011), 446–47.
9. Gregory Newbold, interview with the author.

10. Mark Hertling, interview with the author.
11. Interview with Wolfowitz aide.
12. Interview with CENTCOM planner #2.
13. George W. Bush speaking with four reporters, January 28, 2003, quoted in Robert Draper, *Dead Certain: The Presidency of George W. Bush* (New York: Free Press, 2007), 189.
14. Wolfowitz aide interview.
15. David Rose, interview with the author.
16. John Maguire, interview with the author.
17. Scott Ritter, interview with the author; Scott Ritter, "Dinner with Ahmed," Truthdig, March 17, 2008.
18. Interview with senior Pentagon official.
19. Doug Feith, interview with the author.
20. Tom Greenwood, interview with the author.
21. Peter Rodman to Donald Rumsfeld, "Support for Iraqi Opposition," DOD memo, May 9, 2002, declassified.
22. Donald Rumsfeld to Doug Feith, "Iraqi Opposition," DOD memo, May 17, 2002, declassified; Feith handwrote his note to Rodman on Rumsfeld's memo.
23. Donald Rumsfeld to Dick Cheney et al., "Supporting the Iraqi Opposition," DOD memo, July 1, 2002, declassified.
24. Interview with CENTCOM planner #3.
25. Interview with senior CIA official.
26. Douglas Feith, *War and Decision: Inside the Pentagon at the Dawn of the War on Terrorism* (New York: Harper, 2008), 383.
27. Interview with senior intelligence official.
28. Interview with Pentagon official #1.
29. Luis Rueda, interview with the author.
30. Wolfowitz aide interview.
31. Interview with Pentagon official #2.
32. Wolfowitz aide interview.
33. Interview with CENTCOM planner #2.
34. William Luti to Doug Feith, "Action Plan to Train and Equip the Iraqi Opposition," DOD briefing slides, August 20, 2002, declassified; interview with meeting participant.
35. Feith, *War and Decision*, 280.
36. Stephen Hadley, interview with the author.
37. Christopher Straub, interview with the author.
38. Feith, *War and Decision*, 288. The original version of Rice's memo was written on August 14, 2002, but it went through months of iterations and was finalized in early November.
39. Doug Feith, "The Case Against Iraq," DOD memo, August 22, 2002, declassified.
40. Doug Feith, "Presentation—The Case for Action," DOD memo, September 12, 2002, declassified.
41. Interview with senior intelligence official. A similar account of this meeting was chronicled in Tenet, *Center of the Storm*, 319.
42. Interview with CIA operative.
43. Tom Fingar to Richard Armitage, "Iraq: CIA-Hosted Simulation of Post-Saddam Iraq," State Department INR memo, July 24, 2002, declassified.
44. Interview with CIA peace game participant #1.
45. Interview with CIA peace game participant #2.

46. Bob Grenier, interview with the author.

47. Interviews with two participants in the two CIA chief of station meetings.

48. David Welch, interview with the author.

Chapter Twelve: Ballpark Estimates

1. CIA analyst, interview with the author; Joe Ralston, interview with the author; Joe Wippl (CIA Berlin chief of station), interview with the author.

2. Glen Shaffer, interview with the author.

3. Glen Shaffer to Donald Rumsfeld, "Iraq: Status of WMD Programs," DOD memo, September 5, 2002, declassified; Donald Rumsfeld to Richard Myers, "WMD," September 9, 2002, declassified.

4. Donald Rumsfeld, interview, *Fox News Sunday*, September 9, 2002, transcript.

5. Interview with Blair foreign policy adviser.

6. "Removing Saddam Was Right, Even Without WMD—Blair," BBC News, December 12, 2009.

7. "Deputy Secretary Wolfowitz Interview with Sam Tanenhaus, Vanity Fair," May 9, 2003, Department of Defense transcript.

8. Donald Rumsfeld et al., *Executive Summary of the Report of the Commission to Assess the Ballistic Missile Threat*, July 15, 1998.

9. Robert Walpole, testimony, *National Intelligence Estimate on the Ballistic Missile Threat to the United States, Hearing Before the International Security, Proliferation, and Federal Services Subcommittee of the Senate Committee on Governmental Affairs*, February 9, 2000.

10. Greg Thielmann, interview with the author.

11. Tom Fingar, interview with the author.

12. Dick Durbin, remarks in the Senate, *Congressional Record*, September 10, 2002, S8428-9.

13. Interview with CIA senior official #1.

14. Ibid.

15. Ibid.

16. Interview with National Intelligence Estimate (NIE) coauthor.

17. Interview with CIA senior official #2.

18. Interrogation of Hussein Kamel by Rolf Ekéus, August 22, 1995, transcript, UNSCOM /IAEA briefing notes.

19. Thielmann interview.

20. Interview with senior intelligence official.

21. Interview with CIA senior official #2.

22. Interview with CIA analyst.

23. Central Intelligence Agency, "Key Judgments," *Iraq's Continuing Programs for Weapons of Mass Destruction*, National Intelligence Estimate, October 2002, 10, declassified.

24. Interviews with two CIA weapons analysts.

25. Interviews with two weapons inspectors.

26. Charles Duelfer, interview with the author.

27. Interview with CIA Iraq analyst.

28. Interview with CIA biological weapons analyst. See also Martin Chulov and Helen Pidd, "Defector Admits to WMD Lies That Triggered Iraq War," *Guardian*, February 15, 2011. The best comprehensive account of the Curveball saga is Bob Drogin's *Curveball: Spies, Lies and the Con Man Who Caused a War* (New York: Random House, 2007).

29. CIA, "Key Judgments," 11.
30. Richard Cheney, interview with Wolf Blitzer, CNN, March 24, 2002.
31. Senate Select Committee on Intelligence, *Report on the U.S. Intelligence Community's Prewar Intelligence on Iraq Together with Additional Views,* July 9, 2004, 38.
32. Carl Ford to Richard Armitage, "Niger—Sale of Uranium to Iraq Is Unlikely," State Department INR memo, March 1, 2002, declassified.
33. "[Redacted] Nigerian Denial of Uranium Yellowcake Sales to Rogue States," CIA cable, March 8, 2002, declassified.
34. UK Joint Intelligence Committee, *Iraq's Weapons of Mass Destruction: The Assessment of the British Government,* September 2002, 25.
35. Senate Select Committee on Intelligence, *Report on the U.S. Intelligence Community's Prewar Intelligence on Iraq,* 49.
36. CIA senior official #1 interview.
37. CIA, "Key Judgments," 29.
38. Carl Ford to Marc Grossman, "Niger/Iraq Uranium Story and Joe Wilson," State INR memo, June 10, 2003, declassified.
39. David Albright, "Aluminum Tubes: Separating Fact from Fiction," Institute for Science and International Security, December 5, 2003.
40. John McLaughlin, interview with the author.
41. Interview with CIA Counter Proliferation analyst, via third-party email.
42. Carl Ford to John Bolton, "Assessing the Iraqi Aluminum Tubes," State Department INR memo, September 6, 2001, declassified.
43. Thielmann interview.
44. Interview with DOE technician.
45. Michael R. Gordon and Judith Miller, "Threats and Responses: The Iraqis; U.S. Says Hussein Intensifies Quest for A-Bomb Parts," *New York Times,* September 8, 2002.
46. Condoleezza Rice, interview with Wolf Blitzer, CNN, September 8, 2002, transcript.
47. DOE technical expert interview.
48. David Barstow, William J. Broad, and Jeff Gerth, "The Nuclear Card: The Aluminum Tube Story—A Special Report; How White House Embraced Suspect Iraq Arms Intelligence," *New York Times,* October 3, 2004.
49. Interview with CIA senior official #3.
50. McLaughlin interview.
51. DOE technical expert interview.
52. CIA, "Key Judgments," 9.
53. DOE technical expert interview.
54. Charles Duelfer, interview with the author.
55. Interview with three NIE coauthors.
56. CIA, "Key Judgments," declassified excerpt, available at https://fas.org/irp/cia/product/iraq-wmd.html.
57. CIA, "Key Judgments," 13; CIA senior official #1 interview.
58. Adam Nagourney and Janet Elder, "Public Says Bush Needs to Pay Heed to Weak Economy," *New York Times,* October 7, 2002.
59. Interviews with two Bush administration officials.
60. White House, "President Bush Outlines Iraqi Threat," news release transcript, October 7, 2002.
61. George W. Bush, interview with author, December 2006.

Chapter Thirteen: The Blank Check

1. Brent Scowcroft, "Don't Invade Iraq," *Wall Street Journal,* August 13, 2002; Henry Kissinger, "Our Intervention in Iraq," *Washington Post,* August 12, 2002; James A. Baker III, "The Right Way to Change a Regime," *New York Times,* August 25, 2002.

2. Lydia Saad, "Top Ten Findings About Public Opinion and Iraq," Gallup News Service, October 8, 2002.

3. Interviews with three administration officials.

4. George W. Bush, "President Discusses Foreign Policy with Congressional Leaders," White House, September 4, 2002, transcript.

5. Carl Levin, interview with the author.

6. Bob Hagedorn (Skelton's chief of staff), interview with the author; Ike Skelton, *Achieve the Honorable: A Missouri Congressman's Journey from Warm Springs to Washington* (Carbondale: Southern Illinois University Press, 2013), 109. In his book, Skelton misidentified Keniry as an NSC staffer. But he supplied the same memory much earlier to Thomas Ricks; see Ricks, "Show Me in 'Merica," *Washington Post,* August 25, 2004.

7. Notes from a Rumsfeld meeting attendee.

8. Jeffrey M. Jones, "Congress Sees Record-High Pre-Election Ratings," Gallup News Service, October 15, 2002.

9. John McLaughlin, interview with the author.

10. Interview with Democratic leadership staffer #1.

11. Interview with NIE coauthor #1.

12. Interview with CIA official.

13. Peter Carlson, "The Solitary Vote of Barbara Lee," *Washington Post,* September 19, 2001.

14. George W. Bush, "Remarks by the President at Chris Chocola for Congress, and Indiana Victory Finance Dinner 2002," South Bend, Indiana, September 5, 2002, White House transcript.

15. Scott L. Althaus and Devon M. Largio, "When Osama Became Saddam: Origins and Consequences of the Change in America's Public Enemy #1," *PS: Political Science & Politics* 37, no. 4 (October 2004): 795–99.

16. Tom Daschle, interview with the author.

17. Interview with White House official.

18. Interview with intelligence analyst.

19. Interview with NIE coauthor #2.

20. Levin interview.

21. Interviews with two CIA briefers.

22. Levin and McLaughlin interviews.

23. George Tenet with Bill Harlow, *At the Center of the Storm: My Years at the CIA* (New York: HarperCollins, 2007), 336; Julian Borger, "CIA in Blow to Bush Attack Plans," *Guardian,* October 9, 2002.

24. House Continuing Resolution No. 33, Final Roll Call, January 12, 1991, http: //clerk .house.gov/evs/1991/ROLL_000.asp. One-third of Gephardt's Democratic caucus voted against the resolution, most of them moderates.

25. Gwen Ifill, "Gephardt Makes It Official: He's No '92 Candidate," *New York Times,* July 18, 1991.

26. Interview with Gephardt senior aide #1.

27. Interview with Gephardt senior aide #2.

28. George W. Bush, "President: Terrorism Insurance Agreement Needed by Friday," White House, October 1, 2002, transcript.
29. Notes from a breakfast attendee.
30. Gephardt senior aide #1 interview.
31. Interview with Biden senior aide.
32. Ibid.
33. Bob Graham, interview with the author.
34. Ibid.
35. John Edwards, *Late Edition with Wolf Blitzer*, CNN, February 24, 2002, transcript.
36. John Edwards, remarks in the Senate, *Congressional Record*, September 12, 2002, S8554.
37. Interview with Edwards senior aide.
38. Michael Kranish, "Hillary Clinton Regrets Her Iraq Vote. But Opting for Intervention Was a Pattern," *Washington Post*, September 15, 2016.
39. "One Year Later: Diplomacy and Tracking Terrorists," "Live Online" chat with Richard Holbrooke, *Washington Post*, September 10, 2002.
40. Interview with Clinton senior aide.
41. Hillary Clinton, remarks in the Senate, *Congressional Record*, October 10, 2002, S10289.
42. Daschle and Robert Byrd, remarks in the Senate, *Congressional Record*, October 10, 2002, S10242.
43. Tom Daschle, interview with the author.
44. "Hillary Clinton Talks About Her Vote to Go to War, Saddam, and WMDs," YouTube video of Hillary Clinton speaking at a meeting of Code Pink and Unreasonable Women for the Earth, March 2003, posted by "Kirsten T M M Michel Ecology Productions" on February 2, 2011, https://www.youtube.com/watch?v=HtK9AzcU42g.
45. Clinton senior aide interview.

Chapter Fourteen: A Passing Phase

1. Interview with Bush White House official.
2. John Hillen, "Superpowers Don't Do Windows," *Orbis* 41, no. 2 (Spring 1997). Hillen's essay did not in fact argue that superpowers should *never* "do windows"—only that in a coalition, the peacekeeping tasks should be assigned to partners with lighter capabilities. In an email exchange with the author, Hillen pointed out that in a 1998 paper he wrote for the Washington Institute's *Iraq Strategy Review: Options for U.S. Policy* (Washington, D.C.: Washington Institute for Near East Policy, 1998), he argued that a U.S. invasion of Iraq would necessitate performing such tasks. This paper, "Conquering and Occupying Iraq," also included this pre-9/11 forecast (*Iraq Strategy Review*, 117): "Obviously, the United States and its allies would never entertain such an extreme policy unless Iraq carried out a significant act of aggression." On page 130 of the essay, Hillen envisioned an invasion force of 310,000 to 340,000, or roughly twice the amount ultimately prescribed by Secretary Rumsfeld (*Iraq Strategy Review*, 130).
3. Lawrence Korb, "Defense Expert Korb Says Top Military Officials in Iraq 'Very Frustrated' Fighting Elusive Enemy," Council on Foreign Relations, November 13, 2003.
4. Interviews with three Pentagon officials; this particular quotation appears in one of Rumsfeld's final snowflakes before his resignation as Secretary of Defense: "Iraq—Illustrative New Courses of Action," November 6, 2006.
5. John Batiste, interview with the author.
6. Fouad Ajami, "Iraq and the Thief of Baghdad," *New York Times*, May 19, 2002.

7. Jeanne Godfroy, interview with the author.

8. Simon Webb, "Bush and the War on Terrorism," memo, April 12, 2002, declassified; Simon Webb, interview with the author.

9. Interviews with two Bush White House officials.

10. David Phillips, interview with the author.

11. Interview with State Department official #1.

12. Interview with project participant.

13. Zaah Sethna, interview with the author.

14. State Department official #1 interview.

15. Kanan Makiya, interview with the author.

16. Richard Myers, interview with the author.

17. Greg Newbold, interview with the author.

18. Kevin Benson, interview with the author; interview with two CENTCOM planners.

19. Interview with IPMC participant, confirmed in interview with second participant; also Douglas Feith, *War and Decision: Inside the Pentagon at the Dawn of the War on Terrorism* (New York: Harper, 2008), 276.

20. Tom Greenwood, interview with the author; Frank Miller, interview with the author.

21. Lincoln Bloomfield, interview with the author.

22. Interviews with three ESG participants.

23. Interviews with two individuals familiar with the two conversations.

24. Greg Schulte, interview with the author.

Chapter Fifteen: Inspectors

1. Jerry Watson, interview with the author.

2. Hans Blix, interview with the author; also, Hans Blix, *Disarming Iraq* (New York: Pantheon, 2004), 56–58.

3. Walter Pincus, "Skirmish on Iraq Inspections," *Washington Post*, April 15, 2002.

4. Ibid.; Blix interview.

5. Interviews with four administration officials; Douglas Feith, *War and Decision: Inside the Pentagon at the Dawn of the War on Terrorism* (New York: Harper, 2008), 301; Walter Pincus, "Rumsfeld Disputes Value of Iraq Arms Inspections," *Washington Post*, April 16, 2002.

6. Feith, *War and Decision*, 301.

7. National Security Council, "A Decade of Deception and Denial: Saddam Hussein's Defiance of the United Nations," White House background paper, September 12, 2002.

8. "Iraq Agrees to Weapons Inspections," CNN, September 17, 2002.

9. "Saddam Hussein's Deception and Defiance," Office of the Press Secretary, White House, September 17, 2002.

10. Interviews with two NSC meeting attendees.

11. Interviews with three administration officials with knowledge of these conversations.

12. William Luti to Stephen Hadley, "UNMOVIC: Building in a Disarmament and WMD Elimination Authority," briefing memo, September 22, 2002, declassified.

13. Blix, *Disarming Iraq*, 76–77.

14. Blix interview.

15. Elliott Abrams, interview with the author.

16. John Negroponte, interview with the author; John Bellinger, interview with the author.

17. Negroponte interview.

18. Blix interview; Ewen Buchanan, interview with the author.

19. Blix interview.

20. Blix, "Warlords: The Memoirs of Three War Leaders," unpublished book review of the Bush, Blair, and Howard memoirs provided by Blix to the author, 2011.

21. Blix interview; interview with meeting attendant; Blix, *Disarming Iraq*, 83; Mohamed ElBaradei, *The Age of Deception: Nuclear Diplomacy in Treacherous Times* (London: Bloomsbury, 2011), 52.

22. Paul Wolfowitz to General William B. Caldwell IV, memo, undated, declassified.

23. Blix, *Disarming Iraq*, 88; Blix interview.

24. Blix interview.

25. ElBaradei, *Age of Deception*, 51; Blix, *Disarming Iraq*, 83.

26. Blix interview; ElBaradei, *Age of Deception*, 51.

27. ElBaradei, *Age of Deception*, 52.

28. Condoleezza Rice, *No Higher Honor: A Memoir of My Years in Washington* (New York: Crown, 2011), 185–86. In thinking that the IAEA had erred in its judgment about Saddam's nuclear program in 1991, Rice herself was incorrect: the IAEA's assessment had been based on Saddam's declared nuclear sites. Undeclared sites were beyond its purview.

29. Interview with OVP official.

30. Blix interview; ElBaradei, *Age of Deception*, 53; Blix, *Disarming Iraq*, 86.

31. Blix interview; ElBaradei, *Age of Deception*, 53; Blix, *Disarming Iraq*, 86.

32. Alastair Campbell, *The Burden of Power: Countdown to Iraq—The Alastair Campbell Diaries* (London: Hutchinson, 2012), 369; Alastair Campbell, interview with the author.

33. Interviews with two Bush administration officials.

34. Bill McLaughlin (CIA analyst), interview with the author; Blix, *Disarming Iraq*, 105–6.

35. McLaughlin interview.

36. Interview with senior administration official.

37. Dan Bartlett, interview with the author.

38. Blix interview; Blix, *Disarming Iraq*, 96.

39. Carl Levin, interview with the author.

40. Andrew Liepman, interview with the author.

41. Interview with intelligence official.

42. Liepman interview.

43. Interview with senior administration official.

Chapter Sixteen: The Magician and the Warrior

1. Commission on the Intelligence Capabilities of the United States Regarding Weapons of Mass Destruction, *Report to the President of the United States* ("The WMD Commission Report"), March 31, 2005, 137–38.

2. WMD Commission Report, 134.

3. Interview with CIA weapons analyst #1; Bob Woodward, *Plan of Attack: The Definitive Account of the Decision to Invade Iraq* (New York: Simon & Schuster, 2004), 246–47.

4. Interview with Bush senior adviser.

5. WMD Commission Report, 14.

6. Marc Grossman, interview with the author.

7. Interview with CIA senior manager #1.

8. Interview with CIA analyst #1.

9. Interview with intelligence officer.

10. Interview with CIA senior manager #2.
11. CIA senior manager #1 interview.
12. Interview with CIA case officer #1.
13. Interview with CIA senior official #1.
14. CIA case officer #1 interview.
15. Central Intelligence Agency, "Iraq's Continuing Programs of Weapons of Mass Destruction," National Intelligence Estimate, October 2002.
16. White House, "President Bush Outlines Iraqi Threat," remarks in Cincinnati, news release transcript, October 7, 2002.
17. Interviews with CIA weapons analyst #1 and CIA senior official #2; WMD Commission, 137–39.
18. Bill McLaughlin, interview with the author; CIA senior official #2 interview.
19. McLaughlin interview.
20. Nick Calio, interview with the author.
21. Interview with CIA senior official #3.
22. Interview with CIA senior official #4.
23. Interview with CIA senior official #5.
24. Ibid.
25. Interview with CIA weapons analyst #2.
26. CIA senior official #4 interview.
27. Woodward, *Plan of Attack*, 247.
28. McLaughlin interview.
29. Woodward, *Plan of Attack*, 249.
30. McLaughlin interview.
31. George Tenet with Bill Harlow, *At the Center of the Storm: My Years at the CIA* (New York: HarperCollins, 2007), 361.
32. McLaughlin interview. His notes did not mention Tenet saying "slam dunk." He, Tenet, John McLaughlin, and Florence did not recall him saying it, while Makridis, Card, and Rice did.
33. Woodward, *Plan of Attack*, 249–50.
34. Condoleezza Rice, interview with the author.
35. Interview with December 21, 2002, meeting attendee.
36. McLaughlin interview.
37. CIA senior manager #2 and CIA senior official #2 interviews; Tenet, *At the Center of the Storm*, 364.
38. CIA weapons analyst #1 interview.
39. Interviews with two of the three participants in the meeting; Tenet, *Center of the Storm*, 369–70.
40. Interview with analyst who retained copies of these emails.
41. John McLaughlin, memo to analysts, December 30, 2002, unclassified.
42. CIA senior official #4 interview.
43. Interviews with three individuals with knowledge of this conversation.
44. Interviews with four OVP officials.
45. Interviews with four briefing participants; Woodward, *Plan of Attack*, 289–90; Anna Perez, interview with Michael Martin, "New Memoir Questions White House Loyalty," NPR, May 30, 2008.
46. Karl Rove, interview with the author.
47. Woodward, *Plan of Attack*, 271.
48. Interview with two State Department officials.

49. Interviews with three State Department officials.

50. Jack Straw, interview with the author.

51. Colin Powell, interview with the author.

52. Senate Select Committee on Intelligence, *Report on the U.S. Intelligence Community's Prewar Intelligence on Iraq Together with Additional Views,* July 9, 2004, 241.

53. Interview with State Department official #1.

54. CIA senior official #5 interview.

55. Powell interview; interview with White House official.

56. Interview with OVP official #1.

57. Ibid.

58. Ari Fleischer, interview with the author.

59. Carl Ford, interview with the author.

60. Senate Select Committee on Intelligence, *Report on the U.S. Intelligence Community's Prewar Intelligence,* 423–28.

61. George W. Bush, "President Bush Meets with Prime Minister Blair," White House, January 31, 2003, transcript.

62. Larry Wilkerson, interview with the author; Powell interview.

63. Interview with State Department official #2.

64. Dan Bartlett, interview with the author.

65. State Department official #2 interview.

66. Interview with Langley participant.

67. McLaughlin interview.

68. Barry Lowenkron, interview with the author.

69. CIA case officer #1 interview.

70. WMD Commission Report, 84.

71. Steve Slick, email exchange with the author.

72. Slick email exchange.

73. Bob Drogin, *Curveball: Spies, Lies, and the Con Man Who Caused a War* (New York: Random House, 2007), 149.

74. Jim Pavitt, interview with the author.

75. Interview between CIA source and Bob Drogin, supplied by Drogin to the author.

76. Joe Wippl, interview with the author. Except where otherwise noted, the Curveball passages were derived from interviews with Margaret Henoch, CIA weapons analysts #1 and #2, and two CIA senior officials, and from the WMD Commission Report, 84–104. One source whom the author discounted is now-deceased CIA European division chief Tyler Drumheller, whose book *On the Brink: An Insider's Account of How the White House Compromised American Intelligence* (New York: Carroll & Graf, 2006) and subsequent appearance on *60 Minutes* lent him the status of a whistleblower who had attempted to persuade first John McLaughlin and later—on the night before Powell's speech—George Tenet that Curveball was not a credible source. McLaughlin disputed, both to the author and to the WMD Commission, that such a conversation had taken place, and Drumheller did not memorialize the meeting in writing. He did, however, tell Henoch immediately after the alleged conversation that he had issued such a warning. As for the warning to Tenet, of which Tenet told both the author and the WMD Commission he had no recollection, Drumheller's own rendition in his book is equivocal and arguably unmemorable, particularly given that he allegedly related it late that night, after Tenet had spent hours working with Powell on the final version of his speech. Without calling into question the veracity of Drumheller, who is not alive to defend himself, the author elected to omit Drumheller's account, above

all because the central actor from the Directorate of Operations was not him but his subordinate, Henoch.

77. Interview with CIA senior official #6.
78. Interviews with three CIA senior officials.
79. Lawrence Wilkerson, interview with the author.
80. Lowenkron interview.
81. Martin Chulov and Helen Pidd, "Curveball: How US Was Duped by Iraqi Fantasist Looking to Topple Saddam," *Guardian*, February 15, 2011.
82. Interview with DIA intelligence officer.
83. CIA weapons analyst #2 interview.
84. Ford interview; Colin Powell, speech before the United Nations, February 5, 2003, transcript.
85. Hans Blix, interview with the author.
86. Interview with Rolf Ekéus; "The Case Against Iraq," *PBS NewsHour*, February 5, 2003, transcript.
87. Interview with OVP aide.
88. Dawson Cagle, interview with the author.
89. Interview with UNMOVIC inspector.
90. Fleischer interview.
91. Tom Daschle, interview with the author.
92. Ibid.
93. Mary McGrory, "I'm Persuaded," *Washington Post*, February 6, 2003.

Chapter Seventeen: Truth and the Tellers

1. Patrick Tyler, interview with the author.
2. Warren Strobel, interview with the author.
3. Warren Strobel and Kevin Whitelaw, "The Trap That Suits Saddam—and the U.S.," *Washington Post*, September 24, 2000.
4. Patrick E. Tyler, "Poison Gas Attack Kills Hundreds," *Washington Post*, March 24, 1988.
5. Patrick E. Tyler, "Halabja Journal: In Town Iraqis Gassed, Kurds Now Breathe Free," *New York Times*, November 18, 1991.
6. Tyler interview.
7. Warren Strobel, "Former CIA Director Looks for Evidence That Iraq Had a Role in Attacks," Knight Ridder, October 11, 2001.
8. Strobel interview; John Walcott, interview with the author.
9. Chris Hedges, "A Nation Challenged: The School; Defectors Cite Iraqi Training for Terrorism," *New York Times*, November 8, 2001.
10. Patrick E. Tyler and John Tagliabue, "A Nation Challenged: The Investigation; Czechs Confirm Iraqi Agent Met with Terror Ringleader," *New York Times*, October 27, 2001.
11. Walter Pincus, interview with the author.
12. Ari Fleischer, interview with the author; search of White House press briefing transcripts.
13. Interview with *New York Times* reporter.
14. Jim Hoagland, "Saddam, Iraq's Suave Strongman," *Washington Post*, May 11, 1975.
15. Interview with individual familiar with the conversation.
16. Jim Hoagland, "How CIA's Secret War on Saddam Collapsed," *Washington Post*, June 26, 1997.
17. Jim Hoagland, "From Pariah to Iraq's Hope," *Washington Post*, March 5, 1998.

18. Jim Hoagland and Vernon Loeb, "Tests Show Nerve Gas in Iraqi Warheads," *Washington Post*, June 23, 1998.
19. Jim Hoagland, "What About Iraq?," *Washington Post*, October 12, 2001.
20. Jim Hoagland, "Hidden Hand of Horror," *Washington Post*, September 12, 2001.
21. Jim Hoagland, "Eye on the Goal," *Washington Post*, October 31, 2001.
22. Jim Hoagland, "CIA's New Old Iraq File," *Washington Post*, October 20, 2002.
23. Jim Hoagland, "Hurdles in the Hunt for Weapons," *Washington Post*, November 28, 2002.
24. David Ignatius, interview with the author.
25. Lally Weymouth, "Same Old Saddam," *Washington Post*, November 14, 1997.
26. "Sound and Fury," *Washington Post*, February 15, 2003.
27. Howard Kurtz, "The Post on WMDs: An Inside Story," *Washington Post*, August 12, 2004.
28. Pincus interview.
29. Ignatius interview.
30. Dick Cheney, *Meet the Press*, NBC, September 16, 2001, transcript.
31. Dick Cheney, *Meet the Press*, NBC, March 24, 2002, transcript.
32. Jeffrey Goldberg, interview with the author; Jeffrey Goldberg, "The Great Terror," *New Yorker*, March 17, 2002.
33. Jason Burke, interview with the author; Jason Burke, "The Missing Link?," *Guardian*, February 8, 2003.
34. Goldberg interview.
35. Leon Wieseltier, interview with the author; Mark Brzezinski, email exchange with the author.
36. Christopher Hitchens, debate with Mark Danner, Robert Scheer, and Michael Ignatieff, "American Power and the Crisis Over Iraq," Wiltern theater, Los Angeles, March 15, 2003, transcript.
37. Andrew Sullivan, "How Did I Get Iraq Wrong?," *Slate*, March 21, 2008.
38. Bob Kerrey, interview with the author.
39. Paul Berman, "Why Germany Isn't Convinced," *Slate*, February 14, 2003.
40. Interview with columnist.
41. Bill Carter, "ABC to End 'Politically Incorrect,'" *New York Times*, May 14, 2002.
42. Warren Strobel and John Walcott, "Bush Has Decided to Overthrow Hussein," Knight Ridder, February 13, 2002.
43. Walcott and Strobel interviews.
44. Judith Miller, *The Story* (New York: Simon & Schuster, 2015), 212–14; Judith Miller and Michael Gordon, "Threats and Responses: The Iraqis; U.S. Says Hussein Intensifies Quest for A-Bomb Parts," *New York Times*, September 8, 2002.
45. Colin Powell, *Fox News Sunday*, Fox, September 8, 2002, transcript.
46. Dick Cheney, *Meet the Press*, NBC, September 8, 2002, transcript.
47. Condoleezza Rice, *Late Edition with Wolf Blitzer*, CNN, September 8, 2002, transcript.
48. Elisabeth Bumiller, "Traces of Terror: The Strategy; Bush Aides Set Strategy to Sell Policy on Iraq," *New York Times*, September 7, 2002.
49. Interview with *New York Times* reporter.
50. Interviews with four *New York Times* employees.
51. Patrick E. Tyler interview; Tyler's unpublished August 22, 2002, manuscript; Tyler's emails to Howell Raines and to Cheney's staff.
52. James Risen, interview with the author; interview with additional *Times* source; James Risen, "Prague Discounts an Iraqi Meeting," *New York Times*, October 21, 2002.

53. James Risen, "The Biggest Secret: My Life as a *New York Times* Reporter in the Shadow of the War on Terror," *Intercept*, January 3, 2018.

54. Risen interview.

Chapter Eighteen: Things Fall Apart

1. Charles Duelfer, Iraq Survey Group, "Regime Strategic Intent: Sorting Out Whether Iraq Had WMD Before Operation Iraqi Freedom," *Comprehensive Report of the Special Advisor to the DCI on Iraq's WMD,* September 30, 2004.

2. Kevin M. Woods et al., *Iraqi Perspectives Project: A View of Operation Iraqi Freedom from Saddam's Senior Leadership* (United States Joint Forces Command, 2006), 93.

3. Scott Shane, "In Video, Hussein Uses Slingshots and Bows to Rally Iraqis for War," *New York Times*, November 24, 2006; video of Hussein with generals from Peter Klein, *Beyond Top Secret*, History Channel.

4. Hans Blix, "An Update on Inspection," statement before UN Security Council, January 27, 2003; Hans Blix, interview with the author.

5. Interviews with three UNMOVIC inspectors.

6. George W. Bush, State of the Union Address, January 28, 2003, transcript.

7. George Tenet with Bill Harlow, *At the Center of the Storm: My Years at the CIA* (New York: HarperCollins, 2007), 450.

8. Interview with senior White House official; interviews with two senior CIA officials.

9. Mohamed ElBaradei, *The Age of Deception: Nuclear Diplomacy in Treacherous Times* (London: Bloomsberg, 2011) , 63.

10. Interviews with two senior White House officials; Mohamed ElBaradei, statement to the UN Security Council, January 27, 2003.

11. Senate Select Committee on Intelligence, *Report on the U.S. Intelligence Community's Prewar Intelligence on Iraq Together with Additional Views*, July 9, 2004, 409–21.

12. William Luti to Doug Feith, "Khurmal Options Briefing," memo, January 22, 2003, declassified.

13. William Luti to Paul Wolfowitz, "Action Memo," memo, January 11, 2003, declassified.

14. David Wurmser, memo to unspecified recipient, undated, declassified and retrieved from GWU National Security Archive's Iraq Project.

15. Blix interview; Hans Blix, *Disarming Iraq* (New York: Pantheon, 2004), 128.

16. Blix interview; Ewan Buchanan, interview with the author; Hans Blix, report to the UN, May 30, 2003.

17. Dawson Cagle, interview with the author; Rocco Casagrande, interview with the author.

18. UNMOVIC inspector interview.

19. Casagrande and Cagle interviews.

20. Hans Blix, briefing to UN Security Council, February 14, 2003.

21. Alastair Campbell, *The Burden of Power: Countdown to Iraq—The Alastair Campbell Diaries* (London: Hutchinson, 2012), 459.

22. Blix, *Disarming Iraq*, 192.

23. Ibid., 194.

24. Walter Pincus, interview with the author.

25. Interview with Pentagon official.

26. "German FM makes impassioned plea for peace," video of Fischer's speech, YouTube, posted by AP, July 21, 2015; Kate Connolly, "I Am Not Convinced," *Telegraph*, February 10, 2003; Donald Rumsfeld to Torie Clarke, "Arguments," memo, February 18, 2003.

27. Interview with CIA weapons analyst.
28. John Moseman, interview with the author.
29. Interview with CENTCOM briefing participant.
30. Debra Cagan, interview with the author.
31. John Sawers, interview with the author; David Welch, interview with the author.
32. James Risen and David Johnston, "Threats and Responses: Counterterrorism; Qaeda Aide Slipped Away Long Before Sept. 11 Attacks," *New York Times*, March 8, 2003.
33. Interview with CENTCOM war planner.
34. Doug Feith to Donald Rumsfeld, "Iraq Coalition Update," memo, January 30, 2003, declassified.
35. Interview with coalition-building aide.
36. Hartwig Hummel, "A Survey of Involvement of 15 European States in the Iraq War 2003," revised version, Parliamentary Control of Security working paper (Düsseldorf; Heinrich Heine University, 2007), 7–8; Cagan interview.
37. CENTCOM war planner interview.
38. David L. Lyon, interview with Charles Stuart Kennedy, Foreign Affairs Oral History Project, Association for Diplomatic Studies and Training, 2010; "Tonga Sends 44 Troops to Help U.S. in Iraq," *New Zealand Herald*, June 16, 2004.
39. Coalition-building aide interview; Hartwig Hummel, "A Survey of Involvement of 10 European States in the Iraq War 2003," Parliamentary Control of Security working paper (Düsseldorf Heinrich Heine University, 2007).
40. Hummel, "A Survey of Involvement," revised version, 2007, 21.
41. Coalition-building aide interview.
42. Khadim Al-Waeli, interview with the author.
43. Cagan interview; Nick Thorpe, "3,000 Iraqi Exiles to Train at U.S. Base in Hungary for Secret Role in War," *Guardian*, January 16, 2003.
44. Tom Greenwood, interview with the author.
45. Interviews with three administration officials.
46. Interview with JCS general.
47. Interview with CENTCOM senior planner #1.
48. Interview with Deputies Committee meeting participant.
49. Richard Myers, interview with the author.
50. Interview with CENTCOM senior planner #2.
51. Condoleezza Rice, *No Higher Honor: A Memoir of My Years in Washington* (New York: Crown, 2011), 189–90; interview with senior administration official.
52. Senior administration official interview.
53. William Luti to Douglas Feith, "Draft NSPD on Post-War Planning Office," memo, January 7, 2003, declassified.
54. Robert Blake to Richard Armitage, memo, January 15, 2003, declassified.
55. Interview with party attendee.
56. Tom Friedman, interview with the author.
57. Interviews with two senior administration officials.
58. Ibid.
59. Frank Miller, interview with the author.
60. Elliott Abrams, interview with the author.
61. Campbell, *Burden of Power*, 449; Alastair Campbell, interview with the author.
62. Interviews with two White House officials and one State Department official.
63. Fleisher's notes of White House meeting; Robert Draper, *Dead Certain: The Presidency of George W. Bush* (New York: Free Press, 2007), 187–89; Zalmay Khalilzad, *The Envoy:*

From Kabul to the White House, My Journey Through a Turbulent World (New York: St. Martin's Press, 2016), 157–58; Ari Fleischer, *Taking Heat: The President, the Press, and My Years in the White House* (New York: William Morrow, 2005), 297–99; Kanan Makiya, interview with the author.

64. Makiya interview.
65. Douglas Feith, *War and Decision: Inside the Pentagon at the Dawn of the War on Terrorism* (New York: Harper, 2008), 348; Gordon W. Rudd, *Reconstructing Iraq: Regime Change, Jay Garner, and the ORHA Story,* Modern War Studies (Lawrence: University Press of Kansas, 2011), 1–2.
66. Jay Garner, interview with the author.
67. Rudd, *Reconstructing Iraq,* 130.
68. Interviews with three senior administration officials.
69. Feith, *War and Decision,* 377.
70. Rudd, *Reconstructing Iraq,* 146–47; Feith, *War and Decision,* 386–87.
71. Marc Grossman, interview with the author; Rudd, *Reconstructing Iraq,* 146.
72. Tim Cross, testimony at Chilcot Inquiry, December 7, 2009, 17.
73. Condoleeza Rice, interview with the author.
74. Interviews with two senior administration officials.
75. Paul Pillar, "Principal Challenges in Post-Saddam Iraq," CIA memo, January 2003, declassified.
76. John McLaughlin paper.
77. Miller interview.
78. Bill Burns to Colin Powell, "Principals Committee Meeting on Iraq Relief and Reconstruction," memo, December 19, 2002, declassified.
79. Interview with OVP official.
80. Interview with senior administration official; Khalilzad, *The Envoy,* 153.
81. Interview with NSC official.
82. David Pearce, interview with the author.
83. Ghassan Charbel, transcript of interview with Ahmad Chalabi, *Al-Hayat* (London), March 21, 2009.
84. Khalilzad, *The Envoy,* 163.
85. Interview with Condoleezza Rice confidante.
86. Garner interview.

Chapter Nineteen: Liberator

1. Paul Wolfowitz, "Wolfowitz Says U.S. Would Seek to Liberate, Not Occupy, Iraq," February 24, 2003, State Department transcript; Michael DeLong with Noah Lukeman, *Inside CENTCOM: The Unvarnished Truth About the Wars in Afghanistan and Iraq* (New York: Regnery, 2004), 77; Stephen F. Hayes, "The Horrors of Peace," *Weekly Standard,* March 10, 2003; Rudi Williams, "Wolfowitz Talks to Iraqi Americans About Ousting Hussein, Rebuilding Homeland," American Forces Press Service, February 24, 2003; Rudi Williams, "Wolfowitz Meets Boy Who Survived Assault by Hussein's Troops as an Infant," American Forces Press Service, February 26, 2003; Samer Hijazi, "Questions Loom in Murder of Man at Detroit Gas Station," *Arab American News,* July 19, 2016; Maha Hussain, interview with the author.
2. Carl Levin, interview with the author; "The Invasion of Iraq," *PBS Frontline,* May 9, 2004, transcript.

3. Interview with Defense Department official; Wolfowitz, "Commencement Address at the U.S. Military Academy," June 2, 2001, DOD transcript; Peter Boyer, "A Different War," *New Yorker*, June 23, 2002; Thomas E. Ricks, "Bush Backs Overhaul of Military's Top Ranks," *Washington Post*, April 11, 2002.

4. Interview with senior Pentagon official.

5. Paul Wolfowitz, testimony, *Hearing Before the Committee on the Budget, House of Representatives*, February 27, 2003.

6. Mark Hertling, interview with the author.

7. Wolfowitz, *Hearing Before the Committee on the Budget*.

8. Interviews with U.S. and British military leadership.

9. Jim Garamone, "Wolfowitz Says U.S. Must Encourage Moderate Muslim States," American Forces Press Service, June 5, 2002.

10. Jim Garamone, "Wolfowitz Says Turkey's Example Important to Muslim World," American Forces Press Service, July 15, 2002.

11. Greg Bruno, "Inside the Kurdistan Workers Party (PKK)," Council on Foreign Relations, October 19, 2007.

12. Barak A. Salmoni, "Strategic Partners or Estranged Allies: Turkey, the United States, and Operation Iraqi Freedom," *Strategic Insights* 2, no. 7 (July 2003).

13. Carol Migdalovitz, "Iraq: Turkey, the Deployment of U.S. Forces, and Related Issues," Congressional Research Service, May 2, 2003.

14. "Wolfowitz Visits Turkey to Discuss Military Action Against Iraq," VOA News, July 16, 2002.

15. Marc Grossman, interview with the author.

16. Migdalovitz, "Iraq."

17. Ian Fisher, "Threats and Responses: The Allies; Turkey, in the Middle, Grows More Worried Every Day About a U.S. Attack on Iraq," *New York Times*, October 28, 2002; Bill Park, "Strategic Location, Political Dislocation: Turkey, the United States and Northern Iraq," *Middle East Review of International Affairs* 7 (June 2003).

18. Ambassador Robert W. Pearson to Colin Powell, "Wolfowitz and Grossman Press Turks for Support on Iraq," cable, December 3, 2002, declassified.

19. Vernon Loeb and Karl Vick, "U.S. Official Confident of Turkey's Support," *Washington Post*, December 5, 2002.

20. Paul Wolfowitz, testimony before House Budget Committee, *Congressional Record*, February 27, 2003.

21. Salmoni, "Strategic Partners or Estranged Allies"; Migdalovitz, "Iraq."

22. John Bisney, "Kuwait," CNN Radio, April 1, 2003.

23. Bill Keller, "The Sunshine Warrior," *New York Times Magazine*, September 22, 2002.

24. "Paul Wolfowitz Speaks in Washington," CNN, March 11, 2003, transcript.

25. Steve Ganyard, interview with the author.

Chapter Twenty: A Man in the World

1. Interviews with two OVP officials; Christopher Meyer, *DC Confidential: The Controversial Memoirs of Britain's Ambassador to the U.S. at the Time of 9/11 and the Iraq War* (London: Weidenfeld & Nicolson, 2005), 237.

2. Bob Woodward, *Plan of Attack: The Definitive Account of the Decision to Invade Iraq* (New York: Simon & Schuster, 2004), 251; Condoleezza Rice, *No Higher Honor: A Memoir of My Years in Washington* (New York: Crown, 2011), 186.

3. Donald Rumsfeld, *Known and Unknown: A Memoir* (New York: Sentinel, 2011), 456.

4. Woodward, *Plan of Attack*, 261.

5. Interview with senior White House official #1.

6. Interviews with two senior White House officials.

7. Interview with CIA briefer.

8. George W. Bush, "President Bush: This Is a Defining Moment for the UN Security Council," White House, February 7, 2003, transcript.

9. Alastair Campbell, *The Burden of Power: Countdown to Iraq—The Alastair Campbell Diaries* (London: Hutchinson, 2012), 482.

10. White House, "Global Message on Iraq," statement, March 6, 2003.

11. White House, "President George Bush Discusses Iraq in National Press Conference," news release transcript, March 6, 2003.

12. White House senior official #1 interview.

13. George W. Bush, "President Says 'It is a Moment of Truth' for UN," White House, February 9, 2003, transcript.

14. Interviews with two senior White House officials; Ernesto Ekaizer, "Bush Avisó a Aznar de que Estaría en Bagdad en Marzo con o sin Resolución de la ONU," *El País*, September 25, 2007.

15. Kurt Volker, "Bush, Chirac, and the War in Iraq," *Foreign Policy*, November 15, 2016.

16. Interview with administration official #1.

17. George W. Bush, *Decision Points* (New York: Crown, 2010), 410.

18. Lara Marlowe, "Chirac Attacks U.S. on Death Penalty," *Irish Times*, March 31, 2001.

19. Interview with administration official #2.

20. Bush, *Decision Points*, 233, 245.

21. Volker, "Bush, Chirac."

22. Administration official #2 interview.

23. Daniel Fried, interview with the author.

24. William Boston, "European Leaders, Public at Odds over War with Iraq," *Christian Science Monitor*, January 17, 2003.

25. Sean Loughlin, "House Cafeterias Change Names for 'French' Fries and 'French' Toast," CNN, March 12, 2003.

26. John Hooper, "U.S.-German Relations Strained over Iraq," *Guardian*, September 24, 2002.

27. Peter Finn, "Europe Rifts Widen over Iraq," *Washington Post*, February 11, 2003.

28. Rice, *No Higher Honor*, 213. Though Rice implied that she made this remark after the invasion, Alastair Campbell, in *The Burden of Power*, wrote that Bush had repeated Rice's quip to Blair on March 19 (page 511).

29. Administration official #1 interview.

30. Administration officials #1 and #2 interviews; interview with U.S. diplomat.

31. White House, "President Bush Meets with Prime Minister Blair," news release transcript, January 31, 2003.

32. Alan Travis, "Support for War Falls to New Low," *Guardian*, January 21, 2003.

33. Giles Tremlett and Sophie Arie, "Aznar Faces 91% Opposition to War," *Guardian*, March 28, 2003.

34. Ekaizer, "Bush Avisó a Aznar."

35. "President Bush Meets with President Biya from Cameroon," UPI, March 20, 2003.

36. Interviews with two administration officials.

37. Administration official #1 interview.
38. Ginger Thompson and Clifford Krauss, "Threats and Responses: Security Council; Antiwar Fever Puts Mexico in Quandary on Iraq Vote," *New York Times*, February 28, 2003.
39. Bush, *Decision Points*, 246.
40. Campbell, *Burden of Power*, 477.
41. Campbell, *Burden of Power*, 491; Woodward, *Plan of Attack*, 344; Bush, *Decision Points*, 247.
42. Bush, *Decision Points*, 246.
43. Campbell interview; Jack Straw, interview with the author.
44. White House, "President Bush Announced the Recipients of the Presidential Medal of Freedom," news release transcript, June 21, 2002; interview with administration official #3; "Mandela Attacks Blair and Bush," *Guardian*, January 30, 2003.
45. Eric Lichtblau, "Threats and Responses: Dissent; Tens of Thousands March Against Iraq War," *New York Times*, March 16, 2003.
46. Ari Fleischer, interview with the author.
47. George W. Bush, press conference, March 6, 2003, transcript.
48. Campbell, *Burden of Power*, 505.
49. White House, "President Bush: Monday 'Moment of Truth' for World on Iraq," news release transcript, March 16, 2003.
50. Interview with individual with knowledge of the conversation.
51. Interview with CIA senior official; National Security Council, "Summary of Conclusions: NSC Meeting on Regional Issues," March 10, 2003, declassified.
52. National Security Council, "Summary of Conclusions: NSC Meeting on Regional Issues," March 11, 2003, declassified.
53. "Reshaping the Iraqi Military," DOD briefing slides, March 7, 2003, declassified; Doug Feith, interview with the author; Jay Garner, interview with the author; Frank Miller, interview with the author.
54. George W. Bush, press conference, March 16, 2003, transcript.
55. Interviews with three administration officials.
56. Interview with briefing attendee.
57. Ari Fleischer's notes of meeting with Elie Wiesel, February 27, 2003.
58. Bush, *Decision Points*, 248.
59. "Iraqi Assyrians Meet Top U.S. Administration Officials," Assyrian International News Agency, March 19, 2003.
60. Interview with Oval Office staffer.
61. George W. Bush, "President Says Saddam Hussein Must Leave Iraq Within 48 Hours," White House, March 17, 2003, transcript.
62. Campbell, *Burden of Power*, 510–11; Campbell interview.
63. Dawson Cagle, interview with the author.
64. Interview with VTC participant.
65. Interviews with four CIA senior officials.
66. White House, "President Bush Addresses the Nation," news release transcript, March 19, 2003; interviews with two CIA senior officials.
67. Interview with senior CIA official.
68. Interviews with two of Saddam's interrogators.
69. Colin Powell, interview with the author; John Donovan, "The Fall of Basra," ABC News, April 8, 2003, video; CENTCOM, "Chronology of OIF, Combat Phase, May 14, 2003, declassified document; Rohit Singh, "Gulf War II: Operation Iraqi

Freedom," *Scholar Warrior*, Spring 2011; "Iraq War 2003: Attack on Fort Bliss's 507th Maintenance Company," KVIA, August 31, 2010.

Chapter Twenty-One: The Day After

1. George W. Bush, "Operation Iraqi Freedom," radio address, April 5, 2003.
2. Jacob Bacall, interview with the author; Elisabeth Bumiller, "A Nation at War: The Leaders; Bush and Blair Will Meet in Belfast Early Next Week on Iraq, Mideast and Ulster," *New York Times*, April 5, 2005; George W. Bush, Presidential Daily Diary, April 4, 2003, FOIA document from George W. Bush Presidential Library.
3. Zaab Sethna, interview with the author; interview with Defense Department official #1; Ahmad Chalabi, interview with Ghassan Charbel, *Al-Hayat* (London), March 23, 2009; Marie Colvin, "Nazi Files Incriminate Top Iraqis," *Times* (London), April 20, 2003; Colvin, "Chalabi the Challenger Finds Iraq's Leader in Waiting," *Times* (London), April 13, 2003; Sean Loughlin, "Rumsfeld on Looting in Iraq: Stuff Happens," CNN, April 12, 2003.
4. Jay Garner, interview with the author; Gordon Rudd, interview with the author; interview with CENTCOM official.
5. Interview with Defense Department official #2; Jennifer Frey, "Stars and Stripes," *Washington Post*, April 27, 2003; Tommy Franks with Malcolm McConnell, *American Soldier* (New York: Regan Books, 2004), 346–54; Bob Woodward, *Plan of Attack: The Definitive Account of the Decision to Invade Iraq* (New York: Simon & Schuster, 2004), 530.
6. Garner interview; Margaret Tutwiler, interview with the author; Robin Raphel, interview with the author; Stuart W. Bowen, Jr., Office of the Inspector General for Iraq Reconstruction (SIGIR), *Hard Lessons: The Iraq Reconstruction Experience* (U.S. Independent Agencies and Commissions, 2009), 59; Donald Rumsfeld, interview with David Nummy, "Iraq Experience Project," United States Institute of Peace, October 14, 2004, transcript.
7. Rudd interview.
8. Garner interview.
9. Rudd, Garner, and Sethna interviews.
10. Interview with three senior Bush administration officials.
11. Gordon W. Rudd, *Reconstructing Iraq: Regime Change, Jay Garner, and the ORHA Story* (Lawrence: University Press of Kansas, 2011), 247; Garner interview.
12. Paul Bremer, interview with Charles Stuart Kennedy, Foreign Affairs Oral History Project, Association for Diplomatic Studies and Training, June 16, 2008.
13. Interview with senior administration official.
14. Bob Kerrey, interview with the author.
15. Donald Rumsfeld, *Known and Unknown: A Memoir* (New York: Sentinel, 2011), 505.
16. Donald Rumsfeld to Andrew Card, "Ambassador Paul Bremer," memo, April 24, 2003.
17. White House, "President Discusses the Future of Iraq," news release transcript, April 28, 2003.
18. White House, "President Bush Announces Major Combat Operations in Iraq Have Ended," news release transcript, May 1, 2003.
19. Kevin Tebbit, interview with the author.
20. Bremer, Foreign Affairs Oral History Project interview.
21. Donald Rumsfeld, "Principles for Iraq—Policy Guidelines," DOD memo, May 13, 2003, declassified.

22. Paul Bremer, interview with the author.
23. Garner interview.
24. Bremer interview.
25. Garner interview; Raphel interview; Nummy, "Iraq Experience Project"; Coalition Provisional Authority, Order Number 1, "DeBaathification of Iraqi Society," May 16, 2003.
26. Coalition Provisional Authority, Order Number 2, "Dissolution of Entities," May 23, 2003.
27. Charlie Seidel, interview with the author; Rob Baker, interview with the author.
28. Seidel interview.
29. Interviews with three NSC meeting participants; Bremer interview.
30. Stephen Hadley, interview with the author; Frank Miller, interview with the author.
31. Garner interview.
32. "Saddam Adviser Surrenders to U.S.," *Guardian*, April 12, 2003.
33. Charles Duelfer, interview with the author; Jerry Watson, interview with the author.
34. Richard Myers, interview with the author.
35. Central Intelligence Agency, "Trailers Suspected of Being Mobile BW Agent Production Units," CIA (website), April 23, 2007.
36. Interview with BW analyst.
37. Margaret Henoch, interview with the author.
38. Stephen Cambone, special Defense Department briefing, Pentagon, May 7, 2003, available as C-SPAN video, "Weapons of Mass Destruction in Iraq," https://www.c-span.org/video/?176524-1/weapons-mass-destruction-iraq&start.
39. Central Intelligence Agency, "Trailers Suspected."
40. Bob Drogin, *Curveball: Spies, Lies, and the Con Man Who Caused a War* (New York: Random House, 2007), 199.
41. John McLaughlin, interview with the author; Central Intelligence Agency, "DCI Tenet Announces Appointment of David Kay as Special Advisor," press release, June 11, 2003.
42. Scott Ritter, interview with the author.
43. Judith Miller, "Aftereffects: The Hunt for Evidence; Trailer Is a Mobile Lab Capable of Turning Out Bioweapons, a Team Says," *New York Times*, May 11, 2003.
44. McLaughlin interview; interviews with two CIA analysts.
45. Central Intelligence Agency, *Iraqi Mobile Biological Warfare Agent Production Plants*, May 28, 2003.
46. Interview with Dan; CIA, "Trailers Suspected."
47. White House, "Interview of the President by TVP, Poland," news release transcript, May 29, 2003.
48. Carr Ford, interview with the author.
49. Interview with meeting participant.
50. Hamish Killip, interview with the author.
51. James Risen, "The Struggle for Iraq: Intelligence; Ex-Inspector Says CIA Missed Disarray in Iraqi Arms Program," *New York Times*, January 26, 2004. The accounts of CIA analyst interviews with Iraqi scientists were gleaned from multiple intelligence sources.
52. Tom Friedman, interview with the author.
53. Operation Iraqi Freedom History Brief, May 14, 2003, https://www.esd.whs.mil/Portals/54/Documents/FOID/Reading%20Room/Joint_Staff/09-F-1449_Operation_Iraqi_Freedom_OIF_History_Brief.pdf.

54. Interview with CENTCOM planner.
55. Ibid.
56. Interview with CIA paper author.
57. Interview with Wolfowitz aide #1.
58. Interview with Wolfowitz aide #2.
59. Stephen F. Hayes, "Of Prisons and Palaces," *Weekly Standard*, August 4, 2003.
60. Interview with member of Wolfowitz entourage.
61. Department of Defense, "Deputy Secretary Wolfowitz Briefing on His Recent Trip to Iraq," news release transcript, July 23, 2003.
62. John Batiste, interview with the author; Mark Hertling, interview with the author; Rob Baker, interview with the author.
63. Wolfowitz aide #2 interview.
64. Gary Anderson, "The Baathists' Blundering Guerrilla War," *Washington Post*, June 26, 2003.
65. Department of Defense, "Secretary Rumsfeld Media Availability with Jay Garner," news release transcript, June 18, 2003.
66. Wolfowitz aide #1 interview.
67. Video of Wolfowitz at the New Yorker Festival, September 21, 2003, https://www.c-span.org/video/?178290=1/policy=iraq; Jeffrey Goldberg, "How Did I Get Iraq Wrong?," *Slate*, March 19, 2008.
68. Joel Rayburn and Frank K. Sobchak, *The U.S. Army in the Iraq War, Vol 1: Invasion, Insurgency, Civil War, 2003–2006* (Carlisle, Pa.: Strategic Studies Institute, 2019), 214.
69. Dexter Filkins, "At Least 11 Die in Car Bombing at Jordan's Embassy in Baghdad," *New York Times*, August 7, 2003.
70. Bremer, Foreign Affairs Oral History Project, 2015.
71. "Iraq: Five Years After Baghdad Attack, UN Remembers Some of its 'Best and Bravest,'" UN News Service, August 19, 2008.
72. "Najaf Bombing Kills Shiite Leader, Followers Say," CNN, August 30, 2003.
73. James Kitfield, "Ramadan Offensive," *National Journal*, November 1, 2003.
74. David Ignatius, "A War of Choice, and One Who Chose It," *Washington Post*, November 2, 2003.
75. Donna Miles, "Deputy Secretary Praises Iraqi Women's and Human Rights Groups," American Forces Press Service, October 24, 2003.
76. Miles, "Iraqi Civil Defense Corps Grows in Numbers and Role," American Forces Press Service, October 29, 2003.
77. Rayburn and Sobchak, *The U.S. Army in the Iraq War*, 232.
78. Interviews with two Wolfowitz aides.
79. Entifadh Qanbar (person present for the conversation), interview with the author. Bush's remark was confirmed in an interview with Jordan's foreign minister, Marwan Muasher. Ignatius, in an interview, did not recall some of this dialogue, though his November 2 *Post* column, "War of Choice," contains several of the details, including Bush's profane appraisal of Chalabi.
80. James Kitfield, interview with the author.
81. Donna Miles, "Wolfowitz Vows Al-Rasheed Attack Won't Deter Coalition," American Forces Press Service, October 26, 2003; Stephen F. Hayes, "The Visionary," *Weekly Standard*, May 9, 2005; interviews with four witnesses to the bombing.
82. Rob Baker, interview with the author.
83. Hayes, "The Visionary"; David O. Agbeti, *From Africa to the Heart of the GOP* (self-published, AuthorHouse, 2005), 144.

84. Paul Wolfowitz, statement of retirement at the Pentagon, *Congressional Record,* May 25, 2005, S5916.
85. Elias Nimmer, interview with the author.
86. Interviews with two meeting participants.
87. White House, "Remarks by the President at Ernie Fletcher for Governor Reception," news release transcript, October 9, 2003.
88. Colin Powell, interview with the author; Richard Boucher (who spoke with Powell immediately after the exchange), interview with the author; "Calendar of U.S. Military Dead During the Iraq War," Cryptome (website).
89. Steve Balestrieri, "Operation Red Dawn, Saddam Hussein Captured, 13 December 2003," SpecialOperations (website), December 13, 2017.
90. White House, "State of the Union Address," news release transcript, January 20, 2004.
91. Robert Draper, *Dead Certain: The Presidency of George W. Bush* (New York: Free Press, 2007), 224; Ahmad Chalabi, interview, *Al-Hayat,* March 2, 2009; White House schedule for January 20, 2004, public papers of President George W. Bush, U.S. Government Printing Office.
92. Bremer interview.
93. Interview with intelligence official.
94. Marwan Muasher, interview with the author.
95. George W. Bush, *Decision Points* (New York: Crown, 2010), 259.
96. Bremer interview.
97. Sethna interview.
98. Risen interview.
99. Rob Richer, interview with the author.
100. Senate Committee on Intelligence, *Use by the Intelligence Committee of Information Provided by the Iraqi National Congress,* S. Rep. 109-330, September 8, 2006, 34.
101. Dexter Filkins and Ian Fisher, "The Struggle for Iraq: Ransacking; Iraqis and G.I.'s Raid the Offices of an Ex-Favorite," *New York Times,* May 21, 2004.
102. Sethna interview.
103. Chalabi, *Al-Hayat* interview.
104. "Chalabi Denies Supplying False WMD Information," CNN, November 9, 2005; "Iraq's Chalabi Meets with Cheney, Rumsfeld," Radio Free Europe, November 15, 2005.
105. John Nixon, interview with the author; Bill McLaughlin, interview with the author.
106. "DCI Remarks on Iraq's WMD Programs: Remarks as Prepared for Delivery by Director of Central Intelligence George J. Tenet at Georgetown University," CIA (website), February 5, 2004.
107. Richard Stevenson, "Iraq Illicit Arms Gone Before War, Inspector States," *New York Times,* January 24, 2004.
108. David Kay, statement at Senate Armed Services Committee hearing, January 28, 2004.
109. Killip interview; Rod Barton, *The Weapons Detective* (Melbourne: Black Inc. Agenda, 2006), 374; Rod Barton, interview with the author.
110. Barton, Killip, and Duelfer interviews.
111. Duelfer interview.
112. Interview with CIA weapons analyst who participated in a December 2003 VTC of senior weapons analysts.

113. Central Intelligence Agency, "Key Mobile BW Source Deemed Unreliable," redacted memo, May 26, 2004, cited in Senate Select Committee on Intelligence, *Use by the Intelligence Committee*, 37.

114. Senate Select Committee on Intelligence, *Use by the Intelligence Committee*, 79–81.

115. Bill McLaughlin interview; interview with CIA analyst; "Full Transcript of the Debate Between the Vice Presidential Candidates in Cleveland," *New York Times*, October 5, 2004.

116. Interviews with five CIA officials.

117. Jami Miscik, "DDI's State of Analysis Speech," CIA headquarters, February 11, 2004.

118. Jane Green, interview with the author.

119. Duelfer interview.

120. "Testimony by Charles Duelfer on Iraq WMD Programs," Speeches and Testimony Archive, CIA (website), March 30, 2004.

121. Killip and Barton interviews; Barton, *Weapons Detective*, 379–85.

122. Duelfer interview; Paul Wolfowitz, interview with the author.

123. Special Advisor to the Director of Central Intelligence, *Comprehensive Report of the Special Advisor to the DCI on Iraq's WMD*, September 30, 2004; Nixon and Bill McLaughlin interviews; declassified FBI memo from Piro, Baghdad Operations Center, June 11, 2004.

124. Duelfer interview.

125. Cryptome, monthly tally of U.S. military casualties from December 2003 to October 2004.

126. Cagle interview.

127. Interview with Bush administration aide.

128. Rumsfeld, *Known and Unknown*, 506.

129. Interview with NSC aide.

130. Interview with CENTCOM planner.

131. Rumsfeld to John Abizaid, "Chalabi," memo, May 25, 2004.

132. Interview with CIA senior official who frequently briefed Rumsfeld and Wolfowitz on the insurgent activity during this period.

133. Bartlett interview.

134. Bryan Bender, "Polls Suggest Arab-Americans Gravitating Toward Kerry," *Boston Globe*, August 13, 2004.

135. "NSC on Iraq by SVTC," May 12, 2004, declassified notes.

136. Interview with CIA official.

137. Interview with CIA senior manager.

138. Interview with CIA analyst.

139. Christopher A. Preble, "Iraq and the Election of 2004," Cato Institute, November 26, 2004.

140. Paul R. Abramson et al., "The 2004 Presidential Election: The Emergence of a Permanent Majority?," *Political Science Quarterly* 120, no. 1 (Spring 2005): 33–57.

141. James E. Campbell, "Why Bush Won the Presidential Election of 2004: Ideology, Terrorism, and Turnout," *Political Science Quarterly* 120, no. 2 (Summer 2005): 291–41.

142. Rumsfeld, *Known and Unknown*, 504.

143. Interview with *Washington Post* staffer.

144. Gallup Poll, "Favorability: People in the News," November 19–21, 2004. In the same poll, Rice scored 62, Cheney 53, and Bush and Rumsfeld 51.

145. Interview with reporter who heard Powell's comment; interview with State Department official.

146. Interviews with two State officials.
147. Interview with former ambassador.
148. White House, "President Outlines Steps to Help Iraq Achieve Democracy and Freedom," news release transcript, May 24, 2004.
149. Feith interview; Douglas Feith, *War and Decision: Inside the Pentagon at the Dawn of the War on Terrorism* (New York: Harper, 2008), 492–93.
150. Eric Schmitt, "The Conflict in Iraq: Resignation; Senior Official behind Many of the Pentagon's Most Contentious Policies Is Stepping Down," *New York Times*, January 27, 2005.
151. Doug Feith, "Remarks at My Farewell and Award Ceremony," August 8, 2005, https://www.DougFeith.com.
152. Henoch interview.
153. Bush, *Decision Points*, 87.
154. Interview with senior White House official.
155. Bush interview with author on December 12, 2006, quoted in *Dead Certain*, xiii.
156. Crocker interview.
157. "How Common Is PTSD in Veterans?," National Center for PTSD, Department of Veterans Affairs; Daniel Trotta, "Iraq War Costs U.S. More Than $2 Trillion: Study," Reuters, March 14, 2013.
158. Amy Hagopian et al., "Mortality in Iraq Associated with the 2003 War and Occupation: Findings from a National Cluster Sample Survey by the University Iraq Collaborative Mortality Study," *PLOS Medicine*, October 15, 2013.
159. Nixon interview.
160. Michael Briggs, interview with the author; Jacqueline Trescott, "At Gallery, History is Rewritten; Bush Portrait Caption Had Linked Iraq to 9/11," *Washington Post*, January 14, 2009.
161. Tammy Duckworth, interview with the author; Steve Ganyard, interview with the author.
162. CSIS event witnessed by author; Kadhim al-Waeli, interview with the author.

INDEX

===